A DEAL WITH THE DEVIL

Discovering Chris Watts: The Facts - Part Two

NETTA NEWBOUND & MARCUS BROWN

Junction Publishing

Netta Newbound & Marcus Brown/Junction Publishing United Kingdom

A Deal with the DEVIL - Discovering Chris Watts - Part Two

ADWTD/ Netta Newbound & Marcus Brown – 1st Ed.

We'd like to dedicate this book to four beautiful souls, Shanann, Bella, Celeste and Nico - RIP.

Disclaimer

All the information in this book has been taken from the Colorado Bureau of Investigation (CBI) *Discovery* files regarding the investigation into the disappearance of Shanann Watts and her daughters.

Any thoughts, views, and opinions are solely the authors' own.

Publisher's notes: Although the author's are British and tend to use British English spelling, there are several instances in this book where they have written the words as they have been reported, using American English spelling.

Preface

Following on from *In Cold Blood – Discovering Chris Watts: Book One.*

To recap...

We guess it's safe to say most people will have heard of the Watts case.

Christopher Lee (Chris) Watts, the dashing, seemingly genteel, affable man who murdered his entire family in a calculated attack that shocked the entire world.

Shanann Watts, his pregnant, incredibly beautiful wife whose life was snuffed out because her doting husband decided he wanted a fresh start.

Bella Marie and Celeste Cathryn (CeCe) Watts, adorable sisters who worshipped their father, the very man who suffocated them both in cold blood using their comfort blankets against them. He then went on to dispose of their tiny bodies into huge tanks filled with toxic crude oil.

Nico Lee Watts, Chris and Shanann's unborn son.

No doubt, most of you watched the story unfold on the news, open-mouthed, in total shock. What could push a loving father to brutally murder his family? Surely there was some mistake? We all have preconceived ideas of how a monster should look–

grotesque, hideously deformed, a crazed madman–not this handsome, mild-mannered, shy, polite gent who was often portrayed as the perfect husband and father.

So, what happened?

During this series we will look at the facts, the police investigation, the evidence, hear Chris Watts' explanation and his reasoning. We will try to make some sense of what occurred during the early hours of 13th August 2018.

We will endeavour to present to you all aspects of the case, right from the initial investigation and how it unfolded, to the first and subsequent confessions all transcribed word for word (where possible) from actual video and audio footage obtained from the FBI's Discovery Files.

We will continue where we left off.

At the end of book one, Chris Watts had finally confessed to murdering his beautiful family and disposing of their bodies at an oil field.

In part two, we will focus on…

- … the grim discovery and recovery.
- … the chilling details of the autopsies.
- … the remaining police interviews of NK.
- … the Plea Deal.
- … the sentencing.
- … Chris Watts' Prison Interview.

But first, a little bit about us…

I'm Netta Newbound, a bestselling author and, although true crime has been my passion since I was a youngster, writing psychological thriller fiction has, until now, been the voice of my fascination. I am incredibly excited to embark on this journey with you all.

Like a lot of people, I have been obsessed with this case since the story first broke back in 2018. Although the details, footage, and discovery files are all over the internet, I realised there is very little in-depth information available in chronological order and I jumped at the chance to work on this book when it was suggested at the beginning of the year. My prime objective is to make it easy for anyone unfamiliar with the case to access and read the details as it unfolded.

My name is Marcus Brown, and I am best known for writing in the crime, horror, and supernatural genre.

In Cold Blood is my first foray into true life crime and, like Netta, I became interested in this case as it hit news outlets worldwide.

I've always had the wildest of imaginations, but nothing could prepare me for the horrors written about in this book. No character I've ever created could come close to the monster that is Chris Watts, but his wicked nature does not make the story any less heart-breaking or fascinating.

Marcus and Netta have worked together for a few years now, mainly in a publishing capacity, but in 2019 they joined forces and wrote *Avaline Saddlebags*—the first in a psychological fiction thriller series.

Combining their joint obsession with this case, they studied the files together, often into the small hours.

We want to *stress* that if you have already read the discovery files, then this series of books is probably *not* for you.

PLEASE NOTE: During the transcripts there are a lot of filler words used... um... like... etc. We cleaned a few of these up but decided their excessive use could tell their own story if analysed, so, for this reason, we decided to leave most of them in. It is often the non-verbal utterances and mannerisms that paint the real picture.

We will remain sensitive to both the Rzucek and Watts families throughout this series. The last thing we want to do is to cause them any more heart-ache or sorrow. We cannot begin to imagine their pain. Out of respect, we have chosen to omit any interviews with the family members apart from the victim impact statements from the sentencing.

Introduction

The world was shocked to discover this seemingly mild-mannered husband and father had brutally murdered his own family, and, ever since, there has been a continued interest, resulting in numerous books, films, and television documentaries on the subject. Digging deeper, it is easy to understand why the specifics of this particular case have caused such furore.

In this, the second book in the series, we will once again focus on the facts—actual interviews transcribed mainly from the Discovery Files. We ended the last book with Chris confessing to killing Shanann after *she'd* supposedly murdered their two adorable daughters. Did anybody believe him? Not really. But it was a confession, and it appeared to suit the detectives, who many believe had botched the investigation from start to finish.

We left Nichol Kessinger firefighting—trying her damnedest to get onside with the police, offering explanations of why she'd deleted texts way before the detectives even knew she existed. But was it all an act? She knew *Anadarko*, her and Chris's employer, had contacted the police and informed them about their affair. However, they didn't know *she* knew that. They just thought she'd come forward as a witness of her own free will. After the next few interviews, NK seems to vanish without trace. Did she make a deal of her own?

That's enough from us for now. Settle down, make yourself comfortable and discover for yourself what happened next…

ONE

Discovery and Recovery

******GRAPHIC CONTENT WARNING******

Although we are aware this entire case is upsetting and sickening to most people, due to the content, we feel the following chapters should come with a warning. If you are of a delicate disposition, maybe you should skip to chapter five.

In this chapter we follow the investigation to the discovery of Shanann's body. We did consider leaving the details out, but we have stated earlier that we will provide you with all the facts and so, with this in mind, we shall proceed.

On the afternoon of 15th August 2018, while Tammy and Grahm were interrogating Chris Watts, other members of the investigation team made their way to CERVI 319. According to his GPS, Chris drove to this well site after leaving his house on the morning of the 13th August. They met with an *Anadarko* employee who escorted them down several dirt roads to the well site, which was fenced with barbed wire, and contained a well head, a separator and storage tanks on a gravel pad.

At approximately 3:30pm, they deployed an unmanned drone to

scan the area and obtained real-time video feed, as well as several still photographs. In the brush to the south of the pad they located what appeared to be a sheet lying on the ground. The detectives approached the sheet and just south of the gravel pad they discovered an area of bare dirt that appeared to have been recently disturbed. They promptly left the area to obtain permission to search.

Around 4:15pm they received consent from the owner of the land to allow them to search the area and collect evidence. The detectives cautiously approached the dirt-stained sheet and recognized it to be a fitted bed sheet, the same pattern as the sheet found in the Watt's rubbish bin. There were two black rubbish bags in the brush close to the sheet which also seemed to have been left there recently. A search warrant was requested.

A while later, the detectives were informed that Chris Watts had confessed to killing his wife and dumping her body along with that of his two daughters at the well site. The coroner was requested to respond.

Once the search warrant had been secured, the detectives documented the scene with digital photographs and measurements. Then they collected the sheet and rubbish bags. They also found a rake head protruding from the ground beside the area of disturbed dirt, and a broken wooden rake handle.

Afterwards, one of the detectives climbed the stairs to the top of the holding tanks and managed to peer inside the openings with a flashlight. His vision was obstructed by visible gas fumes. The detective noted that the openings were very small, just eight inches across, and numerous strands of blonde hair were stuck to the rim. Arrangements were made for the tanks to be drained the following morning. Police security was placed at the site overnight.

Upon the coroner's arrival, they proceeded to excavate the disturbed area of dirt. Shanann's body was found just three inches below the surface. She was lying face down in a kneeling-type position, her arms outstretched in front of her and her feet pulled up underneath and behind her and directed up towards the top of the grave. Her chest and face primarily were facing down into the ground while her back was oriented up. Her head was towards the west while her feet were towards the east. Her left arm was extended to the east along side her head. The victim was wearing a blue pair of underwear and a light-coloured shirt. The depth of the grave when the body was removed was approximately twenty-seven inches.

The *Weld County Coroner* took possession of Shanann's body at 12:20 am on Thursday, 16th August 2018.

At 8:30am on 16th August 2018 Agent Tammy Lee met with numerous *Anadarko* employees, as well as several police officers and agents at the battery site to recover the bodies of Bella and CeCe Watts. The CSP Hazmat unit was also in attendance.

During a safety briefing, they were informed the east tank battery contained approximately nine feet of crude oil and the west approximately one-point-four feet. They arranged to proceed with the emptying of the east tank.

While waiting for the tank to be drained, Tammy assisted in a grid search of the area. They were trying to locate the children's blankets and stuffed animals that Chris had mentioned leaving beside the grave site. They could not be located.

It took approximately six hours to drain the first tank. Then the manway cover was removed and members of the Hazmat unit entered and recovered a deceased female child, later identified as Celeste Watts. Celeste was covered in oil and was removed from the tank in a white decontamination box that had been affixed with rope handles. She was wearing a pink nightgown as well as a pull-up (nappy/diaper). Once outside of the tank, forensic pathologist, Dr Michael Burson patted her stomach area down with oil absorbent pads. Celeste appeared to have skin slippage and was wrapped in a white sheet and laid inside an open body bag.

Tammy left soon after and wasn't present for the recovery of Bella's body which was found at the bottom of the west tank a while later. Bella was wearing a pink, multi-coloured shirt and shorts.

TWO

Autopsy of Shanann Watts

******GRAPHIC CONTENT WARNING******

We have been in two minds whether or not to report the autopsy findings to you – as with the previous chapters, the details are graphic and upsetting. We have decided to give you a shortened and condensed summary of the autopsies taken from Tammy Lee's report, followed by more detailed reports for those of you who want to see the content in its entirety.

At 10:00 am on the 17th August 2018, Agent Tammy Lee visited the McKee Medical Centre to attend the autopsies of Shanann, Bella and Celeste Watts. This summary is from her report.

Dr Micheal Burson and his assistant Joey Weiner were present to perform the autopsies. Also attending was Weld County Coroner, Carl Blesch, Weld County Chief Deputy District Attorney, Steve Wrenn, Weld County Deputy District Attorney, Patrick Roche, FBI Special Agent, Grahm Coder, and CBI Crime Scene Analyst, Eric Bryant.
A request by the public defender's DNA expert was put forward for the

necks of the victims to be swabbed, as well as the removal/scrapings of the fingernails and x-rays to be taken.
The first autopsy was performed on Shanann Watts.
Shanann was wearing a purple/grey t-shirt, black bra, and a blue thong underwear. The items were removed and collected as evidence. Shanann appeared to have a large amount of skin slippage and her amniotic sack was protruding from her vaginal area. Dr Burson examined the amniotic sack and removed the fetus which was collected as evidence.
During the autopsy, Dr Burson advised that Shanann's hyoid bone was not broken, although he pointed out bruising to the soft tissue on the right side of the hyoid bone. He also noted bruising to the muscles and tissue in Shanann's neck. The doctor advised he did not note any other trauma to Shanann's body and found no evidence of disease.
Dr Burson advised Shanann's preliminary cause of death was asphyxiation due to manual strangulation (Official autopsy report below)

FULL AUTOPSY REPORT

Name of decedent: Shanann Watts
Case#: AW18-155
Investigation#: WCCO 18-435
Date and time of death: August 16, 2018 at 0005 hrs (pronounced)
Date and time of autopsy: August 17, 2018 at 1030 hrs **Age:** 34 YEARS
Sex: Female
DIAGNOSES:
HISTORY OF BEING REPORTED MISSING AND SUBSEQUENTLY BEING FOUND UNRESPONSIVE IN AN OBVIOUS STATE OF DEATH IN A SHALLOW GRAVE:
ASPHYXIATION DUE TO MANUAL STRANGULATION:
BRUISING OF THE ANTERIOR STRAP MUSCLES OF THE NECK (RIGHT > LEFT)
MILD TO MODERATE DECOMPOSITION CONSISTING OF GENERALIZED DISCOLORATION, BLOATING AND SKIN SLIPPAGE

HISTORY OF INTRAUTERINE PREGNANCY, SECOND TRIMESTER:

A LARGELY DECOMPOSED FETUS AND PLACENTAL UNIT FOUND EXPELLED FROM THE GRAVID UTERUS
TOXICOLOGY:
A. POSTMORTEM – BASIC, SPLEEN BLOOD:
1. ETHANOL28 mg/dL
2. BLOOD ALCOHOL CONCENTRATION (BAC)0.128 g/100 mL

OPINION: Based on the history provided and the autopsy findings, the cause of death is asphyxiation due to manual strangulation by another individual. The manner of death is homicide.

EVIDENCE OF INJURY

EXTERNAL EVIDENCE OF INJURY

Possible patterned abrasions of the neck and left aspect of the face.

INTERNAL EVIDENCE OF INJURY:

A 1 cm area of probable bruising on the anterior subcutaneous neck tissue.
Bruising of the superior aspect of the right sternocleidomastoid muscle.
Bruising of the soft tissue and fascial tissue of the surface of the right thyroid cartilage.
Bruising of the soft tissue associated with the right horn of the thyroid bone, which is intact.

GENERAL EXTERNAL EXAMINATION

… The body is that of a well-developed, well-nourished although decomposing Caucasian female whose appearance is generally consistent with the reported age of 34 years. The body measures approximately 67-inches long and weighs 144 pounds.
The body exhibits mild to moderate decomposition consisting of generalized discoloration, bloating and skin slippage. At the time of autopsy, rigor mortis is released in the major muscle groups. Livor mortis is not readily apparent due to post-mortem artefact. There is however an area of blanching on the right aspect of the abdomen extending along the groin to the right thigh. This is likely consistent

with an area of pressure, based on the body positioning at the time of discovery.

HEAD: Head hair is brown, normally distributed although sloughing from the scalp and measures approximately 30 cm long over the crown.

EYES: The eyes are moderately opacified (post-mortem artefact). The irides appear brown; the pupils are equal at 0.4 cm. The sclerae are dull although white. There are no discernible scleral or conjunctival petechiae.

NOSE: The nose is midline although dried. It does not grate upon palpation.

ORAL CAVITY: The oral cavity contains natural dentition in good repair. There are no discernible buccal mucosal petechiae. The lips exhibit mild drying artefact.

NECK: The neck structures are midline and without palpable adenopathy. There is a linear array of variably sized, purple-black, circular defects which extend from the inferior aspect of the chin, along the jawline, up the left aspect of the face, towards the left temporal area.

CHEST: The breasts and nipples are normal adult female without palpable masses.

ABDOMEN: The abdomen is moderately protuberant and tense. There is no detectable fluid wave.

GENITALIA: The external genitalia are largely normal adult female. However the internal genitalia are protruding through the vaginal vault. This likely represents prolapse of the uterus due to pregnancy and post-mortem artefact. Adjacent to the probable uterus is a largely degraded portion of tissue which is unfortunately covered in sandy debris from the gravesite. Upon further examination of this tissue, it is revealed to be a largely decomposed fetus. Gender and age cannot be determined, however it has the following measurements: crown/rump length of approximately 10.5 cm and a foot length of approximately

0.7 - 0.8 cm. There is an approximate 17 cm umbilical cord extending to a disrupted placental disc. The membranes are ruptured and covered with sandy debris. Portions of the placenta, umbilical cord and membranes will be retained and the fetus will be transferred to the jurisdiction of CBI for subsequent genetic analysis.

EXTREMITIES:
UPPER EXTREMITIES: The upper extremities are well-developed and symmetrical with all digits present. The fingernails are long and in good repair although markedly dirty with sand and debris from the gravesite. The fingernails are pulled and retained as evidence by law enforcement.
LOWER EXTREMITIES: The lower extremities are well developed and symmetrical with all digits present. The toenails are short and in good repair with the exception of abundant sandy debris from the gravesite.
BACK AND SACRUM: The back and sacrum are unremarkable.

GENERAL INTERNAL EXAMINATION

The body is opened with a routine thoracoabdominal incision. The subcutaneous fat measures 2 cm in thickness at the level of the umbilicus.

BODY CAVITIES: There are no abnormal fluid accumulations or adhesions in any of the body cavities. The internal organs however do exhibit marked discoloration and vacuolization due to post-mortem artefact. The internal organs are also markedly dry.

CARDIOVASCULAR SYSTEM: The heart weighs 210 grams. The epicardial surface is unremarkable. The coronary ostia are patent. The coronary arteries follow a right dominant distribution. Sectioning reveals no significant narrowing by atherosclerosis. There is no acute thrombosis. The endocardial surface and papillary muscles are unremarkable. The myocardium is red-brown, firm and without fibrosis. The valve leaflets are thin and pliant. AORTA: The aorta has a normal smooth yellow intimal surface. There is minimal atherosclerotic streaking noted. The major branches, including the celiac, superior, and inferior mesenteric, and renal arteries are widely patent. The inferior vena cava is unremarkable.

RESPIRATORY SYSTEM: The right and left lungs weigh 280 and 320 grams, respectively, and show normal septation. The lung parenchyma is pale tan-brown and markedly atelectatic. There are no masses or gross areas of consolidation. The trachea and mainstem bronchi are unremarkable. There are no foreign bodies or masses. The pulmonary arteries are free of thromboemboli.

SPLEEN: The spleen is soft and weighs 120 grams. The capsule is intact, smooth and glistening. The parenchyma is firm, red-purple and smooth. There are no infarcts, nodules, scars or cysts present.

LIVER AND BILIARY SYSTEM: LIVER: The liver weighs 900 grams. The capsule is intact. The parenchyma is firm and red-brown. No masses are detected.

GALLBLADDER: A thin-walled gallbladder contains one well-formed gallstone.

GASTROINTESTINAL TRACT:

OESOPHAGUS: The oesophagus has a uniform diameter and intact mucosa.

STOMACH: The stomach is empty. The mucosa is smooth, glistening and arranged in normal rugal folds. There are no gastric or duodenal ulcers.

SMALL AND LARGE INTESTINES: The small and large intestines have a uniform dimension and appear unremarkable. The vermiform appendix is not visualized.

PANCREAS: The pancreas is tan-orange with lobular architecture. There is no evidence of haemorrhage or saponification.

ADRENAL GLANDS: The adrenal glands have a golden cortex and grey-brown medulla.

GENITOURINARY SYSTEM:

KIDNEYS: The right and left kidneys weigh 120 and 100 grams, respectively. The capsules strip with ease. The external cortical surface is red-purple and smooth. The cortices are well delineated from the medullary pyramids. The pelves and ureters are non-dilated.

URINARY BLADDER: The urinary bladder is empty. The mucosal surface is tan-pink, moist and smooth.

FEMALE INTERNAL GENITALIA: The fallopian tubes and ovaries are unremarkable. The uterus (480 grams), measuring 19 x 14 x 2 cm, is prolapsed through the vaginal vault. The uterus is opened to reveal a predominantly empty space with membranous fragments remaining. There is also red-brown fluid and discoloration of the endometrial lining.

NECK: Traumatic injury has been previously described. The anterior musculature is smooth and dull. The epiglottis and hypopharynx are unremarkable. The hyoid bone and thyroid cartilage are intact. The laryngeal mucosa is unremarkable. There are no masses or aspirated material. The thyroid gland has symmetrical lobes and appears unremarkable.

SPINE: The spine has normal configuration. There is faintly visible hardware involving the anterior aspect of the cervical spine at the level of C6. There is no soft tissue haemorrhage or other abnormalities associated with this prior surgical site.

SKULL AND BRAIN: Reflection of the scalp reveals areas of congestion and discoloration which are likely associated with post-mortem artefact. There is no evidence of discrete haemorrhage, contusions or lacerations. Reflection of the skull reveals no evidence of epidural or subdural haemorrhage. There is no subarachnoid haemorrhage. The brain is markedly soft and discoloured (post-mortem artefact) and weighs 1080 grams. The cerebrovascular system has normal configuration. The cranial nerves are symmetrically intact. Serial coronal sections through the brain reveal no areas of haemorrhage, contusion or mass lesion within the cortex, white matter, brainstem or cerebellum. The atlanto-occipital joint is intact. The cervical spinal column has normal mobility.

SPECIMENS OBTAINED

SPECIMENS: Specimens retained at the time of autopsy include blood obtained from the spleen. Representative sections of major organs are also retained.

TOXICOLOGY: Blood obtained from the spleen is submitted to NMS Labs for analysis.

EVIDENCE:
The fetus is transferred to the Colorado Bureau of Investigation for genetic analysis if warranted in the future.
Swabs:
The palmar surfaces of the hands
Anterior and lateral neck surface
Face
X-rays: AP and lateral views of the head and neck
Bilateral fingernail clippings
Deoxyribonucleic acid blood spot card (DNA)

HISTOLOGY: Sections of heart, lung, liver, kidney, brain, right sternocleidomastoid muscle, right sternothyroid muscle, soft tissue from the surface of the right thyroid cartilage and right lobe of the thyroid are submitted for histology.

MICROSCOPIC EXAMINATION

ALL TISSUE SECTIONS EXAMINED SHOW MARKED POST MORTEM AUTOLYSIS.

THREE

Autopsy of Bella Watts

******GRAPHIC CONTENT WARNING******

The second autopsy was performed on four-year-old Bella Watts. Once again taken from Tammy Lee's report.

Bella was dressed in a pink nightgown covered in butterflies and a pair of underwear. The items were removed and collected as evidence. Bella also had a large amount of skin slippage. She had been x-rayed and there was concern she might have suffered a broken jaw. The x-rays were sent to a Paediatric Radiologist at Children's Hospital who advised it appeared to be gas in the area of the jaw and not an actual fracture. It also appeared Bella had some scrapes to her buttocks and the tops of both shoulders thought to be where she was too wide to enter the opening of the tank without force.

Dr Burson also pointed out the following:

Bella's frenulum (skin connecting the top lip to the gum) was torn, which created a large hole.

The inside of Bella's gums and inner lip also appeared bruised and it appeared she had bit into her tongue

Bella's injuries were consistent with hard downward pressure on her nose and mouth.

Bella's death was violent. It appeared she struggled to get away.

Dr Burson advised Bella's preliminary cause of death was asphyxiation due to manual smothering. He did not note any bruising or injury to Bella's neck. (Official autopsy below)

FULL AUTOPSY REPORT

Name of decedent: Bella Watts **Case#:** AW18-156
Investigation#: WCCO 18-436
Date and time of death: August 16, 2018 at 1750 hrs (Pronounced)
Age: 4 YEARS
Date and time of autopsy: August 17, 2018 at 1330 hrs **Sex:** Female

DIAGNOSES:

HISTORY OF BEING REPORTED MISSING AND SUBSEQUENTLY LOCATED IN AN OBVIOUS STATE OF DEATH WITHIN AN OIL TANK BATTERY:
ASPHYXIATION DUE TO SMOTHERING
BLUNT FORCE TRAUMA OF THE FRENULUM AND GINGIVAL MUCOSA OF THE MAXILLA
POSTMORTEM ARTIFACT (DECOMPOSITION)
OIL, WATER AND SLUDGE DEBRIS IN THE STOMACH
HYDROCARBON EXPOSURE
TOXICOLOGY:
A. POSTMORTEM – BASIC, LIVER TISSUENONE DETECTED
B. HYDROCARBON AND OXYGENATED VOLATILES PANEL, CHEST CAVITY BLOOD:
1. BENZENEPRESENT
2. ETHYLBENZENEPRESENT
3. TOLUENE3.7 mcg/mL
4. XYLENES (O,M,P)PRESENT
5. N-HEXANEPRESENT
6. METHYLPENTANES (2-,3-ISOMERS)PRESENT
7. N-BUTANOLPRESENT
8. ETHANOL13 mg/dL
9. ACETALDEHYDEPRESENT

OPINION:

Based on the history provided and the autopsy findings, the cause of death is asphyxiation due to smothering. The toxicology results likely represent decomposition and an artefact of being submerged in an oil tank for several days. The manner of death is homicide.

EVIDENCE OF INJURY

EXTERNAL EVIDENCE OF INJURY

A 13 x 3 cm area of vertical excoriations on the left buttocks.
An at least 1.5 cm laceration of the frenulum and upper gum line with associated pink-purple contusions.
Superficial probable bite wounds of the mucosal surface of the tongue
• A 9 x up to 4 cm yellow-tan possible abrasion on the left torso.
A 3 x 1.5 cm faint yellow-tan discoloration on the superior aspect of the left shoulder.

INTERNAL EVIDENCE OF INJURY:
None

GENERAL EXTERNAL EXAMINATION

… The body is that of a well-developed, well-nourished Caucasian female whose appearance is generally consistent with the reported age of 4 years. The body measures approximately 41-inches long and weighs 38 pounds.
At the time of autopsy, rigor mortis is released in the major muscle groups and the muscles of mastication. Livor mortis is not readily apparent due to post-mortem artefact (decomposition). There is post-mortem artefact consisting of bloating, marbling of the abdominal surfaces and areas of skin slippage. Unfortunately, the body was found in an oil tanker containing oil and aqueous fluid. This resulted in abundant skin slippage upon washing.

HEAD: Head hair is blonde-brown, normally distributed and measures up to 15 cm long over the crown.

EYES: The eyes are moderately opacified (post-mortem artefact). The irides appear brown; the pupils are equal at 0.3 cm. The sclerae are dull, however there are no discernible scleral or conjunctival petechiae.

NOSE: The nose is midline and does not grate upon palpation.

ORAL CAVITY: The oral cavity contains natural dentition in good repair. The frenulum is markedly disrupted and there are adjacent pink-purple bruises of the buccal mucosa present. There are also teeth impressions and superficial bite marks on the mucosal surface of the tongue.

NECK: The neck structures are midline and without palpable adenopathy.

CHEST: The breasts and nipples are normal female.

ABDOMEN: The abdomen is mildly protuberant and slightly tense (post-mortem artefact).

GENITALIA: The external genitalia are normal female.

EXTREMITIES:

UPPER EXTREMITIES: The upper extremities are well-developed and symmetrical with all digits present. The fingernails are short, dirty and in fair repair without evidence of tearing. The fingernails are clipped and retained as evidence.

LOWER EXTREMITIES: The lower extremities are well-developed and symmetrical with all digits present. The toenails are short, dirty and in fair repair.

BACK AND SACRUM: The back and sacrum are unremarkable.

GENERAL INTERNAL EXAMINATION

The body is opened with a routine thoracoabdominal incision. The subcutaneous fat measures 1.2 cm in thickness at the level of the umbilicus.

BODY CAVITIES: There are no abnormal fluid accumulations or adhesions in any of the body cavities.

CARDIOVASCULAR SYSTEM: The heart weighs 80 grams. The epicardial surface is unremarkable. The coronary ostia are patent. The coronary arteries follow a right dominant distribution. Sectioning reveals no significant narrowing by atherosclerosis. There is no acute thrombosis. The endocardial surface and papillary muscles are unremarkable. The myocardium is red-brown, firm and without fibrosis. The valve leaflets are thin and pliant.

AORTA: The aorta has a normal smooth yellow intimal surface. There is minimal atherosclerotic streaking noted. The major branches, including the celiac, superior, and inferior mesenteric, and renal arteries are widely patent. The inferior vena cava is unremarkable.

RESPIRATORY SYSTEM: The right and left lungs weigh 160 and 140 grams, respectively, and show normal septation. The lung parenchyma is mottled pink-tan to purple. There are no masses or gross areas of consolidation. The trachea and mainstem bronchi are unremarkable. There are no foreign bodies or masses. The pulmonary arteries are free of thromboemboli.

SPLEEN: The spleen is soft and weighs 60 grams. The capsule is intact, smooth and glistening. The parenchyma is firm, red-purple and smooth. There are no infarcts, nodules, scars or cysts present.

LIVER AND BILIARY SYSTEM:

LIVER: The liver weighs 350 grams. The capsule is intact. The parenchyma is firm and red-brown. No masses are detected.

GALLBLADDER: A thin-walled gallbladder is empty.

GASTROINTESTINAL TRACT:

OESOPHAGUS: The oesophagus has a uniform diameter and intact mucosa.

STOMACH: The stomach contains approximately 75 ml of viscous, green-black fluid which is suggestive of oil and particulate matter from the oil tank which she was in. The mucosa is smooth, glistening and arranged in normal rugal folds. There are no gastric or duodenal ulcers.

SMALL AND LARGE INTESTINES: The small and large intestines have a uniform dimension and appear unremarkable. The vermiform appendix is present.

PANCREAS: The pancreas is tan-orange with lobular architecture. There is no evidence of haemorrhage or saponification.

ADRENAL GLANDS: The adrenal glands have a golden cortex and grey-brown medulla.

GENITOURINARY SYSTEM:

KIDNEYS: The right and left kidneys weigh 50 grams each. The capsules strip with ease. The external cortical surface is red-purple and smooth. The cortices are well delineated from the medullary pyramids. The pelves and ureters are non-dilated.

URINARY BLADDER: The urinary bladder is empty. The mucosal surface is tan-pink, moist and smooth.

FEMALE INTERNAL GENITALIA: The cervix, uterus, fallopian tubes and ovaries are unremarkable.

NECK: The anterior musculature is smooth and glistening. The epiglottis and hypopharynx are unremarkable. The hyoid bone and thyroid cartilage are intact. The laryngeal mucosa is pink-purple, moist and smooth. There are no masses or aspirated material. The thyroid gland has symmetrical lobes and appears unremarkable.

SPINE: The spine has normal configuration.

SKULL AND BRAIN: Reflection of the scalp reveals patchy areas of likely Tardieu spots. These areas are incised to reveal superficial blood collections within the fascial planes. There do not appear to be any contusions present. The skull is intact and without fracture. The dura is intact and without epidural or subdural haemorrhage. There is no subarachnoid haemorrhage. The brain is moderately edematous with flattening of the gyri and narrowing of the sulci and weighs 1300 grams. The cerebrovascular system has normal configuration. The cranial nerves are symmetrically intact. Serial coronal sections through the brain reveal no areas of haemorrhage, contusion or mass lesion within the cortex, white matter, brainstem or cerebellum. The atlantooccipital joint is intact. The cervical spinal column has normal mobility.

SPECIMENS OBTAINED

SPECIMENS: Specimens retained at the time of autopsy include vitreous fluid and blood collected from the peripheral veins, heart and lungs.

TOXICOLOGY: Pooled blood as described above and liver are submitted to NMS Labs for analysis.

HISTOLOGY: Sections of heart, lung, liver, kidney, and brain are submitted for histology.

EVIDENCE:
Swabs of face prior to washing
Swabs of anterior neck prior to washing
Swabs of face after washing
Swabs of anterior neck after washing
Swabs of bilateral hands (palmar surface)
Oral swabs
Vaginal swabs
Bilateral fingernail clippings
Deoxyribonucleic acid blood spot card (DNA)

Radiographs (x-rays):
Full body x-rays are taken and submitted to the Weld County Coroner's Office.

MICROSCOPIC EXAMINATION

HEART: Sections of the heart are without histopathologic abnormality.

LUNG: Sections of the lung are without histopathologic abnormality.

LIVER: Sections of the liver are without histopathologic abnormality.

KIDNEY: Sections of the kidney are without histopathologic abnormality.

BRAIN: Sections of the brain are without histopathologic abnormality.

FOUR

Autopsy of Celeste Watts

******GRAPHIC CONTENT WARNING******

The final autopsy performed was on three-year-old Celeste Watts.

Celeste was dressed in a pink nightgown, *Minnie Mouse* underwear and a pull up nappy/diaper. The nightgown and underwear were collected as evidence.

Celeste also had a large amount of skin slippage. She didn't appear to have any obvious signs of injury or bruising to her neck area. There didn't appear to be any injury to her mouth or face.

Dr Burson advised Celeste's preliminary cause of death was asphyxiation due to manual smothering.

During the autopsies, Dr Burson measured the hip and shoulder width of both Bella and Celeste and advised the smallest width was on Celeste at nine-and-a-half inches. The opening of the hatch to the oil tank was only eight inches in diameter.

The items of evidence collected were packaged and turned over to Detective Baumhover.

FULL AUTOPSY REPORT

Name of decedent: Celeste Watts Case#: AW18-157

Investigation#: WCCO 18-437
Date and time of death: August 16, 2018 at 1540 hrs (pronounced)Age: 3 YEARS
Date and time of autopsy: August 17, 2018 at 1730 hrs **Sex:** Female

DIAGNOSES:

HISTORY OF BEING REPORTED MISSING AND SUBSEQUENTLY LOCATED IN AN OBVIOUS STATE OF DEATH WITHIN AN OIL TANK BATTERY:
A. ASPHYXIATION DUE TO SMOTHERING
B. MILD POSTMORTEM ARTIFACT
TOXICOLOGY: A. POSTMORTEM – BASIC, SPLEEN BLOOD-NONE DETECTED B. HYDROCARBON AND OXYGENATED VOLATILES PANEL, SPLEEN BLOOD:
1. N-BUTANOL4.4 mcg/mL
2. ETHANOL31 mg/dL
3. N-PROPANOLPRESENT
4. ACETALDEHYDEPRESENT
C. ETHANOL, LIVER TISSUESEE COMMENT
1. COMMENT: THE CONCENTRATION OF THE ETHANOL INCREASED FROM 99 MG/100 G TO 174 MG/100 G OVER THE COURSE OF MULTIPLE ANALYSES. THE NATURE OF THE SPECIMEN AND/OR THE CONTAINER TYPE WHICH MAY NOT CONTAIN PRESERVATIVE, MAY EXPLAIN THE VARIABLE QUANTITATIVE RESULTS.

OPINION:

Based on the history provided and the autopsy findings, the likely cause of death is asphyxiation due to smothering. The toxicology results likely represent decomposition and an artefact of being submerged in an oil tank for several days. The manner of death is homicide.

EVIDENCE OF INJURY

EXTERNAL EVIDENCE OF INJURY:

No significant trauma is noted.

INTERNAL EVIDENCE OF INJURY:

None.

GENERAL EXTERNAL EXAMINATION

... The body is that of a well-developed, well-nourished Caucasian female whose appearance is generally consistent with the reported age of 3 years. The body measures approximately 37 ½ inches long and weighs 37 pounds.
At the time of autopsy, rigor mortis is released in the major muscle groups and the muscles of mastication. Livor mortis is not readily apparent due to post-mortem artefact.
The body exhibits mild post-mortem artefact consisting of generalized bloating, areas of marbling, skin discoloration and skin slippage.
During the washing procedure, the majority of the skin is sloughed from the surface.

HEAD: Head hair is red-brown, normally distributed and measures up to 15 cm long over the crown.

EYES: The eyes are opacified (post-mortem artefact). The irides appear brown; the pupils are equal at 0.3 cm. The sclerae are dull and there are no discernible scleral or conjunctival petechiae.

NOSE: The nose is midline and does not grate upon palpation.

ORAL CAVITY: The oral cavity contains natural dentition in good repair. There are no buccal mucosal petechiae.

NECK: The neck structures are midline and without palpable adenopathy.

CHEST: The breasts and nipples are normal female.

ABDOMEN: The abdomen is mildly protuberant and tense (post-mortem artefact). There is no detectable fluid wave.

GENITALIA: The external genitalia are normal female.

EXTREMITIES:

UPPER EXTREMITIES: The upper extremities are well-developed and symmetrical. The palmar surfaces of the hands were previously sloughed off during the body recovery process and are packaged separately. The palmar surfaces of the hands and digits and the accompanying fingernails are retained and transferred to the jurisdiction of the Colorado Bureau of Investigation.

LOWER EXTREMITIES: The lower extremities are well-developed and symmetrical with all digits present. The toenails are short, slightly dirty and in good repair.

BACK AND SACRUM: The back and sacrum are unremarkable.

GENERAL INTERNAL EXAMINATION

The body is opened with a routine thoracoabdominal incision. The subcutaneous fat measures 1 cm in thickness at the level of the umbilicus.

BODY CAVITIES: There are no abnormal fluid accumulations or adhesions in any of the body cavities. The internal organs all exhibit marked discolouration and vacuolization due to post-mortem artefact.

CARDIOVASCULAR SYSTEM: The heart weighs 80 grams. The epicardial surface is unremarkable. The coronary ostia are patent. The coronary arteries follow a right dominant distribution. Sectioning reveals no significant narrowing by atherosclerosis. There is no acute thrombosis. The endocardial surface and papillary muscles are unremarkable. The myocardium is red-brown, firm and without fibrosis. The valve leaflets are thin and pliant.

AORTA: The aorta has a normal smooth yellow intimal surface. There is minimal atherosclerotic streaking noted. The major branches, including the celiac, superior, and inferior mesenteric, and renal arteries are widely patent. The inferior vena cava is unremarkable.

RESPIRATORY SYSTEM: The right and left lungs weigh 180 and

160 grams, respectively, and show normal septation. The lung parenchyma is dark pink-tan to purple and markedly atelectatic. There are no masses or gross areas of consolidation. The trachea and mainstem bronchi are unremarkable. There are no foreign bodies or masses. The pulmonary arteries are free of thromboemboli.

SPLEEN: The spleen is soft and weighs 40 grams. The capsule is intact, smooth and glistening. The parenchyma is firm, red-purple and smooth. There are no infarcts, nodules, scars or cysts present.

LIVER AND BILIARY SYSTEM:

LIVER: The liver weighs 320 grams. The capsule is intact. The parenchyma is firm and red-brown. No masses are detected.

GALLBLADDER: A thin-walled gallbladder is empty.

GASTROINTESTINAL TRACT:

OESOPHAGUS: The oesophagus has a uniform diameter and intact mucosa. STOMACH: The stomach is empty. The mucosa is smooth, glistening and arranged in normal rugal folds. There are no gastric or duodenal ulcers.

SMALL AND LARGE INTESTINES: The small and large intestines have a uniform dimension and appear unremarkable. The vermiform appendix is present.

PANCREAS: The pancreas is tan-orange with lobular architecture. There is no evidence of haemorrhage or saponification.

ADRENAL GLANDS: The adrenal glands have a golden cortex and grey-brown medulla.

GENITOURINARY SYSTEM:

KIDNEYS: The right and left kidneys weigh 50 and 40 grams, respectively. The capsules strip with ease. The external cortical surface is red-purple and smooth. The cortices are well delineated from the medullary pyramids. The pelves and ureters are non-dilated.

URINARY BLADDER: The urinary bladder is empty. The mucosal surface is tan-pink, moist and smooth.

FEMALE INTERNAL GENITALIA: The cervix, uterus, fallopian tubes and ovaries are unremarkable.

NECK: The anterior musculature is smooth and glistening. The epiglottis and hypopharynx are unremarkable. The hyoid bone and thyroid cartilage are intact. The laryngeal mucosa is pink-purple, moist and smooth. There are no masses or aspirated material. The thyroid gland has symmetrical lobes and appears unremarkable.

SPINE: The spine has normal configuration.

SKULL AND BRAIN: Reflection of the scalp reveals no areas of laceration, contusion or hematoma. The skull is intact and without fracture. The dura is intact and without epidural or subdural haemorrhage. There is no subarachnoid haemorrhage. The brain markedly soft and edematous (post-mortem artefact) and weighs 1280 grams. The cerebrovascular system has normal configuration. The cranial nerves are symmetrically intact. Serial coronal sections through the brain reveal no areas of haemorrhage, contusion or mass lesion within the cortex, white matter, brainstem or cerebellum. The atlanto-occipital joint is intact. The cervical spinal column has normal mobility.

SPECIMENS OBTAINED

SPECIMENS: Specimens retained at the time of autopsy include pooled blood from the iliac veins and heart, blood obtained from the spleen and liver tissue.

TOXICOLOGY: Pooled blood, spleen blood and liver tissue are submitted to NMS Labs for analysis.

HISTOLOGY: Sections of heart, lung, liver, kidney and brain are submitted for histology.

EVIDENCE:
Swabs of face prior to washing
Swabs of anterior neck prior to washing
Swabs of face after washing
Swabs of anterior neck after washing
Swabs of bilateral hands (palmar surface)
Oral swabs
Vaginal swabs
Skin (palmar surfaces) and fingernails from the bilateral hands
Deoxyribonucleic acid blood spot card (DNA)

Radiographs (x-rays):
Full body x-rays are taken and submitted to the Weld County Coroner's Office

MICROSCOPIC EXAMINATION

HEART: Sections of the heart are without histopathologic abnormality.

LUNG: Sections of the lung are without histopathologic abnormality.

LIVER: Sections of the liver are without histopathologic abnormality.

KIDNEY: Sections of the kidney are without histopathologic abnormality.

BRAIN: Sections of the brain are without histopathologic abnormality.

FIVE

Second Police Interview - Nichol Kessinger

(TAKEN FROM THE DISCOVERY AUDIO FILES)

16th August 2018

***Koback* -** Agent Kevin Koback
***Martinez* -** Agent Tim Martinez
***Nichol* -** Nichol Kessinger
***Duane:* -** Duane Kessinger

Koback: Um, we introduced ourselves in the lobby and... earlier so we're just gonna do that again real quick. My name's Kevin Koback, I'm with the Colorado Bureau of Investigation and, uh, we're assisting the Frederick Police Department with this case involving Chris Watts. And this is Tim Martinez...
Martinez: Also an agent for CBI.
Koback: Sir, if you'd just introduce yourself?
Duane: Duane Kessinger. I'm Ni… Nichol's father.
Koback: Duane what's your birthday?
Duane: November 3, 1958.
Koback: And home address for you, sir?
Duane: Duane provided his home address.
Koback: What city?
Duane: And that's, uh, Arvada, 8004.

Koback: And a cell phone or, uh, home phone or where we can reach you?
Duane: Duane provided his phone number.
Koback: Thank you. And Nichol can you just introduce yourself for the recording?
Nichol: Nichol Kessinger. Do you need all the other stuff too?
Koback: Yes, please.
Nichol: Nichol provided her address and phone number.
Koback: Is that... I think we determined it was Northglenn, right?
Nichol: Yes.
Koback: Do you know your zip code?
Nichol: (zip code).
Koback: Okay. Can you speak up just a little bit so the recorder...
Nichol: Yeah.
Koback: I know you're tired and you're stressed, um, and we won't be here any longer than we have to be. Uh, you've already had a conversation with people before. You came here on your own free will to talk to us. We picked you up at... at your request and brought you here. Um, you can get up and leave at any time. You don't have to talk to us. If there's a question you don't want to answer don't answer it. If you don't want to talk anymore, just tell me I want to... I... tell me, 'I want to leave,' and I'm kind of in the way of the door but you're not being... uh, you're... you're not being, uh, interrogated as a criminal suspect, we're here to understand your relationship with Chris and what you know about Chris and his family and, uh, events relating to Chris Watts. Um, and do you know him as Chris or Christopher?
Nichol: Either one.
Koback: Okay. Um, so the phone number that you reached him on, can you tell me what that number was?
Nichol: I think I deleted that out of my phone too. I just, like, cut him out of my life. It's a 910 number, you guys have it.
Duane: Well we gave it to Mark yesterday.
Nichol: Yeah. So...
Koback: I... I probably have it but just in case...
Nichol: ... he'll have it. I don't have it anymore.
Koback: If I recited it to you would you know it?
Nichol: Just the first three numbers.
Koback: Okay. But you...

Nichol: 91...
Koback: ... know it as a 910 number?
Nichol: Yes, that's what I do know. I... I mean that's...
Koback: Okay.
Nichol: ...what I've got.
Duane: North Carolina or something.
Koback: Yeah, North Carolina.
Nichol: That's what it is.
Koback: Okay. So, let's just start with, like, a timeline of your, um, getting to know Chris, how you guys met, where you met, all those things. Let's just run... and I... I'm not gonna ask you specific questions unless I think it's necessary. I'll let you just tell me your story. I think it's a little bit easier that way. So I just want to know how you met him, where you met him, how long you guys were dating, uh, and those kind of things initially.
Nichol: Okay. Um, I think I met him sometime in June, probably early June. It might've been May, it was just talking at work, it was pretty casual. Um, and, uh, he didn't have a wedding ring on his finger and every time I talked to him he didn't tell me that he was in a relationship, he didn't even mention his kids right away either. Um, and then one day he told me that he had two kids. I was like, that's pretty cool. And, uh, so he was telling me about his kids...
Koback: That sounded like a sarcastic comment.
Nichol: No, I thought it was kind of cute. I was like, oh he's a dad. It was right around Father's Day too so whenever that is, is that in June? Yeah.
Koback: Okay. I'm not good with holidays.
Nichol: So that's... he told me he had kids and then it was Father's Day shortly after that so...
Koback: Okay.
Nichol: ... that's what I do know. And I was like... no I thought it was cute. And then, um, he was telling me about 'em, he was pretty excited about 'em. And then he mentioned that he did have a significant other and then he told me that those two were in the process of a separation.
Koback: Did he mention the children's name or his significant other's name?
Nichol: Um, I didn't know his significant other's name for a while.

And then, I think he told me his kids' names pretty quick but to be honest with you on an exact date of when that happened, I don't know.
Koback: So in May and June... first of all. Where do you work?
Nichol: I work at *Anadarko Petroleum Corporation*. I'm contracted to *Anadarko Petroleum Corporation.*
Koback: Okay and you work out of an office setting, where?
Nichol: In Platteville, Colorado.
Koback: Okay. And Chris also works out of that location, per se?
Nichol: Yes. Yes. He's in the field but he comes into the office with his team.
Koback: So you work... uh, what is your job responsibility?
Nichol: I do healthy- health, safety, and environment.
Koback: Okay. So you work in the office and you take care of health safety for... *Anadarko* is an oil and gas company, right?
Nichol: Yes.
Koback: So you're doing health safety in the office and Chris works in the field...
Nichol: Yes.
Koback: ... as a... what... what kind of job does he do?
Nichol: He's an operator so I don't know all of his daily duties but he's a field operator, so he works with the oil wells.
Koback: So he goes out and does work on those, whatever...
Nichol: Yes.
Koback: ...uh, that work might be? But he comes into the office frequent for...?
Nichol: In the mornings. His team meets in the mornings. They don't... they're not all in there every day. Some days some of 'em are in there, some days other ones are in there but in the mornings typically from like six-fifteen to probably seven, somewhere around there.
Koback: And is that where you met Chris?
Nichol: Yes.
Koback: Okay. So can you just take us through, kind of, a little bit of, uh, the early part of how you guys... how he courted you or you courted him. I don't know which one happened, um, how you guys got to know each other?
Nichol: Um, I guess we just started talking, he actually... um, so, part of my job is to manage the gas monitors that we have so *Anadarko* requires all of their field personnel to carry like, uh, gas monitor

sensors for toxic gases and it's my job to control all the inventory, any issues, anything like that. Um, and we were havin' some pretty serious equipment issues and we had, uh, numerous amounts of people coming in my office one day and he happened to be one of them. Um, and I had seen him before, like, they meet in the... in the lunchroom and that's where I go put my lunch in the fridge so I had seen him but I didn't never talk to him. Um, so that day we just started talking and then every time I saw him in the hallway after that and it was always hit or miss, like, it wasn't an everyday thing. It was just when I saw him we just started talking and we just, kind of, had a lot in common and just hit it off. So we'd always have, you know, pretty good conversations. And then I don't know, one day he just... he... he told me that he had kids and started talking about his kids and then mentioned, 'Yes, that I have a wife but we're getting separated.' I said, 'Okay,' and then...

Koback: When do you think that was?

Nichol: When he said all that?

Koback: So specifically, when he told you he was getting separated from his wife, was that within the first couple weeks that you knew him, or was that later on? You said you met him around May or June...

Nichol: Yeah it was still in June.

Koback: Okay.

Nichol: It would've been before Father's Day.

Koback: So had you guys ever gone out on any kind of, um...

Nichol: No.

Koback: ... date at that time? You just were...

Nichol: No, no, no, no.

Koback: ... conversing at work?

Nichol: Yeah that's all it was. And then, um, I don't know, we started hanging out. We hung out. We went to... we went to a park, hung out at a park.

Koback: Let's go back real quick. So he took... why did he tell you that he was getting a divorce? Did he ask you out at that time?

Nichol: No, he didn't. I think he was probably interested in me and so, um, he talked to me a couple times, uh, via his work phone and I was like, uh, no. Like, it was still very, like, friendly conversation. But then when I realized this man is interested in me, I'm interested in him, this is personal, so we got away from the *Anadarko* thing 'cause I really don't want those guys affiliated with any of this. And...

Koback: So you have a work phone that's specifically...?
Nichol: No. I have one phone that I do both on. He has two phones.
Koback: Okay. So he had your phone, the 720-656...
Nichol: That's the only number that I wrote with all the time.
Koback: Okay.
Nichol: So *he* has two phones.
Koback: All right. And one of those owned by *Anadarko* and...
Nichol: Yes, sir.
Koback: ... one personal.
Nichol: Yes, sir.
Koback: Do you know what his *Anadarko* phone number was?
Nichol: Nope.
Koback: Okay.
Nichol: It's been so long, and, I mean, I'm sure I could, like, look it up, but I tried to look it up for those guys yesterday and I couldn't find it.
Koback: Okay.
Nichol: Um...
Koback: We can find it, that's okay. I just wondered if you knew it.
Nichol: Um, but at that point we just took it to his phone 'cause I just felt it was better that way. Um, and we just continued to talk and then, um...
Koback: Let me go back to the park, where was the park?
Nichol: It's down the street from my house, it's called East Lake Number Three.
Koback: Your... your house...
Nichol: Yes.
Koback: ... in Northglenn?
Nichol: Yes.
Koback: And that was in the June timeframe?
Nichol: I... yeah. Well, like, the beginning of July, it was right around my birthday, like, so sometime in the very end of June, beginning of July.
Koback: Okay. And that's the first meeting you had outside of work?
Nichol: Yeah.
Koback: Um, basic conversation for a first date?
Nichol: I mean, we kept it pretty simple, I guess, you know, um. I don't even remember everything we talked about...
Koback: Sure.

Nichol: ... we were there for a few hours, um, but...
Koback: Understand my... so if... if I ask about conversation what I'm looking for… was he talking about his family during any of these meetings? Those are the kind of… I understand, uh, there, you know, whatever you guys were talking about relationship, your life, your interest, those things, I... we don't need to know that. What I'm interested in is knowing is when he brings up his children, when he brings up his wife, when he brings up financial information, when he brings up his home, when he brings up anything that may have been… and… and it's been a few days so you've had a chance to reflect on, um, some articles that you may have read and you know unfortunately that you're in a situation where somebody has been murdered. And that information when you look backwards, um, in your memory with the conversations with Chris, anything that he might've said that would be relative to that… and I'm not just, you know… and even if one day he was mad and he said, I want to do this or do that, um, you know, anything like that. If he ever made any kind of statements that you were like, whoa that was weird, um, or why would he say that or why did he mention that. Do you understand what I'm... I'm looking for?
Nichol: No, I completely understand, I just feel like some of this happened so long ago that I can't tell you, like, the exact words of the exact conversation at the exact time and place...
Koback: Sure.
Nichol: ... because it's, like, we had a lot of conversations. I mean, we talked every single day so it's like...
Koback: So if there's a...
Nichol: ... I'm trying to help you guys with the stuff, like, the stuff that's more current I can give you guys a lot more detail and exact times but when you're asking me about something that happened six weeks ago and exactly what was said it's, like... I mean I'm sure I can give you a general idea but to be honest with you, like, to pinpoint exact words it's not gonna happen.
Koback: I'm not lookin' for exact words, um, just more… let's say six weeks ago he said something that triggered with you last night, um, that's what I'd be looking for—or something four weeks ago. And if you don't remember where it was, or the specific words, that doesn't matter, just he said something that was off the wall or he said this or he said that, that has caused you a moment to pause and you go wow I

wonder why he said that, now knowing what you know today. Do you understand where... where I'm goin' with that?
Nichol: I completely understand and, to be honest with you, I mean, there were several discussions that we had about his current relationship and where it had gone and what it had caused, um, and he talked about his kids from time to time. But the thing is he was never hostile, it was never anything aggressive. Like, even when he spoke of his wife and the fact that they were separating it was never ill, it was... it was very... it was still very kind, it was just like, 'This is not working', you know, and would explain why but it wasn't anything out of the ordinary or anything that I think would scare me. And to this day, even after everything that I found out I still look back at that and I don't see any red lights with the way that he spoke of his family.
Koback: Okay.
Nichol: At all.
Koback: Can you just describe his de… overall demeanour over the eight, ten, twelve weeks that you guys knew each other?
Nichol: It wasn't that long. It was like six weeks that we were hangin' out. Well, I guess we knew each other longer but...
Koback: Okay, but you met him in the office and just his overall persona of who he was... was he aggressive, was he mellow, was he calm, was he outspoken? Well… who was Chris?
Nichol: He... I… you know, I think he's an introvert. I would consider him to be a pretty… I don't want to say he's a very reserved individual, I think he's probably more reserved around other people. I think he emphasized to me that one of the reasons that he really enjoyed talking to me is because if… he felt like he could get out of his shell. He said around most people he just didn't really feel the... the need to... to, like, talk and converse. And it wasn't just in his home life, just in general, it wasn't something where he... he's an introvert. And he said with him... with me it made him feel like he could really just start talking about things that excited him and I think a lot of that had to do with the fact that we had things in common. Um, so with me, I think he was a little bit more outgoing but even then I would still consider him to be an introvert. I mean not...
Koback: So...
Nichol: ... on the extreme end. If an introvert went to like one to ten I'd put him at like a four or a five, so on the lighter side of introversion.

Koback: ... so, pretty even keel?
Nichol: Yes, like really relaxed all the time, he was never really, like, worked up about anything. Just...
Koback: Mellow...
Nichol: ... chilled.
Koback: ... easy-going guy?
Nichol: Very much.
Koback: Okay. And he was that way with you... did you ever... did he ever have any kind of, uh... did you guys ever have arguments?
I mean...
Nichol: No.
Koback: ... pretty short relationship, no arguments during that time?
Nichol: No.
Koback: Did he ever lose his temper at any time?
Nichol: Never.
Koback: You guys never had a yelling match?
Nichol: No.
Koback: So, you never saw him upset or mad?
Nichol: No. And there was a couple times that we had some disagreements on some things that, as we, like, further progressed into this story, you know, but it was never... like, I am very calm when I talk to people, it's like extremely rational when I handle situations that there's a disagreement in. And he always was the exact same way, like, always. Like, I never stress anything. I think one thing that actually kind of drew me to him was the fact that he was very open with communicating with me if there were any, like, differences on how we saw things or… or just like open-minded about things. It was... it was... actually I... I personally thought it was kind of unique because usually most of the men that I've ever met are typically very closed off and I didn't get that from him, at all. But it was always, like, kind. Very kind.
Koback: So, no sense that this guy had a temper or...
Nichol: Not at all.
Koback: ... wasn't... was aggressive or he never lost his mind and yelled and said crazy stuff or anything like that?
Nichol: No.
Koback: Okay.
Nichol: No.

Koback: So can we just kind of go back to your relationship, you say you guys had a lot in common. What... what was that?
Nichol: Well, I mean, like, were both really into fitness, I think that's important, it's a lifestyle. Um, both of us ate pretty healthy so I think that was important as well. Um, he is a total gearhead. He likes cars a lot and I don't know nearly as much about them but it's always been something that I've been pretty interested in so we'd definitely talk about stuff like that. Um, and I... I guess he was always willing to learn new stuff, and vice versa. I like to travel a lot, it's not something that he's done a lot but he seemed, like, really interested in what I had to share with him and vice versa. So, even if it wasn't something that we originally had in common together, it was just like, hey I respect what you have to say, and vice versa.
Koback: So you guys just yin and yang, you got along pretty well?
Nichol: Very well.
Koback: And no tim… he never gave you any indication that...
Nichol: None.
Koback: ... that he was having issues, um, so you... when... during your guys' dating time did you guys spend most of the time at your place?
Nichol: Always.
Koback: Okay. Always at your place.
Nichol: I told… well or we'd go out but, um, I told Mark yesterday. He asked me if I went over there and I told him about one time that I went over to that house. I've been to that house twice, but it was very, very brief and it was not an extended stay. I did not feel comfortable there or, like, I just didn't want to be there, it's not my life. That is somebody else's life and somebody else's existence and I respect that… that's their space. So I used to tell him, 'Well, come to my house because this is, like, this is our space. This is my space.' And so for me out of respect just for, like, whatever situation he had going on and the fact that it's not my home, um, I felt that it was better to... to be in my place. And I... I live alone. I don't have any roommates or anything so it's pretty easy to do that.
Koback: So, during June and July did you… were you aware that he, uh... his family was not… his… did you meet his children...
Nichol: No...
Koback: ... during June and July?

Nichol: ... I didn't want to. And he didn't ask me to.
Koback: Okay.
Nichol: I mean not that I didn't want to ever, it was just not now, it's like, you're not finalized with your separation and not only that, we've barely been dating, like, you can't introduce kids to somebody new in a situation like that, that's something that takes time. I mean would I have liked to have met them? Of course. They, you know, I mean that would've been a... a great honour for me to have somebody introduce their children into my life, you know, and... and... but not then. It was something that it was like, okay well let's see where we're at in six months. Let's see where we're at in a year and if we're still doing this and you and me are still, you know, happy with where we're at and you think that this is something that is gonna be long term and is worth bringing your children into the picture then yes I would love to meet them. But it's like, not right now. You are still in this situation when you're not even completely out of it and I'm getting in it and that's not fair for them. And that was kind of the policy that I had with him was it was just like, yes but not yet.
Koback: So did he ask to introduce you to his children?
Nichol: Not at that time.
Koback: Okay.
Nichol: I think both him and I were on the same page of eventually, if things went as they should in a relationship...
Koback: I understand you guys' relationship is very new and young and, um...
Nichol: Yeah.
Koback: ... so although it was short I... just laying everything out helps us understand what actually was going on with him and...
Nichol: Yeah.
Koback: ... some... we may... I might ask her a question and you're going, why the heck would he ask her that, probably because I have information that I'm not willing to share with you and I'll tell you that right now. I'm not gonna tell you... some questions I'm gonna ask you and you'll go, 'What the heck?' I won't... I won't share some information with you, just it protects you and it protects our investigation so if it seems weird there's a reason I'm asking it and...
Nichol: That's fine.

Koback: ... it's usually relative to what I know. Um, so don't... don't take offense to it. Again, it's just part of what we need to know. Um...
Nichol: Understood.
Koback: So, just… you went to his house on two occasions...
Nichol: Yes.
Koback: ... were... was that recent?
Nichol: No that was like pretty early into it and I did not like it and did not want to go back.
Koback: Do you recall where the house was?
Nichol: Yeah, it's right off the highway in Frederick.
Koback: Okay. And you know the streets?
Nichol: I mean, I'm sure I could figure it out again if I really had to, like, off the top of my head no.
Koback: Do you know the street name?
Nichol: No.
Koback: Okay.
Nichol: I would have to drive around in there to get there.
Koback: Okay. Um, did it look like anybody else lived at that house at that time?
Nichol: Oh, definitely.
Koback: Okay.
Nichol: I mean the whole thing...
Koback: So, is that what freaked you out?
Nichol: I mean, he told me that he was living in the basement, um, and said, 'We're separated but we're not divorced and we're gonna get ready to sell the house.' And that was the impression that I was under. And I was under the impression that they were taking everything pretty slow with this with, like, getting ready to sell the house. I mean, those are big things. So that's what I was informed, and I mean if you think about it this whole thing happened in a six week stretch, like, that's really that much of a timeframe. So in that sense, like, it's believable to me. Um, yes, I went... I went to the house and, um, the first time I was there, um, I hung out in their front living room. I just sat on the floor and it was on the 4th of July, it was the morning of the 4th and I was helping him, uh, to set up *My Fitness Pal* app and like track his food and his calories and stuff 'cause he does pretty good with the working out and stuff and he asked me, he's like, 'Can you help me just, like, get this dialled in?' I was like, 'yeah I can do that.' So that... he invited me

up to the house and I was already kind of hesitant to do it 'cause I was like, there are other people that live here. I just felt like it was an invasion of space. And so I went up there and we just stayed in that front room and I helped him out with that, um, and got him all set up with that. And then, uh… oh, he asked me if I wanted lunch and he grilled chicken and carrots. Chicken and carrots. And then, uh, that's all he had and I was like, okay. So we, uh… so we ate and then I left. And then there was another day about… I can give you the date-ish, let me look at a calendar. I think it was the weekend after my birthday.

Duane: Um, just a thing on the courtesy for the phone for... what was that guy's name, Don?

Koback: This gentleman...

Nichol: Oh.

Koback: ... ((Unintelligible)). I just met him today.

Nichol: Um...

Koback: Do you want to do the phone...

Nichol: ... I forgot about that.

Duane: For TPD?

Koback: It's not for them. They're doing it for us.

Duane: Yes.

Koback: We just didn't... we don't have the equipment with us to do it and I asked them to do it for us. They're not involved in this investigation. He would just be a, uh, computer person. He would not be looking at any of this stuff. That, uh, would fall to myself. So keep that in mind, he's not involved in this investigation. Thornton PD has nothing to do with this other than lettin' us use their facility and, um, helping us with some electronic download. He's not gonna look at your phone right now. He's gonna put it on a disk and they're gonna give it to me.

Nichol: Gotcha. I don't know. What do you think? I really want to help you guys, I do.

Duane: It's up to you.

Nichol: I feel like I'm... I'm... this whole thing is just gonna be crazy regardless of whether I give you my phone or not. I mean, that's kind of how I look at it, like it's happening, it's gonna happen.

Duane: Well the texts reiterate what you've been...

Nichol: The media is just gonna...

Duane: ... saying all along so it's not like...

Nichol: Well, they do, that's the only thing too. I mean that's kind of a good backup. Yeah, I'll give it to 'em.
Koback: I think you hit the nail right on the head. There is reasons why we want everything. Um, it validates things that we know. I'm not gonna come out and tell you that I… if you tell me something today, we'll validate it with your text messages. Whether it's the ones we have now...
Nichol: Yeah. Yeah, yeah. I will...
Koback: ... or the ones you're gonna give us. Certainly.
Nichol: I'll give it to 'em. If you want to go get him... I was...
Koback: I want you to read… this is what I want you to do before you decide that, okay? Um...
Nichol: So, the second time I went to the house, I'm not sure what day it was, but it was the weekend of the 14th.
Koback: On... of August?
Nichol: July.
Koback: July.
Nichol: I don't know if it was the 14th or the 15th, um, one of those two days. But we had went out and we stopped there just real quick on the way back. And we were there not very long but that time I saw a picture of his wife and one of his kids. And I remember thinkin' to myself like wow she's so beautiful, and I took a step back and I was just like, this man has a gorgeous house, he has beautiful babies, he has a beautiful wife, he has an awesome job. Why would he want to leave this? And I remember talking to him about it and that was the first time that I tried to actually say, 'What do you think about not separating from your li… wife? What if you really try to work on this?' And he had expressed to me that, 'We've tried to work on this and it's not working, so that is why we're separating.' And I spent some time just, you know, kind of... 'cause it... it almost made me feel bad where I was… like to the point where I'm engaging in a relationship with a man who, the way he described it, is in a contractual agreement but was not in an emotional relationship with somebody. Um, and for me the way I would have preferred to do this is to avoid it 'til that contractual agreement was also done and he was done. And he could've approached me and said, 'I'm… just had a divorce, you know, maybe we could take this slow. What do you think?' But instead it was, 'Oh we're separated and we're working on a divorce,' and that is the part that I feel bad about

because I should've waited on that and I didn't. And, you know, I was just like, well they're already there so, you know, but then being in that house I was just like, 'Why? Fix this. Find a way to fix this, make it work,' you know, and I would... I would… I was, like, trying to push him to do it and he seemed pretty reluctant to do it. He didn't want to. And, um, I don't know, we were still seeing each other fairly frequently but, I kind of like backed away so we weren't hangin' out quite as much and we were still close but it was just like, I really wanted him to try. I wanted to know that he tried and it didn't work and then he moved on. Not that, you know, they both kind of tried and then he got himself into a situation with somebody else. And I don't know, I just thought he had a beautiful life goin' on and he could have made it work. That was the way I looked at it from the outside.

Koback: So, is this something you reflected on since this event or was this you...

Nichol: No, I was doing it then, like you can see it in my...

Koback: You said this… this doesn't look right, he's kind of, um... I don't want to be responsible for breakin' up a marriage, especially with two children, is that kind of the gist I'm gettin' here?

Nichol: I didn't think it didn't look right. I mean I… I think he was legitimately sleeping in the basement and I don't... I didn't think that these two were... I mean I think it was like hey we're both stuck in this house for now, we gotta sell this, in the meantime you live here, I live here, we sleep in different rooms, take care of the kids. That's just like kind of...

Koback: Okay.

Nichol: ... how I took that. And, um, no I didn't think it didn't look right. I just thought it just seemed like he had so much going on and it was just beautiful that it was like, 'why don't you just try this out, you know, and see if you can fix it.' And he'd always be like, 'well what about us? What about us?' I'm like, 'don't worry about us. That is more important. Like, try to see if you can salvage whatever it is that you have going on with your wife,' and… and, you know, he… I always got the impression that he was a great father to his kids, like always. And so, you know, and I was like, 'and be the dad that you want to be,' I was like, 'and see if you can make it work.' And he just, like… we kind of talked about it off and on for a few weeks and I was just kind of like, I don't know, like I think I was kind of cold feetin' about it when I went... after I went over to his house. And so this was pretty early on. And then, um, he told me that, uh, oh he went to, um... he went to North Carolina and he was like, 'I'm gonna talk to her when I'm in North Carolina and see if I can get her to do this, to, like, try to rekindle the flame.'

Koback: Okay, so try to, uh, salvage his relationship as you've been asking him to do?

Nichol: Yes. And… and then if he decided...

Koback: When did he go to North Carolina?

Nichol: Um, I think it was like the last week of July, somewhere around there.

Koback: Okay.

Nichol: So I mean this was like a couple weeks that I was just kind of like trying to push him to do that.

Koback: So let's... let's pause that North Carolina and we'll come...

Nichol: Okay.

Koback: ... back to that real quick. I want you to read this. If you don't understand what it means then ask me the question. But basically, what it says is you have the right not to let me look at your phone. I am asking to look at your phone for the purposes we previously discussed for the text messages and your phone log and unfortunately the photos that are attached therein too. Um, that information is only rel… relative to this investigation, I'm not lookin' at anything else except for the conversations between you and Chris Watts, and the phone, um, data between you and Chris Watts for phone calls for times and dates for those phone calls. Um, and then the content of the text messages that... that are there. And we can... we'll write that specifically down here, understand that if...

Nichol: I just don't want anybody to get some of those texts, like they have nothing to do with this case and they are just like...

Koback: Between you and Chris?

Nichol: Yes they're just... they're just...

Koback: So just tell me what you're...

Nichol: They're just kind of raunchy.

Koback: Okay, well...

Nichol: I don't need anybody... I don't need that...

Koback: Everybody's an adult...

Nichol: ... posted like...

Koback: We're not gonna post it.

Nichol: ... somewhere.
Koback: Um, it... the...
Nichol: I don't need...
Koback: ... the only ones that...
Nichol: ... I don't want the newspapers to get that. That's all I want.
Koback: The only ones that...
Nichol: I just need them to not get that.
Koback: ... we would be looking for, again, is the same kind of questions we're getting to here is things about his children, things about his wife...
Nichol: Understood. Understood.
Koback: ... that the questioning of did he ever, you know, has he ever said something to you that might indicate maybe not then but now that there was something like this in his mind. Or you... you know what we're lookin' for? I don't need to come out and tell you that. I understand the embarrassment of particular photos or potential, um, sexual types of conversations you may have had with Chris, uh, it's... it's not relative to... to the investigation we don't care, okay? You're an adult, I'm an adult, everybody in this room's a… even your dad and I give it to you for saying that stuff in front of your dad 'cause I'm not sure many women could do that. Um, so that's not what we're... we're after. We're after the... the information that corroborates things that you've told us and also that corroborates or, um, may tend to prove that things that Chris told us were a lie. You understand that?
Nichol: Mm-hm.
Koback: Um, and that's maybe going a little bit far, I usually won't tell people that but because of your reservations that's what I'm lookin' for. If I can disprove something he's told me by a phone record, phone records don't lie—people do. Okay? So, if I can disprove something that may be important that's what I need it for. I'm not saying I can. Has it happened before? Absolutely. Is it critical in cases that I've worked in the past? Yes. So that's why I want it. Okay? Um, again, you don't have to give it to me, you can tell me, 'I don't want you to have it, go get a warrant'. I'm not even gonna tell you if I go get a war… try to get a warrant right now. I'm just asking for you to consent and... and again we can write right here what you're willing to give me which is the text messages and the phone log and unfortunately again the... the attachments on some of those text messages. And I'll write it on there

and then you'll just sign it, okay? Do you under… do you understand the questions there? Do you have questions about any of the things that it says? You understand you don't have to do this...
Nichol: Mm-hm.
Koback: ... you're doing it of your own free will? And I know you're tired, so if you want to let your dad read it too, um...
Nichol: He will, thank you.
Koback: ... that's... that's a good idea.
Nichol: Can you fill it out before I sign it?
Koback: Yep. And just you read it and if you have any questions then we'll... we'll put on there what we're after.
Nichol: I'm so hungry.
Koback: You should've told me. I would have got you some food. I got food in my car.
Nichol: It's not staying down, it's coming up...
Duane: She hadn't been feelin' good. Not 'cause of any... just...
Nichol: Like, I got sick prior to this...
Duane: The gym.
Nichol: ... whole... whole thing happening, and then I think ev… all of this compounding with the fact...
Koback: Stress.
Nichol: ... that I'm sick it's just not good. I have not really been eating or sleeping much at all.
Duane: Yeah. I... I am with you. We... we definitely need to accelerate the case because the more lo… the more it takes the less sure that they are of situations. But, on the other end, I think if we... if you do just that only...
Koback: You tell me what you're willing to provide to me and we'll write it on...
Duane: I… is that good enough?
Nichol: Mm-hm. I just want our text conversation and then our phone call records.
Koback: So I'm gonna put, um...
Nichol: So the time and date of the phone call records and then our text message on those.
Koback: Text...
Martinez: Could we get photos of him?
Nichol: Huh?

Martinez: Could we get photos of him?
Nichol: Off of that?
Martinez: Would you mind if we got his photos that he sent to you?
Nichol: Well, they'll be in that text message thing.
Koback: So, all of his photos were sent... there was no apps or anything else...
Nichol: No. No, no, no, no, no.
Koback: ... you used that you guys were sending?
Nichol: No.
Koback: It was all just text messages?
Nichol: Yeah.
Koback: Okay. So it'd be an attachment to a text that he sent you?
Nichol: Pretty much.
Koback: But...
Nichol: Ev… everything is in the text and the phone call records.
Koback: So...
Nichol: Like, all of it.
Koback: ... because we don't have it on tape, we discussed prior to turning the tape on, um, on Tuesday which would've been the 14th of August, um, you had read some newspapers articles on the 13th and the 14th that regarded this case, you had also had a conversation with Chris at some point during the day on Monday, uh, and on Tuesday because of what you found, specifically what you said was... and don't let me put words in your mouth but, you kn… you found out that his, um, wife was pregnant.
Nichol: And I... yes.
Koback: And you did not know that prior?
Nichol: No.
Koback: And you found that out via the newspaper articles and that caused you concern. Um...
Nichol: Well, I just realized that he was lying to me and I was like, 'Well if you can lie to me about this, what else are you lying to me about?' And it made me realize that maybe his wife was in danger at that point and it was day two, too, and she still wasn't home.
Koback: What did that cause you to do with your phone though?
Nichol: Oh, what, when I deleted those? I was just kind of grossed out by him to be honest with you. I was just like, 'I don't know what's going

on right now, but you just lied to me and I don't want to see this come over my phone anymore.' So I removed it.
Koback: So you re… just... you already said, but you removed text messages?
Nichol: I deleted all of his stuff because he lied to me. I mean that's what it was, it was hur… it was the hurt that made me delete it. And then it was the lie that made me start questioning everything else he had been telling me for the last few days.
Koback: And that's when you decided to come forward?
Nichol: Yes.
Koback: Okay. So, just for context...
Nichol: Yes.
Koback: ... when people delete stuff off phones usually we go, hold on a second...
Nichol: No, no, no, no, no it wasn't malicious at all.
Koback: And... and... and that's why I want to (unintelligible)...
Nichol: It wasn't malicious at all.
Koback: ... and no I'm not saying it was malicious.
Nichol: He... he... he lied to me, it just hurt. I had never felt like he had ever lied to me before and it was a big lie...
Koback: Right.
Nichol: ... I mean telling somebody that you're in the midst of a divorce and then you have a wife that has a fifteen week old baby on the way is a huge, huge thing and I was very taken back and I was just... it was hurt. And so, at that point, I just… I, like, deleted it. I had a... I had a few more quick things to say to him and then I just got rid of him. That's literally what I did. I just cut him out of my life. It would have honestly been like a bad breakup kind of thing. Like, if none of this other stuff would have happened that's what it would have been, that would have been the end of it.
Koback: The information was not destroyed because there was anything in there that would be, uh, harmful to you or potentially to Chris at this point, but harmful to you in particular, that's not what you did?
Nichol: No. No, no, no, no, no.
Koback: You did it out of… uh, excuse my language… this guy's an asshole so I'm gettin' rid of him and I'm gettin' this stuff off my phone.
Nichol: That was like me kicking him out of my life.

Koback: Okay.
Nichol: And then... like I said and then realizing that he lied, that was when I was like, okay maybe his family is in danger and they're not coming back and they're not staying with a friend.
Duane: Yeah, when'd I go over there? Tuesday morning?
Nichol: Wednesday morning.
Duane: Wednesday, yeah.
Nichol: I called you Wednesday morning.
Duane: That's when we started discussing you guys need to get everything that... I just...
Koback: You can understand the importance of...
Duane: Oh, no question. We were...
Koback: Like I said, people lie, phone records don't. Um, and they really help specifically, um, establish dates and times.
Nichol: Mm-hm.
Koback: I think we have a... have a very good grip on that in this case already but there may be a time when we go, 'We need to know something else,' and then we would have it, we don't want to lose it. And that's... that's really what it is for us is if we lose information that later on we go, 'Man, I wish we would've got that,' and we may never even use these. We may never even look at 'em but if... if we have it now then we don't worry about losing it. So I appreciate you being cooperative and giving it to us.
Nichol: Yeah.
Koback: So, the first thing I wrote was text messages between Chris Watts and attachments. Okay, so 'cause we're talking about the photographs unfortunately that caused you much disdain. And then, I am gonna put, uh, phone log for calls between, uh, yourself and Chris Watts. Your phone number is, uh...
Nichol: Nichol confirms her phone number.
Koback: And this right now is located at... we're at the Thornton Police Department, it's gonna be moved to my... so this is kind of... doesn't make sense but we're here, it's gonna be moved to the Colorado Bureau of Investigation. He's gonna download it here but I'm gonna take it with me, just so you know, it's not staying here.
Nichol: Okay.
Koback: They're not gonna retain any of this, this comes with me.
Nichol: Okay.

Koback: Okay.
Duane: Is there anything else you want on there? I think that's about...
Nichol: That's it. I mean I don't have social media. I don't really have anything else you guys can pull.
Koback: Okay.
Martinez: Is there anything else you know of that could help us with this that we... that is not on this sheet?
Nichol: Uh, as far as like data?
Martinez: That's on your phone.
Nichol: No. No, I mean everything we did was like text and talk pretty much. I mean and like I said, any pictures that I had, like, even if you were to restore all my regular photos there's so many pictures in there and you wouldn't even know which ones were for him and which ones weren't. But the one... any picture that I wanted to send to him I sent via text so if you guys go through the text in the attachments you will have... you will have everything that wasn't said verbally and was done via text. But I think that's it, like I don't have... I don't have anything else as far as, like, no Facebook, no Instagram, no... no Twitter, no LinkedIn, like, none of it. So, um, there was never any of that kind of correspondence. So I think that should probably cover everything you guys will need.
Koback: Is there any particular messages that I... would help me so I don't have to look at... 'cause whatever is on your phone I don't know how long we're gonna get back to but let's say there... is there a particular date or time or message that stands out to you that would be relative to... specifically to the investigation into this case that might assist me in understanding why something like this could have occurred?
Nichol: I'm still in shock that this whole thing happened, I...
Koback: I can imagine.
Nichol: ... I, like, that's why I gave him the benefit of the doubt for the first day 'cause I was just like, no way. Like, I didn't even think about that, I mean, murder was not on the top of my mind when somebody doesn't come home for an evening. Especially if they just, like, had some sort of, like, heated conversation. It's like, okay you guys are separating, you have a heated conversation, you leave for a night, like I didn't even think this guy killed his wife. I mean that... that, like... murder is not something on the top of my mind when I call one of my friends for three or four hours and she doesn't answer the phone. Like

that doesn't even process to me as, like, a real thing that is a possibility at that point. And so that's why I gave it a day and then the second day I was talkin' to him he was just like a hot mess I could tell. And then with, like, the way he was talking to me and then that's kind of when I cut him off and I stopped talking to him. And then...

Koback: So remember what you just said and we're gonna get to that 'cause that's probably a very important conversation. So, but...

Nichol: Yeah. So if you want to know days I would probably honestly just start at like Sunday and work your way forward. I mean all the rest of that stuff it's just like the small talk of, like, hey this, this, this, you know. I mean...

Koback: And your relationship building through the first weeks...

Nichol: Yeah, I mean, like, and if you go, like, maybe a week further back, like, there's times I was trying to help him find an apartment, like, just for him, not for me, but for him and his kids, um, to get set up. And there's times where I'm, like, 'Well where's your wife moving to? Like, how close is she gonna be to you? You should be within thirty minutes of your kids so they're close. And you want to be close to their school and close to your gym. And, like, what's your price range?' Like, I was helping him get all of this stuff set up and it was in a very decent manner and I don't know if all of that is in text, some of it's probably on the phone. Like, at this point I've talked to him so much that I don't even know which parts are verbalized and which parts are texted at this point...

Koback: Right.

Nichol: ... but we can figure it out.

Koback: Okay. The... you see what I wrote, uh, text messages between Chris Watts and attachments. Uh, and then the phone logs for calls between your phone number and Chris Watts. That's... those are the two things that we'll ask to be extracted from your phone. So if you're okay with that, if you...

Nichol: Why does that say, 'As removed, cell phone data'? Isn't that this?

Koback: That is that and that's what he's gonna remove.

Nichol: Oh.

Koback: And then that officer is gonna fill that out.

Nichol: Gotcha. What is the date? I don't even know what day it is.

Koback: Today is the 16th.

Nichol: And you want to add anything to this?
Koback: If you give... get your phone we'll get him started.
Nichol: Oh, other than we... yeah we just... we wanted to give you everything but we also want to be protected in doing so, is more of the...
Koback: Sure.
Nichol: ... was more of the thing. It… it's just...
Koback: And when he's done we'll give you our copy of this.
Martinez: Is there a password or anything like it... will it lock up after a period of time?
Nichol: Yeah. Yeah, yeah. ((Unintelligible)).
Martinez: That's his notes.
Duane: And...
Martinez: Make sure there's nothing written on the back. I'm just teasing.
Nichol: There's not. I checked before I ripped it off. Okay.
Koback: Let's go back to North Carolina.
Nichol: Okay.
Koback: He went to North Carolina and he was trying to rehab his marriage with his wife?
Nichol: Uh, he said he was...
Koback: Do you know her name at this point?
Nichol: Yeah.
Koback: Okay. Are you okay saying her name?
Nichol: It's Shanann.
Koback: All right. And do you know the children's' name?
Nichol: Yes, it's Bella and Celeste—CeCe.
Koback: She went by... they called her CeCe?
Nichol: Mm-hm.
Koback: All right. So he went to... were they in North Carolina already?
Nichol: They were already there.
Martinez: If you want something.
Nichol: I don't know if my stomach will do that. Um, yeah, they were already out there. He just flew out there to go meet up with...
Koback: Do you know why they were there?
Nichol: They're... they're all from there.
Koback: Okay so they were... they're from...

Nichol: They were visiting her family for the most part until he got there. And then they still were mostly visiting her family.
Koback: Okay. And do you know how long they had been there?
Nichol: A while. Like, weeks.
Koback: All right. And he flew out to join his family there?
Nichol: Yep.
Koback: Do you know specifically where you flew to?
Nichol: What airport?
Koback: No, no, no, what city.
Nichol: No not off the top of my head.
Koback: Okay.
Nichol: I'm sure if I thought real hard maybe I could think about it but I mean come up with it, no I don't know.
Koback: All right. So he goes there, how... do you re… you said it was, like, the last week of July?
Nichol: I think so. I think it was like one of the last days of July. I'm almost positive. I think it was a weekday.
Koback: Okay.
Nichol: Um, yeah he flew out there and I thought I had convinced him to try to make peace with her and I was like, 'If you guys work on this, like, I'm out 'cause what's the point? I'm not trying to be with somebody that's in another relationship,' which I know that sounds silly given the whole relationship that we had in the first place but I really was under the impression that they were separating. I mean it was, like, reiterated to me so many times that that's what I thought it was. And it made sense to me too because he could pretty much call me whenever he wanted. I was the one that would tell him like, 'Hey when your kids are awake you need to spend time with your kids. Like, do that. And then after they go to bed if you want to talk to me you can talk to me.' But it was never like this super, super restricted thing. Like, sometimes right after work if I was still talking to him I'd get kind of bummed out and I'd, you know, I'd tell him, I'd just be, like, oh it's frustrating sometimes having to wait. But at the same time I was never like, this is horrible or, you know, it was always, like, I understood why. But then once his kids were asleep he never had any… it was like he could do what he wanted. Do you know what I'm saying? Like, he was in...
Koback: Sure.

Nichol: ... his basement and she's upstairs and they're not speaking. So, it kind of made sense, it wasn't, like, sneaky...
Koback: And you guys are just texting and...
Nichol: We're talking or whatever, you know...
Koback: Sure.
Nichol: ... I mean and it was just... it was, like, I said, it was at certain times but that ti… and originally it wasn't but it was me that put that timeframe on there because I thought he should hang out with his kids. Um...
Martinez: Those two times that you were at his house did you see any evidence of that, him living in the basement? Did he ever show you that area… (unintelligible)?
Nichol: I've seen it, yeah. I went down there and saw his... his little workout equipment and there's a bed down there all set up, and the basement was all clean and organized and stuff so, um, like a... like a decent bed setup so it made sense to me, like, hey this is... this is what's happening down here. Um, so I saw it. Um...
Martinez: Even though his family was in Nor… North Carolina for multiple weeks it appeared that he was still living in the basement?
Nichol: Mm-hm.
Martinez: Hm.
Nichol: Well… and he told me sometimes he would like go upstairs and sleep if – if, like, he was home alone 'cause I know she'd like go on business trips and stuff. But he's like, 'I don't like that bed anyways,' so he didn't really like to sleep up there. I was like, okay. Um, even when it was just him. So that was the impression that I got. Um, I don't know what we were talking about, North Carolina?
Koback: Let's... yeah go... go back to North Carolina.
Nichol: So, North Carolina. Um, so he still made very frequent communication with me when he was out there and at one point he told me that they sat down and they talked about it and he told her that he wanted to either fix things or, like, to try to fix things and if she didn't want to fix them then they needed to move forward with the separation and actually file for a divorce at this point, was... was the impression that I got from this and just what he told me. And so, um, he said that she was, like, pretty receptive to just not trying. He was like, 'She seemed like she just wants me to go.' He's like, 'When she has her mind made up, she has her mind made up and that's what she

wants,' and he's like, 'She doesn't want to try anymore,' and he's like, 'And neither do I really.' And he was like, 'It's done,' and he's like, um... and then the next day... I don't even know what days these were, some time when he was out there, he told me, um, 'We're putting the house up for sale as soon as we get back.' And I was like, 'Whoa that was quick.' And he was like, 'It's her, she's ready to go.' And I was like, 'Okay.' And so I left it at that and then, um, he got back and I started askin' him like, 'What are you gonna do? Because the Colorado housing market is fire and you guys are gonna sell this house real fast,' and I'm like, 'You need to start looking for new places to live.' And I'm like, 'Where do you want to live?' And I was really trying to help him out, I'm like, 'Do you want to get a house? Do you want three bedrooms, so you have one and each of your girls have one?' I'm like, 'Do you want to, you know… do you want an apartment? Like what do you want, you know, where do you want to live?' Because he's in Frederick but that whole area over there is just a bunch of small towns and you can kind of just pick and choose, everything's kind of, you know, and so, um, he told me, 'Well, I like Brighton,' and I was like, 'Okay.' And then he told me he wanted a two-bedroom apartment and he said he wanted one room for him and the other room for his two girls. And I thought it was kind of cute, like, I remember telling him, I was like, 'Yeah me and my sister had bunk beds at my dad's house,' and I was like, 'When we were little girls.' When we were... me and my sister are the same age apart as him and his... I mean as his two daughters, you know, so I told him, I was like, 'They're gonna love it.' I was like, 'They might be like stuck in... in one room together,' I was like, 'But, they'll become like best buddies.' And it was really exciting, like I liked helping him and I just wanted him to like... I don't know. This is what he told me he wanted so I was like, 'Well I will help you do the research.' But another thing that I really took care of was to be like where is she moving to? I was never like, 'You know what, screw your wife, try to get full custody,' none of that bullshit. It was always just like, you know, I'd ask him, I'm like, 'Well what kind of custody are you guys gonna have,' 'cause he sa… he... at work they're about to switch his schedule so right now he's like a Monday through Friday and they're about to switch these guys to eight days on, six days off...

Koback: Mm, that's tough.

Nichol: That's awesome. And I... and I was... so I was tellin'... I was

askin' him, I was like, 'Are you gonna have your kids on that set of days off?'
Koback: Mm-hm.
Nichol: I was like… 'cause that would work perfect, one week on, one week off,' and I was just like, you know, we had just talked about it and I'm like, 'What is your plan?' And he's like, 'We haven't figured out exactly what we're gonna do about the kids yet,' but he told me, he's like, 'Colorado's a 50-50 state and she's okay with everything 50-50.' Like, he said that she was on board with this because she wanted it too, like she was checked out of this relationship. So that was how he made this sound, that it was like a very kosher we're done kind of thing and...
Koback: Did you ever give him books or articles or anything to read about saving your marriage? Did you ever provide anything to him like that?
Nichol: About saving his marriage?
Koback: Yeah, like, how to recover a marriage or how to save a marriage or, you know, there's... there's all sorts of publications and books out there.
Nichol: No. No but I did tell him... and I don't know if I did this through text or phone, that will be something you guys will I'm sure figure out. Um, but I would tell... I told him a few times like, 'I think that you should take the time to read some articles, uh, about, um, what separation does to kids.' You know, and I told him, I said, 'When my parents separated, we were literally like 3 and 5,' we were almost the exact same age as these little girls. And I told him, I said, 'You know, I was so young when it happened that it didn't really have a big negative effect on me because I was so small that I really didn't process it too well.' I was like, 'But I do have cousins that their parents got divorced when they were like 10, 11, and I think that it hit 'em a little harder, you know,' and I... and he's like, 'Oh they'll be fine,' you know, and I told em, I was like, 'Even though they're small and you think that they'll be fine,' I was like, 'I think you guys should just read about it just so that you guys are prepared in case, you know, one of these two starts having a hard time with the fact that you guys aren't in the same house anymore.' You know, an… and... and I would tell him, I was like, 'You know, there's pros and cons to it, like,' 'cause he was getting ready to do it and it would be like, you know, it's kind of cool havin' two Christmases and, you know, like your parents get to go, you know, be happy doing whatever it is they want to do with their lives and they don't have

to be in a situation that's probably not good for the kids because it's not good for those two. You know, but at the same time it was, like, just read, like that's what I always used to tell him, I'd always tell him to, like... I... I tell people to read about everything, reading is so good for you.

Koback: So he at this time is telling you that yeah I am the guy trying to save the marriage and she doesn't want it?

Nichol: That's what he told me. That's what he told me so...

Koback: Okay.

Nichol: ... um, and he... yeah and then he was like, 'She doesn't want it so I'm not gonna do it.' And then it was like, 'We're filing for divorce, we're selling the house,' and this was like all as soon as they were comin' back from North Carolina, like boom, boom, boom, boom, boom. And...

Koback: Well do you recall when he gets back from North Carolina?

Nichol: No. I don't even know how long he was out there. I know it was less than two weeks and more than one.

Koback: Okay.

Nichol: I don't remember.

Koback: So he's... he comes back early August, would that be fair?

Nichol: Oh yeah, it was definitely in the first two weeks somewhere.

Koback: All right.

Nichol: Probably the second week of August at some point. And then I don't remember when...

Koback: Does his wife come back with him at that time or does he...

Nichol: Yeah, they all came back.

Koback: They all come back at the same time.

Nichol: They all came back. Um, and then, uh, yeah so he... he continues to just, you know, tell me that this is, like, what he wants and... and so I took the time... and you will see that in the text too where I, like... like there – like, I found this apartment, it was perfect, it was so cute, I was like, 'It's in your price range, it's six miles from the gym, it's twenty-three miles from work,' I'm like, 'You know, it's super close to Frederick, it's gonna be by your kids' school, like this is... this is the spot,' you know. And... and... and I told him, I was like, 'I'll keep looking for more places,' and he's like, 'Well there some that I want to go see too.' And he actually had me thinking that he was gonna go look at these places this week before all this sh… stuff...

Koback: Oh, so this is fairly recent then if we're talking...
Nichol: Oh, this just happened like in the last couple weeks.
Koback: He's gonna go look at apartments during...
Nichol: He wanted me to go with him.
Koback: When you say this week are you saying...
Nichol: Like this... this week.
Koback: ... Monday was the 13th...
Nichol: Like this week.
Koback: Okay.
Nichol: Yeah. So I told him, I was like, 'Well pick out a few spots and if you want me to come with you I'll go look at 'em but you, you know...'
Koback: You said earlier that he had never, um... or that the... the apartment wasn't for you and him. It was just for him and his children.
Nichol: Oh yes.
Koback: It wasn't... you weren't in… had no intentions of moving in with him?
Nichol: No. I have my own spot. I still have a lease there 'til July, and even then he never asked me to move in with him...
Koback: Okay.
Nichol: ... and I never tried to move in with him. I mean I told him, I mean, I really tried to take everything with this whole situation very slow. The only part that I screwed up on was the fact that he wasn't completely separated from her when him and I decided to spend time with each other. That is where I screwed up. But other than that everything else it was always like, you know, you build your life, I'm gonna build my life, we will intertwine them but I am not ready to, like, do this. And he respected that and I... and I, um, I even said that and I don't know, I... that might be in the text but (unintelligible) that Chris like, 'You need space, you're just getting out of a divorce, like, personally I think jumping into a new relationship is a little quick.' I was like, 'I was in a relationship earlier this year and I think this is also a little quick.' And I'm like, 'So why don't we take our time?' And I'm like, 'If you guys end up doing a week on, a week off with your kids,' I'm like, 'The week you have your kids be with your children. And the week that you don't,' I'm like, 'I don't even want to see you every day,' I'm like, 'I think we should spend like a few days of that together,' I'm like… 'cause I like my space and I think you need your space, I think you

need your space to develop your identity again and, like, get it back,' because I think he's just been like so wrapped up in this whole thing that he's got in his own life... in his life that he... I mean he doesn't remember probably what it's like to be single or have time where it's just him.

Koback: Sure.

Nichol: And so I was just like, you know, like embrace that. I think it's a beautiful thing and I really try to take it smart with all that. And it was the same thing with his kids, I was just like, you know, like... and I... and we'd talk about things every once in a while where I... you know, I'd be like, 'Hey if I ever meet,' you know, 'cause like I have a lot of house plants is a good example, so I have a lot of house plants and I told... I told him, I was like, 'One day if I ever meet your kids,' I was like, 'I'm gonna show these girls how to like paint pottery and plant some plants.' I was like, 'I think they would love to see something grow that they build, I think it would be really, really cute.' And like, little stuff like that but it wasn't very frequent, it wasn't, 'Hey we should get married,' and, 'Hey we should have babies,' and, 'Hey I want to live with you,' and, 'Hey I need to meet your children now,' and, 'Let's cut the mom out,' it was never like that.

Koback: Okay. And that was... it... there was never any conversation about, you know, 'We can't do this with her around, we can't do this with the kids around'?

Nichol: Never.

Koback: He never said that...

Nichol: No.

Koback: ... you never said that?

Nichol: No. No.

Koback: So there... there... the way you guys were trying to make this work was just, you know, slowly trying to come together because of his current situation and by your account your own...

Nichol: Mine. I mean I don't want to rush.

Koback: ... you're... you're just a... an independent person it sounds like, pretty much.

Nichol: Yeah.

Koback: And, uh, but through text message or through conversation he never said, uh, 'Hey, uh, you know, this is gonna be financial able...

I'm not gonna be financially able to do this,' or, 'This isn't a good thing, I got these kids,' none ... none of those conversations ever came up?
Nichol: No. I mean, he told me he had a budget restriction so for his apartment, and I'm pretty sure this is in the text and this will probably be in the last couple weeks. Um, he told me $1100 to $1400 when I was asking him. Like, 'cause I told him I'd help him do homework, I was like, 'You do some homework, I'll do some homework, we'll knock this out because if you guys are for real putting the house up you gotta figure it out.' Um, and so that was his budget and I remember asking him, I was like, 'Are you sure you don't want to just get a house?' And he's like, 'I never thought about a house.' I'm like, 'Yeah you can rent houses man, like it's a thing,' and he's just like, 'I don't know if I can afford that.' I was like, 'Okay.' And I knew that those two had been some financial trouble, I definitely found out a lot more about that situation in, uh, newspaper recently. Um...
Koback: Okay so prior to the newspaper how did you know he was in financial difficulty?
Nichol: 'Cause he, I mean, I... when I went to that house everything in there is very, very, very, very nice, it looks like it all comes with a very expensive price tag. And, uh, I didn't say anything to him about it, but I could kind of tell then where I was just looking at everything like how do you guys afford this? And then he has that car, that's... I don't even know how much that car costs, but I bet its...
Koback: What car... what car is that?
Nichol: That Lexus. I'm sure that thing cost like eighty grand. But just like money, like everything just looked like it cost a lot of money in that house.
Koback: You probably have a decent idea of how much money he makes.
Nichol: Yeah and it's not enough money to pay for all that, not even close.
Koback: And did you have any idea what, um, Shanann did for a living or how much money she might've made?
Nichol: I mean, I had an idea, I don't... I mean, I would consider her like a sales rep, I don't know how else to describe that. Um, for the company that she worked for and, uh, I don't know exactly how much she made. He said that she was really competitive and she liked to try to keep up with him. He's like, 'She gets close sometimes.' So I don't know how much those two brought in. I mean off the top of my head

if I could guess, probably somewhere around like $140K a year. I mean I don't know. 'cause I don't know exactly how much he makes and I don't know exactly how much she makes. But based just off of what I know about the oil field, like, yeah, I... I would say that's probably an accurate estimate.
Koback: So he... even if they're makin' let's just use the figure $100,000, they're living above their means or below their means?
Nichol: Oh... oh my God, like...
Koback: Way too much?
Nichol: Way, way, way, way too...
Koback: Did he ever discuss with you any of those issues?
Nichol: I mean, a little, I mean, I didn't know about the bankruptcy or any of that 'til I read on the newspaper about that but he just... he... I think he was really frustrated with the situation. Um, he told me, he's like, 'You know, I feel like my pay-check goes in my bank account and I just watch it go like this,' he's like, 'But it doesn't have to,' he's like, 'She makes it like that.' And I was just, like...
Koback: So was he resentful for that?
Nichol: I don't know if he was resentful, I just think he was frustrated by the fact that they could be doing a lot better financially and she… from the vibe that I got… had really bad spending habits.
Koback: So she was a spender. Um, the car hers or his?
Nichol: I think it's hers.
Koback: Okay.
Nichol: I'm pretty sure that that's hers.
Koback: Do you know what other car they might have?
Nichol: Well I mean his APC pickup truck.
Koback: And that's... that...
Nichol: That's it, I think.
Koback: ... and that's owned by *Anadarko* though, right?
Nichol: Yeah.
Koback: So...
Nichol: But so I don't... I don't think they own any other vehicles as far as I know. I think it's just that thing.
Koback: And... and... and *Anadarko* who doesn't allow him to drive that on his own personal, right?
Nichol: No. No.
Koback: So he's just got one vehicle...

Nichol: Yeah.
Koback: ... um, and it's a very expensive Lexus. Um, and then they live in a pretty expensive house, I...
Nichol: It's a huge house.
Koback: Yeah. Yeah.
Nichol: I was very taken back, when I saw it. I was just like, whoa, how do you guys...
Koback: And then the fixtures inside caused you to pause...
Nichol: Everything. Everything was just like...
Koback: And you mentioned today you read something about, uh, bankruptcy...
Nichol: Yeah.
Koback: ... what did you read?
Nichol: That those guys filed bankruptcy for a lot of money and...
Koback: Who are those guys?
Nichol: Two tho… that couple.
Koback: Okay.
Nichol: In 2015. Oh Shanann and Chris...
Koback: Thanks.
Nichol: ... filed bankruptcy in 2015.
Koback: Okay. And you said for a lot of money, do you recall the amount?
Nichol: No because it was different in each of the newspapers and I don't know which one to believe so...
Koback: Okay.
Nichol: Hundreds of thousands of dollars. So, um, yeah I didn't know that.
Koback: So, let's go just back though, him and the financial, he tells you... or he has a concern enough to at least express some con… something to you that he's frustrated with the way she spends or he's upset with working so hard and never having any money and she's kind of the responsibility, she's the responsible party for spending most of the money?
Nichol: I... I pretty much got that vibe. I mean he just told me, he's like, 'We're house broke all the time.' And I was just like, 'That's unfortunate,' and I asked him, I was like, 'Do you have 401K,' and he was like, 'Yeah.' And I mean the reason I ask him this is because if I get in a relationship with somebody I want to know like what kind of

baggage that they have, I think that's important if I walk into a situation where I'm like, hey I have good credit and I have all of these things that I've been building and you don't have your stuff together, like, what are we gonna do with this. And it's important for your... your long-term thing.

Martinez: You're smart.

Nichol: So I'm preparing. And so I just asked him, I was like, 'Well do you have 401K?' And he was like... he's like, 'Yeah I do have that.' And then I asked him, I was like, um, I... I didn't ask him like how much that they had or anything, but I just said, 'Is your lifestyle sustainable?' And he was like, 'No.'

Koback: Okay.

Nichol: And I was like, 'How long do you think that's gonna take?' He's like, 'I don't know but it's not sustainable.'

Martinez: Where did his girls go to school?

Nichol: I don't know. He never actually told me, like, when I gave... I asked him once, it was like… when I was trying to find him an apartment I was like, 'Are you comfortable telling me where your girls go to school,' that's in the text too, I was like, 'So I can figure out what distance from the apartment it is.' I was trying to just make his life convenient with, like, him, his ex, his kids and all the stuff that he needs to do and work. Um, and he was like, 'Don't worry about it, their school is pretty centrally located so anywhere in the area that we were discussing will be fine.' And he just left it at that. So he didn't even tell me which was fine, I respect that.

Koback: Day-care is obviously very expensive for a two and... three and five-year-old.

Nichol: Oh yeah.

Koback: Right. So...

Nichol: I understand.

Koback: ... did he ever bring, uh, any... did he ever discuss that?

Nichol: Never.

Koback: Okay.

Nichol: Never. Um... uh, like the only... like I said, the only financial thing he ever said is just like, 'She just likes to spend money. Like a lot of it.'

Koback: Okay.

Nichol: So that was just kind of the vibe that I got from that and that it was just, it was a lifestyle that she liked to live, like very like materialistic kind of lifestyle. Like it was...

Koback: Wanted to project a certain image...

Nichol: Yes. All the time. And he said that that was why they got that house too, he's like, 'She wants everybody to think that we live a certain way and that we can sustain all this stuff,' and he's like, 'And we can't.' And I told him, I said, 'When you're in those situations why don't you…' I'm like, 'Do you... do you voice your concern about this?' And he told me, he's like, 'When I try to talk to her,' he's like, 'She's really bossy and she usually shuts me out,' and he's like, 'When she does that,' he's like, 'I just let it go.' And I was just like, 'All right,' I mean I don't... I don't try to interfere with how those two interact. But I didn't ask about it 'cause I'm just curious 'cause I would never put myself in a situation where someone was like, 'You know what, we're gonna live in this house that costs double what we can afford and that's how it's gonna be 'cause I want everybody to think we're fancy.' 'Cause I wouldn't do that. I mean to me, like, I wouldn't put up with somebody doing that to me, and I'm not saying that that's what she was doing. I mean for all I know he could've been completely lying about this. He could be the one spending all the money.

Koback: Sure.

Nichol: You know?

Koback: This is just what he told you.

Nichol: Exactly. So I mean that's as far as I can interpret it so I can't be like, 'Well oh she needs to do this and she needs to do that,' but he... he, you know, he just... he voiced his concern where it's just like, 'Financially I'm in a very bad spot that I...

Koback: Okay.

Nichol: ... don't need to be in but I'm stuck in,' and that was kind of where he was at. So... but I mean he was never mean when he talked about her. He was never hostile, nothing like that. He just… I… very calmly like, this is the situation and I think the only reason that he even provided me with that information is because I asked.

Koback: Okay. You said something, um, about her being controlling or...

Nichol: Bossy.

Koback: ... bossy...

Nichol: That's what he said, bossy.

Koback: ... um, in like a lot of aspects of their life or what... do you know exactly what he meant by that, how that affected him?
Nichol: I think he was just saying when he voices his opinion it's not heard, is... is the gist of that. Which I thought, from what it sounded like from their separation, from them trying to separate that that was a big deal for him where he was saying that the reason that they don't really get along anymore is because he feels like he's not heard.
Koback: Okay.
Nichol: He says that he, you know, he comes home from work and he tries to talk to her and she'll just be like, 'One minute, I'm on the phone.' Or she'll, like, scroll through social media and she doesn't acknowledge him. And, um, he said that he had addressed it with her a few times and they're calm, he said they don't really fight, like, they don't scream and yell. Um, and he said he had addressed it with her a few times and he said it just fell on deaf ears, he's like, 'She just seems like she's not interested anymore,' and I think it made him sad because, I mean, he was like all about his kids and he seemed like he was trying to be all about her but it just wasn't reciprocated and I think at that point he was just like, I don't... that it's just they just kind of like fell apart.
Koback: Okay.
Nichol: Just kind of drifted apart. But it was...
Koback: Was that your wor… was that your words or his?
Nichol: What, that they...
Koback: Fell apart.
Nichol: That... I... those are mine.
Koback: Okay.
Nichol: Those are mine. He just said that they didn't communicate very well. And it wasn't in a... an aggressive way communicate, it was just the fact that they didn't communicate at all.
Koback: They just...
Nichol: They didn't talk.
Koback: And they had children and they... did... did... do... was there ever mention that he was trying to resolve or, uh, save his marriage to... for the children's sake? Yo… a lot of people talk...
Nichol: Yes.
Koback: ... about that, did he talk about that?
Nichol: Yes. I mean he told me that he believed that the only reason

that those two had still been doin' it as long as they've been doing... 'cau… he told me that her and him have had communication issues for about six years where she just seems really, like, detached and uninterested in like trying to build something with him. Um, and he said... and I said, 'Six years is a really long time for you guys to not fix that,' considering they were married for what, eight? I mean that's like the majority of their marriage. And he said, um, 'Sometimes I think we just do it for the kids,' or something like that. I mean, it's been a long time since I've seen...

Koback: Sure.

Nichol: … these conversations so I don't know, like, verbatim but...

Koback: And that's... we're trying...

Nichol: ... it was pretty much just like...

Koback: ...get you to remember sometimes.

Nichol: Yeah, like, but he said it wasn't just him though, he was like, I think she does that too...

Koback: Okay.

Nichol: ... you know, I mean, and it was, like, this equal part where they are just kind of like goin' through the motions, I think.

Koback: Mm-hm.

Nichol: And so, like, when he told me that she was cool with like the 50% everything and just, like, breakin' it off and being really civil about it… it... it kind of made sense to me 'cause I was like, the way he made this sound it wasn't oh she's this horrible person or oh I'm this horrible person, it was, 'Her and I have drifted so far apart that it's kind of a mutual agreement that this is not gonna work.'

Koback: So in those six years though they had two children...

Nichol: Yep.

Koback: ... um, and you said earlier you did not know she was pregnant until reading the newspaper...

Nichol: Yep.

Koback: ... so, um, that never came up in any conversation...

Nichol: Never.

Koback: ... um, there was no... no indications that that was going on...

Nichol: None.

Koback: ... um, he never hinted to anything like that?

Nichol: Nothing.

Koback: As far as you knew, um, he was just leading her, he had two children and, um, that was the final take on that?
Nichol: Yes.
Koback: Okay.
Nichol: I think... I know why he lied to me. He lied to me because if I'd have known that he had a child on the way I would have never wasted my time with him in the first place, like, none of this would have ever even occurred if he would have just told me the truth.
Koback: So do you think if he found out that you, um… if, let's say this week you guys were to go look at some apartments—and this is hypothetical—but you, um, you've never found out that his wife was pregnant, would... would that have changed anything? Uh, like you just said, 'If I knew he was… his wife was pregnant, I wouldn't be in this picture,' so, if his wife was not pregnant, um, and forgive me but if... if he takes her out of the picture you're never gonna know that she was pregnant, right?
Nichol: What do you mean takes her out of the picture, like...?
Koback: If... if he murdered her, she's out of the picture, you're never gonna know if she was pregnant. If he can get away with murder you're not gonna… I got divorced from my wife...
Duane: Wait...
Koback: You said... do you understand what I'm saying here? If... if she's gone...
Nichol: But this...
Duane: Don't lead.
Koback: Hypothetically...
Duane: Please. Don't lead on.
Koback: Yeah hypothetically if she...
Duane: Okay.
Koback: ... you understand where I'm going? If you didn't know...
Duane: Right but you're... you're leading...
Koback: Okay.
Duane: ... into questions that are nothing with your...
Koback: If you didn't know though...
Duane: Wait Nic.
Koback: ... that she was there...
Duane: Did you hear what I said?
Koback: I'm not... I'm following you, I just want her to answer a ques-

tion that relates to… she said something that's important that if he didn't have a child on the way sh… or if he didn't... if she didn't know that she would've continued the relationship, right?
Nichol: But he killed his kids. At what point does he think that I'm gonna be in a relationship?
Koback: I'm not t… I'm not talkin' about the children. I'm just talking specifically about her. If i… and if... if you only knew... if the kids were still here and he called you and said, 'I'm divorced from my wife,' and he gets away with this... do you understand what I'm thinking, from his aspect?
Nichol: I still wouldn't do it. I still wouldn't do it, 'cause I'd be like, 'Where did she go?'
Koback: Okay.
Nichol: Because I'm under the impression that she's a really good mom. Like, he never bashed her momming skills. Like, he... no. S… no. I wouldn't... no.
Koback: Okay.
Nichol: No.
Koback: And that's... that... you see where I'm tryin' to take that?
Nichol: Yes.
Koback: So he never... you guys never had a conversation about the child, period?
Nichol: I didn't know.
Koback: Okay.
Nichol: At all.
Koback: All right. And, by your words, if you did know, you would've ended the relationship?
Nichol: Well, because it wouldn't of made sense to me. That he's, like, 'I'm getting separated. Oh, by the way, I have a baby on the way.' It's, like...
Koback: That's fifteen weeks.
Nichol: '... you are a liar. You're just tryin' to sleep with me.' That's what I would've probably interpreted that as, and I'd a just shut that off at work, and that would've been the end of it.
Koback: Okay. Um, all right. We can move past that. Um, the week that he comes back from North Carolina, you... you don't remember, somewhere in the first couple weeks of August?
Nichol: Yeah. I think it was the second week, but I don't remember...

Koback: Okay.
Nichol: ... off the top of my head.
Koback: So we'll just use August as a timeframe. Is that fair? Because you know...
Nichol: Mm-hm.
Koback: ... he left in July, and he comes back in August. How many times do you think you see him?
Nichol: I saw him a few times. I saw him this past Saturday. I saw him the Wednesday before that. And he wanted to see me more. I was the one who wanted my space. I was, like, 'Nope. Your kids are home. Go hang out with your kids.' And even on Wednesday, I cut it short. Like, he came and hang out with me for a few hours and then I was, like, 'Go chill with your kids.'
Koback: Okay.
Nichol: Um, I was always, like, really respectful of his kids.
Koback: Do you know, specifically, where you guys me… went? Did you meet at your house? Did you guys go to, uh, any restaurants? Did you go to establishments? Where'd you go?
Nichol: Um, last Wednesday, he came to my house and this past Saturday, we went to, um... what is the name of that bar that we used to go to? It's not the same... The Lazy Dog, but it's the one off of 144th and I-25. I think it's 144th. Up there.
Koback: And it's The Lazy Dog?
Nichol: Yes.
Koback: Um, did he ever mention a Rocky's game that night?
Nichol: Um, no. I don't think so. But there was a... there was a, um... the Broncos were playing.
Koback: Okay.
Nichol: Which we couldn't see, 'cause they sat us in really crappy spots. But it's okay, 'cause it's pre-season. But, um...
Koback: So you we… do you recall what time you went there?
Nichol: Hm, no. I remember... well, kind of. So he had to get a babysitter that night.
Koback: Do you know who that was?
Nichol: Uh, somebody who's really young. I remember I asked him who his babysitter was, and he's, like, 'We have two. This girl's only seventeen, but the other one's out of town. So this girl's gonna stay, and she doesn't do overnights. So I gotta be back by ten.'

Koback: Okay.
Nichol: And I remember her sayin' that, and him sayin' that. And I... I don't know what time he got to my house. It was between I want to say, like, five-thirty. It might've been five, but I don't think so. 'Cause I think the babysitter, if I remember correctly, showed up at, like, four-thirty or something and he was, like, 'I want to spend time getting my kids acclimated to her. And then I will come
Koback: So her chi… his children didn't even know her?
Nichol: Oh, no. They knew her, but he was saying, like, he likes to, like, stay there for a little while. While... he doesn't just, like, walk out the door...
Koback: Okay.
Nichol: ... when they show up. It's, like, a transitional thing. And so, um, that's why I'm sayin' I don't know how long that was. I want to say, like, five-thirty. And then he had to be back by ten, so he left at, like, nine-somethin' to be back by ten.
((Crosstalk))
Koback: So how did he show up? What was he driving?
Nichol: No. He didn't pick me up. He came to my house. We drove my truck.
Koback: Okay. So you... he gets to your house. You know what he was driving to get to your house?
Nichol: Um, off the top of my head, I don't remember. Um, h… I'm pretty sure he usually drives that Lexus, but he doesn't always park it in my complex, 'cause the parking... there's not good spaces. So where you guys picked me up at, a lot of times he'll just park out there, because there's room.
Koback: Okay.
Nichol: Um, so that kinda works so that he's... 'cause there's just not a lot of room in my apartment complex. Um, but off the top of my head, I don't know what he was driving.
Koback: What kinda truck do you drive?
Nichol: I drive a, uh, Toyota 4 Runner.
Koback: Okay. So you guys take your 4 Runner to The Lazy Dog?
Nichol: Yep.
Koback: And you said they sat you in crappy location? And where...
((Crosstalk))
Nichol: It just...

Koback: Where were you put inside the bar?
Nichol: We were... when you walk in, you just hang a right and we were, like, one of the first two booths on the right, when you walk in the door.
Koback: Okay.
Nichol: You just... it's just not a good... it's a good spot, but just not for the TVs. And we actually went to the other Lazy Dog. We went to the one that you and me go to. Where's that at? Federal and 100...
Duane: 20th.
Nichol: It's 120th and Federal, and we went there, and they have a different menu. And I was, like, 'I don't want to eat this food. So, we should go to the other one.'
Koback: So initially you go to the 120th location?
Nichol: Yes.
Koback: Did you actually...
Nichol: And...
Koback: ... get seated?
Nichol: Uh, kinda, sorta. They were, like, cleaning off a table and we were standing there, just kinda lookin' at the beer menu and the food menu, and I was, like, 'I don't want this.' And he... and so we left.
Koback: Six o'clock?
Nichol: Probably, somewhere around there. six, six-thirty. And then we left and went to the other one, and we ate dinner.
Koback: All right. And you were in the first or second booth, right...
Nichol: Ah-huh.
Koback: ... to the right of the door?
Nichol: Ah-huh.
Koback: I'm just askin', 'cause if they have video, we want to be able to verify that.
Nichol: Ah-huh.
Koback: So that's why it's important.
Nichol: Ah-huh.
Koback: Um, and you were there for how long?
Nichol: Uh, I don't know. Probably... we didn't stay for dessert, so I don't know. How long's the restaurant take? Like, an hour-and-a-half?
((Crosstalk))
Martinez: I don't know.
Koback: I've never been to The Lazy Dog.

Nichol: I don't know. Probably about an hour-and-a-half, and then, uh, we went back to my house for a little bit. Hung out at my house, um, for a little while, and then he had to leave. And then he left.
Koback: Do you recall what time he left?
Nichol: Off the top of my head, no. I remember he was, like, gonna be late to be back at ten. I think there's a text message where he starts texting me when he's home at his house.
Koback: Okay.
Nichol: So you can probably figure that out. And I remember th… I texted him back and I was, like, 'Damn, that was quick.' Or 'Wow, that was really quick.' He's, like, 'Yeah, I even had time to stop at the ATM,' or 'Stop at the gas station.' Stop somewhere to get money to pay the babysitter.
Koback: Okay.
Nichol: Um, and I was just, like, thinkin', like, 'Whoa, that was really fast.' Um, but I think he was still, like, a little late coming back, but nothing too drastic. So he probably left my house, like, somewhere around nine-thirty-ish.
Koback: All right. And you n… he goes straight home. He texts you. Um...
Nichol: Well, I was already home.
Koback: Right. No, he text you. He goes straight home from your house and he texts you that he's home?
Nichol: Mm-hm.
Koback: So that should be in your text messages.
Nichol: Uh... uh, it should be. I'm pretty positive that was not a phone call. I'm almost positive that was a text. Sometimes I get them flip-flopped, or I don't remember, but sometimes I know. I'm pretty sure that one was a text.
Koback: Saturday, during your dinner, um, what... what kinda conversation did you guys have?
Nichol: Uh, I don't even remember. Oh. I, uh… so, he's been tryin' to eat a little healthier than he normally does. And he's always, like, been in the… workin' out since I knew him and he tries to eat clean. But he was tryin' to step it up a little bit. And nothing like the people who do, like, the competitions and the shows that are all super restrictive. I mean, it was nothin' like that. It's just, like, day-to-day general maintenance, but it's how I eat and it's pretty healthy. And, um, he's been

losin' a lot of weight. He lost, I want to say, like, thirteen pounds in the time that we were hangin' out. And, honestly, when you start eatin' a little bit cleaner and you start workin' out a little bit harder, the first couple months... especially for a man, 'cause they lose weight faster... it's not something that's, like, that drastic, to me, but it did stand out that it was, like, a little much. And so I was, like, 'Whoa. Like, maybe you're not eating enough macro nutrients. So let me look at them.' So he had been working on his *My Fitness Pal* app and, like, programming, like, all the stuff he eats. And I just started going through them and I was tryin' to figure out where his ratios were wrong. We actually spent a lot of time doing that, 'cause he had asked me to do it for him. Um, because I just was at the point where I was, like, if his weight loss slows down in a few weeks, he'll be fine. And if it doesn't, then his macros are a little off. It's not that big of a deal, like, in the workout community. This is a very normal thing, but I just...

Koback: Did you have any other outside concerns? Like, potential drug use? Alcohol use? Any of that stuff that... that led you to go, 'Hey, he's lost an extreme amount of weight in such a short period of time'?

Nichol: No, and I wouldn't call it extreme. It was just, like... it w… it was... it was a lot but, I mean, I... when I first started workin' out, I dropped, like, twelve pounds in two weeks. When I first… first started, like, hittin' it hard with the diet. So the fact that he lost that much weight, it wasn't... like I said, it was... it was not a surprising amount. I just didn't want it to be, like, a sustained amount. But no, I didn't think anything weird of it just because of, like, how interknitted I am with the workout community and I know, like, this is possible. But it just... he... the thing that concerned me about it, I guess... and it wasn't even concern, but the thing that, like, kinda red-lighted me, like, 'Hey, this might be con… carrying on,' is the fact that his macros were, like, pretty dialled in. Like, I had wrote them and he didn't stay exactly on them, but his calorie intake was about where it needed to be. My experience, anyways, for, like, what he was trying to achieve. And so I don't know. He didn't seem to have a problem with it. He liked where he was at with all of that.

Koback: So that was your main conversation Saturday?

Nichol: That was, like, a big chunk while we were there. Is, like, us actually going through... 'cause I was, like, going through each item. Like, 'Why do you have... why are your ratios off?'

((Crosstalk))

Koback: Do you know where his kids or wife were that night?
Nichol: On Saturday?
Koback: Yeah. His ki… well, you know his kids are with the babysitter. Do you know where his wife is?
Nichol: She's in Arizona.
Koback: Okay. How do you know that?
Nichol: 'Cause he told me.
Koback: Okay.
((Crosstalk))
Koback: Do you know what she's doing there?
Nichol: I think she's on a business trip. He didn't even tell me right away. He actually told me, I think, like, on Saturday, or somethin'.
((Crosstalk
Koback: Like, during...
((Crosstalk))
Nichol: Friday or somethin'. I don't... I honestly don't remember. I just remember I was, like, really surprised. Where he's, like, 'Hey, I'm gonna try to get a babysitter if you want to hang out or somethin' like that.' And I was, like, 'Why do you need a babysitter? Like, your wife's home.' He's, like, 'No, she's out of town.' I was, like, 'Oh.'
Koback: Okay.
Nichol: 'Okay.'
Koback: Was there much conversation regarding that? Her on... bein' on a trip, or the children on... during those conversations?
Nichol: Not really. I just asked him what time she was comin' home on Sunday and he just said, 'Really late.'
Koback: Okay.
Nichol: And that was it. I mean, there… there's nothin' really to talk about with that.
Koback: Okay. So your conversations mainly health-related?
Nichol: Mm-hm.
Koback: Um, you guys returned to your house and then he goes home. And then you talked to him for, um, a few hours on Sunday.
Nichol: Did I? Are you asking me or are you telling me?
Koback: I'm asking you.
Nichol: Oh. I was, like, I don't even know. Sunday... honestly... oh, on s… so wait a minute. That was Saturday. This is the... we're talking about Saturday. We're not talking about Sunday right now.

Koback: Okay. So, you're still on Saturday?
Nichol: Yes. This...
Koback: You guys have a phone conversation when he gets home?
Nichol: That was the day that he got the babysitter, and I went out to dinner. Not on Sunday.
Koback: Okay.
Nichol: Okay. Sorry, I just want to make sure you got...
Koback: That's okay. Yep.
Nichol: ... your days right. So Saturday, yes. We went out. He had the babysitter. He went home. I'm sure we did. We always talk on the phone and, honestly, I mean, Mark asked me that the other day. He's like, 'How long were you on the phone? Fifteen minutes? Twenty minutes?' Like, you're gonna have to look at the records, to be honest with you. Like, I'm... so much.
Koback: You like to talk. I can tell a little bit.
Nichol: Yeah.
((Crosstalk))
Nichol: A little bit.
Duane: Four hundred... when she was young, she'd crank out about four-hundred words a minute. Gusts, up to six hundred. That little thing can yack, man.
Koback: You're a talker. So I'm... I'm lettin' you talk. Um...
Duane: I need to use a restroom. If I can use...
Koback: Let me show you where it's at.
Nichol: Can you get me some water...
Koback: So...
Nichol: ... while you're out there with them, please?
Duane: Sure.
Nichol: Thank you.
Duane: And another bottle?
Koback: That's...
Nichol: Yeah. At least one.
Koback: Let's move to...
Nichol: Sunday.
Koback: ... Sunday, right? Well, let me reverse somethin'. Your conversation with the children... or about the children, was there ever any talk about medical concerns with either of the children?

Nichol: All I know is CeCe is allergic to pea… not peanuts. Like, pine nuts. Pine nuts.
Koback: So she has a nut allergy?
Nichol: Yes.
Koback: Did they take meds?
Nichol: He... I know that she had, like, an epi-pen, but as far as I know, she didn't have any meds. But I never asked. Like, I was just told, like, she has a pretty severe allergy. And...
Koback: Enough to carry an epi-pen. That's pretty severe.
Nichol: Yeah. While we're on this, so, when he was in North Carolina, um... this is all, like, hearsay now, because it's, like, this is in a conversation. Like, he's telling me this stuff, but who knows exactly what happened? But he went out there to go see his family and her family, and while he was in town, before he went out to North Carolina, I guess his mother had accidentally, like, not exposed her to something with nuts, but had, like, given a product... I think it was, like, ice cream, to a different kid that could have traces of nuts. Or something… I don't know. But it was, like, his daughter was fine, but she was, like, in the range of contamination and I think his wife was very upset about that. And when he got to North Carolina, he told me that he was supposed to spend, like, half time with them, half the time with her family, and that was supposed to be what it was. I don't know. But he said that he went to go see his family, and they weren't answering the phone for, like, a day or two before he went out there. And then, when he got there, there was a note on the door that said, uh, 'Son, if you stop by, we're at the beach.' And they ignored him for, like, most of the time that he was out there. And...
Koback: His own family?
Nichol: Yes. His mom, his dad, and his sister.
Koback: What'd he... what's the significance? Do you know under... do you know why?
Nichol: Yeah. He said... and, again, I don't know what is true...
Koback: Mm-hm.
Nichol: ... with this man anymore, and what's not. But he told me that... like, leading up to it, I was, like, 'Well, why are your folks ignoring you?' And I was really concerned about this. Like, every single day he would talk to me when he was out there and I was, like, 'You talk to your family today? You talk to your family today? Did you talk

to your dad? What happened? Did you talk to them?' 'No, I didn't.' Or, 'Yeah, I talked to my mom.' 'Well, what'd she say? Are you gonna hang out with them?' Like, I wanted him to see his people, because it's important. Family is an important thing, you know. It just needs to function properly and...

Koback: Sure.

Nichol: ... and so I was, like, 'Well, um'... and he was, like, 'Well, they're ignoring me.' And I was, like, 'What do you think happened?' And he was, like, 'I'm not really sure, but I think, um, something was said between my wife and them during that incident.' And he's, like...

Koback: The...

Nichol: '... because every time I...'

Koback: ... peanut or...

Nichol: Yes.

Koback: ... fruit and nut...

Nichol: That happened before he got there. Yes. And he was, like, 'Because every time that I try to, um… I talk about possibly going over there to see if they're home, she gets upset about it.' And I was, like, 'Okay.' And he told me that his mom and his wife did not get along at all. He said that his mom didn't even show up to his wedding, because she's, like, really… did not care for Shanann. So again, I don't know what's true and what's not, but I just know that there was some tension there.

Koback: Mm-hm.

Nichol: And, again, like, that part is, like... I feel like it's almost third-party, so that's why it's, like...

Koback: Sure.

Nichol: ... I didn't even worry about...

((Crosstalk))

Koback: Well, but it came from him to you, so it's not. It is somethin' that I, um... is... whether it's important or not, we can validate that. Uh, I'm sure we will be having some conversations with family. Um, you know, it... what does it mean? I don't know. Um, but...

Nichol: Yeah. I don't know, either. But I just know...

Koback: So...

Nichol: ... like...

Koback: Maybe she n… I don't know.

Nichol: Well, and then, um, he ended up seeing them on the last, like, full day that he was there, and they told him, supposedly, that she had gotten really upset and then screamed and yelled in front of his… Chris's sister's kids that are very young. And that his mom and his dad had said, like, 'You're never gonna see Chris again. You're gonna see me. You're never gonna see the babies.' And just, like, threatened them. And then walked off. And I guess that was the incident that happened prior to him coming out there. And then she didn't tell him about it.

Koback: Mm-hm.

Nichol: She just, like, let it go and then he just spent all week tryin' to figure out why his family was, like...

Koback: Hm.

Nichol: ... not tryin' to be involved.

Koback: Gotcha.

Nichol: Um, so again, I'm not sure. That was i… like, it... it just feels really third-party, so it's hard for me to talk about. Because...

Koback: Sure.

Nichol: ... I don't know how much...

Koback: That's okay.

Nichol: ... validation...

((Crosstalk))

Koback: So be… beyond the… the nut allergy for CeCe, did you know of any other... did she take meds that you know of? Other than carrying an epi-pen?

Nichol: His kids or his wife?

Koback: No, hi… his children.

Nichol: No.

Koback: And now... well, if you know anything about his wife's medical conditions, if she had any.

Nichol: No. I've, like, read in the newspaper. They keep sayin', 'Oh, she had medical conditions.' And I'm like, 'Is that a misprint? Are they talkin' about CeCe? Or is that just somethin' else I don't know?'

Koback: So you don't know anything about...

Nichol: Nope.

Koback: ... uh, Shanann having any kind of medical problems?

Nichol: Nope.

Koback: Okay. Covered Saturday. So there's a phone call Saturday night, actually. Um, from... uh, it can't be Saturday. It had to be Sunday. I wrote that down quickly. Sunday night. Is there anything else you think... let's... let me just back up. From the Saturday, where you guys had a meal at... at The Lazy Dog, to prior for the six weeks that you guys were serious, and, um, although your dad's here and I think you're probably pretty comfortable, your relationship with Chris was... can you describe your relationship?

Nichol: I mean, when he was with me, I considered it to be fairly healthy. Was open communication and it was, what I thought, was honest. And it was very calm. It was respectful. Uh, we got along really well. He gave me my space when I needed it. I gave him his. And any time he wanted to take care of hi… like, any time that his kids could be in his life for hours or days or whatever... whenever they were home, I made sure that I wasn't a presence in his life. So that he could be the best dad that he needed to be. Um, and, I mean, I thought, what we had, it was very comfortable for me. I enjoyed it. I think he did very much, as well.

Koback: Your guys... you... six to eight weeks, two mo… whatever it was, you guys have an intimate relationship during that time?

Nichol: Yes.

Koback: Okay. So you're... and you're pretty serious. Um, d… did he ever tell you that he loved you?

Nichol: Yes, he did.

Koback: Did you ever tell him the same?

Nichol: Couple times.

Koback: Okay. Um, notwithstanding that today, 'cause that may... those thoughts may have changed for you, but on… let's go Mon- Sunday into Monday or Monday, did you... did you still love him on those days?

Nichol: I think it was something where it was, like, I s… I said it a few times and I meant it, but he definitely felt the urge to say it to me a lot more than I did to him. Because it was just all very new to me and it was, like, 'Take your time with this. Like, you don't need to... to, like, rush that, you know?' Like, I remember when he was in North Carolina and he was, like, tryin' to patch things up with his wife. And he told me he loved me. And I was, like, 'Don't say that to me. Like, please go try to fi… and I mean it.' And that might be in the texts, too. Where it's, like, 'Don't. Don't. Like, don't say those words to me and then go try to make peace with you li… wife and lay in bed with another woman. Like, just don't do that.' And I was, like, 'It's not that I don't appreciate what you're saying to me.' It's, like, just... it just didn't sit right for me, you know? So I'd just be like...

Koback: Almost like an insecurity where he had to say that to you? Or...

Nichol: I... I don't... no. I think he... he, like... looking back at all this now, I don't think he was trying to fix things with her. So saying 'I love you' to me seemed like probably something that he genuinely meant. Like, 'I love this woman.' And regardless of where he was gonna end up that night. But, to me, in the way that I was perceiving things, he had told me that he was tryin' to fix things with her. So it's just, like, 'This is an inappropriate time.' And I wasn't mad at him. And I'm pretty sure that's in the texts, too. Where it was very, like, calm but it's just, like, it's almost disrespectful. Where it's, like, 'Please don't.' I'm like, 'You know, if we get to that point where it is you and me, like, yes, you can say that. But don't... not then. Like, that's...'

Koback: So you thought he was very genuine when he said that?

Nichol: I... yeah. I did. I mean, and he wrote it and sent all those cards I gave you. Not in all of them, but, like...

Koback: Hm.

Nichol: ... the later ones.

Koback: And...

Nichol: Thank you.

Koback: When you said it to him, you said you meant it, when you said it.

Nichol: Yes. I just didn't say it as frequently as he said it. Like, sometimes he would say it and I was just, like... for me, it was still, like, very, very new. So I kinda, like, took my time and only said it when I was just, like, 'This is a really important moment.'

Koback: So you go… I mean, in the short period of time that you guys were together, he...

Nichol: Yes.

Koback: ... wa… became very attached to you.

Nichol: Yes. Very, very attached.

Koback: I mean, he's sending cards...

Nichol: Flowers.

Koback: ... he's tellin' you he loves you. He sends you flowers. Does he buy you any other gifts?

Nichol: Nope. I wouldn't have wanted them anyways. It's... flowers is enough. You can't... I don't need expensive stuff.
Koback: Okay. But he becomes very attached to you.
Nichol: Yes.
Koback: Um, you guys are talking multiple times a day, at least. You're...
((Crosstalk))
Nichol: All the time.
Koback: You're seein' each other on a regular basis.
Nichol: Yep.
Koback: Um, so i… it... it's a very, um... and... and his wife is not around, nor are his children. So there's a lot of time for you guys to build your relationship in this first four... four weeks or so. Is that fair?
Nichol: Yeah. And even when she... she was back, I mean, it was still, like, we were still spending time together. He was still spending time with his children, and I have my own life. Like, I mean, there was one week where I just, like, went out of town for my… with my friends for my birthday. I wasn't even around the whole, like, th… last few days of June, up until the 3rd of July. I was, like, gone. You know? And then there was another... like, a f… last weekend, I had a friend impromptu come in town from out of state, and I hosted her, uh, for a few days. And it's, like, it... like, I still did my own thing all the time. Like, whether he was there or not. Like, if my friends were, like, 'Hey, we want to make plans,' I would tell him, like, 'We're not hangin' out today, 'cause I want to go see my mom or my dad.'
Koback: Did your friends know about him?
Nichol: Nope.
Koback: Why?
Nichol: 'Cause it's, like, he's with two women right now. They don't...
Koback: Okay.
Nichol: ... need to know about that.
Koback: So if you had a boyfriend of four to eight weeks, on a regu… I don't know if you ha… were married prior or if you had a boyfriend before, but if you had a steady boyfriend, you would let people know... I think you told me before we got started that y… you just told your dad about Chris, um...
Nichol: No, I wouldn't of told him.
Koback: ... recently.

Nichol: I wouldn't of told people.
Koback: Okay.
Nichol: It's too early. I mean, people...
Koback: So you don't tell your friends, 'Hey, I have a new boyfriend'?
Nichol: No, 'cause they... i… people come and go.
Koback: Okay.
Nichol: I mean, dating, seeing these days is, like... it sucks. I mean, so no. I wouldn't. I mean, it would have to be somethin'... even with Shawn. I think I was with Shawn for probably, like, six or seven months before I brought him home to my family. I mean, I really... and same with...
Koback: Okay.
Nichol: ... the... that was the guy I was in a previous relationship with. But I mean...
Koback: But this one, you were a little bit more... you said he's with two women. Did that... was that one of your considerations for not telling anybody about him?
Nichol: Y… yes. Well, I mean, it was, like, 'Okay. Like, this'... to me, it wasn't gonna be an ex… extended thing. Like, if it got to the point where we were, like, dating for, like, three or four months and he's still talkin' about, 'Oh, I'm gonna move out and I'm gonna sell the house,' I think at that point I probably would've just been like, 'I don't think you're really, like, doing these things you say you're gonna do.' And I probably would've just, like, left, because, at that point, it's not fair. It wasn't fair to me in the first place. It wasn't fair to her in the first place. It wasn't fair to any of us in the first place. You know? It wasn't fair to his family, for him to have an affair. It wasn't fair to me to have him lie to me and make me think that everything is going to plan and, still, to this day, I don't even know what's a lie and what's not. I don't even know if they were, like, filing for divorce. I don't know if they were putting the house up. I don't even know... I don't even know anymore what is real and what is not.
Koback: Sure.
Nichol: But what I do know is it's just, like... you know, that wasn't fair to me, either, because if I'd a known not even all the truth but, like, obviously, some of it, I wouldn't have even engaged in any of this in the first place. And it just... and I mean, and that's the part, for me, just, like, on my personal level, outside of everything that is happening. That

is gonna affect me long-term. It's, like, you know, I'm gonna wake up every day and know that, like, this mom and her unborn child and these two little girls are not around anymore. And it breaks my heart. It is so... oh my god. And... and he... and then I have to think about, like, the consequences of his actions, and how they affect everybody else. Like, all of these... her family's impacted. My name is about to be, like, slandered for probably a while. I don't know how long it's gonna take to heal, but I would not be surprised if it's gonna be hard to go out in public sometimes for a couple of years. And that really hurts me. I'm just, like, this is a horrible, horrible thing. Like, how dare you? You know? And... and people aren't gonna understand that. You know? They're gonna say, 'Oh, you know, you're the woman that had an affair with this man who took out his whole family.' And I take a step back and it's just, like, I didn't know. Like, I... I... uh. It's... he's so disgusting. I am so ashamed of him and everything, and I just... oh, those little girls. They're so little. They're so little.

Koback: We talked to... we talked a little bit earlier about gettin' some help for these things, and we can provide that.

Nichol: God.

Duane: Okay.

Koback: At… at really, no cost. Through the state.

Duane: Oh, one more can... we just want to make sure, uh, there's resolution.

Koback: Absolutely.

Duane: That's why we come to you guys.

Koback: Yeah.

Duane: To pound this sh...

Koback: And...

Duane: ... pound it down until there's...

Koback: Yeah, I... I'm...

Duane: ... nothin' left.

Koback: ... sorry that you're talking again today. I really am. I don't want to put you through any more trauma than you've already been through. There is, um, reasons for everything that we're doing today and what... what occurred. And I'm sorry. I genuinely am sorry. I... it... these are not things that we like to do twice. It's the same thing with other types of victims from other crimes. We want to do it once, and we want to be done. Unfortunately, we didn't know yesterday, uh, what we know today. And that's why we're here, because we need this video. And I'm... I am sorry, 'cause I know it's hard to talk about it. But it... it's...

((Crosstalk))

Nichol: ... so sad, and she's pregnant.

Duane: And... and wo… on our end, we didn't...

Nichol: God, they're so cute. They're so little. Like, wow. Why? Why? Why? Why? How? I don't even understand how you could bring yourself to do that to somebody who's, like, that big. Oh, Jesus.

Koback: Take a minute. Do you want to step out for a minute?

Nichol: No, I just need to chill with my eyes closed for a sec. I still cannot believe this is happening. All right. Let's keep goin', 'cause we're just...

((Crosstalk))

Nichol: ... gettin' to, like, the meat of this whole...

Koback: Let's... let's...

Nichol: ... situation.

Koback: ... get to the phone call on Saturday, from nine to eleven.

Nichol: Uh...

Koback: What did you guys... or s… pardon me. On Sunday from nine to eleven.

Nichol: Yeah. We talked a few times. So Sunday...

Duane: You okay?

Nichol: I think so. I need to think. I can't even think.

Koback: Take a couple breaths and take a... take a second.

Nichol: Sunday night. I don't even know. I don't think I was that concerned about anything at that point.

Koback: You guys had had a meal... a nice meal the night before. You knew his wife was probably coming home late that evening.

Nichol: Oh. Um, you know what? I still don't remember what we talked about. I, like... honestly, we talked about so much random stuff. Like, it's so hard to pinpoint some of these things. Um, I don't remember what we talked about. I do remember that was a long phone conversation, though. We probably talked about all sorts of stuff. Um, one thing...

Koback: Anything...

Nichol: ... I do remember, though, um, that I didn't remember earlier when I was talking to Mark... so this is where I'm starting to remember little bits and pieces.

Koback: Mm-hm.

Nichol: I... I don't remember...

((Crosstalk))

Nichol: Yeah. No. This was a phone conversation. I don't remember what was in the phone conversation. Probably nothing of relevance, to be honest with you. But, um, usually he talks to me when he's, like, down in the basement, in his bed, before he goes to bed and before I go to bed. And I could hear the TV on, which I thought was kinda weird. I didn't ask him, I just heard it in the background, and I remember thinking... and it was right before we got off the phone. I was, like, 'Why the hell is he up?' And there's no TV downstairs. So I was, like, 'Well, maybe'... I don't know.

Koback: So no TV in the basement, where he usually calls you from?

Nichol: Yeah. And I don't know how many TVs they have. Like, I've never been in their bedroom. I went upstairs once and it was to their little playroom and I just looked at it. And I was, like, 'That's super cute that your girls have books.' And that was it. And other than that, I have never been in any of those rooms in that upstairs. Like, to me, it was just, like, you don't... no. Like, ever. I had no... so I don't know if he has any other TVs. I'm assuming by how much other nice stuff they have in their house, it wouldn't surprise me. So I'm not quite sure what room he was in at that point. Um, but I just remember hearing the TV, and I was, like... it was just weird to me, 'cause I was, like, 'Why are you watching TV right now? It is super late.' And that was the only thing...

Koback: And he... and he had phoned you or were you guys already talking when the TV was goin' or just...

Nichol: I just remember, like, I... like, go… picked up on it, like, later, but I don't think it was, like, throughout the whole conversation.

Koback: Okay.

Nichol: I just remember it being towards the end, 'cause I remember thinking, like, 'Wow, it's really late.'

Koback: The... the, um, somethin' I didn't ask you about the house, 'cause you'd been there twice and it just, uh, made me remember. Do you remember how you guys accessed the house?

Nichol: Uh, that's a good question. Uh, so once through the garage, and I think once through the front door.

Koback: Uh...
Nichol: I think the first time was through the front door. I think. And I think the second time was through the garage.
Koback: Is there anything unique about either of the doors when you went into the house? That might not be typical of another house?
Nichol: Like, a unique door? I know they have a...
Koback: Not the door itself.
Nichol: ... camera on their door.
Koback: Okay. There's... there's...
Nichol: I mean, I know that.
Koback: There's a camera on the... which door?
Nichol: I... it's on the front door, isn't it?
Koback: Um, I don't know. I'm asking you.
Nichol: I think so.
Koback: Okay.
Nichol: Uh, I don't know. Um...
Koback: Was… did he use a key to access the house?
Nichol: No. Um, he did not. The first time I went over there, he just let me in. And then the second time... did we go through the garage? I don't remember. I've been through his garage before. I went through his front door once, though. 'Cause I remember he had just cleaned... it was the first time I went through his front door. 'Cause he had just cleaned his carpets, and he had moved all the furniture out of the way, and the furniture was kind of in the way of the door. And he's, like, 'The door doesn't open all the way right now. I'll move all the furniture back when the carpet dries.' So I do remember that, just kinda offhandedly. Uh, and the second time, I want to say we went through his garage, 'cause I remember his garage. I remember... yeah. Yeah. So...
Koback: So he was at the house when you went there? Um, you were never there by yourself, correct?
Nichol: He was at... yeah, no.
Koback: Or he took you there?
Nichol: He... the first time, he was already there...
Koback: Okay.
Nichol: ... and I met up with him. And the second time, we went there together.
Koback: So the front door... I asked if he had used a key.
Nichol: He let me in.

Koback: Okay. So there's a, um... you know, those key pads...
Nichol: Mm-hm.
Koback: ... where you can enter a access code. Do you remember seein' that on his door?
Nichol: Oh, like, I want to say vaguely, but to be honest with you, I don't remember. Like, he let me in that day. That's... that was so long...
Koback: So he never gave you...
Nichol: ... ago.
Koback: He never gave you the code to access his home?
Nichol: No.
Koback: Okay.
Nichol: Not at all.
Koback: Um, you talk about a security system. Uh, there was a s… uh, camera on the front door?
Nichol: Mm-hm.
Koback: Was that just, like, a... you know what a ring doorbell is? That goes to your phone.
Nichol: I don't even know what it looked like.
Koback: Okay.
Nichol: I only know that it existed, either because A, I wasn't paying attention the first time I was over there but, B, because of all the stuff that's going on right now. That's the only...
Koback: Okay.
Nichol: ... reason I know it's...
Koback: Okay.
Nichol: ... e… it exists.
Koback: Do you remember seeing any cameras anywhere in the house?
Nichol: No.
Koback: Okay. Did he ever tell you about the alarm system or give you an access code...
Nichol: No.
Koback: ... to the alarm system?
Nichol: No, no, no. I wouldn't have asked for that. I wouldn't of wanted that anyways.
Koback: Sorry to regress to that.
Nichol: No, you're okay.

Koback: We can go back to the... the phone call. Or where you noticed the television in the background...
Nichol: Yeah.
Koback: ... of the phone call.
Nichol: Yep. So I didn't know what room he was in, but I was just, like... I just thought it was weird. 'Cause he's always, like… before I go to bed and I lay down, he's always, like, kinda tryin' to do the same thing. We just talk. It's, like, a really chill thing 'til one of us is about to pass out. Then that's the end of it. Um, but it was strange. 'Cause I was, like, 'The TV's on.' And I remember what I was thinkin'. I was, like, 'Maybe he's waitin' up for her.' And then I was, like, 'Maybe not.' I didn't know. I didn't... it wasn't something that alerted me. It was just different from his...
((Crosstalk))
Nichol: ... standard operating procedure. Because he... whether his wife is home or she's gone, he's always got kinda, like, the standard op when he calls me. So that's why it was kind of, like, unique.
Koback: Okay.
Nichol: Because it doesn't really fluctuate when she's there and when she's not there. He's pretty, like, free rein with what he does.
Koback: Mm-hm. So anything i… anything important that you recall during that conversation about the children, about his wife, about what he was doing the next day, what he had planned? Anything like that?
Nichol: No.
Koback: Did he tell you any of that information?
Nichol: I remember he told he had to go to the field and not to the office on Monday morning.
Koback: Okay. Did he specifically say where he needed to go on Monday morning?
Nichol: No. I don't ask him for those sites. There's li… *Anadarko's* got thousands of sites. If he were to tell me, I wouldn't of... I wouldn't even tell...
Koback: They're just random numbers and stuff, right?
Nichol: Well, he told me... he said, 'I gotta go to a site. I gotta go, um, check out, like, a valve' or somethin' where they think that they had a release. Somethin' like that. Uh...
Koback: Did he mention the town or anywhere...
Nichol: No. No. He just told me that that's what he had to go do.

Koback: Okay.
Nichol: He's... 'cause, yeah. He was, like, 'I won't see you in the office in the morning.' 'Cause I usually... I see him, but I don't actually talk to him. I'll go in the cafeteria. I will put my lunch in the fridge, and him and his whole team are sitting in there, and I don't talk to any of them. I just walk out. Um, but anyways, yeah. He's, like, 'So I won't see you. I'm goin' to the field.' Which is not an uncommon thing for the Ops guys to just go straight to the field. Like, it happens. Like, typically, they go to the office. I would say three or four days a week. But there are days where him and his other team members are not there. Or, like, I'll get in there and some days the... the cafeteria's packed, and they're all there. And other days, I get in there, and there's only three or four of them.
Koback: So it didn't cause you any concern that he said...
Nichol: No.
Koback: '... I'm goin' to the field on Monday. I won't see you'? That wasn't...
Nichol: No. It didn't...
Koback: That's happened before?
Nichol: Yeah, I mean...
Koback: Okay.
Nichol: ... it wasn't something... I mean, and it's not just him. It's that whole team. Like, you can just tell when they've got, like, a lot goin' on. 'Cause I'll walk in and there'll be two of them as opposed to six or seven.
Koback: Do you know what he did Sunday, during the day?
Nichol: Um, I don't even know what I did on Sunday during the day. I am so tired. Let me just think about this. Daniel came over Friday. I hung out with him Saturday. And then Sunday...
Martinez: When did Jim come in?
Nichol: Monday.
Martinez: Huh.
Nichol: Jim got here Monday. What did I do on Sunday? I am drawing a blank. I'm really tired. I don't know. Can I get back to you on that?
Koback: Did you guys have any conversations on Saturday night during your meal, what he might be doing on Sunday?

Nichol: I'm sure we did. I don't know why I'm drawing a blank, 'cause I haven't slept.
Koback: I… if I say that his... he may have, uh, done something with his children, would that refresh...
Nichol: Oh, yes.
Koback: ... your memory?
Nichol: He went to a birthday party.
Koback: Okay. Um, do you know whose house he was going to?
Nichol: Nope, but I know that they had a water balloon fight.
Koback: Okay. He... he had one or his children?
Nichol: His children did.
Koback: Okay.
Nichol: He said he used to get really into it. He said he got really interactive with his kids. He's, like, 'So many adults don't really spend a lot of time playing with the kids, but I always do.'
Duane: We went to the museum on what day? Saturday or Sunday?
Nichol: Sunday.
Duane: Okay
Nichol: That's right.
Duane: Okay.
Nichol: So... yeah, that's what I was, like, 'Was I hanging out with you?' God. Uh, so...
Koback: Very memorable event, huh?
Nichol: Uh, we hi...
Duane: That was, uh...
Nichol: Me and him and my... my m… stepmother...
Duane: My wife and...
Nichol: ... and my sister went...
Duane: Yeah.
Nichol: ... to, uh, the museum. And that's right.
Koback: What museum?
Nichol: Uh, the Denver Museum of Nature and Science. And they went to brunch prior to that, and I skipped brunch. Um, and I went to the gym.
Duane: You shouldn't of. It was good.
Nichol: I had to do core day. That was the last time I worked, actually. Um...
Duane: That's what we did Sunday. Okay.

Nichol: And... yeah. So core day, and then we went... we went to the museum, and
then, um...
Koback: When did you... did he tell you about the water balloon fight on Sunday evening, during your conversation on the phone?
Nichol: I think so.
Koback: Okay. So...
Nichol: I think so.
Koback: ... you don't know whose house he went to on Sunday?
Nichol: No.
Koback: Um, but you knew it was for a child's birthday?
Nichol: Yeah. And he had told me about that in advance, really. So I don't know if it was Saturday that he had told me that he was gonna go to the birthday or Friday. I just remember he was, like, 'I gotta go to this birthday party...'
Koback: Okay.
Nichol: '... with my kids.'
Koback: Um, any other conversation that makes sense?
Nichol: I mean, honestly, at this point, I'm really tired, so I know there are certain things that I need to tell you guys that we'll get to as these days progress.
Koback: Yep.
Nichol: Um, but in all honesty, if it doesn't stand out to me now...
Koback: Today?
Nichol: ... it probably wasn't...
Koback: That's fine.
Nichol: ... relevant.
Duane: What about that 9 o'clock thing you were tellin' me on Monday?
Nichol: Oh, what he told me? Oh, yeah. Well, we'll get there. We'll get there. We're still on Sunday night.
Koback: So we're on Sunday.
Nichol: We're... we're gonna go...
((Crosstalk))
Koback: We're gonna get... we're gonna get to...
Nichol: This is gonna be a long day.
Koback: We're gonna get there to Monday. We're... we're getting

there. So Sunday night... or Sunday during the day, you had your own personal, um, stuff going on...
Nichol: Mm-hm.
Koback: ... with your family.
Nichol: Mm-hm.
Koback: You never see him on Sunday. Is that accurate?
Nichol: No. I didn't see him. What did I do the rest of the day? I came home. I think I might've just chilled at my house. I don't remember. I think I cleaned my house. I don't know. I didn't see him, though.
Koback: Okay. And...
Nichol: Yeah. Saturday was the last time I saw him.
Koback: Okay. Sunday, you're at home. You talk to him from... we know he – you have a conversation...
Nichol: Mm-hm.
Koback: ... in the late evening hours, and then...
Nichol: Mm-hm.
Koback: ... you go to sleep?
Nichol: Mm-hm.
Koback: Um, on Sunday night?
Nichol: Mm-hm.
Koback: When's the next time you talk with Chris?
Nichol: Probably Monday morning.
Koback: Do you know what... what time?
Nichol: No. I mean, so we used to randomly text each other throughout the day. But we both get really busy. So some days I don't hear a lot from him, and some days I don't text him until 2 o'clock in the afternoon. 'Cause I'm just busy. And I... I remember, I didn't hear a lot from him that day. Uh, which was, like... that's not out of the normal for either one of us, um, during the day. Um, but at one point, I do remember he text me and he's, like, 'Oh, it's been a really busy day.' And then said some other stuff. Which I'm sure you will find in my text. What he said, I don't know. It wasn't obviously, anything that was alerting to me. I... that's what I'm sayin'. Like, at this point I remember really key things. But if it's a conversation then I'm like, 'I don't remember exactly what was discussed.' It's 'cause it was probably just bullshit. Like, just...
Koback: Just...
Nichol: ...talkin' to each other. Yeah.

Koback: ... small talk stuff?
Nichol: Yeah. Um, but I remember he was busy that day, and we didn't talk that much. And then I... I clocked out at 3:00 is what my timecard says. That's what I was showing, um, Mark, the other day. And I got home to go meet my buddy. One of my good friends was comin' over to my house. And he actually has a key to my house. So he was actually there when I got there. And...
Koback: Who's that?
Nichol: My friend, Jim. Um, and so, Jim came over and I got home. He was there. He had just walked in the door, and, um, I remember briefly, after he got there, I checked my texts. I mean, briefly after I met up with Jim, I glanced at my texts and Chris said something about, 'My family's not home.' Or, like, 'My wife and kids aren't home.' Like, something to that effect. And I told Mark... 'cause he asked me for a time, and I don't have an exact time, but I remember it was right after I walked in the...
Koback: That was a text message, though?
Nichol: Yeah. It's in a text. And it's, like... it was briefly after I walked in the door. So based off how long it takes me to get home from work and when I clocked out, it was probably about 3:45 PM. Um, text me and tells me that. And he knows when I get off of work, too. So he doesn't always bug me if I'm busy. So, I don't know what's up with that, but that's when he that's when he sends that to me. And, um...
Koback: So you're saying that he... he would've known that you would've had your phone available to you and not been at work when he sent you that text message?
Nichol: Uh, yes. That's what I'm trying to say.
Koback: So, looking back at it, you think it was purposefully sent at that time?
Nichol: Oh, I'm sure.
Koback: Is... I'm... the... I'm just asking your feeling on that.
Nichol: Yes. And then he said, 'Call me when you can.' And I was, like...
Koback: There was no other communication between you and him that morning, on Monday morning, at all?
Nichol: Well, there w… there was, but it was random, like...
Koback: It... but nothin' about this event?
Nichol: No. No, no, no, no, no.

Koback: About, like, 'My mo… my wife's missing' or...
Nichol: No.
Koback: '... my'... w… anything?
Nichol: Nothin'.
Koback: Okay.
Nichol: Nothin'.
Koback: And you knew he wasn't comin' to the office, 'cause he had told you that Sunday night.
Nichol: Yeah. And then he goes... and so they're only in the office for the morning. Like...
Koback: Right.
Nichol: ... some days it's longer than others, but I would say by a maximum of 7:30, every single morning, they are all gone. And they don't come back unless they have a meeting or something that they have to attend. So not seeing him for the rest of the day is not an unnormal thing.
Koback: Okay.
Nichol: Like... but, like, I'm saying we don't really... the only reason we interact was kind of, like, by an off-chance thing. Like, I don't work with him.
Koback: Mm-hm.
Nichol: Um, so he, uh... yeah. We talked randomly throughout the day, but it was really sporadic, and he seemed pretty busy. So we didn't talk too much. Like I said, didn't put too much thought into it. It happens all the time. Um, waited 'til about 3:45, then sent that text to me. And, yes, he does know that I will be home at that point, or getting home. Like...
Koback: Did you give Mark Jim's information?
Nichol: No. I would really, not like to involve him in this.
Koback: Okay.
Nichol: He does not know about this. He didn't... and he was not, like, he doesn't know any of this is occurring.
Koback: Okay.
Nichol: Like, I was literally tryin' to...
Koback: So he... he knows, certainly, through the media that somethin's occurred?
Nichol: Yeah.
Koback: With...

Nichol: He's, like, out of town.
Koback: ... Chris.
Nichol: He's probably has no idea.
Koback: Okay.
Nichol: He doesn't know...
Koback: Okay.
Nichol: ... who Chris is. Like, he's not... I do not... no.
Koback: So he's just a friend of yours...
Nichol: Yes.
Koback: ... um, that was...
Nichol: He does not need to be dragged into this.
Koback: ... coming to your apartment and doesn't know anything about Chr… does he know anything about Chris?
Nichol: No.
Koback: Okay.
Nichol: Nothin'. Absolutely nothin'.
Duane: Yeah. We've known Jim for...
Nichol: He... yeah.
Duane: ... ye… years and years.
Nichol: Yeah.
Koback: You're not datin' him or anything like that?
Nichol: No.
Koback: He's just a friend?
Nichol: He's one of my very good friends. Like, my dad knows him. He's a great guy. He just... he... he works out of state a lot. So when he's in town, um, we hang out. But when he's in town and he's off of work, to save time... I... so I... I gave him a key to my house one, 'cause I trust him and he's one of my best friends, and two, 'cause, uh, sometimes he will just meet me there. Because I'll be, like, 'Hey, I'm gettin' off of work.' And then if I get stuck in traffic or something, he ends up sitting outside of my apartment waiting for me to get off of work. So I'm like, 'Here's a key.' And my dog loves him and stuff. So no.
Koback: Okay.
Nichol: He's not involved with it...
Koback: So he's just a family friend?
Nichol: Yes. I don't even want him dragged...
Koback: The only reason I ask...
Nichol: ... into this.

Koback: A- and I'm not really concerned, uh, about your location. Um, I think we already have your cell phone records. Um, at some point, i… did Mark ask you to supply... uh, did they ask for consent to get cell phone records. That'll probably be done by warrant if we...
Nichol: Isn't that what you just did?
Koback: Nope. What I'm talkin' about is your movement.
Nichol: Oh.
Koback: Um, by GPS or by cell phone tower. To show where you were, obviously, and I don't want to cause you concern. We want to know where you were that day, too. You're dating a man who did some egregious stuff, and we want to put... we want to show that you were never near him that day, period.
Nichol: Oh, I mean, you guys can...
Koback: So...
Nichol: ... track my stuff.
Koback: No, I… I mean, that... that was somethin' we will have to get a warrant for, anyways, to... I'm just saying if... if we asked for it, would you have any objections...
Nichol: Yeah, you're...
Koback: ... to that?
Nichol: No. You can have it.
Koback: All right. So, um, we'll...
Nichol: I'm... I'm a pretty boring person. I don't...
Koback: Well, it sounds like...
Nichol: ... go too many places.
Koback: ... you just went to work that day and then you came home and you were there at 3:45.
Nichol: Yeah, give or take...
((Crosstalk))
Nichol: ... like, five minutes.
Koback: Yeah. Right.
Nichol: But yeah. So 3:45 I meet Jim there. Yeah, I would totally do...
Koback: And so, Jim is a... understand from an investigative point, he could be a person who could say, 'Yeah. I was there at 3:45. I don't'... he doesn't know Chris. He doesn't know anything. He could say, with one phone call, 'Yeah, she came in at 3:45.' Done.
Nichol: Totally.
Koback: Do you know what I'm sayin'?

Nichol: Yeah.
Koback: And I don't have to ask anything more than, 'Hi, Chris. My name's Kevin.
I'm...'
Nichol: Oh.
Koback: Or... or... or Jim.
((Crosstalk))
Koback: And I'm not saying you have to...
((Crosstalk))
Nichol: Just leave Jim alone. Just leave Jim alone.
((Crosstalk))
Nichol: Jim does not need to be wrapped up in this.
Koback: ... some point... if at some point I needed Jim's info to... let's say we couldn't find your phone records. Would you tell...?
((Crosstalk))
Nichol: You can have them. I will give them to you.
Koback: Would you tell me who Jim was if I couldn't get them?
Nichol: If you had to.
Koback: Okay.
Nichol: I don't really want to involve him in this.
Koback: Perfect.
Nichol: That is not fair to him. That's not... no. If I do not have to do that...
Koback: That's fine.
Nichol: Um, yeah. So anyways, Chris was, like, 'Call me.'
Koback: And this is the 3:45 text?
Nichol: Yeah. He sent me a few. There were... I think there was three of them, and I don't remember what the other one said. But something about, like, 'Yeah, my family's gone.' Or... I don't remember verbatim, but 'Call me when you can.' Or have... 'Call me when you have a chance.' Something to that effect. And so when he told me, 'Call me,' I was kind of alerted. Where I was, like, 'Okay. What's goin' on?' You know? Um, but first when he told me, like, his family was not home, that didn't really seem odd to me. That his family wasn't home. It was really vague. I'm like, 'Okay. Like, are they at the grocery store? Like, elaborate.' And so you know... and then but he says, 'Call me,' like it's an emergency, but then just says that they're not there. And so I am really floored by the... well, I'm not floored but just kinda, like... he

says, 'Call me,' so I'm concerned, and then he's really vague. So I'm like, 'Maybe he just wants to talk to me.' I don't know. I think it took me a little while to really process the severity of the situation, just because this is not something that you expect to see every day. And the way that he talked to me made me believe that this is not what was goin' on, at all.

Koback: Okay. So you make a phone call to him and you guys have a conversation?

Nichol: I did. I stepped outside. Um...

Koback: This is three-forty-five?

Nichol: Ish. I mean... well, like, I think I actually interacted with Jim for probably a good fifteen or twenty minutes. I mean, he's my guest. He's in the house. Um, so I don't think I called him right away. But, like... I mean, I'm tryin' to balance the fact that I have my friend here, and then Chris is saying that something needs to be addressed. But, to me, it didn't sound like an emergency. I mean, it was all the time. Like, people aren't home right now. You know? So it just... it wasn't, like, 'Oh my god. I have to take this call. It's an emergency.'

Koback: It didn't register as being serious?

Nichol: No. No. I mean, it just... it was the way he said it. And I was, like, 'Okay.' So I, um... I remember hangin' out with Jim for a while, and then I stepped outside, and I made a call out on my back patio. And I called him. And he didn't answer the phone. And then he texted me back? Oh, no. Did he answer the phone? I don't remember. I think he missed my call, and then he called me back. Or he just answered. Either way, it was a very short talk to him where he was just, like, 'I have to go. The cops are here.' And I don't remember if he said that on the phone or over text. I don't...

Koback: That's okay.

Nichol: ... even... I'm so tired.

Koback: That's fine. You don't need to...

((Crosstalk))

Nichol: But either way, like, the cops...

Koback: It's... it's the context.

Nichol: Yeah. I mean, you guys'll figure it out. 'The cops... the cops are here.' And I'm just like, 'All right.' And then I remember we were in a... like, we were texting, but I was hanging out with my company. So it wasn't a non-stop text. It was just kinda, like, I would check my phone every once in a while, and we would communicate with each other. And he was just saying they weren't there and that her friend, Nicky, was there. And that her friend, Nicky, had called the cops. And I'm like, 'Why would this girl call the cops?' And I'm like, I honestly do not remember the order of operations on all of this, but I'm pretty sure the majority of our conversation that night, until my friend, Jim, left the house... which was probably pretty late. I don't even know what time. Like, nine or ten... was all via text. So you should have this via text.

Koback: Okay.

Nichol: Like, I don't think we started talking again on the phone until after my company left. Um, and he was, like, uh... I don't know. He just started giving me details about stuff, and I don't remember what order. But he was sayin', like, Nicky was really upset, and that the cops were there, and that they were searchin' the house. And I was just, like, 'What?' You know, like, 'What? Why?' And he was tellin' me that, um, they had had a disagreement or something like that and then, um, he told me she was gonna go to a friend's house. And I was, like, 'Okay. Well, maybe she left. You know, maybe she just went to her friend's.' And then I think he... I don't remember, but I think he was the one that told me that her cell phone and her purse were still there. I think he told me that.

Koback: He told you her cell phone...

Nichol: I'm...

Koback: ... and purse were still there?

Nichol: I think he did. I don't remember.

((Crosstalk))

Koback: What's the significance of that, in your mind, at that time?

Nichol: At that point, I thought this woman was really tryin' to get out of this house.

Koback: Okay.

Nichol: That's what I thought. 'Cause he said that they'd had a disagreement, and I was just, like, 'Okay. Well'... I mean, I leave my cell phone at home, sometimes.

Koback: But he... he said disagreement. What... did he tell you what it was about or...

Nichol: Not at that point. Not at that point.

Koback: Okay.

Nichol: So, um, again you guys are gonna have to check these texts, 'cause it's all, like... I don't know. My brain's...
((Crosstalk))
Koback: That's okay.
Nichol: ... mashed potato right now. Um, but I remember him sayin' that and I'm just thinkin', like, 'Well, maybe she was in a rush, you know? Like, maybe she was just, like, 'I'm goin' to my friend's. I'm leavin' my cell phone here because I don't want you callin' me. I don't want anyone else callin' me.'' I mean, there are days where, when I'm outside of work, I will just shut my phone off. I just do it and it's, like, my way of getting peace. So, to me, that… I mean, it was weird that she... w… it wasn't even that weird to me that she left her phone, just because I leave my phone. But it was weird to me that she left her purse. But knowing the fact that that girl was always on her phone, then yeah. I guess it is kinda odd.
Koback: Like, she lived on her phone, I think.
Nichol: Uh, yeah.
Koback: Pretty much is my understanding of her and a phone. So...
Nichol: Yeah.
Koback: ... I don't know if you knew that...
Nichol: I did.
Koback: ... until prior to the media stuff or just from Chris.
Nichol: I did.
Koback: So did that... so did that strike you as odd? But if you were thinking...
Nichol: Kind of. I mean, agai...
Koback: ... maybe she just left?
Nichol: I just thought she needed to get away from the situation. I mean, I... that didn't seem that awkward to me, that a couple that is going through a separation would be, like, 'We're... I need to leave.'
Koback: Mm-hm.
Nichol: 'I just need some space.' Like, it didn't even process. I was, like, 'Okay. Like, give her some space.' You know? And, um, on that note, too, um, when he was in... we're gonna jump back for just a second.
Koback: That's okay.
Nichol: I had a thought. So when, uh, he was comin' back from North Carolina, that was when he officially told me, 'We're gonna get a

divorce and we're gonna put the house up for sale.' Like, he told me they were separating, and they were gonna put the house up for sale, but they hadn't done it yet. And then, when he got back from North Carolina, that was when he was, like, it was, like, a sealed deal.
Koback: Okay.
Nichol: Um, and the reason that is of significance is because at some point over the weekend... I don't remember when... he told me that they were putting the house up. I... I don't know if it was they were putting it up on Monday. Like, the day they went missing. Or if it was that they were calling the realtor to verify some stuff so they could put it up that week. Like, I don't... I don't quite remember. I just remember the house was supposed to be on the market that week.
Koback: Did he name a realtor ever?
Nichol: Yeah, he did, and I don't remember her name. It was a female.
Koback: Okay.
Nichol: And I don't remember her name.
Koback: That's fine.
Nichol: Like, at all. I was tryin' to think of that for you guys not too long ago.
Duane: Is it a company? Do you got the company name?
Nichol: No. He never gave me that. He gave me her name and he's – it was the same name twice. He gave it to me once when he was in North Carolina, and then once... the other time... 'cause I remember askin'. I was, like, 'Who's that?' 'Cause he was, like... he's, like, 'I'm gonna have to have her call so and… so today and make sure everything's still good to go.' I was, like, 'Who's that?' He's, like, 'The realtor.' I was, like, 'Oh.' Or not today but Monday.
Koback: If it ever comes to your mind, just...
Nichol: Yeah. I doubt it.
((Crosstalk))
Nichol: That was such a...
Koback: Yeah.
Nichol: I will try. I don't...
Koback: Lots of names.
Nichol: ... remember what it was.
Koback: That's fine. It's not that critical. Um, that person may come forward to us

anyways, um... uh, perhaps. So...
Nichol: Okay.
Koback: ... don't worry about it. Let's go back to the phone calls on Monday afternoon.
Nichol: Yeah. So, um... so he's texting me a lot of this information, and I'm startin' to kinda freak out. And it's not like I'm freaked out, like, 'Oh, she got murdered.' I mean, that is not what I thought. It's, like, 'Okay.' Like, the way I looked at this, like, apparently his wife had been gone since midday. Well, was when she got reported missing. I didn't know that. Like, here's the way I looked at this, it was, 'I got home from work just now.' I mean, he didn't say that, but I interpreted, 'I just got home from work, and my family is not here.'
Koback: Okay.
Nichol: So when we're texting for a few hours... like, the cop thing was kinda weird but he's, like, Nicky insisted they call the cops. Nicky insisted they call the cops. And I'm like, 'Okay.' You know? And I'm just tryin' to figure out, 'Well, what role does this woman play in this situation? Like, is she...'
Koback: Did you know who she was?
Nichol: No. I don't know any of his people. Um, like, this has been pretty, like, tight wrapped for a while, which is probably a really good thing. Um, but anyways, um, I didn't know, like, who she was. And so, um, I started askin' him. I was, like, 'Well, where do you think your wife is at?' And he's, like he's, like, 'I think she'll be back tonight. Like, I think she's out with somebody.' And he was tellin' me that they had had a disagreement. So I was, like, 'Well'... I remember s- telling him... I was, like, 'You should make sure that you have a f… oh, um, wait a minute. No, no, no. So all that happened, and then it starts gettin' kinda late out. And I remember we talked for text for a while and part of this conversation. Then it moved to the phone. Um, and I remember tellin' him... 'cause he was, like, 'I think she'll just be back tomorrow. I think she's just gonna be gone for the night with a friend.' You know? And I...
Koback: Did he name the friend?
Nichol: No. He didn't. And I... well, and 'cause I... I don't think... he made it sound like he didn't know what friend's house she would be at. And I remember talkin' to him and I was, like, 'Well, maybe it's that Nicky girl.' And he's, like, 'Well, Nicky called the cops. So why would she be at Nicky's house?' I'm like, 'I don't know. Kinda throws her off

the trail of where she's at, you know?' And it's, like... it sounds kinda weird but it's, like, I... he really made this sound like this woman was just upset, left the house, and that was probably what he thought happened to her. And so I... I didn't really put too much, like...

Koback: Did he tell you the kids were missing, as well, with her?

Nichol: Yes. I knew...

Koback: Okay.

Nichol: I mean, which made sense to me, 'cause I was, like, 'Well, if you were at work all day.' I mean, he didn't tell me he got home early. He didn't say that to me. So, I mean, it made sense. Like, if she's gonna leave, they should probably go with her. Um, and... and so, uh, I don't know. I wish... I feel like I wish I should've processed all of this earlier, but I just don't feel like, when one of my friends is gone, I'm, like, 'Oh my god. They got murdered. We should address this. Like, I haven't heard from them for four hours.'

Koback: It's not a typical thought when somebody...

Nichol: No.

Koback: ... just checks out for a day.

Nichol: No. So it got late at night and I remember telling him... I was, like... he's, like, 'I think she'll be back tomorrow.' And he was gonna go into work. And I told him not to. I was, like, 'You need to stay home, and you need to help the cops.' I'm like, 'And you need to wait for her to come back.' And he's tellin' me, like, 'Well, what if, like, she comes back and she sees my truck?' And I was, like, 'You know what I would do?' I was, like, 'I would ask one of your good friends who's off of work tomorrow, to come over to this house and hang out with you while you're here.' I was, like, 'And go park your truck down the street.' I was, like, 'So she's upset at you and she wants to come back.' I was, like, 'But she doesn't want to be here if you're here, maybe?' I was, like, 'If she comes back,' I was, like, 'and she doesn't see your truck, maybe she'd be more willing to come in the house.' I'm like, 'You know?' I'm like, 'But don't be alone with her.' I was, like, 'Because if she's upset enough to leave,' I was, like, 'you don't know what kinda confrontation you're gonna have when you get back in the house.' And I was, like, 'So that's why you should have a friend there, so that you're not alone with her.' And I was, like, 'And if, for some reason, you are alone with her,' I told him, I was, like, I really thought she just left. I did. I was, like, 'Get your phone, put it on video, and put it in your pocket.' And I was, like, 'And just zip it up.' And he's, like, 'Why?' And I told him. I was, like, 'Cause you can voice record.' I was, like, 'So if she comes home,' I was, like, 'and you two are still, like, you know, if there's some choice words being said because you guys obviously got into, like, something that's, you know...'

((Crosstalk))

Koback: Did he ever articulate what their argument was?

((Crosstalk))

Nichol: He did, and I will get there, but you know, I told him, like, 'Just be prepared.' You know, 'cause at this point it wasn't, like, I was tryin' to make her to be a bad person. It was just, like, I didn't know what was going on. I assumed that she had left, so I was, like, 'Well, when you get back,' because I knew that they were going through a divorce. It was, like, 'Just cover your bases. You know, try not to be alone. And if you are, just record what you guys are talking about. So at the end of the day nothing bad happens to you, you know?' And that was kinda how I processed that whole situation. And so, um, he was, like, 'All right.' And then, uh, she didn't come home that night. That was Monday night, right? Yes.

Koback: We're talkin' about Monday.

Nichol: Monday? Monday night. Yes. Um, and he told me, um, what he... this is what he told me they talked about, and I realize that this was total bullshit. And I think he's telling you guys a different story. And I think the reason that he's telling me what he's telling... I think the story he's telling you is probably slightly more accurate than the one he told me on this case, and the reason is because I think he was tryin' to save his ass with the fact that she's pregnant. So he told me, um, that they... that she had asked him to wake her up before he left for work on Monday morning. And so I don't know if she did that in a text or how it was supposedly communicated. Um, but he said that he went to get her up... which I also found weird. 'Cause she's still sleepin' when he leaves. 'Cause he... she gets up with the kids, and they get up shortly after that but it's just him in the mornings, you know? And so she w… he supposedly... he said that she woke up and those two kinda just got in a disagreement, and I don't know what all was said, but he was, like, 'She was bein' pretty mean.' And then he said, uh, 'She told me that she's pregnant, and she told me that the kid is not mine.' That is what he told me.

Koback: So he... 'She's pregnant, the kid's not mine...'

Nichol: And that she s...

Koback: Like, he's playin' he didn't know she was pregnant?
Nichol: Yep.
Koback: Until that morning?
Nichol: Yep.
Koback: And that it's not i… she had an affair with somebody else.
Nichol: Yes. And this is before I knew she was fifteen weeks pregnant.
Koback: Okay.
Nichol: Like, all the stuff on Monday that I read i… from my recollection... 'cause I didn't find out she was pregnant 'til Tuesday. So anything that got posted on Monday did not emphasize the fact that she had a baby on board. Um, so then, um...
Koback: Let me ask you somethin'. You said that he usually s… gets up in the morning and just it's him and she gets up and takes care of the kids. Is that the routine that you know for them? Um, or do you know him to get up and prepare meals prior to him leaving the home?
Nichol: Oh, he gets up and he goes to the gym and he, I mean, works on his basement.
Koback: Uh, what... okay.
Nichol: And makes breakfast. And I don't know his whole routine.
Koback: Does he make breakfast for himself or does he make breakfast for his children?
Nichol: D… I don't know. I think... I don't know. They're still sleeping at that point. Like, all I know is he, at one point in some time in this whole thing, he told me that they usually get up at six-thirty and she gets... she gets them ready and takes them to school and does all the morning stuff with them, as far as I know. And then in the afternoons, when he gets home from work, he kinda does more of the afternoon stuff.
Koback: Okay.
Nichol: So it's kinda, like, a tag-team operation that they have going on, but I think she does more in the AM and he does more in the PM.
Koback: Right.
Nichol: Is kind of how I process that, but I don't know.
Koback: Okay.
Nichol: Um...
Koback: So then, she's mean to him and then throws this out?
Nichol: Yes.
Koback: That she's pregnant from another man?

Nichol: And I said, 'Do you believe her?' And he was just, like... he said somethin' about, like, 'Oh, yeah. Like, she's... she kinda looked like she was showing when we were in North Carolina, but I wasn't sure.' And I'm like, 'So you think she's pregnant?' And he's, like, 'Yeah.' And I was, like, 'Do you think she's having an affair?' And he's, like, 'I think she said that out of spite.' And he's, like... and I was, like, 'Okay.' And then... and, again, like, I think he's just saying all this to me to try to cover his tracks with me. I think w… I don't know what he told you guys, but I bet it's probably very different, and I think that what he said to me... it... it was directed towards me. Like, this whole bullshit little box lie that he had right there was the lie directed at me... at me.
Koback: Did he say when the arguments started?
Nichol: Nope.
Koback: Um...
Nichol: He just said it was in the morning.
Koback: Did he say i… did...
Nichol: He said he woke her up in the morning.
Koback: Okay. Did he say when she came home? Did he ever let you know that?
Nichol: Uh, I think he w… I want to say he said around two, but I don't know.
Koback: Okay.
Nichol: Um...
Koback: And then he woke her for what purpose?
Nichol: 'Cause she asked him to.
Koback: Okay.
Nichol: So I was under the impression that he was asleep. I'm assuming this is how it went and what he was tryin' to tell me. Is that he was asleep by the time she got home, and she sent him a text and said, 'Wake me up before you leave.' And then he woke her up and they got in an argument, and then he went to work.
Koback: Okay.
Nichol: That is how I processed it.
Koback: And the context of that argument, again, was just that she's pregnant and is there anything else that he shared with you?
Nichol: He did not elaborate on it, and I didn't ask. I didn't ask.
Koback: W… what were you thinkin' at that time?
Nichol: Uh, this was on Monday. I don't... I mean, I... again, at that

point, I was, like... I still thought she left. I mean, this was all on Monday. I legitimately thought this woman left the premises with her kids and just wanted nothin' to do with him for, like, twenty-four hours.
Koback: So his story was believable? That she was pregnant from another man and maybe she took off for that guy or...
Nichol: I... he... he... I mean, he said several times, like, 'I think she just said that out of spite.'
Koback: Okay.
Nichol: Like, he thought she was with one of her friends.
Koback: So he sto… held true to that story? Uh, she's...
Nichol: Pretty much.
Koback: She's just leavin', and she's with a friend?
Nichol: That was kinda what he thought. And that's kinda what he had me believing. And, at the time, I wasn't really alarmed, because it'd been, like, a half a day.
Koback: Sure.
Nichol: Um, and so then Tuesday rolled around, and...
Koback: Did you see him at all on Monday? You said you didn't. I...
Nichol: No.
Koback: Right. Or...
Nichol: I did not see him.
Koback: Okay.
Nichol: And I went to work Monday and Tuesday.
Koback: Did he ever try to convince you to come see him? Or say he wanted to come to your house?
Nichol: No, not at all. We were supposed to go look... pick out apartments to go look at on Wednesday... so yesterday. Um, but, uh, that obviously...
Koback: Right.
Nichol: ... didn't work.
Koback: So, on Monday you never... he never tried to be convincing to get you to come up to see him?
Nichol: No, no, no, no, no, no.
Koback: Nothin'?
Nichol: Not... not that I'm aware of. I don't think so, because he... I had – my buddy, Jim, was over Monday and Tuesday, and he knew Jim was over Monday and Tuesday. And that's why we were gonna hang out on Wednesday.

Koback: Okay.

Nichol: Um, so no. He didn't ask me. Um, so Tuesday rolled around, and she still wasn't around. And this is when I started gettin' kinda sick. My friend, Jim, was sick on Monday when he came up and I don't know. I just started feelin' like crap as it was. And then, um, I was just kinda havin' a hard time focusing and thinking about what was going on. 'Cause... and I'd asked him a few times. I'm like, 'Where's your family, Chris? Like, where's your family?' You know? And he would tell me, 'I don't know.' Or, 'I want them home.' Like, I... it... it... I asked several times. So I think I got different responses, but each time he didn't know where they were. You know? And I'm like, 'She's still not home?' And he's, like, 'No.' And oh, and I had also asked him to, like, um... he said he had a friend, Dave, named that was a cop, which I also find convenient that there's another Dave working this case, who's a cop. Um, but he would... I was, like, 'Well, Dave's off. Why don't you just have him post up outside your house, too, and see if she shows up?' You know? And he told me on Tuesday morning... he was, like, 'I called Dave and asked him to sit outside my house, and he's gonna do it.' And he's, like, 'And then my friend, Nick, is coming over later on this afternoon.' And I was, like, 'Okay.'

Koback: Did you ever hear Nick's name before?

Nichol: I've actually heard that name a few times. Like...

Koback: Okay.

Nichol: ... around him. Like, there's certain... I never heard *Dave* before. Dave was new. But I've heard the name Nick a lot, so I don't know if that's real or what, but if I was to guess friends that he legitimately has, I would assume that he was one of them. Um, but yeah. Because I know he's told me before, like, when we first started hanging out, that Nick lived kind of in the area and he's, like, um... he's, like, 'He actually goes'... he's a trail runner. And he's, like, 'He runs at East Lake Number Three.'

((Crosstalk))

Koback: ... in your area?

Nichol: Kind of.

Koback: Okay.

Nichol: And I remember him saying that to me once. He's, like, 'You know that park that we hung out at?' I was, like, 'Yeah.' He's, like, 'My

buddy runs over there. We should not go to that park anymore.' And I was, like, 'Okay. Um, that's cool.' And, uh, anyways, where were we at?
Koback: Tuesday morning.
Nichol: Tuesday morning.
Koback: We're almost done.
Nichol: I know. I'm just... I'm just... I'm tryin' to just keep it all together here for you guys. Um, Tuesday morning. Oh, so he said Dave was gonna stay outside of his house and Nick was gonna come over that afternoon. I was, like, 'All right.' And then, um, I don't... I think most of the texting throughout that day was kinda, like, 'Have you heard anything? Like, what's going on?' It was kinda like, me checking up on him. Um, and I don't remember everything, but it wasn't a... a... I didn't even make it through the entire workday. Like, I was feeling really, really sick. Um, like, in general. And then I decided on my lunch break to get on the internet and look at what was going on with all the reports. And I saw a report that was, like, this woman who's fifteen weeks pregnant and her two daughters are missing. And I was like, 'Whoa. What?' And I was just so floored and I read a couple other articles, just to make sure that... you know how the newspapers are. And just double check. Like, am I really reading this right? And then I'm like, 'Okay.' And sh… he had told me previously, like, 'She says she's pregnant with another man's kid.' But he'd said, like, he could kinda tell in... in North Carolina. But that girl is obviously pregnant. I mean, in her photos. I mean, fifteen weeks. That's, like, four months. That's pretty far along. And so it's... that's like, how would you not know if she's showing? Like, you totally know she's showing. And so oh my god, I got so sick. I was just like, 'I need to go.' I just packed my stuff and I left work, and I went home and, uh... I remember I told Jim that I was gonna get home early. And he wanted to come over right away, and I was just, like... I just needed some time to process what was going on. But I did tell him... I was, like, 'You can come over earlier than you did yesterday.' 'Cause he didn't want to wait in traffic. That was the thing. He's like, 'Save me some time.' So I don't remember what time he got there. Um, I probably still have that text, 'cause I don't have any reason to delete those. Um, but he... so he came over a little early, but I did have a gap of time in there. I don't know how long it was. I bet it was after I got... from the time I got home to the time Jim got there, I bet it was probably, like... I don't know. Hour-and-a-half, maybe. Somewhere around there. Um, and, uh, I remember talking to Chris during this

time, and it was all text. I did not talk to him on the phone at all on Tuesday. And I was pretty upset, where I was just, like... you know, I was going back and forth. Like, 'Where's your family?' This and this and this. But I'm like, 'She's pregnant.' You know? And this and this... and he's like, 'The baby's not mine. The baby's not mine.' And I'm just like, 'You told me yesterday that you think that when she said she cheated on you, she did it out of spite.' And he was like, 'Yeah.' And I'm like, 'So then it's your kid.' And he kept denying it. And then he started kinda worrying about us. He'd just be like, 'Well, does this ruin everything with us?' This and this and this. And I'm like, 'No.' I'm like... and I'm, like, just trying to, like... his situation is so much more important right now than, like, our situation.

Koback: But his main concern is you and him.

Nichol: Kinda, sort of. I mean, and I keep askin' him. Like... I'm like... and I told him numerous times, which is also in the texts that you guys will pull I'm just like, 'You need to focus on finding your kids and your wife right now.' And I was like, 'And you need to focus on finding all three of your kids.' And I kept emphasizing to him he had three kids, you know? And I wasn't even mad about it. I was just like, 'You need to find your family. You need to f...

Koback: Did he ever go look for them that you know of?

Nichol: Uh, I don't know. I don't think so. That doesn't even ring a bell to me so I don't think so.

Koback: 'Kay.

Nichol: Um, but, uh... oh and I forgot something else that's really important. I will add it in there, too. But let me just finish this thought. So then, um, Tuesday – were we talkin' about – oh, yeah. So I kept tellin' him, I was like, 'Chris, I know it's yours. It's okay.' I was like, 'Go find your family,' you know? And I was, like... was I... was I hurt? Yes. But at the time, I realized his situation with what he had going on was way more important than our situation. And so that's why I was just, like... like, I had... I confronted about it and then I was like, 'You need to go find them.' And we talked about it for a little while and then I was just like... I don't remember exactly how it went but something along the lines where I was like, 'Why can't you just be honest with me?' I was like, 'Stop lying to me. Like, stop lying.'

Koback: Did... did you have an inclination... you've talked to this man a lot. And during this Tuesday, Wednesday conversation, did you feel like he was bullshittin' you? Uh...

Nichol: A little bit, kind of, yeah. I mean because he was... not Monday. Monday, I did not. But Tuesday, yeah. That's when it all started to click. I was like, 'Oh, my goodness,' because he was like, 'Well'... like, he just didn't seem as concerned as he should be and he was super worried about shit with us. And I'm just like...
Koback: So concerned about his family and overly concerned about your relationship?
Nichol: Yes.
Koback: 'Kay.
Nichol: And I kept tryin' to put it on the back burner. And shame on me for bringing it up in the first place. I was just really taken back. Like, 'Wait a minute. She's fifteen weeks. Like, how would you not notice that?' I was just... I was confused. And I was also like, 'Is he lyin' to me?' And I kinda wanted to know because I realized that there's a situation at hand here and I'm just like, 'What is going on?' You know? And for part of it, it wasn't even me trying to find out 'cause I'm upset. It was almost, like, me tryin' to find out 'cause I'm like, 'Is there something else I'm missing here?' I felt like there was pieces to this puzzle that I didn't know existed that were not in place and it was strange. And so, um, anyways I told him, I was like, 'Be honest with me.' I was like, 'Don't lie.' And I don't remember exactly how it went but I was tryin' to emphasize like, 'Stop bullshittin' me.' So he told me the truth. And he told me it was his and then he knew about it.
Koback: 'Kay.
Nichol: I was like, 'Okay.' And then he asked me again, 'Did that ruin everything?' And I was like, 'No, it didn't.' And in the back of my head, it's like, 'Yeah, I'm done. I'm not dealin' with that. Don't lie to me.' But his situation is so critical right now that it's like, I'm not gonna ruffle his mental feathers because they're already really ruffled because of the situation. So out of respect for his mental health, I just dropped it. And I just kept telling him, 'We're okay. We're okay. We're okay.' But then I, uh...
Koback: How many times do you think he asked you during these phone calls...?
Nichol: Oh, it wasn't a phone call. This was text.
Koback: Pardon me.
Nichol: Text Tues...
Koback: Text...

Nichol: Text Tuesday.
Koback: Text Tuesday. How many times did you think he brought up your relationship and if you guys were okay?
Nichol: Probably two or three times.
Koback: And how many times did he bring up concern for his children or his wife?
Nichol: I think he brought it up a lot, too. I mean, he kept tellin' me that he was worried about them.
Koback: Okay.
Nichol: I mean, it happened. It wasn't like he was just spaced out. I mean, he was definitely showing that, too. I was just surprised that he was also showing it for me. 'Cause at that moment, if I had some crazy stuff goin' on with somebody in my family, I would be putting all my relationship stuff on hold like, 'Look, like, baby, I gotta deal with this. Someone in my family's missing. When I find them, we will talk.' And that would just be it. But that's just me. I mean, that's how I would address the situation. And that's kinda how I've been gauging how I handled Monday, Tuesday and Wednesday as, like, 'What would I have done?'
Koback: Sure.
Nichol: You know? And... and kind of, like, that's why I didn't contact you guys on Monday, because I probably wouldn't have done that for one of my friends. And not that I'm cold hearted, it's just, like... it's just... uh... uh, that's just not how me and my friends work. So it didn't... you know, so anyways...
Koback: There was a... there was extenuating circumstances that you wouldn't have known that caused her friends to be concerned.
Nichol: Mm-hm.
Koback: Just so you know. I… there's nothing wrong with you for not goin', 'Oh something's wrong,' and not callin' the police. The people that provided the information to the police initially had way more information about her than you do. So that's why they came forward. So I can see a... I can feel a little reservation that you're like, 'Why didn't I do something? Why didn't… you didn't know enough. I think a normal person on Monday... a reasonable person is just goin', 'Shit, this woman's in a w… whacked out relationship with her husband, she's got two kids. Now she's pregnant. She just takes off.' So don't blame yourself for not making a phone call to the law enforcement or goin' to the

poli… you didn't know anything. So I'm just tryin' to help you get past that. Don't worry about it.

Nichol: Okay.

Koback: It's... it's not... the... the people that came to us had way more info than you did regarding what was happening with her life.

Nichol: Okay.

Koback: Okay? So...

Nichol: So... thank you.

Koback: Don't get... don't... don't blame your… beat yourself up over that. Please don't.

Nichol: Okay.

Koback: Okay?

Nichol: And then, uh, so, Tuesday, after that conversation, I told him... I was like… I told him to delete his texts 'cause I knew he was going crazy texting me. And I didn't want any of his friends to see him texting me because they didn't... I don't think they knew about me. It had nothin' to do with you guys. It was just, like... I mean, and you'll see 'em, you know? But it was...

Koback: The secrecy of your relationship.

Nichol: Pretty much. And I... I just feel like he was texting me so much openly and he had friends there that I was like... I didn't want them to see that. And so I was tryin' to get him to slow down. And then I told him, too, like, um, after he lied to me, I was just kinda like... I was done. And I was tryin' to find a way to get away from the situation without alarming him or panicking him. So I told him, 'Everything is all good. I'm still here for you.' And I feel bad 'cause I lied to him but I mean, I just tried to keep him calm and then I told him, 'Contact me once they find your family. And then we'll talk.'

Koback: That was Tuesday?

Nichol: That was Tuesday.

Koback: Okay.

Nichol: And he sent me a text back saying something along the lines of… what did he say? Something like, 'Please just think of... of'... oh and, I kept tellin' him I was scared. I was really frickin' scared. In fact, that's another thing I'm missing. I'm so tired. Monday night I called him back in the middle of the night. 'Cause I could not sleep. I could not sleep at all. And I remember when I called him, he sounded like he was sleeping. And I was like, 'How the hell can you sleep right now?' I think that's exactly what I said to him. And he was just like, 'I'm just kinda dozin' off and on on the couch.' And I just remember thinkin', like, 'I haven't shut my eyes yet and this is not even my family.' And so that happened on Monday night. Um, so then I was going somewhere with that that had to do with Tuesday, and I forgot what it was. I'm so sorry.

Koback: Take... take a breath and relax.

Nichol: Um...

Koback: We're... we're almost to Wednesday and then we're out of here.

Nichol: Yeah. So then, um, yeah, so then once he... he lied to me, I just really tryin' to push him away and he was like, 'Just don't forget, like, the person that you knew me to be when you were with me,' or something like that. And it was almost...

Koback: That's... was that strange?

Nichol: It just kinda sounded almost like a farewell. And I didn't think it was too weird because I was like, 'I think he realizes that I'm up… really upset that he lied to me and I think he's aware of the fact that I'm probably about to walk away from him.' So I think that was his way of saying goodbye. So it didn't really seem strange in the context of what was going on between the him and I part of stuff. And then, um, and I kept asking him, too, like, 'What did you do, Chris? What did you do?' And he was like, 'I didn't do anything.' And I'm like, 'Where's your family?' And I asked him that. I don't know if I started doing that on Tuesday or if I started doing that on Monday. But I definitely... I think it was Tuesday. 'Cause I don't really think I was that alarmed on Monday. And then, um... uh, so that was supposed to be our final sign-off text. And then Jim got there at my house and I was hanging out with Jim. But I was still in my head, just kinda stressed out. And I remember I walked to the room, went in my bedroom and texted Chris one more time and I told him, I was like, 'If you did something bad,' I was like, 'you're gonna ruin your life.' And I was like, 'And if you did something bad,' I was like, 'you're gonna ruin my life.' I was like, 'And I promise you that.' And he responded back to me and he's like, 'I didn't hurt my family, Nikki.' And that was, like, the last text. That was the last time we ever talked. And I never said another word to him after that.

Koback: That was Tuesday?

Nichol: That was Tuesday. And then he left me alone. He gave me the space that I asked him. He respected it. And he didn't mess with me at all.

Koback: Was that a phone call where you said it? F...

Nichol: No, that's all Tuesday... text Tuesday.

Koback: Text Tuesday.

Nichol: Just call it text Tuesday.

Koback: All texts. Okay.

Nichol: Everything was texts. I did not talk to that man on the phone at all that day. I mean, I don't think so. I'm pretty sure it was all texts.

Koback: 'Kay.

Nichol: Um, and then, uh...

Koback: So, at that time in your mind, if you said that, what... what are you thinking? What... were you thinking that he maybe did something to his family?

Nichol: Yeah. I started gettin' really scared.

Koback: What... what caused that thought?

Nichol: The fact that he lied to me.

Koback: Okay.

Nichol: And that she still wasn't home, and it was day two. I figure if you're upset for a day, you leave for a day, but you come back. And she wasn't back. And it was midday. And not only that but, like, she doesn't have her phone, she doesn't have her... her car, she doesn't have the kid's EpiPen. She doesn't have any of that. So what I'm thinkin' in my head is like, 'For a night, if you're really upset, somebody comes, pick... one of your friends picks you up, like, okay.' But I can't explain that for two days. Like, that just doesn't logically process in my mind as something that any woman I know would do. The one-night thing, I know women that would do that. But the two-night thing, no. And so I'm like, 'She's still not back and he just lied to me. And it made me... like, I just started getting scared. And I remember telling him that throughout the whole day. Like, I... I don't even know how many times I texted him that. I wouldn't be surprised if it's eight, ten times. I'm just like, 'I'm scared. I'm scared. I'm scared.' And one of the last texts that I sent to him, too, I told him... I said, 'I'm scared because I feel like I don't know who you are anymore.' And I s...

Koback: And his response to that?

Nichol: I don't even remember to be honest with you. I think that was, like, in that sign-off text that I sent to him.

Koback: Okay.
Nichol: Um, but I mean, I was. I was kinda scared. I was... what I was really scared for was scared for his family's wellbeing because I don't know where these people are at this point and it's scary. I mean, it's scary that she's gone but it's even more scary to me that these little girls are gone. Like, that was the part that really freaked me out. Like, if it was just her, I'd be like, 'Well, maybe she took off with somebody. Maybe she didn't. I mean, I don't know because she's a grown woman and she can make those choices.' But if...
Koback: Well were some of the scared... was there fear in you that people were gonna find out about your relationship, too?
Nichol: No, I didn't even care about that at that point.
Koback: At that point, there was n...
Nichol: I was just, like...
Koback: Okay.
Nichol: ... scared of the situation. It was just getting escalated and it was freaking me out. And he was just, like, not... he was strange. So, another thing, so, that was Tuesday. And that was it for Tuesday, but I forgot some stuff on Monday that I did need to bring up to you guys. So Monday, um, when we were on the phone, at one point he mentioned to me... I can't even believe I have to say this. She left her wedding ring here and I said something along the lines of, 'Does that mean you two are done?' And he was like... uh, oh my God. He said, 'How much do you think it's worth?' And I r… remember hearing him say that and being like, 'What the fuck?' And I remember thinkin' to myself, I don't even know how to respond to this. And so, I was like, 'I don't know. Pawn it, man.' And I was just, like... I was like, 'I pawn jewellery all the time.' I was like, 'I pawned jewellery a few times.' I was like, 'It's not worth shit though.' And I was like, 'So I don't know if you really wanna do that.' And he's like, 'No. No. I think I'm gonna get it appraised. It's a nice rock.' And I was just like, 'Okay.' And it was really awkward. And then he, like...
Koback: And that was on Monday?
Nichol: That was on Monday night. And that, to me, was, like... it was kinda strange. And then the Tuesday lying thing... like, I'm telling you, it started Monday night, him saying that, that was why I couldn't sleep. 'Cause he made the comment about the wedding ring.
Koback: Okay.

Nichol: And then Tuesday, her still not comin' home and then him lyin' to me. And I was just like, 'Oh my God. Oh my God. Like, what if something happened?' And it was really hard for me to put...
Koback: When... when you say, 'What... what if something happened?' What were you thinking?
Nichol: Like, what if somebody took her? Like, could he possibly hurt her? And that was the first time that I really, I think, genuinely considered, 'Did this man hurt his wife?' And it was hard for me to grasp. And, uh, I thought about it a lot and I... I waited for the night 'cause I wanted to see if she would come home. And it was already pretty late. And I had company and I was just, like, 'Let me just see how this plays out.' And, um, my buddy, Jim, left, I don't know, probably nine or ten. Probably just the same time he always leaves. And then, um, I couldn't sleep then. It was really bad. And I woke up in the morning and I saw the interview that he had with the newspapers. And he just looked really different to me.
Koback: How so?
Nichol: The white in his eyes is gone. They're a different colour now. It's like he has no soul. I swear to God. I saw it and I was just like, 'Look at his eyes.' I saw his mugshot. They're not even the same colour. Like, when you guys retrieve the pictures that are on my phone, look at his eyes then compared to now. Like, it's the scariest shit I think I've ever seen in my life. It freaked me out. I was like, 'That's not even the same man that I know.' And it was really uncomfortable. Um, but anyways, I saw that report in the morning and I was just to the point where I was just like, 'All right. Like, something happened.' This woman is missing. Whether it was him or someone else, I know a woman went missing not too long ago in Longmont. Like, I think it was two months ago or something like that. And you guys... not you guys. But somebody up there called off the search on her. I don't think they ever found her. So I was like, 'I don't know, maybe that's connected, maybe somebody came and got her. Maybe he did something. I don't know.' But I knew it was a problem. And at this point, I was like, 'I'm in a very messy situation with this man. And I don't know what to do.' And so I called my dad 'cause he's, like, the only person that I trust with everything in the whole world and I was just like, 'I have a problem.' And I told him everything and my – I was like... we just discussed it and it was like, 'We need to go to cops.' Definitely. Because I figured you guys would find me eventually, but I was like, 'I feel like they need

to speak to me. I feel like I'm a very important person for you guys to communicate with.'

Koback: You are.

Nichol: And so, you know... and again, I wish I'd have done it sooner but it just, like it just kinda took the sequence of events of his lies and all of his bullshit falling apart for me to process that I needed to address the situation. And so, you know, and the time. And so that, to me... and another thing he lied to me on, I caught him on Monday night, he was like... oh it was right after the wedding ring thing. He was talkin' about... it might've been before. One of the two. But he was... he was talkin' about how, um... he reflected on North Carolina and he was talkin' about how he wanted the separation and all this stuff. And I'm like, 'Wait a minute. Wait a minute. Wait a minute. I thought you were the one tryin' to make peace with her and she's the one who didn't want it.' He's like, 'No, I wanted it.' And I was just like, 'Okay.' And another thing on Monday night, his breathing was, like... uh, it was like his voice would crack sometimes. But I didn't condemn him for anything like that because I was like, 'Well yeah, he's probably stressed the hell out. His family's gone,' you know what I'm saying?

Koback: Sure.

Nichol: So I don't know. So that happened. And then, um...

Koback: He never made any admissions to you about anything that he had done?

Nichol: Nope.

Koback: Um, he never said anything about doing... or at any time, not... not just in these days but during your relationship, did he ever say anything about hurting his wife, his children?

Nichol: Never. Never.

Koback: Did... in... in... on these conversations from Monday to Tuesday, um, did he ever say that, um, you know, somebody did something to them? Or did he ever give s… uh... um, an excuse to you how this could've happened?

Nichol: No. I mean, he... he was...

Koback: Other than they just were goin' to a friend's house.

Nichol: Yeah, or he was like, 'Yeah, I think she's with one of her friends. She doesn't wanna talk to me,' kinda thing.

Koback: So...

Nichol: But other than that, no. I mean he told me, like, 'Yeah, she said she was with another man. But I think it was out of spite.' Like, he never really held that she was with another dude. Like, sh… he never was like, 'Yeah, she's with some guy.' Like, she said it but I don't think she meant it.

Koback: Mm-hm.

Nichol: Is kinda what he was directing towards me. But no, he... I think that's why I gave him the benefit of the doubt so long. Like, he has always been such a civil, gentle man to me. And he's always been pretty calm and level-headed when he talks about the d… like, the differences between him and his wife. And, I mean, that's a sensitive subject. And he never, ever seemed like he was aggressive about it. I mean, he was always just chill. And he never talked ill of his children. He was always so bubbly about them. Like, those were his babies. So, when all this happened, I was just like, 'What the fuck?' And...

Koback: S- so that brings me to a question real quick. I mean, you got... you – I don't think anybody over the last six or eight weeks knows this dude better than… than you. I really don't. You guys probably spent more time together than anybody.

Nichol: Mm-hm.

Koback: Um, conversation, whatever. Relationship. Um, what do you think... the... what's the catalyst for this event? Do you have any... have you had... and I... I know it's a hard question but I wanna get it out now we're here. If... if there's a thought that you have, um, that might lead us to understand a little bit why he might've done something like this, um... like I said, I don't... I met Chris on... on Wednesday. Um, so I don't know Chris. Not like you do.

Nichol: Um, you know, I've thought about this. And sometimes I think to myself if I wasn't in that man's life, would his family still be alive? And I've thought about this a lot. And I think I can give myself different responses. But in all honesty, I think they might be alive but not permanently. I do not think that this man just snapped. I don't think that he just met some fuckin' amazing woman and he was just gonna try to fuckin' murder his family and then think that I was okay with building a relationship with somebody who did something like that. Like, at what fucking point, you know? And not only that I always try to say, you know, like, 'When we get to a point where we've been together long enough, I would love to meet your children.' Like, I never discluded them from anything. Like, I remember comin' back from Colorado Springs and I was like, 'Oh my God, they got the Cheyenne

Zoo down here. You gotta take your kids. And the... you can feed the giraffes and they would love it.' Like, I always tried to, like, in… like, show him cool things like, 'Hey, man, would your kids like this? 'Cause my nephew would like this. Like, check this out.' You know? I sent him a screenshot of some rainbow u… unicorn Lucky Charms the other day. I was like, 'Do your daughters know about these? 'Cause I bet these are epic.' Little things like that where it's genuinely... like, I care. I do. Despite how messy this is and how I'm sure I'm gonna be portrayed in the media and everything, like, I care about his wellbeing with his children and all of that. And so for me when I think of, what was he… going through his head? I find it really hard to believe that I am the catalyst for all of this. I will be willing to say that I think me being in his life accelerated what was inevitably about to happen. But I don't think people just snap. Love does not murder. Hate and resentment murder. That's the way I look at that. I do not know what is the truth anymore and what's not and I don't have all of the details. But this is just my opinion but I'm pretty convinced that that woman and him did not get along very well and the reason they stuck together was, 'Hey we're gonna do kids.' And I think they also stuck together because they were in a very bad financial bind. And I think that she continuously disregarded it. And I think he messed up because he was too passive to say anything to her about it and really address it. And it just got to the point where it's just like, you file bankruptcy and then what do you do? Just wait 'til you file the next one? I don't know. I don't know what their finances look like now but from the way he made it sound, it's probably a pretty stark situation. And I don't know if hundreds of thousands of dollars in debt over and over and over again are enough to lead a man to wanna take somebody out, but I don't know. I've heard of people committing suicide over that shit before. And I would never justify what he did. I think it's fuckin' disgusting. It's... ugh. Like, he's such a fuckin' pig. But I just... I try to be like, 'Why?' I try to come up with the why. And I really think that he was struggling with her really bad and not only that, he's got a third child on the way and I know he was probably just like, 'I can't fucking afford a third kid.' Wants it but can't afford it, you know? And he always told me he wanted a little boy. You know? He wanted a third child.

Koback: Mm-hm.

Nichol: And so I think that it was just something, like, I think they were in a financial situation and I think she was very non-responsive to him trying to... to solve problems and get out of the situations that they were in. And I think people just get complacent is what it is. And then, you know, I think, uh, he met me and I think I was like a breath of fresh air for him where it was, like, he could get away and just be like, 'You know what? I can be myself. I don't have to worry about money right now.' Like, you know, and this girl, like... I have my shit together. Like, my life is so very in order.

Koback: You seem very, uh, organized and independent and dialled in for a 30 y...

Nichol: Always. Like, I do really good at... I do really good at work, I have almost a perfect credit score. I've been savin' money for a house. Like, I don't mess around. I mean, I did. I screwed up. This is my one screw up ever and it's about to be on, like, n… national news. But, um, just very dialled in. And I think it was a breath of fresh air for him to be around something like that because I don't think that he knew that that was a real thing. And he had told me that, like, numerous times. Like, 'I didn't know women like you, like, existed.' I was just like, 'All right.' Like, I don't... and I... when he meant it, it was just like... like, just the way you run your life. And so... 'cause he got married really young, you know? And so to answer your question, I think inevitably it was going to happen. I think it just got propelled faster. I mean, I don't think... I don't understand what he would've achieved with... if he wanted to be with me that bad, what he would've achieved with me by doing what he did. I think his situation at home was way, way deeper than anything him and I ever had, and it led to that. And I don't know what happened in that conversation that they had. But I kinda have a feeling that it wasn't even about her pregnancy or another man or me. I have a feeling it was about money.

Koback: So, drillin' down, you think money...

Nichol: I think it's...

Koback: ... for him is the... the biggest downfall? Uh, you guy… I mean, beyond the relat… really, I don't know that you know too much about the relationship or the particulars just other than monetary issues, financial issues. That sounds like what you guys talked about when you talked about their relationship.

Nichol: I mean, he told me other things. Like, they really didn't sleep together too much, stuff like that. But I feel like a lot of husbands and wives don't do that. But it was like, 'Well of course you don't. That's why you're coming to me.' You know? Um, but, um, no. I think... I

think I just... like, me being in his life just pushed that forward. I honestly think that there's probably a good possibility that this would've just happened further down the road where it would've just got...
Koback: So did you see that i… before yesterday or Tuesday? Or was that just kind of something that you have reflected on and you've thought about this now goin', 'Man, I... now that I see that in this guy'... or just because of the lifestyle he was living? And if you didn't get removed from it, h… this was gonna happen sooner rather than later like you said?
Nichol: Um, you know, if I was to reflect on anything over the past few weeks besides the stuff, the last few days where you're like, 'Hey is there, like, any red flags?' um, I would say, no. But one thing I did notice one time is we were sittin' on my couch and I was tellin' him, 'My house' – I have a really beautiful house. Like, it's set up really nice. But everything I have is from Craigslist or Goodwill. Like, I have pieced it together and it's all, uh, markdown stuff. And I have pieced it together in a way like, 'It's pretty, huh? It's a pretty house.' But you would never guess that everything I got is super discount. And, um, one day we were sittin' on my couch and we were just bullshittin' about some stuff. And I was tellin' him like, 'Oh yeah, you know, I got this marked down, American Furniture 'cause the corner was dented. And I got this one off a guy on Craigslist. And I put it all'... and I was tellin' him, I was like, 'I put it all together.' And I was like, 'To me,' I was like, 'material things don't make a home.' I was like, 'It's the energy and the love that you bring to the home.' I was like, 'It's not about what it looks like.' I was like, 'It's about what you bring to it mentally.' And he collapsed in my lap and gave me the biggest, most genuine hug I think that man has ever given me. And he just laid there. And he was just like, 'You are so different.' I didn't even say anything. I just put my fingers in his hair and just let him chill there. And I assumed that it had to do with the finances. But it didn't stress me out. It was just, like, this relief sigh where he just dropped into my arms. And I didn't really think too much of that event except for that I was like... this was, like, a... it was a really genuine hug. Like, collapsed into my lap just so relieved. And I didn't really think much of it until I started reading about their bankruptcy and all this other shit and I was like, 'Oh.' So I think it might've been bigger than he let on 'cause he never told me about his bankruptcy.
Koback: Sure.

Nichol: You know, he just told me about his current financials, and he didn't even get that in depth but I'm assuming they're trash. And so yeah, I think... I think her spending all that money and not listening to him and him not standing up for himself in a calm and, you know...
Duane: Just elevate?
Nichol: Yeah, manner just kinda...
Koback: La… last hard question regarding this.
Nichol: Go ahead.
Koback: And... and then I... I have just two cursory questions regarding some... something else and then I think maybe Tim has a few questions for you. But the... I think what you, um, say about the finances directs... direct… ra… dir… directly at his wife. Do you think that goes to the children as well? Because she took, uh... did she treat them like that, like they were gold and they got everything as well that you know of? Or do you think there's a separate issue for why he may have, um, done what he did to his children other than financial?
Nichol: That part, I don't have an answer for. I can't fuckin' explain that. I don't even think there is an answer. I don't... I don't even think there's any sort of, like, computing up here that could possibly give a rational explanation for why that would've happened.
Koback: 'Kay.
Nichol: I mean, the only thing that I've honestly thought of when I play the scenario over in my head is that maybe they woke up and saw him doin' in their mom. And he was like, 'Fuck.
Koback: 'Kay.
Nichol: Now, I gotta do this, too.' I don't know. I'm like... I'm like, 'Why?' Because they were his little lifeline, you know? He... he... that was everything to him, you know? And I get those two have problems.
Koback: But he had a great relationship his... but from what you're accounting is he...
Nichol: With his kids.
Koback: ... he loved his children.
Nichol: Yeah. Like, I'm... that part... it just... it's... oh my g… that's the worst part of this whole mess. The worst part of this whole mess. And...
Koback: We won't dwell on it. We don't have to do that.
Nichol: No.
Koback: Let me ask you, um...

Nichol: But... so no, I don't... I don't have an explanation. That's the only thing I can possibly, plausibly think of is maybe they saw it. But other than that, I don't know what the fuck.
Koback: Okay. Who's Charlotte?
Nichol: Are you asking me who Charlotte...
Koback: Mm-hm. Mm-hm.
Nichol: Like, one of my friends?
Koback: Mm-hm.
Nichol: Uh, she's a really good friend of mine. Why?
Koback: Did you have some conversations with her regarding another boyfriend?
Nichol: No.
Koback: That you might have met on eHarmony? Or did she meet somebody on eHarmony?
Nichol: No. She's gay, she doesn't...
Koback: Okay.
Nichol: She's engaged.
Koback: So there's some text messages that... between... that we got off your phone obviously.
Nichol: Mm-hm.
Koback: Um, and the only reason I'm asking this is because he found out maybe you had another boyfriend, you understand the... my l… uh, m… my line of questioning that looked like maybe you had another boyfriend. And I don't know if that's this Jim guy...
Nichol: No.
Koback: ... that maybe you guys were... no, I'm not sayin' that he's your boyfriend. That... that when we were interpreting the text messages, that it seemed like he might... you know, 'This man came to my house, he has a key to my house,' that you're saying right now.
Nichol: Oh.
Koback: When I look at that from my perspective, Jim may be another boyfriend for you.
Nichol: Oh no, no, no, no, no. Charlotte is my oldest friend. I love that girl.
Koback: So did you have a conversation with Charlotte about Jim?
Nichol: I mean, sometimes we talk about him. We're all friends.
Koback: W… did... or would... did you guys ever have a conversation about eHarmony? That's the... an online...

Nichol: I mean, possibly. I was on there for a while.
Koback: Okay.
Nichol: But I didn't actually ever go out on any dates f… with guys from eHarmony.
Koback: Okay.
Nichol: Not one.
Koback: Okay.
Nichol: I talked to a couple guys on there, but I was like, 'No.' I didn't go on any dates.
Koback: So another... s… the only reason n… would be another potential reason for him to be upset.
Nichol: No.
Koback: And...
Nichol: He knew about Jim. He's always known that Jim is one of my good friends.
Koback: Okay.
Nichol: And I lay it out at people at the beginning, like, 'I have friends that are male, I have friends that are female. These are my friends. That's what it is.'
Koback: Okay.
Nichol: Like, he never to me seemed jealous of Jim by any means. So no, I'm curious what texts you're talking about with Charlotte.
Koback: I have m… I have, like, a hun...
Nichol: I wanna look that... I talk to that girl so much.
Koback: I have one-hundred-and-fifty-three pages of text messages so I can't r… if I could pull it up, I would but I don't know where it is.
Nichol: I thought you guys just got my texts.
Koback: We got, uh... when we asked for everything, we... for seven days, they give us everything.
Nichol: Oh, so why did you need to just do that if you just had 'em?
Koback: 'Cause I don't know that it's... they're completely accurate. Again, what they send me is... I don't have any way to verify that they're accurate.
Nichol: Got ya.
Koback: And... and if you delete a text message, sometimes those are not retained by carriers. Um, they... they're still on your handset. There's a way to recover 'em from your phone.
Nichol: Got you.

Koback: But they may not be held... there are certain carriers that don't even keep text messages. And I won't tell you who those people are, but they don't keep 'em. We can't even get our hands on 'em because they don't have a database, they won't pay the money. They're stored on your stuff and your stuff only. So that's why we ask for it. And some of those things disappear in three days. Five days. Seven days. Unless we ask them to keep 'em. And sometimes we don't know in time. So that's why we do it, too. 'Kay? So just, uh, a q… it was a question because it also would provide potentially a motive for what Chris did if... if he found out that you had another boyfriend. And...

Nichol: Why would he kill his family 'cause I have a boyfriend?

Koback: Well, he wigs out that he finds out that you have a boyfriend and just loses it altogether. Do you understand? 'Cause he's already losin' his wife and now his new girlfriend has another boyfriend. And he just... he can't... there's multiple reasons why it just... it was a concern that...

Nichol: His cheese slid off his cracker. So sad. I don't know. He's not even the same. I look at those mugshots and it's... they're scary. They scare me.

Koback: Yeah...

Koback: Tim?

Koback: ... that's what you said about that video, too. It didn't... I had noticed it was – I would've been a wreck. Woof.

Nichol: I don't know, I mean, I volunteer with some guys for... when I did the arm… military stuff that had PTSD and they were tellin' me when they went through trauma that they, like, kinda locked up. So I didn't even think it was the fact that he was calm that freaked me out. It was his...

Martinez: Oh, when you were helpin' those guys out...

Nichol: ... eyes.

Martinez: ... when the... from the...

Nichol: Yeah.

Martinez: Oh yeah.

Nichol: It was his... like, that part didn't... 'cause I was like, 'I... I've seen'... there's these guys that have been at battle that I've worked with that are like, 'Yeah, I've experienced this. This is how I handle my trauma.' And they're very, like, just kinda like zombies. But... so I didn't

hold that against him. It was just his eyes. Um, the... just the... the light is g... gone from him eyes.
Martinez: So, let me just finish just with a couple quick questions here but besides the obvious, you know, and... and what he's done, uh, do you... was there... what's the worst thing about this guy? Did you ever have just some sense – you seem to be pretty together with who you date, the people you, you know, hang around with. You... you seem to know a lot about people. Was there some impression he gave you that was negative?
Nichol: The whole time, like, the whole time we were together?
Martinez: Yeah. Anything negative that sticks out?
Nichol: I didn't think anything negative. I mean, I have preferences. I thought he was, like... I don't wanna use the word clingy 'cause that's fucked up. He was really... he was a lot more into me than I was into him. And it didn't make...
Martinez: The entire time?
Nichol: Yeah. I mean, I really enjoyed his company though. I mean, enough so that I kept everything going despite the situation. And I mean, like, it didn't scare me or anything. It's just, like, I don't move that fast.
Martinez: Okay.
Nichol: So I think things were moving...
Martinez: What were his longterm plans with you? What did... what did he discuss with you?
Nichol: Like, I mean, we'd bullshit about it every once in a while and be like, 'Oh yeah'... I asked him, I was like, 'If you didn't have that big house,' 'cause he didn't wanna live in it and he had made it very clear he didn't pick that out, he didn't... none of that. I was like, 'Well, if you could have a house that you wanted, what would your house look like?' And he would tell me, 'I want a little ranch home. Like, it doesn't need all these floors. Just a few bedrooms. Enough space for my kids. Maybe some property so they can run around. You know, two-car garage, maybe three. Put the old sports car in there,' 'cause he liked cars. Stuff like that. You know, I'd tell him, I'm like, 'I'm simple, too. So if you end up doing that and we end up staying together, let's do it.' But it was never like, 'Sell your house. Let's go buy a house.' Like, it was very...
Martinez: He ever say anything about gettin' married?
Nichol: To me?

Martinez: Yeah.
Nichol: I mean, w… it was, like, a thing where it was, like, offhandedly, like, 'One day, maybe this will happen.' But again, it was like, these were... I did not take these as very deep, deep conversations. It wasn't like, 'This is when we're gonna get married. This is what's gonna go on.'
Martinez: Okay.
Nichol: You know? Um...
Martinez: And you knew him for how long?
Nichol: F… brief.
Martinez: In total. Just... not even... not dating him but I mean, when did you... when were you first aware of him? How long?
Nichol: I don't know. Probably the beginning of June or maybe May. So, two and a half, three months tops. I mean, this is all really fresh. Like, all of this is compounded into a very small timeframe.
Martinez: Very quick.
Nichol: Yes.
Martinez: Has he worked for the company for a while?
Nichol: Yeah. I don't know how long. I wanna say, like, five or six years off the top of my head but I don't know. But he's...
Martinez: Did he supervise people? Do you know anything about that?
Nichol: Uh, yeah, kind of. So he was an operator and the way that operators are set up at *Anadarko* was they have operator one, operator two, operator three. But then each operator is, like, broke down into the basic guy, the medium guy and the foreman. And then it starts all over again. So he is still on level one of the operators but he's the top dog on the level one of the operators.
Martinez: Okay. The whole time you known him is two or three months? Did he ever complain of anything, any medical issues whatsoever? Or did you ever pick up on anything? Does he... is he allergic to anything? Does he have any... you know, a s… a special diet? Anything that's... that's messin' with him physically?
Nichol: Not that I'm aware of. Not at all.
Martinez: Okay how about psychologically? Did you ever think, 'There's... there's something wrong with this guy'? I mean, was it...
Nichol: N… I wouldn't have dated him if I did. He... honestly... I mean, maybe because I thought he was one of the most laid back and

decent men I'd ever met and I just haven't met a lot of people like that. But I mean, no. Not up until all this stuff started happening. Then I was like, 'Whoa. You are not the person that I thought you were.' Um, but prior to that, n… no. Not at all.

Martinez: Okay.

Nichol: I really didn't. I enjoyed his company.

Martinez: You think he was datin' anyone else?

Nichol: No.

Martinez: No way?

Nichol: No.

Martinez: Okay.

Nichol: He was way too invested in that.

Martinez: Um, was the relationship pretty... was it sexual right off the bat?

Nichol: Pretty close. I mean, once we got it to be where we're hangin' out outside of work, yeah. I mean, it wasn't, like, immediate but shortly following that, yes. And then it just continued.

Martinez: Okay. Pretty consistently throughout the relationship?

Nichol: Mm-hm.

Martinez: So kinda hot and heavy. Um, you mentioned that maybe you guys were sendin' some photos back and forth. What did... what kinda photos is he sending you?

Nichol: Well see, he would send me workout photos, stuff like that. He sent me a couple of inappropriate pictures. I did not request those. I didn't even want 'em. I was just like, 'Why do men do this?'

Martinez: What... what were they?

Nichol: Oh, it was of his... his package. And I'm just like, 'Okay cool.' Um...

Martinez: Like, his face and everything? Or just...

Nichol: No, no, no.

Martinez: Okay.

Nichol: Um, no. That's it. But I think he only did that, like, one time. It was just like, 'I don't even really want this.' But usually he would just send me pictures, like workout pictures, like, progress picture stuff. And I would just kinda keep him updated. Like... 'cause he... he had some fitness goals in mind. So I was kinda tryin' to help him out with that.

Martinez: Okay.

Nichol: Uh...

Martinez: When was the last time you guys were intimate?
Nichol: Uh, Saturday. Saturday.
Martinez: Was that the Broncos game?
Nichol: Uh-huh.
Martinez: Where... where would that have taken place?
Nichol: At my house.
Martinez: When he went to go pick you up before headin' up to, uh...
Nichol: He didn't pick me up. We drive my vehicle. But, um, yeah. Prior to and immediately following afterwards. So it was like, he...
Martinez: So when he dropped you back off...
Nichol: ... he came to my house...
Martinez: ... you... you did...
Nichol: ... it happened and then we went out to dinner and he came back to my house, happened again and then he left.
Martinez: Okay. Any other stressors in his life besides finances and... th… that he mentioned? And his wife?
Nichol: I mean, just the fact that they just... that she doesn't let him openly communicate. I mean, but other than that, no. I mean, nothin' that I really know of. He was... I mean, we didn't dive super deep into that stuff. It was just, like, occasionally there'd be a conversation where it would come up and I mean, he... it wasn't even really information that he wanted to provide. It was just me being curious like, 'Why are you separating from her? This is good to know.' Or, like, 'What are your finances like in case I end up building a life with you?' But it was usually me doing the inquiries. But I used to try not to be super invasive about that stuff.
Martinez: Mm-hm. What are the... in your mind again, just real quick, what are the things that... that really pop out to you that he would complain about, about his wife?
Nichol: Just that she didn't listen to him. She never listened to him. She always just shut him up. Oh, and he told me once that she used to kinda, like, talk shit to him in front of his kids and his kids were startin' to repeat it.
Martinez: Did he give you an example?
Nichol: Yeah, uh, she said... what did she say? He said he tried to ask her for something and ask her a question. I don't know. Something he... he didn't dive super into this. This was pretty early on. And he... she said, uh... she told him to shut up and that he didn't know anything.

And his kids started, like, repeating it. And he said that it made him really sad and he realized that that was when he needed to separate from her.
Martinez: So... and... and he'd never though... he said she was a good mom?
Nichol: Yeah. I mean, he never complained about her bein' a bad mom or neglectful, anything like that.
Martinez: Abusive, anything like that?
Nichol: Nothing. Nothing. When it comes to violence or anger or any of that, nothing. I mean, and he even said, like, 'Yeah, like, so she... she kinda, like, gets bossy with me sometimes but as far as arguing back and forth,' he's like, 'that never happens.' He's like, 'We don't fight like that.' So I don't know. He seemed pretty even-keeled with stuff so...
Koback: And just, uh... did they talk about how they disciplined their kids at all?
Nichol: I never asked. I felt like that was not my place.
Koback: Di… and he never mentioned it?
Nichol: Nope.
Koback: That's all I was (unintelligible). Just making sure nobody else...
Nichol: What time is it? I bet it's so late.
Koback: It's eight o'clock.
Nichol: Damn.
Martinez: Yeah, it's...
Koback: It's time to go. You have my card. Y… things will probably come to your mind in the next day, week, month, year. Especially as you get some sleep and... and recover here. Please don't hesitate to call me. My email's on there. You can email me. The business phone number on there is not accurate. I used to work in our Pueblo office until...
Nichol: So what is it?
Koback: ... July. Just call my cell phone. I'm never in my office anyway. So...
Nichol: Okay.
Koback: Okay? My cell phone will always be the same. So just call my cell phone. Um, and... and I will respond to you as soon as I can. If... if you need, uh, you know, to send me an email, again, you can send an email to me. Okay? If I can help you in any way with some services to

deal with the obvious trauma that you face, let me know and I'll get you in touch with the people that can help you. Um, also, uh, if you have issues with anybody intimidating you in any fashion, I will tell you right now, I have zero tolerance for that. Zero. I will charge anybody if I can prove it and I will take them straight to jail. Period.
Nichol: Thanks.
Koback: You are not... you're not a suspect in anything, you're merely a witness. Unfortunately for you, you met a man who did some terrible things. And I will not... I... I won't stand for it. I... through my career period, zero tolerance. Uh, you will go straight to jail. You call me immediately and I will handle it.
Nichol: I appreciate that.
Koback: 'Kay? And finally, you probably eventually are gonna get media inquiries.
Nichol: When are you thinking this is gonna happen?
Koback: I don't think it's gonna happen soon. I really don't. I will tell you today that there was an inquiry from a media member requesting to know if there was any other people involved in Chris's life. Um, you know, is... I think they're...
Martinez: Fishing.
Koback: ... the story is... they're... they're searching. But... but there is no... there's only a multiple couple of time... reasons that somebody would think what would cause this. Are they...?
Nichol: Well, uh, they're seein' the financial stuff, they're postin' it.
Koback: Right. And...
Nichol: I'm seein' it.
Koback: So I think there's a buffer for you for a couple of reasons. I told you today I – I did not see the affidavit. I don't think your name was mentioned in it. I... there's no reason for it I don't think at this time for his arrest. When, uh, the affidavit becomes public, which I think they mentioned may be early next week, um, that'll keep the m… media busy for a while. Um...
Duane: Oh, so her name wasn't in it that you think?
Koback: I don't think your name was in it.
Nichol: Mark said he didn't publish that thing yet.
Koback: Right.
Nichol: So if he hasn't...
Koback: He... um, so I talked to Mark this morning and I know he

has not written a report. Now I do know that he did talk to, um, the people yesterday just regarding her because it was important for some of the things we were doing yesterday. Again, I don't think your name appears in that report. Um, so... but don't hold me to that. I... I didn't write the affidavit. But, uh, a… from... from what I know, it doesn't. So at some point, this... your name is gonna come out. I mean, there's just no way it's not. And... and I told you, I won't...
Nichol: So when do you think that is? Like, when we take this to trial?
Koback: Um...
Nichol: Like, at what point... because nobody knows about this.
Koback: Right. But Chris does.
Nichol: Yeah. I don't think he's in any rush to tell the media anything. I mean, maybe.
Koback: These are mi… mitigators that he... in his mind or... uh, y… and you got a phone call from the public defender's office. Whether you talked to them or not, that's your business.
Nichol: I did not.
Koback: You didn't?
Nichol: I did not.
Koback: Oh, I thought you did.
Nichol: I did not.
Koback: Hm.
Nichol: I didn't know what to do. Mark said to ask you what to do.
Koback: Okay so they... did they reach out to you?
Nichol: Yep.
Koback: Okay. You can... your decision. You don't have to talk to 'em or you can. Um, I... I won't say either way. Uh, you have to make that decision for yourself.
Nichol: I don't really know what to do. I feel like if I talk to them, they're either gonna try to find some holes in my story or try to get me to be Chris's only ally and I don't really feel like dealing with either one of those.
Koback: Then I think you've made up your mind.
Nichol: Yeah. I don't want to...
Koback: So then maybe confide in your father.
Duane: No, that's... we were talkin' about that.
Koback: Yeah.
Nichol: Sh… we already talked.

Koback: Um, I can't really give you legal advice. They have every reason to want to talk to you. Just like if they got to you before I did, I would wanna talk to you, too. You understand what I mean? And I won't hamper with their investigation is or anything. They... they want information, too. Certainly. They have a client that they're tryin' to protect and... and make sure that everything that we're looking at is... is the same thing that they would wanna look at.

Duane: But they can get it from you.

Koback: They will get it from us.

Duane: So...

Koback: It'll be, uh... in discovery, they'll get, um, everything that we've talked about here.

Duane: It's in discovery.

Koback: And that's... so when that happens, which is pretty short order, uh, the reports that we will generate, everybody involved in this case will be sent to the public defender's office. I think at that time, you might, uh, find that that, um, i… y… there could be some exposure for you. Um, so, uh, I am not gonna tell anybody who you are. If somebody called me today, I... I don't talk to the media. I don't have any business talkin' to the media. Mark has no business talkin' to the media. They don't need to know who you are. It... your part in this is not relative to anything they... you know, to the story. I… for me. It... it... it's nothing that they need to know. And, um, I don't ever give information to anybody.

Duane: Okay.

Nichol: They're gonna dwell on it though. They're gonna try to use that as his why. I don't think it's his why. I really don't.

Koback: That's why we a… I asked you that question.

Nichol: You know...

Koback: 'Cause you think his why is financial.

Nichol: Yeah.

Koback: Uh, and whether or not we ever know what his why is, I don't know.

Nichol: Did he tell you guys what his why was?

Koback: I can't tell... discuss it with you.

Duane: So, um, just a... a quick open question, the way the legal system runs, is it, um... if he totally confesses and pleads guilty, is there a reason for a trial? Or do they just pack enough discoveries together that this proves what he said and...

Koback: S... so the purpose of...

Duane: ... and he goes to a kinda court and it's done? Or...

Koback: The purpose for discovery is we have to sh... we're obligated by law to share everything that we know with, um, the public defender or a private attorney.

Duane: Absolutely. Right. Okay.

Koback: Um, it doesn't go the other way. Uh, they don't have to share anything with us. So we are obligated to give them everything we have. No matter what happens. Um, I can tell you right now, probably sometime early this week will be his, you know... he's gonna enter a plea. Either I'm guilty or not guilty. That will probably be sometime Monday, Tuesday, Wednesday of this coming week. W- I would imagine, uh, from what I heard today. Now it might be a little more delayed. And then that starts the legal process. So, uh...

Duane: But if he pleads guilty though...

Koback: If he pleads guilty, um, you know, could that happen today? Cer... certainly. I mean, he could go to his attorneys... you've seen it happen before. Um, if he pleads guilty, is that information still available? Absolutely. Because there's still, uh, got to be legal process...

Duane: Mm-hm.

Koback: ... regarding is he competent to stand, uh, for... can he make that plea? I... are, are the attorneys gonna allow him to do so?

Duane: All the stuff.

Koback: You... you know what I'm talkin' about.

Duane: Yep. Okay.

Koback: So tha- all that information still goes to them. Um, and then that would play into, you know, potentially what is the sentence? What... what could be the penalty? All those things have to be looked at by attorneys. So, um, there is no not them ever getting her name. Uh, it is gonna be there at some point. And, um, I don't know... I... I understand your fear. A... and that's why I told you that if anybody m... I don't care if somebody calls you and says, you know, anything minor, you call me and let me know please. I won't...

Nichol: I appreciate that.

Koback: I will not stand for that, okay?

Nichol: Well I'm (unintelligible)...

Duane: So it's the... it would be... the news people would be the only ones that... and of course they already know what to...
Nichol: God, work is gonna be such a mess, too. That's gonna be, like, a whole 'nother level. Like, everybody at my work I heard was so, like, just damaged and broken today. And then it's like, 'Let's just add Nikki into this whole mix.' It's not gonna be good for all of their m… like, mentally either. It's just gonna be a mess.
Duane: Maybe your employer could transfer you to another business.
Koback: I think that's a fair state… I will tell you right now that I... *Anadarko* has been very, very helpful with us and is very concerned about their employees in this event. Um, and I... I'm tired, too. Uh, but you may... uh, your employ… your employer definitely n… is… has an indication of your relationship with Chris I would think.
Nichol: They're not my employer.
Koback: Oh, that's right, you work for a different company.
Nichol: Yeah, but...
Duane: But...
Nichol: ... you're saying...
Koback: I think...
Nichol: ... *Anadarko* has an in… has knowledge of that.
Koback: Well f… maybe...
Nichol: Who are you talkin' about? *Tasman* or *Anadarko*?
Koback: Uh, I don't even know what *Tasman* is.
Nichol: *Tasman* is the people that cut my check and I'm contracted out to APC.
Koback: So, I think people n… um, sus... have suspicion that there was a relationship Chri… with Chris. Not saying you but they may know that... I think there was some suspicion that he was havin' a relationship with somebody else. Not your name specifically. But if you went to your bosses and said, 'I have an issue that I don't'... you know, like your dad's saying, I think that you might find that they'll just get you out of there.
Duane: See, that's what... and... and that's what we were talkin' about today 'cause they probably have a policy for, um, psychological health, they probably have a policy for, uh, inquisitive, you know, people buggin' other employees. Uh, that's a big company with a lot of HR and there's...
Koback: Do you have an employee assistance program? EAP?

Nichol: I don't... uh, oh yeah. That... so that... they were there all day today. But it's like, I got so many calls today from people I work with.
Koback: Those are questions that you can ask them anonymously and that information is retained.
Duane: See, that's what I was sayin' because if...
Nichol: So what am I supposed to do, tell my boss?
Duane: Well... well what... no, but they're... your boss isn't gonna want rumour mongers, they're not gonna want, uh, people f... stressin' you out, they're not gonna wait... they don't want erratic workflow, they don't want any of that. So they'll... they'll probably do a broadcast letter of, 'Anybody that was friends, acquaintances of it...
Nichol: They already did. They already dealt with all the (unintelligible) stuff today.
Duane: ... or anything else, please respect that employee's feelings.' And right there, 'Oh and by the way, if any of you have a problem (unintelligible), you can call Mickey Mouse at'... you know, and that... and that's probably...
Nichol: See, but...
Duane: ... they probably have a policy with that.
Nichol: Here's the problem though.
Duane: And I'm hopin' that they do.
Nichol: I don't work for them.
Duane: But they can still protect you under that.
Nichol: But if they transfer me, like, they're gonna be like, 'You're not even our employee.' Like, I'm pretty sure I'm about to lose my job over this.
Duane: No, I...
Koback: No, you're not gonna... why would you lose your job?
Nichol: I don't know, 'cause I feel like people are just gonna complain about being uncomfortable with working with me. Like, I... I am not gonna have any respect from anybody there. I think I'll have two people that still...
Koback: You really didn't do anything wrong.
Nichol: I had an affair with a married man who lied to me and made me believe that he really wasn't, like, as married as I think he was. But the media is not gonna be so kind to let everybody know that. I think people are gonna think I'm the reason that he went off the deep end.
Duane: Well when...

Koback: That's prob… probably a fair statement. I would probably agree with you to some effect but if these people, you know 'em at work then you...
Duane: And the company will...
Koback: Protect you at some point.
Duane: The company will buffer that as much as they can because if not, it'd be... it'd be chaos amongst employees, and they can't have that.
Nichol: I'm just so sad. Like, this is, like...
Duane: It's just not good in their... their best interests.
Nichol: ... the job of all jobs I've ever had in my life and I fucked it up.
Duane: It's really...
Nichol: Aw...
Duane: Well she been out in the field... what, you been home, uh, three months of the year on an average...
Nichol: Not even.
Duane: ... in s… staggered amount out in the middle of nowhere on oil rigs. This little thing was out hangin' on oil rigs and now they got her in environmental where she's able to clean up stuff.
Koback: Right.
Duane: And it's a hot job, man. It's just a hot job. And...
Koback: I... y...
Nichol: I mean, would you advise me...
Koback: I wouldn't start...
Nichol: ... talking to, like, my head higher-up?
Koback: I can't give you legal advice. Maybe the best thing to do on that is talk to your EAP, whoever the... the employee's assistance people are. They're anonymous, they know all your HR rules, they know all your policy and procedure stuff and, 'How do I... h… h… how can I mitigate this?'
Duane: Fair (unintelligible).
Koback: And also… the... your problem, too, is not just… i… is this gonna become, uh, an environment where you can't work? Um, you know, so you have to call those people and say, 'I don't want this to happen so how do we take care of it? I wanna continue to work for you guys. I love my job.' Whatever. Um, you know, just be proactive. I don't know, um, your bosses on site.
Nichol: Yeah, she's pretty cool. I don't know. She's...
Koback: I think that's a personal decision you have to make.

Duane: Yeah. But I... I don't think...
Nichol: Yeah. I mean, I didn't even think about talkin' to them at all but I keep thinkin' about 'em like, 'Man, when my name gets out in the news, this is about to be crazy.'
Duane: No, like, uh, w...
Nichol: I had people call me all day. Like, my office mate would not shut up. She just called me today and she was just like, 'Oh my God, did you read this article and this article? And what did you think? And, oh my God. And this and this,' and I'm just like, 'I don't... I don't wanna talk about this. Please leave me alone.' And it was really overwhelming. And my project manager called me and he's really chill so we made it a very quick conversation. But some people just didn't get it. And it's so hard to me 'cause I feel like I'm...
Koback: I would get in front of it.
Nichol: ... lying to them.
Koback: I'd get in front of it. N… don't...
Duane: Yeah, because the company...
Koback: Make a decision.
Duane: It... I don't think it would be in their best interest legally, morally or profit-wise to have a bunch of junk goin' on. They would suppress it to keep it at least where everybody's treated with respect throughout the company. This is a tough situation. It d… l… you know, they'll put the... the presidential speech in it but...
Nichol: I mean, I could do that job, like, 75% of that at home.
Duane: Yeah, I would...
Nichol: I've already been thinkin' about that. I was thinkin' about just askin' (Unintelligible) like, 'Hey, man, just let me come in at five in the morning and deal with the gas monitors two days a week. No one will even know I'm there.
Duane: And I believe that...
Nichol: And let me just work at home.'
Duane: ... they probably made a statement on that... what do you call it? OHP or...
Nichol: EAP.
Koback: EAP.
Duane: EAP.
Nichol: They put out a notice today.

Duane: If they put that out and it says your confidentiality will be respected...
Koback: It has to be.
Duane: If that got leaked through an HR department and that got out after you told 'em something, that would not be good for...
Koback: Em… employment law is very strict on that kinda stuff and...
Duane: Yeah, so I... I think you should just atta… not attack it but be proactive in it and snuff it because...
Nichol: And what, just go tell my boss, like... not what I told you guys but a summed-up version of it like, 'Hey...
Koback: But they... they...
Nichol: ... my name is about to get released in the media and there's a lot of stuff tied to me that's tied to'...
Koback: I don't know if I'd do that in that fashion. I might j… you just need to figure out a tactful way to do that. And perhaps an employment... there's attorneys that deal with employment law. Um, and maybe you wanna reach out to one of them. That might help you. I don't know. Um...
Nichol: Ah, damn.
Koback: You know, uh, it... it's... it's a decision that you might need to make or you might wanna talk... I think I would talk to EAP first 'cause it's not gonna cost you any money. Um, but...
Nichol: See if they'll do something... I hope so 'cause they're not actually my employer so that...
Koback: Well, they're an outside, uh, agency that just knows what's going on.
Duane: But both c...
Nichol: So yeah, I don't know so sh...
Duane: Both companies, it would be in their best interest to protect everybody including all the foremen he worked with, apprentices he worked with. I mean, all of those people have a lot of information, too.
Nichol: Not like me.
Duane: But again, they don't wanna hear it, they don't wanna have... you know, they don't wanna talk about it. They have the same rights. So it would be a company-wide thing. So I would just...
Koback: On the media stuff...
Duane: We'll work on that.
Koback: Yeah, I think you've got a grip on that. Um, on the media

stuff for you, I wouldn't talk to the media. Just tell 'em you don't have any comment and for you, probably the same. And if they just persist, um, you... you know, maybe per… put somebody... it... it seems like your dad is your... your biggest confidante here and maybe make a brief statement. If... you know, 'My daughter doesn't wanna say anything. Have a nice day.' Whatever. You know, 'cause if you appease 'em a little bit, sometimes they'll go away. Um, that would just be my suggestion. Um, don't talk to them. The... you don't need to.

Nichol: I'm not going to. I guess they're gonna make their own assumptions. You, uh...

Koback: But, um, so...

Duane: So does your neighbour, so does the p...

Koback: Right.

Duane: ... guy that's stopped at the red light.

Koback: There'll be talk… as soon as they figure out who you are, they're gonna talk to your neighbour and they're gonna say, 'Oh yeah, I saw Chris, you know, and her together, you know?' Whatever. You know it's gonna happen. Just prepare yourself and then it won't be... there... there... there's an...

Nichol: Are they gonna swarm my house?

Koback: I don't think so.

Nichol: No? They were swarmin' his. He told me that, he's like, 'There's media everywhere.' And it's just like, 'I hope that does not happen to me.'

Koback: Well... yeah.

Nichol: I mean, I have a little... I have a safe house in Denver that I can go to that I have the keys to...

Koback: There you go.

Nichol: ... that has nobody there ever.

Duane: That's what we're... that's what we're thinkin' for the next couple weeks.

Nichol: And that's... all I have to do is check the mail and there's no questions asked and nobody knows where it is and I'm not telling anybody. But it's a really nice spot for me to hide out...

Koback: Go there.

Nichol: ... and I don't have any friends in that building. I mean, it's an apartment but it's... it's safe.

Duane: And we will answer your phone calls, but the safe house is from...
Koback: Go... go there.
Nichol: The safe house is the safe house.
Duane: ... people bangin' on her apartment door.
Nichol: When should I go there? When do you think all this is gonna start happening? I mean, it's kinda...
Koback: I mean, might be just good for you to go there anyways for your sanity. And stay away from this place that you had a connection to this man with and get your thoughts in order and...
Nichol: That's so sad. That was my nest. It was such a warm little place.
Duane: That was your...
Nichol: And now it's like, I haven't even slept in my bed. I've just been sleeping on the couch with the dog. I don't even wanna do it.
Koback: What other questions can we answer before we go? I... I kn… I don't foresee talkin' to you again regarding this. Now an attorney might review something and go, 'Hey can you ask her another question?' Um, and that would be a long ways down the line. I don't think there's anything else. I let you talk for a long time today to get it all out. Um, so we don't have to do this again 'cause I don't wanna traumatize you again. Um, but if there is important things that come up, please know that I do wanna talk to you about those. Other things that we haven't talked about today or if something just... I mean, 'I gotta tell him,' just call me.
Nichol: I mean, like, some things I thought were really important, like, the other day I didn't mention the wedding ring thing and then I was like, that was really creepy. I should probably tell them about that.
Duane: And yeah, the...
Nichol: And you got those cards.
Koback: Yeah, um...
Nichol: I gave you those cards.
Koback: So you gave me cards and there was clothing in there.
Nichol: Yeah, I just... I don't care what you do with it all. I just don't want it.
Koback: The clothing... wa… was any of the clothing anything he wore this weekend? Or is it stuff that was from...
Nichol: No, no, no. It was stuff that he brought over prior to that.

Koback: Okay.
Nichol: None of that... some of it's been washed and folded since then. Yeah, I just wanted it out of my house and didn't wanna throw it away.
Koback: We'll... we'll take care of it.
Nichol: So you guys can deal with it.
Koback: We have it. We'll take care of that. Um, if I have questions on the context of a text message, I might just call you and say, 'The hell does this mean?' 'Cause I might not understand what you were talkin' about.
Nichol: Okay.
Koback: If that's okay with you. Um...
Nichol: Yeah, that's fine.
Koback: If... if it's... I'm not gonna bother you unless it's really important. I... 'cause I think I have everything I need from you today.
Duane: Okay yeah, we just wanted to make sure you guys had it so that...
Koback: Well and we don't... I d… I don't...
Duane: You could find the right person or something and get it done.
Koback: We don't wanna do it again. Yeah. And we know we have the right person. And I'm sorry that you're involved. I am. It's never a good time to say anything like that but it's... it's a bad deal, this whole thing is. And this is one of the tougher cases that I think... I've been doin' this a long time. It's… you know, it's tough. So for you to... it's even tougher and don't forget to reach out to somebody for your sanity. Like I told... I asked you, downstairs, a question, and you said, 'No.' You remember what question I asked you, right?
Nichol: No. You know how many questions you've asked me tonight?
Duane: Did you want a pizza?
Koback: Well he'll a...
Nichol: Pizza. I love pizza.
Koback: Well, I want food, too. I asked you if you had any, um conce… I asked if sh… I should be concerned at all about you hurt... hurting yourself.
Nichol: Oh. No. I don't feel the need to do that.
Koback: Right.
Nichol: I just want people to leave me alone.
Koback: And if you...

Nichol: I just feel like I wanna hide for a little while, while all of this is happening.
Koback: Just please reach out to your family or even me and if there's any – if you have any things that's struggling, I w… like I told you, there's people I could put you in touch that will talk to ya. I'm not a psychologist, I'm not... that's not what I am. But people sometimes that get caught in these situations, they end up having lots of emotional issues and you need to address 'em. Don't just hide that stuff, okay?
Nichol: All right. Um, are you guys gonna help me if we go...
Koback: You're super... you're super, super intelligent so...
Nichol: I appreciate that. That's a nice compliment. When we go to trial for this, if that's what he so feels the need to take this to, um, are you guys gonna help coach me through these questions?
Koback: Of course. So we would be there, um, to re-discuss our conversation today, the conversation you had with Mark and then an attorney would, um, talk to you prior to any questioning on the stand regarding what kinda questions they're going to ask you. And r… really the only thing you have to remem… I mean, if you're worried about your recollection or your recall or, you know, how you might remember this, everybody worries about that. Even we do. We spend hours on the stand and it's very difficult. But the only thing you have to remember is tell the truth. And the truth will never change in your mind. You know what happened during these six weeks. You know what happened on Monday and Tuesday. And as long as you tell the truth then d… you there's nothing to be worried about. If you don't remember something, you don't remember it. Um, might they pick on ya a little bit about that? Absolutely. They usually pick on us a lot more than they do you guys. So, um... but that's so far down the road. I mean...
Nichol: I mean, how long are we talkin'? Like, how long is this whole process gonna take?
Koback: That could be... well... so he has the right to a speedy trial once he makes a plea, which is forty-five days. Do I think that's gonna happen? Absolutely not. I can tell you that the majority of the homicides that I work on average somewhere between one and three years.
Duane: Yeah, look at the clown man.
Nichol: So I gotta just deal with the media like...
Duane: With the theatre.

Nichol: ... knockin' on my door like that for three years? 'Cause that's, enough to go cr...
Koback: Your... this case will be hot until the next unfortunately crazy case comes up. And... and you know it's true.
Nichol: That's just...
Koback: I don't know if you watch the news. There's a reason I really don't.
Duane: Every week.
Nichol: I don't watch American news.
Koback: But you know there's something new every week that's the hot topic. This one might be hot for a week, two, three, whatever. And then something else is gonna happen. And... and they're gonna forget all about this one until it comes back to court. And then it's gonna be revived. If it... if it ever does. I don't know if that...
Duane: So...
Koback: You know, he has all sorts of... he could plea. He could say, 'I wanna go to trial. I didn't do this.' Whatever. He could say whatever. Um, so it could be tomorrow, it could be five years. It's... it just depends. I mean, there's a lot of things that can slow cases down. Um...
Duane: Yeah, look at that theatre thing. I mean, that was a whirlwind for, what, a month or so?
Koback: Sure.
Duane: And then all of a sudden it... as soon as people started figurin' out what that guy was all about, all the sudden they started just, like, 'Man, he's weird. He was psycho. Look at him.' And... and he just kinda just...
Koback: And then it petered off and then...
Duane: But then he also shows up every...
Koback: Y… a huge... that's a huge, huge event.
Duane: Yeah.
Koback: Um, you know, certainly un… unprecedented.
Duane: But it shows up every six months or year here.
Koback: Sure.
Duane: Um...
Koback: You know, I mean, you look at... I... I just... there's no way to... to know that.
Duane: Okay.
Koback: But if... like your dad's saying, you know on that, that guy

was sent to the state hospital for evaluation and that takes a long, long time and that can draw out cases if there's evaluations. There's all sorts of things that come into play that really, don't worry about. Um, I… put this thing out of your mind as much as you can and when the time comes, if it ever does, that you had to testify, you will be in good hands. We'll take care of you, the att… the attorneys handling this case are gonna (unintelligible). 'Kay?

Duane: Okay.

Nichol: So, um, I don't...

Koback: And if you have questions that you (unintelligible), just call me.

Duane: Yeah, I don't... I don't think we're gonna talk to the other side, from what we were discussing.

Nichol: I don't...

Duane: They can get the discoveries from you guys and it's...

Nichol: I don't wanna deal with him anymore.

Duane: ... it's... it's the last thing...

Nichol: Mark already said... he's like, 'He might try to call you.' I think I'm gonna just ignore that.

Koback: Who?

Nichol: Chris. I don't know if he will try to call me. I hear… did they find those little girls yet? I know they've been lookin' for 'em.

Koback: We don't... we don't know.

Nichol: And they thought... or they knew where they were at. You don't know yet?

Koback: I don't.

Nichol: 'Cause you've been in here with me?

Koback: Right.

Nichol: Ah, my God.

Duane: I find the whole thing very weird if they close... as much as you told me that he doesn't... he was as normal as he was but yet some c… very close friend would call within a couple of hours of her not answerin' the door or what was it, a... just...

Nichol: Well I think she was on meds or something. Like, so I think he... she wasn't concerned about Chris.

Duane: But to call the... but to call the police within just, like, the same day and yet he acted normal on this end, that is just... that is weird.

Nichol: Yeah.
Duane: Somebody... there's... the... two different lives there or something.
Nichol: Oh, there's definitely two different lives there. That's why sometimes I have to... I feel... when he's like, 'Well, what did she…?' People are like, 'What did he say about her?' And it's just like, 'I don't even know if I wanna say it 'cause who knows if that's what's really happening.'
Koback: Mm-hm.
Nichol: I mean, maybe. Maybe not.
Duane: Uh, Molly called me back, so we'll call her from… ((unintelligible)).
Nichol: Okay. I think I might need to approach *Anadarko*. I really don't wanna go to work tomorrow. I don't think I'm going to. I think I'm gonna just take the week off and then we can sort things out on the weekend and then I can reach out to my supervisor and EAP or whatever.
Duane: Yeah, you need a little sleep and some time.
Koback: Yeah, you definitely need some sleep. Don't drive tonight.

SIX

Third Police Interview - Nichol Kessinger

(TAKEN FROM THE DISCOVERY AUDIO FILES)

21st August 2018

***Koback* -** Agent Kevin Koback
***Nichol* -** Nichol Kessinger

Koback: Today is August 21, 2018. This is Agent Kevin Koback from the Colorado Bureau of Investigation placing a phone call to Nichol Kessinger, also known as Nikki. The current time is 6:45pm.
Nichol: Hello?
Koback: Hi, Nicky, it's Kevin.
Nichol: Hi, Kevin.
Koback: How are you?
Nichol: I'm okay.
Koback: All right. Um, can you… I… I'm running a recorder so you know, um...
Nichol: Okay.
Koback: ... I… I just want you to introduce yourself again for the tape recorder, just say your legal name for me, and then we'll get started.
Nichol: Okay. Okay. It's Nichol Lee Kessinger.
Koback: And your birthday, Nichol?
Nichol: July 3rd, 1988.

Koback: And you go by Nicky, correct?
Nichol: Yes, sir.
Koback: Okay. All righty. So you text me this morning, we had a brief conversation regarding some new information that you remembered, uh, from just reflecting on what's been going on with this case.
Nichol: So... he'd been going down by the time I met him, um, but he was still doing Thrive on top of it.
Koback: Okay.
Nichol: So the thing that caught my… yeah, so the thing that caught my attention about this recently when I was thinking about it is the fact that, um, I think maybe the reason he was doing the two a day, and this is just speculation, is because it had plateaued so maybe he was doubling up because he thought it had plateaued. So the reason that this comes to my attention is because of this weight loss. So, um, he lost thirteen pounds in about five weeks. In fact, I can give you the dates. He lost thirteen pounds from July 4th to August 11th is how much weight he lost, because August 4… I mean, July 4th was the day that I went to his house and sat down with him and asked him, 'How much do you weigh?' And he asked me, 'Can you just look at my macros and see how much protein people my size would usually eat and all?' And just asked me to glance at it. So that's why I went over was to...
Koback: So that's...
Nichol: … kind of, like, help him.
Koback: … when you say his house, that's his house in Frederick that he, uh...
Nichol: Yes.
Koback: … Shanann?
Nichol: Yes. That's the...
Koback: Okay.
Nichol: … one that I told you guys I went to...
Koback: Right.
Nichol: … on the 4th, and that was why I went there was to… to sit down with him that morning of the 4th and just discuss his goals, you know, and again, I'm not a fitness trainer so he already had a de… he… an idea in mind, he was just asking me, like, can you just glance at this and tell me what you think since you pay atten…
Koback: Right.
Nichol: ... close attention to these things? So anyways, um...

Koback: So, wh…
Nichol: … uh...
Koback: … I'm gonna ask ya - I think I already asked ya and we discussed this one, but July 4th was the first time you went to his house? And then I think...
Nichol: Yes.
Koback: … you said, like, the following Monday or Sunday was the… the fin… the second and final time you'd been to his home?
Nichol: Um, I… well, I have to… it was a Saturday and I'll have to look it up. It was either the Sat… it was… hold on, let me pull out a calendar. I really just wanna, like, uh, that's July. So the 4th and then that weekend and the… I think – I think, and I will double-check this, but I'm pretty sure… I know for a fact I was at his house on July 4th...
Koback: Mm-hm.
Nichol: … and I think the second time I went to his house was Saturday the 14th.
Koback: Okay. And… and do you… those are… if I remember right, you only had been there two times, right?
Nichol: Yeah. I didn't wanna go back. After that second time that I was there it's just, like, 'I don't wanna be at this house. Like if you wanna hangout, come to my house.' So… so yeah. So the 14th was the last time I was there.
Koback: Okay.
Nichol: Uh...
Koback: Great.
Nichol: … but back to this… so the… the Thrive thing, so I… I was… I was kind of concerned that he was losing so much weight, um, but I also wasn't because he was kind of fine tuning his diet, but it was enough for me to look at it, um, because I was like, well, I mean, it's… it wasn't, like, a… a… a severe weight loss, but it was… it was kind of fast. So, like, okay, 'Well, are you getting enough calories? What's going on?' And I couldn't figure it out 'cause I was looking at what he was eating and it was healthy proteins and vegetables and… and he was eating a decent amount of food and I'm just, like, 'How is this man losing so much weight?' And then I started thinking about it the other day and I'm, like, 'Oh, my God. It's because he was doubling up on all the Thrive stuff and he was starting to eat really healthy.' So that, I think, is where the weight loss comes from.

Koback: So did you see change in him, personally, during that time from July 4th… or, pardon me, July… July 4th to August 11th when he lost that kind of weight?
Nichol: What did you say? What was the question you asked because I...
Koback: Did… did you s… did you see a lot of change in him, like, um, not physical change, but was his personality different or was it just the weight loss?
Nichol: No, it was just the weight loss, like...
Koback: Okay.
***Nichol:* …** I didn't think he was any different, but this is the one thing that I wanted to point out to you guys was that… that he was always this way, I just wanna state that right now this was not something that started at any certain point, but from the first time that we started hanging out, he always had a ridiculous amount of energy. And it wasn't that he was super high strung and bouncing off the walls, it was that he could stay up. He didn't need to sleep. And he was always that way when we would hang out, he… oh, my God, I would try to get him to go to bed at ten every night. I'm, like, 'If you're gonna stay here, you need to go to bed at ten because I have to get up and go to work in the morning and so do you.' And he… he would keep me up every night and we… usually I would say, I mean, it kind of fluctuated, but typically I would say that we went to bed somewhere when he stayed the night at my house on those nights, somewhere between eleven and midnight every night. And it used to bug me because it was, like, I was so tired. I'm so… I wanna go to bed.
Koback: What time did you wake? What time...
Nichol: I'm sorry?
***Koback:* …** what time did you usually wake up?
Nichol: Um, it kind of depended on the day and what I had going on at work, but I would say in between four-thirty and five is a pretty accurate assumption of when I'm supposed to get up for work.
Koback: Okay. All right.
Nichol: So, I mean, and then so what I would do is I would go to work all day and then when I would get off work, I would sleep. I would go home and nap and I would… and my naps varied in time. Sometimes it was a half an hour, sometimes it was, like, an hour and a half. It was whatever my body needed and then I would get up and I would go to

the gym. And then after I got back from the gym, he would come over to my house and it would be the same thing where it was, like, he would keep me up. And I will tell you without those naps, there's no way I would've been able to keep up with him. No way.
Koback: Okay.
Nichol: And… and an… and another thing about that too, and he was always like that, always, and - and it used to… he… I could tell his body wanted to sleep, but his mind couldn't sleep. And the reason that I say that is because he… I… he… sometimes I would see him, like, he would keep me up so I'd be, like, 'All right, well, let's watch a movie, you know, uh, if you wanna hangout.' And so we'd be up and I'd see him doze off, and then wake right back up and doze off and wake right back up.
Koback: Okay.
Nichol: And there was a few times… there was a few times that we were having a conversation and he would be talking to me, Kevin, he would fall asleep mid-sentence and wake up...
Koback: Okay.
Nichol: … like, snap… yeah, and he would snap out of it five or ten seconds later and keep talking right where he left off.
Koback: That's weird.
Nichol: Yeah. It always blew my mind. I was like, 'This guy must really like me if he's avoiding sleep to be with me.' And it was, like, I just… I couldn't do it. I napped probably almost every, single day...
Koback: Right.
Nichol: … after I hung out with him.
Koback: Right. Okay. I get… so I get...
Nichol: So it was just… honestly, it was all...
Koback: … so...
Nichol: … it was like he was on speed.
Koback: … so you think the Thrive thing contributed to that or at least his own drive for losing weight and getting in shape and maybe his, um, attraction to you, um, drove him? Because you're pretty physically fit and he was kind of motivated by that? I think I remember you saying that earlier, um, but you were trying to help him get in better shape.
Nichol: Well, and, I mean, he was already in good, physical shape and he was already taking care of his health and his diet and the gym. I just

think he was, like, 'Hey, since you're already in the, uh, live a healthy lifestyle, uh, would you be willing to just give me some input?'
Koback: Okay.
Nichol: Maybe I can fine-tune it.
Koback: But do...
Nichol: You know, I never (unintelligible)...
Koback: ... you think that was some of the motivation for him to...
Nichol: Uh...
Koback: ... stay awake long hours and, um, you know, maybe use multiple patches of Thrive to try to impress you, for lack of better terms?
Nichol: No, I think it was the Thrive and I think his body wanted to sleep. I think it really wanted to sleep. I think he legitimately was trying to lose weight and I think that's what was keeping him up...
Koback: Okay. Cool.
Nichol: ... because at the end of the day, I wanted to sleep, but he just was really restless and didn't seem like he wanted to, but he always seemed really respectful of my wishes, so you would think that he would be onboard with that, but it was almost like he couldn't calm his brain, you know, and...
Koback: Mm-hm.
Nichol: ... like I said, he wasn't acting high energy, he just wouldn't sleep and I almost think that's what it was. It was almost restless where it's, like, 'Hey, I can't turn off at the end of the night. Stay up with me.' And he never said that, but that was kind of the impression that I got.
Koback: Okay.
Nichol: And so...
Koback: All right.
Nichol: ... and again, the double Thrive patches, I mean, maybe, but I don't really think he was trying to impress me. I mean, he told me, like, 'I plateaued on this stuff.' So I think maybe he was, like, 'Whoa, what if I double dip?'
Koback: Mm-hm.
Nichol: So...
Koback: Right, so he's trying to get over... I get it. Okay.
Nichol: Yeah. So I don't... I don't think that was a... a Nicky motivated thing for him. I think that was... he ... 'cause he was already

working on the Thrive thing and, like I said, and his fitness. He was doing all that prior to me being in his life.
Koback: Okay.
Nichol: So, and… and so… and I don't know if he was double patching before I met him. He double patched the whole time I knew him, so I don't know if that occurred once I came into his life, or if he had already started doing that once he plateaued.
Koback: Right.
Nichol: I never asked.
Koback: Okay. All right.
Nichol: I just found that really interesting, so...
Koback: Yeah.
***Nichol:* …** I just wanted to bring that up.
Koback: Yeah, and I appreciate it and your… that's the kind of things that...
Nichol: Yeah.
***Koback:* …** I want, uh, when we talked prior, uh, just to… re- get you to recall things that didn't seem out of place then that… but when you reflect back, may have seemed out of place now with what you know. So, what's the next...
Nichol: I agr… I mean, it was scary to me. It was scary that he lost that much weight on that stuff, but I guess a lot of people do and I keep thinking about it.
Koback: Yeah, I mean...
Nichol: I'm, like, it almost seems like it's a drug.
***Koback:* …** if you look at any diet though, I mean, I… I'm not a fitness guy, if you read about Atkins or any of these other diets, people lose excessive amounts of weight in short periods of time, so, um...
Nichol: Yeah.
***Koback:* …** yeah, but, whatever. I… I think it's interesting that, uh, this Thrive played a part in it, um, and quite frankly, I… I am gonna get one of these patches, uh, to try to figure out what it is. Um, so we'll… we'll… we'll figure that out, um, at some point. So...
Nichol: Okay.
***Koback:* …** what's next on your list?
Nichol: Um, let's see, let's see, let's see. Um, oh, okay. So this is Saturday. This is when I made...
Koback: So Saturday...

***Nichol:* ...** a reference to...
***Koback:* ...** would've been...
Nichol: This is Saturday the 11th of August.
Koback: Okay.
Nichol: Was that the 11th?
Koback: Okay.
Nichol: This is the night that we attempted to go to the Lazy Dog on 120th and Federal and we walked in and I looked at their menu a bit, like, trying to seat us, and I looked at their menu and I was, like, 'I'm not eating here.'
Koback: Right.
Nichol: Um, and because… yeah, so we went to the other Lazy Dog, which is actually owned by somebody else, so they have a different menu, so we went to the Lazy Dog off of… I think it's 144th that I told you guys, and we sat down and we ate. And we were attempting to watch the...
Koback: It's on Highway 7, right?
Nichol: What's that?
Koback: Is it on Highway 7?
Nichol: I don't think so. It's on I-25 and, like, 144th.
Koback: Okay.
Nichol: I mean, I can look it up and I can...
Koback: No, that's okay...
***Nichol:* ...** screenshot it and send it to you.
Koback: I think, uh, there's...
Nichol: Um...
***Koback:* ...** two of 'em and I think there was some confusion. One of our guys went, and I just wanna make sure he went to the right one, um, I don't… I don't… I don't know the Lazy Dog, but I'll ask him tomorrow. 144th is right by...
Nichol: The...
***Koback:* ...** Highway 7.
Nichol: Okay. Well, I… I don't know that. I don't know.
Koback: Yeah.
Nichol: I'd just… I had never been to that one, so, um, I think it's 144th. It might be 135th. I will it up tonight and...
Koback: Okay.
***Nichol:* ...** then will just screenshot you the address and I will send it

so that you guys if you guys need to pull those videos you can find it.
Koback: Okay.
Nichol: Um, but one thing that I noticed about this is that, um, so normally when we went out, um, I try to keep things pretty cheap, just to be respectful. I never went to expensive places or anything and sometimes I would pay for things, sometimes he would, but when he paid, he would always use these *Anadarko* gift cards, um, these little, grey gift cards, and they were always, like, $25 or $50 and they always came in denominational increments that made sense. And he told me that he got these from *Anadarko* as rewards for doing really good stuff at work. And is that true? I don't know. I don't know if, I mean, I know that him and his wife have a lot of financial issues so I don't know if maybe he's the one who actually wanted to spend all the money and maybe he was cashing his paycheck in the, uh, gift cards so that his wife couldn't track it. I don't know. I don't know...
Koback: Okay.
Nichol: … but I think it's something you guys will need to confirm with *Anadarko*.
Koback: So were they actually in the name of *Anadarko*? Do… do you remember… or did he just tell you that they were gift cards?
Nichol: They… they would say… no, no, no, no, I've seen 'em.
Koback: Okay.
Nichol: They say *Anadarko* on 'em. They're, like, little sil… dark silver credit cards, but they're gift cards.
Koback: So, you're… you're...
Nichol: Um...
Koback: … just suspicious that potentially he was hiding money from his wife with these gift cards?
Nichol: Honestly, no, I think *Anadarko* legitimately gave him these, but oil industry is pretty good about - when our operators do things that are safe, um, or they do a really good job at something, um, they… they, uh, they usually provide gift cards or some sort of incentive for… it's just a safe… (unintelligible)...
Koback: So they bonus these guys out if they're doing a good job or being extra, like, they have no safety violations and stuff?
Nichol: Yeah, yeah, yeah, stuff like that, so it's, like, they're safety rewards, so...
Koback: Okay.

***Nichol:* …** um, yeah, so… so do I think they were legitimate? Honestly, yes. I… I… I do. That's something you need to confirm with *Anadarko* though, because I wasn't one of their employees, so I don't know.

Koback: Okay.

Nichol: Um, but I did think to myself, like, if they do have money issues, maybe he was possibly concealing it, but the thing… it's not even the gift cards, I think, that are the main focus on this right now. For me, the main focus, uh, I wanted to bring your guys' attention is he always paid with those. Always. And then...

Koback: Every time you guys...

***Nichol:* …** on the night...

***Koback:* …** so you… you… we talked about this, um, prior and let's just revisit it, um, you guys never really went out on a date per se, with the exception of this Saturday night on the 11th? Usually you guys...

Nichol: No, we went...

***Koback:* …** spent time at your home, um, versus going out? Un… unless I'm mistaken on what you're saying.

Nichol: You are. I...

Koback: Okay.

***Nichol:* …** so we on most nights would hang out at my house, but we went out a few times and I have dates for everything and...

Koback: Okay.

***Nichol:* …** I can give you that, once...

Koback: Yeah.

***Nichol:* …** I'm done with this. Um, so, um, the reason that this caught my attention was not because of the gift cards, it was the lack of the gift card. So when we went out to dinner, he went to pay the check and I noticed that instead of using one of the *Anadarko* gift cards, he had a baby blue credit card in his hand that he used to pay.

Koback: Okay.

Nichol: And I just remember thinking to myself, why isn't he using any of those gift cards? I'm pretty sure he still has a balance on one of those, but I couldn't remember. And then I was just, like, I was maybe… 'cause, you know, at this point… at this point he had made it clear to me that they were filing for divorce, like, it was done. So I was, like, well, maybe he just doesn't really care anymore, you know. And… but then another part of me was like, but technically, they're still

together so why would he do that? And I just… I didn't ask because at… he had made it sound like by that Saturday that they were so far removed from each other that I was like, it's plausible that now he's just not, like, has nothing to cover up, you know. But then, at the same time, I still feel like, until your divorce is 100% completely final and you're out of that house, why would you do that?
Koback: Sure.
Nichol: I mean, so, again, I didn't ask him, like...
Koback: So you just found it was a little bit suspicious, um, that he used a credit card versus the, um, the gift card?
Nichol: It was like he had nothing to hide...
Koback: Right.
Nichol: … or nothing to lose. He...
Koback: He...
Nichol: … was just, like, 'Yeah, I'm gonna pay with this...'
Koback: Right.
Nichol: '... and I don't care.'
Koback: Okay. So… and that would certainly be, uh, if it was a credit card, um, just thinking, uh, would be something that maybe his wife would see at some point and he would have to then...
Nichol: Yes.
Koback: … try to have to explain that. So in your mind, he's, like, 'Oh, well, we're divorced or I don't care anymore. Um, she's gonna find out that I have a… a… a girlfriend.'
Nichol: I don't really know what he was thinking. I mean, I can't think for that man, I mean, I don't even… I can't even process half the shit he's done or the lies he's pulled at this point, so I don't know. I just think that… that was extremely peculiar because he had never done that before...
Koback: Okay.
Nichol: … and it didn't seem like a big deal to him.
Koback: All right. I… I get where… where you're going. Um, so it kind of made you think that he didn't have anything to hide anymore?
Nichol: No, not at all. And again, you know, I mean, there was other parts of our relationship where it's, like, he talked to me on the phone pretty freely all the time, you know, so for me he never really seemed… it never really seemed, like, on the phone, he had to hide anything at all. And that's why, you know, when he's telling me, 'Yeah, we're getting

separated. Yeah, I'm sleeping in the basement.' Like, it didn't even, occur to me, like, maybe this isn't happening because it was, like, he was so liberal about his communication with me, even if they were in the same house together at the same time. And so for me, I was, like, 'All right. Well, maybe she's upstairs, he's downstairs, they're separated. It doesn't really matter if he makes a phone call.' And so that he was always liberal with, but when it came to paying for things, it was always the *Anadarko* gift cards. And again...

Koback: Mm-hm.

Nichol: ... I don't know if that's 'cause he was hiding it from her or if that was because he happened to have these gift cards and why not spend those as opposed to the money in your bank account. I mean, I don't know. I just noticed that that one last time that we hung out, that he paid with a credit card and I was confused because I was pretty sure that he still had a balance remaining on one of those *Anadarko* cards, but I... I...

Koback: Okay.

Nichol: ... I don't know.

Koback: Got it.

Nichol: I don't know.

Koback: All right. What's next?

Nichol: So... all right. And then, uh, let me just give you dates real quick...

Koback: Sure.

Nichol: ... um, for the thing when we were out in public. So I think I have these rights, I hope I have these right, um, but on Sunday... I think it was Sunday... I think it was Sunday the 5th. I think.

Koback: July 5th?

Nichol: Um, yeah, that's what I meant. I'm sorry. I'm glad that you're paying attention to this 'cause... yeah. So July... I think July... I'm gonna start at the beginning.

Koback: Okay.

Nichol: So I went out of town for my birthday. I came home on July 3rd, which is the night of my birthday. On the 4th of July, I went over to his house in the morning and then - and helped him with his meal plan thing, and then after that I went to the 4th of July Rockies game with one of my friends. And then on the 5th? I think it was the 5th, I don't remember, um, we went to go see a movie, um, and we went to the movie theatre that is up by that *Lazy Dog*, I think, on 144th and I-25. Um...

Koback: What movie...

***Nichol:* ...** he wanted to go...

***Koback:* ...** did you see?

Nichol: That new *Jurassic Park* movie. I don't know what it's called.

Koback: Okay.

Nichol: And I remember, um, we got there and the first showing was sold out I think? I don't remember. I think either we were gonna go see another movie and it was sold out, or that one was sold out. So… but when we went up there to start with, it was sold out and so we… we left and we, um, we went and walked down to these benches that were right across from the *Victoria's Secret*. Um, and I don't know what corner of the building that would be on, um, if you guys need me to go to there and try to figure out, I can do that.

Koback: No, we- I'll figure it out. That's okay.

Nichol: Um, yeah, and we sat in these benches - on this bench under this tree and just bullshitted until the next showing of the movie. Um, and they we went to the second showing of the movie. And it was really late. I wanna say...

Koback: Do you… uh...

***Nichol:* ...** it was nine something.

Koback: PM?

Nichol: Yeah, it was late.

Koback: On… on the 5th?

Nichol: And I wanna say… I don't… I… I just… I just don't even wanna say it's Sunday 'cause I feel like it was, like, not Sunday. I don't think it was my birthday though. I don't know.

Koback: Okay.

Nichol: I don't know. I might have all my dates mixed up. If I have all my dates mixed up, just...

Koback: That's okay.

***Nichol:* ...** (unintelligible) … camera or something, just...

Koback: That you get… you're getting us close.

***Nichol:* ...** you… you'll find it. Okay. So then, um, let me go back to, um, no. I was looking at August, that's why the date - the date sounded weird. It was… it was, like, it was either the 6th of July or the 7th of July.

Koback: Okay.
Nichol: I was looking at the wrong month on the calendar.
Koback: So Sunday the 6th - pardon me...
Nichol: No, it's… it's either… I think… 'cause on this one I'm saying I didn't think it was a Sunday, so it is either Friday the 6th...
Koback: Okay.
Nichol: … or Saturday the 7th...
Koback: Uh, the...
Nichol: … of July. I'm sorry. I was...
Koback: That's okay.
Nichol: … looking at the wrong calendar. Um, so one of tho… well, 'cause I remember that was our first outing. That was our first date and it was the weekend right after my birthday week, so...
Koback: Okay.
Nichol: … um, so it had to have been, yeah, either probably the 6th or the 7th. And then...
Koback: Okay.
Nichol: … we didn't go anywhere again until the next weekend. And that weekend, on Saturday the 14th, that's the day that I went to his house. Um, we went up to Boulder and we went to the *Shelby Mustang Museum*, so this was July 14th.
Koback: Okay.
Nichol: Yeah. So we went up there, took a tour and then, um, after that we left and, um, we went to his hou…
Koback: Do you remember time that would've been?
Nichol: That we left?
Koback: Mm-hm.
Nichol: I don't know. It was probably...
Koback: Well, what time do you think you got to the museum?
Nichol: Uh, God. I don't even remember, um...
Koback: Morning? Afternoon? Night?
Nichol: I think it was pretty, like, a decent time in the morning. I bet you we got there at eleven or so, 'cause I remember it took us probably an hour, an hour and a half to walk through it I think. It was… it's a small museum. And then after that we were gonna go to lunch in Boulder and then we decided not to. And then, um, we just went to… we went to his house and I dropped him off 'cause I had picked him up to go to the museum, so I dropped him off...

Koback: So you're dri…
***Nichol:* …** at… what?
***Koback:* …** you're driving your 4Runner?
Nichol: Yeah. We… we drove my 4Runner all the time. I told you I was only in his vehicle one time and I think...
Koback: Right.
***Nichol:* …** it was so he could go get gas or something, like, everything… all of these adventures were all done in my truck.
Koback: Okay.
Nichol: Um, so then, uh, we went to his house and, um, we were over there for a little while, but then I was just, like, 'I don't really wanna be here.' So I left and I left him there. He didn't go with me.
Koback: At his home?
Nichol: Uh, yeah, I left him there.
Koback: Okay.
Nichol: Um, and I left by myself. And then on the weekend of the 21st? And this is how you'll know if my dates are lined up. I would base it off of this date and work your way backwards, but, um, this weekend I went to *Bandimere Speedway* with him. As I we… and saw… think it was called the *Mopar Mile High Nationals.*
Koback: Mm-hm.
Nichol: It might've been called *Thunder on the Mountain*. I don't know. It was the drag races though and it was on… yeah, Saturday the 21st.
Koback: Okay.
Nichol: And were there the majority of the day. I think… I think we got there early afternoon and we were there till it ended pretty much.
Koback: Was that, uh, late in the evening?
Nichol: Yeah. Those things go pretty… like, it gets dark.
Koback: Okay. So you guys… so you...
Nichol: So (unintelligible)...
***Koback:* …** dro… did you pick him up again and then drive your truck or… or your 4Runner, right? It's a 4Runner? Drive your 4Runner?
Nichol: I didn't pick him up. No, I didn't… I didn't pick him up again because I never went back to his house. He came to my house and then we carpooled.
Koback: Okay. So he drove to your house, you guys...
Nichol: So...

***Koback:* ...** carpooled down to the *Mile High Nationals* and you stayed a majority of the day? Is there anybody...
Nichol: Yes.
***Koback:* ...** with you guys on any of these dates, or is it just you two?
Nichol: It's just us.
Koback: Okay. Did you, um...
Nichol: Um...
***Koback:* ...** have meals anywhere after you left there? Did you stop at any bars or anything?
Nichol: God, um, okay, so that day, I'm glad you brought that up, um, prior to going to, uh, *Bandimere*, we went to, um, what is the name of that little town… it's not Evergreen, it's in between Lakewo… Morrison.
Koback: Morrison? Okay.
Nichol: We went to Morrison. And there's a patio bar there, um, I do not know what it is called. It's on top of an Italian pizza place. I think it's literally called the Morrison Grill or Morrison Patio Bar, something real simple. Um, and we went… it… it's just a rooftop bar, um...
Koback: And you went before the...
***Nichol:* ...** and it's above...
***Koback:* ...** drag races?
Nichol: Yeah, we went before the drag races...
Koback: Okay.
***Nichol:* ...** and we hung out… yeah, and we hung out there probably for a while. I think we were there for a little while and we ate there, so that's where we got food. I totally...
Koback: So you - you ate lunch there?
***Nichol:* ...** spaced it out until just now. Yeah, we did.
Koback: Okay.
Nichol: Tacos.
Koback: Okay.
Nichol: Um, this is really a bar by the way. Um, yeah, so we… we… we ate… we, um, we did that and then we went to Bandimere and then I don't know what we did after Bandimere. I think we just went to… (unintelligible). I'm almost positive, like, I don't think we did anything after that 'cause it was pretty late. And then on weekend of July 28th through the 29th, um, we went to the sand dunes… we went to the Great Sand Dunes National Park.

Koback: Down in, uh, Alamosa?
Nichol: Yes.
Koback: July 28th, 29th. Did you guys stay anywhere?
Nichol: It was the 28th. What did you say? I'm sorry.
Koback: Where did you… where did you stay?
Nichol: Oh, we camped.
Koback: Okay.
Nichol: We camped. I don't remember the name of the campsite, but if you just let me go through probably my old phone navo or go through just the internet and try to look up campsites, I can probably come up with a name for you.
Koback: Let me… let me ask you this. There was, um, some attachments that, uh, when I was looking at some of your phone stuff today, although very limited, there's a… a man with a backpack, um, he's got a beard. He… he does not look like Chris to me… in… in your photos. Do you know who I'm talking about?
Nichol: Yeah. Is he a little, heavier set?
Koback: Yeah, I'd say he's a little bit bigger.
Nichol: Yes. That is my friend, Jim. That is the one that I was with on the Monday and Tuesday of last week.
Koback: Okay. So there is some photographs… you mentioned the museum… the car museum. I think I remember seeing a couple photos of… of cars and it didn't strike me as anything then. Um, so there may be a little bit more on your phone than what I think, uh, but there is definitely no photos of Chris, and I don't remember seeing, um, any pictures of the sand dunes, but… so did you camp inside the National Park there?
Nichol: No. It was outside. I think we camped at Zapata Falls. I think that's the name of the campsite.
Koback: Yep, Zapata Falls?
Nichol: I think it was the Zapata Falls.
Koback: Mm-hm.
Nichol: Yeah, it's Zapata. We...
Koback: It's before you come to the… you… you turn off 160 and you're going towards the sand dunes and then you turn off and kind of go up a 4-wheel drive road to Zapata Falls?
Nichol: Uh, yeah, that really gnarly… one with all the switchbacks...
Koback: Yep.

***Nichol:* …** and the rocks?
Koback: Mm-hm.
Nichol: Yeah...
Koback: Okay.
***Nichol:* …** there. And so we… we camped there. Um...
Koback: Was it an established campground, or was it just dry camping?
Nichol: No, it was an established campground. There's a campground up there, like, you hang that left to go to Zapata Falls Trail, and then you go right and there's a big campground loop.
Koback: Okay. So that's where you guys were there?
Nichol: Yes.
Koback: All right. Keep going.
Nichol: And then, um, we went to the sand dunes… not the first day, so we got there, uh, fairly late on… how did I do… how did we get… no, no, no, no, no, that's right. So I just… I need to think about this… (unintelligible) … this was Saturday we got there, we set up camp and then after we set up camp, we went to the National Park.
Koback: So ac… you went and hiked the… whatever, the… the sand dunes?
Nichol: Yeah. Yeah, we tried, and I just remember it was super windy. Oh, my God, the sand hurt so bad. I was… it was… it started raining, um, and we stayed. We stayed even though the weather was bad 'cause there was nobody else there. Um, and so we did that for most of the afternoon. And then, um, we came back to the campsite and I showed him how to light a fire 'cause he'd never done it before. Um...
Koback: He'd never lit a fire?
***Nichol:* …** he lit… no, he's never been camping before. He told me he'd never been camping before and I was...
Koback: Oh.
***Nichol:* …** like, 'Well, if you wanna go, I'm trying to go to sand dunes.' So that's why we went 'cause he said he'd never done it.
Koback: Okay.
Nichol: Um, so we...
Koback: Did you guys visit any, um, there's not really very much stuff around there, uh, there's no restaurants or anything in that area...
Nichol: No...
***Koback:* …** so...

***Nichol:* ...** no, we did stop at the... I think it's called The Oasis or something. Um, it's this little... it's, like, on the way to the Dunes. It's not in the Park, but it's on that road that you take to get to the Dunes and it's it's almost, like, a little gas station. And we stopped there and we rented a sand board, um, to go sandboarding on and, um, we got... I think we got more ice for cooler, I think, and we got firewood for...
Koback: So it's a gas station?
Nichol: Kind of, but it's the one-stop shop that everybody goes to 'cause there's nothing else around there.
Koback: Right.
Nichol: Like, you wouldn't... I'm almost sure... I'm almost positive it's called *The Oasis* and they actually have their own campground back there too.
Koback: Okay.
Nichol: It's, like...
Koback: I know where you...
***Nichol:* ...** on that road.
Koback: Mm-hm. It's right before you get to the...
Nichol: Yeah.
***Koback:* ...** entrance to the... the Park?
Nichol: Yep. Yep, yep, yep.
Koback: Okay.
Nichol: On the right-hand side when you're driving in. Um, I'm glad that you know what I'm talking about...
Koback: Well, I worked, uh...
***Nichol:* ...** because, um...
***Koback:* ...** I worked in Southern Colorado for the last five years and I spent a lot of time around Alamosa and - and The San Luis Valley, so...
Nichol: Oh...
***Koback:* ...** I know...
***Nichol:* ...** gotcha.
***Koback:* ...** I know a lot of... about that area, unfortunately. Um, so I...
Nichol: Oh, well, that's... that's good. That helps me.
***Koback:* ...** know where you're talking about. So you... you got ice...
Nichol: So...
***Koback:* ...** um, and, uh, firewood...

Nichol: Yeah. And I got - I'm not sure if we got ice. I think we did just 'cause I like to re-up ice every time I go camping.
Koback: Who… who paid for it?
Nichol: He did.
Koback: Okay. Do you think he used the debit… or the, um, gift card again?
Nichol: Probably. 'Cause that was the plan in the first place. He was just, like, 'Well, hey, I've got these gift cards if you wanna use 'em. You don't even have to spend any money and we can just use these.' And I was, like, 'Well, that's great.' So I remember for the trip I filled up my gas tank and I paid for gas and I bought a little bit of groceries, uh, for the cooler. And then, um, he took care of the campsite and the board and the firewood and all of that.
Koback: Okay.
Nichol: I didn't actually go into that Oasis place I don't think. I'm almost positive I didn't go in there, he did. I - I got in line for the board, I remember that. But their… their little board rental shop is outside of the building.
Koback: Okay.
Nichol: Or he went inside 'cause he went and got firewood. Um, and then we went… went to the Dunes...
Koback: And I'm just...
Nichol: … and we hung out...
Koback: … looking at your dates so you know you're right. *The Bandimere Speedway, the Mile-High Nationals* was July 21.
Nichol: Yeah...
Koback: So...
Nichol: … uh, that's what I was gonna say. Get online and see if that matches.
Koback: Yep, it does, so...
Nichol: Okay. So the… so then all...
Koback: … we're good.
Nichol: … those other dates… all those other dates should be good. The only one that I'm not 100% sure about is the movie. It was that weekend, that movie...
Koback: Okay.
Nichol: … on the 6th and the 7th. It was that weekend. I just remember what day...

Koback: Okay.
Nichol: … of the weekend. I think… I don't think it was a Sunday though. I really think it was a Friday or a Saturday, like, I'm almost positive I didn't have to work anyway.
Koback: All right. So what's after, uh...
Nichol: Um...
Koback: … the *Great Sand Dunes?*
Nichol: Okay, so we went to the… the dunes and then, um, we went and returned the board and then we went back to the campsite and we lit a fire and we ate and we just hung out by the fire for a few hours and just visited and then it started raining really hard. So we put everything in the tent and put out the fire and we went in the tent and I remember he was wide awake and I was so tired, like, oh my, God. I wanted to sleep so bad and he just would not sleep and it was kind of bugging me. I would… I think I would… I would almost, like, wake up and half subconsciously have a conversation with him for a sec and then, like, doze back off. And I just remember being so tired and he was up… probably for a while.
Koback: Okay. And...
Nichol: And then...
Koback: … so you guys...
Nichol: Go ahead.
Koback: … come back to the Denver metro area on Sunday?
Nichol: Kind of. Yeah, but we… so we went, um, one of my friends wanted us to go to the *Renaissance Festival* and she didn't know who I was with, but she was with uh, the *Renaissance Festival* in Colorado Springs, and she's, like, 'Oh, you should stop by.' And I made up and excuse to not go over there. I just her, I was, like, 'Yeah, I don't really know, you know.' And I kind of got out of it because I didn't want her to meet him.
Koback: I got it.
Nichol: Um...
Koback: What friend was that?
Nichol: Charlotte.
Koback: Okay. So did Charlotte ever meet Chris?
Nichol: No, none of my friends ever met him.
Koback: Okay.

Nichol: And then, um, uh, on the way back up, we stopped in Colorado Springs to eat, and we stopped at a restaurant called BJ's.
Koback: On Nevada and I-25?
Nichol: Uh, honestly, I don't know. I mean, I just remember...
Koback: Right by the col…
***Nichol:* …** what it's called, like...
***Koback:* …** *University of Colorado*? There's a bunch of buildings, uh, and it's a big, strip centre.
Nichol: Uh...
Koback: There's a *Costco*...
Nichol: Oh, wait, I think I remember the *Costco*. I think I remember *Costco* 'cause don't kind of have, like… like from the highway you can, like, see it...
Koback: Yep.
***Nichol:* …** from the highway, but that main road, you can see the *Costco* and then you have to kind of, like, turn in and around into...
Koback: Yep.
***Nichol:* …** shopping centre?
Koback: Mm-hm.
Nichol: Yeah, that's the one.
Koback: Okay. *BJ's*, it's more like a, um, Brewhouse, I guess, kind of?
Nichol: Yes. Yes. And it's really nice… that place. It's just, like, it's a nice restaurant. I mean, not nice, but it's just… it's… it… yeah, it's...
Koback: Okay.
***Nichol:* …** it's a decent place, so we...
Koback: So that would've been...
***Nichol:* …** the… it's a big place. That's what I was looking for.
Koback: Yep.
Nichol: It's a big restaurant.
Koback: Sunday...
Nichol: Yeah, so...
***Koback:* …** July 29th?
Nichol: That… what, uh, what… what… what days did you want to know...
Koback: Would… would that have been...
Nichol: Yes, it was Sunday.
***Koback:* …** Sunday, July 29th?
Nichol: Yeah, it was Sunday, July 29th. And if you walk in the restau-

rant… so picture walking in, um, and the front doors are behind you, we were sat to the right on the first level, like, there's… there's a few different levels so we were sat on the right side and then in the right side, we were on the left portion of the section on the right side, there's… there's little, single seater booths.
Koback: Okay.
Nichol: There' really small.
Koback: Okay.
Nichol: So almost in the centre of the restaurant. Almost, but just kind of on the right section of the… the main floor.
Koback: Okay.
Nichol: Okay. So there was that and...
Koback: Did you pay… did he again pay with a gift card at that time?
Nichol: Yes. Yes.
Koback: Okay. All right.
Nichol: And then we went home.
Koback: Okay. Did you see him the following weekend?
Nichol: Uh, no, 'cause he was out of town.
Koback: Okay. Do you know where he went?
Nichol: He… yeah, he went to North Carolina.
Koback: Do you remember the dates?
Nichol: Uh, no, I think… I think, uh, I wanna say that he left on the 31st of July. I'm almost positive 'cause we hung out the weekend prior at the sand dunes and then I came into work on Monday the 30th, I remember that. And then I think he left on Tuesday the 31st of July. I think. And I don't remember when he got home.
Koback: Okay. Next time you guys go out?
Nichol: Uh, it was that Saturday...
Koback: Saturday?
Nichol: … uh, the 11th...
Koback: And you guys...
Nichol: … and that was...
Koback: The Lazy Dog?
Nichol: … yeah, the st… yeah.
Koback: Okay. So we got that all down. What's next on your list?
Nichol: Um, sorry, I was not… I forgot about all of that stuff and I didn't...
Koback: That's all right.

***Nichol:* ...** (Unintelligible), um...
Koback: So we ran through something that I... on... you know, the first time we talked you were really tired. The second time you were overly stressed and you had thought of some very important stuff that you wanted to talk about, so it's fine. And it... I don't mind talking to you as many times as I have to talk to you to get everything down that could atten... you know, at some point be very important. It's fine.
Nichol: Understood.
Koback: So just don't... don't...
Nichol: Understood.
***Koback:* ...** worry about that. I, you know, my job is to talk to you and make sure that this stuff is, um, you know, placed in... in a... a report so it's there forever, so it's... it's fine. Again, I... I just keep telling you every time, you... when you remember things, just call me and... and we'll get it down, all right?
Nichol: Okay. Okay. Yeah, and I hope you guys pull cameras on all that 'cause I'm trying to help you. I'm... I'm really, honestly disappointed that you guys don't have all my text messages or don't think that you do. It makes me sad. I really... I want you guys to have them, like, you need them and it's... it's frustrating to me, but it's, like, I'll just tell you everything I know and we'll go from there.
Koback: That's right.
Nichol: Um, hold on. Uh, hold on. What else? (Unintelligible). Oh, okay. So now let's go to this last week.
Koback: Okay.
Nichol: Um, uh, let's see... (unintelligible). Okay. Um, so Monday. I think probably the most important conversation that I've had... I had with him after all of that took place was that first phone conversation on Monday night, like, the later one. Remember I told... you were telling me there's two big ones?
Koback: Right.
Nichol: And the first one was the one where he mentioned the sheets... the smelly sheets with his kids, and that was also the one where he was telling me he was gonna go get his wife's wedding ring appraised. Um, that same conversation, he... I don't remember exactly how he phrased this. I don't remember what led to this, but he told me, um, something about, like, he mentioned that he had told... I don't know what he said. He said something about the separation and how,

like, she was okay with… with the fact that he wanted a separation or that, um, something like that. And I remember thinking to myself, like, wait a minute. Wh… oh, God, I don't… I'm drawing a blank. It… here's the deal is, like, he had been telling me the whole time that I was spending time with him. That he was getting separated… getting separated and he kept saying that he was the one who initially initiated the separation and then that it was more of a mutual thing. He said that he was the one who had initially brought it up...

Koback: Okay.

Nichol: … uh, like, before we had met, and then she was onboard with it where she was just, like, 'I'm not happy either. Let's do this.' Um, and then I, um, I remember telling you guys that when he was gonna go to North Carolina, I kind of, like, backed away from the situation and I was, like, 'Hey, I think you should try to fix things with her because you have a really beautiful life with her and I think you should try to fix stuff.' And he kept telling me, you know, 'I don't want to. I don't think she wants to.' And I was just like, 'Please try… just please try.' I just thought he had such a beautiful life and… and, you know, and I was willing to just leave, like, leave his life. I was, like, "If you work things out with your wife, I'm gone.' And, like, I… and… and that's fine, you know, and… and he's always be, like, 'Well, what about us?' I'd be, like, 'Don't worry about us, like, try to fix stuff with her.' And he said, 'Okay, I will.' And then when he went to North Carolina, he told me that he sat down and had a conversation with her and that he told her that he wanted to fix it. That is what he said to me. He told her that he wanted to fix it and she said, 'No'. That she still wanted the separation and that she was ready to file for divorce. So I was under the impression, when he got home from North Carolina, that the divorce was filed. That was what I was under the impression. And so then on Monday when we were on that one phone call where he was just saying all sorts of weird stuff, he's, like, again, I don't remember exactly what was said, but it was something along the lines of, um, 'She was okay with the fact that I wanted the separation'.

Koback: Right.

Nichol: And then I remember asking him, I was, like, 'Wait a minute. When you were in North Carolina, you told me that you tried to fix it with her and she was the one who said that she didn't wanna fix it'.

Koback: Okay.

Nichol: And he's, like, 'no, I just…' and then he goes, 'No, I just told her that I still wanted, you know, to continue with the separation.' And I'm just thinking in my head, 'He lied to me. God, he fuckin' lied to me.' He lied so much. I… it's… it's...

Koback: Okay. So that just struck you as another lie?

Nichol: Yeah, so that one I don't - well, it… it… yeah, well, and then now I'm seeing the news where he's telling everybody that he separated from her on… that he said he was… he told her he wanted a separation on the Monday that she went missing and I'm just thinking in my head, he told me that he had already had that conversation with her before I was in… even in his life.

Koback: Well, and so not to 'cause you anymore stress, but so when you're talking to him on Monday, this is Monday, right? This isn't Sunday, this is Monday...

Nichol: No, this is Monday.

Koback: … so this is after the event? This is after the murders?

Nichol: Yes.

Koback: He… he...

Nichol: Yes.

Koback: … is telling you that he… she mentioned, uh, that it was o… she was okay with the separation, although you know now...

Nichol: Yes.

Koback: … that, um, that wasn't accurate with those… that was something different than he had previously told you and certainly she couldn't've been really saying anything unfortunately. So, I… I mean, he's making… he's making up stories after his wife is deceased. Do you… is that a fair statement?

Nichol: Yeah, well...

Koback: Is that… I'm… I'm kind of trying to follow where you're going.

Nichol: I… I don't honestly, I… it just struck me as odd because I don't know if he was talking about the conversation they had had that day, or...

Koback: Okay.

Nichol: … he was talking about North Carolina. So either way...

Koback: It just struck you as a lie?

Nichol: … it was weird… it… it… it struck me weird because he said that he was the one that was pushing for it now. And I was just thinking in the back of my head, he… he made it sound like when I first got

into his life that he was the one who had brought up the separation, but that she was super gungho about it. He made it sound like she was all onboard with it. And then when they were in North Carolina, he's the one who said that he tried to fix it and she wa… didn't want anything to do with it, so it was weird to me when he was saying that he was the one that initiated the separation. 'Cause I'm, like, 'Wait a minute.' Like… and I think he… it… it was weird to me because I think he was referring to… to either whatever happened on Monday morning, or he was referring to whatever happened in North Carolina. And I was just really confused because I was, like, 'Well, at that point, I thought she was the one pushing you away, like, not you pushing her'.
Koback: Gotcha. Okay. All right.
Nichol: Um, so I… I don't… it's just a lie.
Koback: Yep.
Nichol: I mean, honestly, I don't know if it has any significance or it's just… it was just a lie that I caught him. I don't, I mean, I think everything he told me was a lie, but it was a lie on top of… it… it's a lie that contradicted the previous lies that he had told me.
Koback: I understand. What's next on your list?
Nichol: So, uh, uh, let me see. Okay, so then in that same, exact conversation two more things happened.
Koback: Okay.
Nichol: One, um, I was asking him about his daughters EpiPen because I know that CeCe has that tree nut allergy...
Koback: Okay.
Nichol: … and I was, like, I was, like, a… again, I don't remember word for word, but it was something along the lines of, 'She didn't take your daughter's EpiPen?' And he was, like, 'No.' And I was, like, 'Well, aren't you a little worried?' 'Cause I was trying to do my own reconnaissance and I was, like, 'Aren't you worried about that?' And he's, like, he's like, 'Well, we have a stash of them in the basement.' Or something like that. And he's like, 'She probably just took one of those'. And I just thought it was weird because several weeks earlier he had told me how expensive EpiPens were so I'm, like, 'If they're that expensive, how the… how do you have a stash? You don't have a stash. Nobody can afford a stash of EpiPens'.
Koback: Right, they're very expensive.
Nichol: And… yeah, so I almost was, like, so at the time I didn't think

anything of it, and now that I'm thinking about it I'm, like, well, that was a lie too. And so...

Koback: Okay.

Nichol: … so there's that. And then, um, also in that same conversation… so then I started questioning him about why he didn't go to the office on Monday. And I was like, uh, you know, and again it's not an abnormal thing for him to not go to the office, but it's less common. I would say it happens maybe once every couple weeks or maybe once or twice a month, like it's… it's pretty in, like, it occurs so it's not extremely abnormal, but I just thought it was ironic that his wife was missing and he wasn't at the office that morning.

Koback: Okay.

Nichol: And so… and he… or here's the deal. So Sunday night he had told me, 'I have to go straight to the field'. I mean, I guess that's something else you probably wanna know...

Koback: Okay.

Nichol: … so I didn't think of that. So Sunday night...

Koback: So Sunday night… during which conversation? The… so the one we're talking about now...

Nichol: Um, I don't...

Koback: … is your first… you referred to it as your first conversation. Um, I don't remember, uh, you had two that were lengthy. One, I believe, was from nine to eleven at night, um, and we had talked a little bit...

Nichol: It was...

Koback: … about this previously, about him saying that he wasn't gonna go to the office, um...

Nichol: Yeah, so… so he… okay, so… I'm… I'm sorry. It's, like, I jump around sometimes...

Koback: That's okay.

Nichol: … when I start remembering stuff. So he, um, the big conversation that we're talking about, the really important one where he gave me all those weird, uh, one off details, that was the first, long conversation on Monday night. I don't know what time that was, but that was, like, the first long one where he said all of that stuff, like, all of that was in one conversation.

Koback: That… and when you say all that stuff, like, the smelly sheets, uh, talking about...

Nichol: The ring.
Koback: … the ring?
Nichol: … the wedding ring...
Koback: Okay.
Nichol: … the weird part where he slipped up about him being the one to push...
Koback: The se… okay, gotcha.
Nichol: … them separating and not her...
Koback: So...
Nichol: … and… and then the EpiPen thing and then, um, all of that. And then so… so back to Sunday the… August the 12th, that night I believe we only had one phone conversation. I looked at it. I pulled up my phone records today and I'm pretty sure we only had one phone conversation, and then I think I just went to bed.
Koback: Okay.
Nichol: Um, but on Sunday night, um, that phone conversation… that's the one where I heard the TV on in the background and I was, like, maybe he's staying up and waiting for her. Do you remember I told you guys that?
Koback: Yes.
Nichol: I was, like, I think it was really weird that the TV was on, because he talks to me when he's in bed and he wasn't in bed. Um, so that… that's… this is the same conversation. In that conversation, he told me, 'I have to go straight to the field tomorrow.' And he was just, like, you know, like, 'I… I'm not gonna get to see you in the morning.' And I was just, like, 'All right.' And I was like, 'Why?' And just like, I gotta go, um, he's like, 'I gotta go check out a site.' And, uh, like a release in the morning and a release is, like, when… when the oil industry has, like, like, a release of any type of, like, oil products or anything, like, from any of our equipment. And I was, like, I remember asking him, I was, like, 'Well, why would you have to go check out the release? You're not part of the environmental team'.
Koback: So when you say release, is that...
Nichol: He was...
Koback: … like, a spill?
Nichol: Kind of, yeah. I mean, I don't wanna call it...
Koback: Or, like, something's leaking or...
Nichol: … 'cause… yeah, something's leaking, like...

Koback: Okay.
Nichol: … any… anything that's involved with the oil and gas industry, anytime, like, so… like if a piece of equipment leaks. I mean, you gotta think they've got millions and millions of pieces of equipment, like...
Koback: Sure.
Nichol: … it happens. And so he's, like, 'I have to go check out a release'. And I remember asking him, I was, like, 'Why do you need to go do that? You are not part of the environmental team'. Because our field operators, they will find releases and they'll call… they'll call our environmental team, which is who I work for. They don't call me though, 'cause I'm not the one that deals with that stuff, but they do call people in my department and they say, 'Hey, I'm on this - this jobsite and, you know, like, a tank battery's leaking or, like, a… a oil tank's leaking,' or something like that. And then we go out and assess it and clean it up and so on and so forth. So… (unintelligible) ...
Koback: So those are actually specialists that go out and clean this up and he's not one of those people?
Nichol: No, he's not, but sometimes those guys, like, his job is important to shut in oil wells if there's a leak or, like, shut valves if there's a leak, he… he manages the equipment, so… so when he was, like, he's, like, 'I gotta go check out a release.' And I was, like, 'Why are you going to do that? That's not your job'. And he was just, like, 'I just need to go check out some of the equipment where the release occurred'. Now that part didn't really seem too odd to me because, I mean, it make sense that they're, like, 'Hey, we have a release. Send an operator out and make sure all…' oh, he said he had to do a lockout/tagout on the site, um, so that means that depending on where the release is, if it's near a piece of equipment that could be pote… have, like, potential energy to be hazardous, what we do in the oil industry is what's called lockout/tagout. And certified operators, such as himself, um, will go out there and they will pull a lock with a tag on the, like, the… on the piece of equipment where you operate it, um, so that it cannot be in use, like, they'll de-energize the piece of equipment and shut it down, and then they'll put a lockout/tagout tag on it and then the point is… is, like, so then if the environmental team comes in to clean up the mess, nobody accidently reenergizes this piece of equipment while we're trying to clean up the mess because it could injure somebody. Does that make sense?

Koback: Yes. I got it.
Nichol: Okay. So… so now I'm remembering this just now and he was like, 'I think I gotta go do a lockout/tagout on some of that equipment for the release.'
Koback: Would that be something that would've been tracked? Certainly, um, there's a lot of, uh, paperwork and safety requirements and all sorts of things with each site, so if he was actually going to do a lockout/tagout, would that be something that I'd be able to look at… record at *Anadarko* and… and know that he was actually assigned to do that?
Nichol: To be honest with you, probably. Again, I do not work with him, um, but if there's one thing that I do know about *Anadarko* and I love and I'm gonna miss those guys so much, it's the fact that they're very safe, that is they're one of the best oil and gas companies because of how safe they are. Um, so with that being said, I would be willing to bet that there's typically...
Koback: Well, like, you...
Nichol: … a protocol.
Koback: Right. So I… I mean, th… there would have to be a known problem for him to do a lockout/tagout, right?
Nichol: Yes.
Koback: So...
Nichol: Yes.
Koback: … somebody would've had to call and said, hey, there's a… in your guys' words, release, um, at this site and then some boss or whoever it may be would call Chris and say, 'Hey, Chris. I need you to go check this out. If it's so, you're a skilled, um, equipment operator, you make the decision. You lock it out if you have to.' Then the environmental team comes and cleans it up, so there's gotta be, like, a track...
Nichol: Yep.
Koback: … record of all that going on? Um...
Nichol: Uh, I'm assu… I'm assuming that there probably is because lockout/tagout...
Koback: … because if...
Nichol: … I mean, it's… it's to save lives so it's a very serious thing...
Koback: Right, it's a safety thing...
Nichol: … and, like, certainly… certain people… yeah, and only

certain people are authorized, like, I couldn't lockout/tagout something, like, I don't have...
Koback: Right.
***Nichol:* ...** that certification.
Koback: Plus you're shutting down...
Nichol: It's not...
***Koback:* ...** a piece of equipment that makes money. So, um...
Nichol: Yes.
***Koback:* ...** somebody wants to know that, right?
Nichol: Yes.
Koback: Somebody… there...
Nichol: Yes.
***Koback:* ...** there is a, I mean, there… it… it's a business. I'm just trying to think as a businessperson how they would… would do that because certainly if you're doing that, they wanna get the team out there and clean up whatever is going on as soon as possible so...
Nichol: So...
***Koback:* ...** they can piece of equipment back in order and running so they can continue to pump oil.
Nichol: Understood. Understood. Well and, too, the thing… the other thing too is the, like, he hadn't even looked at the site yet so it's, like, how do you know that you need a lockout/tagout? I don't know. Um...
Koback: That and that's what I'm saying.
***Nichol:* ...** that is - that's (unintelligible)...
Koback: I mean, I would like to… it's something for me to investigate. I'm just kind of trying to get a… 'cause you obviously know a lot...
Nichol: Yeah.
***Koback:* ...** more about the oil industry. I don't know anything about it. That makes sense to me...
Nichol: And that's good.
***Koback:* ...** um, so that's good. Cool. Thank you.
Nichol: Yeah. I… I didn't even think of that till just now, so anyways, that is a question for *Anadarko*. That is not a question for me.
Koback: Yep.
Nichol: Um, but, um, anyways, so he told me that he was gonna have to do that and I was, like, 'All right. Cool.' You know, and then, um, and then… so he didn't show up for wo… I mean, well, he did show up for work on Monday, but supposedly he was in the field. Um, and then

Monday evening, um, after my friend, Jim, left, he… that's when, uh, Chris and I spoke on the phone in that first, really extended conversation. Again, I don't know exactly what time it was. It was late, but that first, really extended conversation. That's when he started saying kind of all that really creepy stuff and then, um, he… in that conversation I started questioning him. And I was, like, I was, like, did you really… I don't even remember exactly what I said, but I asked him, I was, like, 'Did you really go to a job site this morning?' And he was, like, 'Yeah'. I was, like, 'And who told you to go there?' And he - I think he said that his foreman had asked either him or his… his, like, co- cowing man is this guy named Troy. I don't know Troy. I don't even know what he looks like, but I do know he - he exists, so he… he… I guess their foreman relies on Chris and Troy to kind of, like, run their little part of the field. And so Chris was, like, he was, like, 'Yeah, my foreman asked either he or Troy to go out there and go look at it.' And...

Koback: Do you know his foreman's name?

Nichol: Um, I don't… he's got a few of 'em I think.

Koback: Okay.

Nichol: I wanna say...

Koback: That's okay.

Nichol: … I wa- wanna say Luke Eppel, but I don't know. You're gonna need to find that out with *Anadarko* too.

Koback: Okay.

Nichol: That's an *Anadarko* question.

Koback: That's all right.

Nichol: Um...

Koback: And I know… I know who...

Nichol: … but I...

Koback: … Luke is and I know who Troy is, so we probably have already answered that. Um...

Nichol: Okay.

Koback: … all right?

Nichol: Yes.

Koback: Great.

Nichol: So, um, anyways, um, so I told him to prove it 'cause at this point, I mean, the things he'd been saying, like, the sheets was kind of weird. You know what it was? It was the wedding ring comment that freaked me out, like, the sheets did, like, was kind of weird at the time, um, and the fact that I thought he had maybe had just lied to me about their separation, but it was, like, the wedding ring comment, like, he was so callous, like, he was just ready to cash it in and get some money...

Koback: You were telling...

***Nichol:* ...** and I was just, like...

***Koback:* ...** him to prove what?

Nichol: To prove that they had told him to go to the field right away.

Koback: Okay. So...

Nichol: And he's, like, 'How do you want me to do that?' And I was, like, 'You take screenshots of your *Anadarko* phone and you text them to me'.

Koback: And did he do that?

Nichol: And I ma… yes, he did.

Koback: Okay. All right.

Nichol: And he didn't… he didn't send me the whole conversation, but it… there was two pictures of a release, um, followed intermittently with, like, there was texts on either side of the picture and, um, it looked… I, like, I… I didn't get everything. He just sent me part of their conversation and I didn't have dates and times on either, like, you couldn't see the dates and times of what he was sending me, so he could've been sending me something that was not recent. It could've been something from weeks ago and I wouldn't've known, but, um, he sent it to me. And he sent it quick, like, it just, like, instantaneously when I asked him for it, like, I was still on the phone with him and...

Koback: Right.

***Nichol:* ...** then I looked at it while I was still on the phone, and it looked… it… it made sense with what he'd been saying, but...

Koback: Okay.

***Nichol:* ...** the only thing in there… yeah, like, it almost looked like someone else was originally gonna go to that site and th… it looked like the conversation someone I interpreted it, the conversation that he had had with his foreman and with Troy or whoever was in that… that conversation, it looked like the conversation had occurred probably at some point over the weekend. And then it looked like Troy, I think, or somebody else in the field was originally gonna go out there on… first thing on Monday and he told them not to worry about it and that he would do it. And… and I, again, I don't know the exact words, like, I don't have that whole conversation. Again, that is something that you… you need to go to *Anadarko* for that.

Koback: Yep. Okay. What's next?

Nichol: Uh, um, and yes, well, then that was… and that conversation… that's the end of that and then...

Koback: Okay.

Nichol: … um, what else… what else… what else? Oh, um, so, uh, okay, and then that same night, um, remember I told you we had that one, big phone conversation that you and me just discussed, and then we Face Timed for two minutes...

Koback: Right.

Nichol: … and then… and then we had another big phone conversation?

Koback: Yep.

Nichol: So when… when we Face Timed, um, I don't know… I don't know. I'll just… I don't know if it's relevant but you say, just say it anyways. Uh, he was wearing a black, wife beater, um, I think it was black. And I told you guys that he was laying on a mattress that had no sheets? And, um, so I've been in his house, but I've never been in his kids' room or the room where his wife slept, like, I went upstairs once, but it was back to that little playroom where all the books are at?

Koback: Right.

Nichol: But I did not go in any of their rooms up there, like, ever. But I remember that the time I did go upstairs, his... the bedroom door to the upstairs bedroom, like, the main room was open and I really, like, I didn't wanna look, but, just when I was walking by, I noticed that they have a really, big bed, like, uh, it was, like, a tall, pillory… just a big bed, uh, frame. And so, um, I don't really know exactly what it looked like. It just looked like a quick glance or whatever… it's just, like, that looks really big and, um, nice, you know.

Koback: Sure.

Nichol: Uh, but again, I didn't go in there so I didn't get a good view of it, but I noticed that night that we were Face Timing, I was trying to figure out where the hell he was because I was, like, I was, like… he was laying down talking to me and he didn't have any sheets on the bed, um, but the background didn't look like the basement. And I've seen the basement and I've seen the bed in the basement. I've seen his little dwelling area down there and it didn't look like that. And I saw, um, it kind of looked like he was, I mean, he was laying down and he had the phone facing him, but you could kind of see in the background, the bed and it looked like… like a really, elegant, really tall bedframe.

Koback: So you think it was the master bedroom?

Nichol: Yes, I do.

Koback: Okay.

Nichol: I think it was. I didn't… I didn't ask, but I'm assuming it was and just no sheets on there.

Koback: Okay.

Nichol: I remember the mattress… if I remember pro… properly, I think it was blue, but I don't remember, um, 100%, but he was just, like, laying on it in a black, wife beater and I just remember seeing this… and… and again, like, I am not… I've never been in that room, so I don't know...

Koback: Okay.

Nichol: … 100%, like, oh, that was it. It just… it… it kind of looked like something very elegant and it definitely was not what was in the basement.

Koback: Okay. What's next? Um... Keeping you on track. I'm trying to go in order. I think that's it. I think that's all I've got. So, I asked you a couple questions, um, when I was driving, when we talked earlier today, and since we weren't...

Nichol: Okay.

Koback: … on tape, I'm gonna just ask again, um...

Nichol: Okay.

Koback: … which was, uh, when… when I… I called you after we looked at your phone download and told you that the messages you deleted, um, like, right now, they don't look, I mean, I can't see them, so I'm trying to recover them, like I told you, through uh, some computer forensics. We'll see if we… we can get that done. But, um, one of the questions that I had for was if you ever social media and you said you did not. So...

Nichol: No.

Koback: … you don't use...

Nichol: I… I don't. I...

Koback: … any social media, you've never used Facebook or Facebook Messenger, uh, with Chris?

Nichol: No, nothing. I've never used any social media with him at all. I have LinkedIn, um, when him and I first started hanging out, um, for business purposes, but it was something that I was, like, never on and then, um, honestly, once all this… all of this news media stuff and everything started happening, I deleted the… the LinkedIn just so that it's… it's harder for these people to try to come track me down and ask me a million questions, um, but I...
Koback: Okay.
Nichol: … never, ever spoke to him on that. I don't even think he has it. I don't even know. I never used it...
Koback: Okay. And then...
Nichol: … so I don't know. But as for actual social media, I haven't had any of that other stuff, like, Twi… I've never had Twitter, I've never had Instagram, I haven't had Facebook since 2016 so no, him and I never had any connection on any social media.
Koback: Do you know when he closed his Facebook?
Nichol: No, no, I'm glad you brought that up because I forgot to write that down the other day. He mentioned that to me on Saturday when we were at dinner. I think it was either when we were walking in the restaurant or walking out of the restaurant.
Koback: Okay. And what did he say?
Nichol: He just, like, offhandedly was, like, uh, 'I shut down my Facebook'. And I was, like, 'What? Why?' And he's like, 'Cause I'm never really on there'. He's, like, 'She used to be on there all the time, uh, for work'. And he's like, 'But I don't need it'. And he just like, it was very random, nonchalant comment. And I was...
Koback: So do you… was...
Nichol: … surprised. Oh, and then I… no, no, no, no. And then I asked him, I said… I said, 'Did you… did you shut it down all the way?' And he kind of, like, gave me this puzzled look and I was, like, 'You have to actually write Facebook with a letter, I mean, not, like, a letter, letter, but you need to send them an email. You can't just deactivate it'. I was, like, 'You need to send them an email that says I want you… I am so-and-so. I want you to shut my account'.
Koback: So what was his response to that?
Nichol: Um, um, I don't remember what he said to me.
Koback: So do you think he...
Nichol: I really don't...

Koback: **...** just deactivated it...
Nichol: ... I don't think he did it.
Koback: ...not shut it down?
Nichol: That's what I think he did... but I don't think he... he... I don't even think he knew that he hadn't completely gotten rid of it.
Koback: Okay.
Nichol: 'Cause I've done it so I know what you have to do to do it.
Koback: Okay. Anything else?
Nichol: Uh, no, but that was just kind of offhanded that you... you mentioned that, so, yeah...
Koback: Okay.
Nichol: **...** but we... no... no, we never... we never talked on Facebook.
Koback: And then I... I asked you, um, if... if necessary... if for some reason I needed to get your phone, um, that, uh, you would be willing to provide me the handset if... if necessary and you s... you were in agreement to that?
Nichol: Yeah, I mean, just... you guys just give me something else so that I can get ahold of people in my life that I need to get ahold of and, um, that's fine.
Koback: Okay.
Nichol: Can I have it back when you guys are done though? I mean... and if you need to keep it I can go get another phone if I have to.
Koback: Well, we... we can work that out should that come up, um, I'm...
Nichol: Okay.
Koback: **...** still waiting...
Nichol: Okay.
Koback: **...** waiting for a call from the, uh, computer forensics expert to... to...
Nichol: Okay.
Koback: **...** give me an idea because of your... your phone's an iPhone, which makes an... my knowledge of this is that if you deleted something of... off an iPhone, it's gone. Now I... I don't know if that's true or not, so I asked you also, uh, to call Verizon, 'cause that's your provider, and to see if they could give you some advice on that. Did you happen to do that?
Nichol: I did. So, um, I... I got on their online chat and I... I saved

that in case, for some reason, you guys need it you can see that I asked them. Um, I was able to they told me that there's several cloud storage devices. They said that Verizon has a cloud and iPhone has the cloud, um, and I checked and, of course, my iPhone cloud backup is not, uh, it's not active...

Koback: Okay.

Nichol: ... so go figure? I just… I don't… I don't pay attention to that stuff, I really don't.

Koback: Well, that's...

Nichol: Um...

Koback: ... why I asked you if you used any cloud stuff earlier, um, so none of that was active?

Nichol: No, that was not… and then I asked 'em, they're, like, 'Well, your… your phone works with Verizon, uh, Verizon iCloud'. And I was, like, 'Well, how do I activate that? Like, how do I open that… open that? Where do I find that in my phone?' And he's, like, 'Oh, it's an app. You have to download the app'. And I was, like, 'Well, is anything from previous conversations gonna be on there if I haven't downloaded the app yet?' And he said, 'No'.

Koback: Okay.

Nichol: But I'll let you guys look at that conversation and my phone and maybe...

Koback: No, no, no.

Nichol: ... you guys can figure out something...

Koback: It makes perfect sense to me.

Nichol: ... that I can't.

Koback: I know exactly what they're saying. So that was their only...

Nichol: So...

Koback: They were saying if you had the cloud it would've been backed up to the cloud, but since you didn't, you… the messages are gone. Yeah. And my iPhone Cloud is not backing anything up either...

Nichol: Right.

Koback: ...so… I...

Nichol: ...it… it's just not active so I'm really sorry about that. But...

Koback: That's okay.

Nichol: ... um, on a good note… so then, um, I found this thing under data usage. I'll show you. I was gonna bring my laptop in when I come, um, not that you need anything off of there, but just so I can show you the… my Verizon account and maybe we can see if we can dig up some stuff on there, but I found a, um, I found, uh, messages and it wasn't the actual body of the text message, but it was, like, the date and time and the phone...

Koback: Okay.

Nichol: … number that it went to, and I received it and I got really excited. I was, like, 'Oh, my God. It's a message log.' And even if it wasn't the body of the message, it would probably help us to figure out what's missing and what's not. And I was super excited and then I started scrolling through it and realized the last ones that they have are from 8-14, so I think they keep 'em for a week and then they get rid of 'em.

Koback: Okay. So did you screenshot that?

Nichol: I wish I would've known that two days ago… what's that?

Koback: Did you take a screenshot of that or anything like that?

Nichol: I mean, I can if you want me to.

Koback: Or is it… is it in your...

Nichol: It just...

Koback: … is that in your personal Verizon account?

Nichol: Yes.

Koback: Yeah, so would you just, um, print that page or do something for me? 'Cause in the event that they are just, you know, computer generation deletion, uh, if there is something there, I'd like to try to save it as much as we can.

Nichol: Well, I mean, I wish you guys would've told me this two days ago because if they're only saving… it looks like they're not saving the body of the messages. It looks...

Koback: Right.

Nichol: … like what they're doing is they're saving the date and time, it's a timestamp for the text messages...

Koback: Sure.

Nichol: … and who they came from, and it looks like they're only saving 'em for a week, like...

Koback: Right.

Nichol: … today they went to 8-14, and I'm afraid that if I wait, tomorrow they'll only go to 8-15.

Koback: Right.

Nichol: You know what I'm saying?

Koback: Yeah, so if you print those tonight...
Nichol: So, and - and I was...
Koback: ... that'd be great.
Nichol: ... just, like, I know, I was so bummed. I was, like, the two days I needed, like, right before where they cut it off.
Koback: Yeah, that's okay.
Nichol: Um...
Koback: I think we're gonna be okay with what we have, um, like I said, I'm just trying to make sure we have as much information as possible. And sometimes it takes a little bit of extra work to get to that information, but I'm okay with that because it could be very important later on down the line. It could be very important now, um…
Nichol: Uh…
Koback: … but I just don't wanna lose…
Nichol: ... I agree. Well, and 'cause it's, like, I know that sometimes, like, I can miss some things, but also, like, I want you guys to see those texts because maybe there is something important there that I can't even think of, you know...
Koback: Sure.
Nichol: ... or not only that, but, like, it validates everything that I'm saying to you guys...
Koback: Right.
Nichol: ... you know?
Koback: Okay.
Nichol: Um...
Koback: Well, I'll work on the texts and, um, like I said, I'm gonna talk to, um, the other agent who, um, is kind of the… the lead agent on this case, and I think that she's gonna wanna sit down with you and kind of, go through the contexts of the messages to get a better idea, you know, 'cause text messages are just words, you… you… we don't know what was said before that in a phone conversation, or what might've been followed up in a phone conversation or what started… prompted a text message to be sent, either from a prior meeting or something like that. So it… it'll be very helpful. Um, I don't think that's gonna happen this week 'cause I know she's super busy, so just be patient with that. Uh, that information isn't going anywhere, we have that retained. And… and I appreciate you saying that you'll, uh, cooperate in doing that.

Nichol: No, I mean, I really wanna help you guys, I mean, I… I have no reason not to help you guys. I, uh, I… I'm… I can't even believe he's trying to blame this on his wife. I… I just… I can't even imagine how hard he's making this on the family right now. It's just… it makes me so sad. It's so sad.
Koback: Right.
Nichol: I, uh...
Koback: All right. Well, keep taking...
***Nichol:* …** we…
***Koback:* …** notes as new things come to mind.
Nichol: Okay. Um, but I was gonna tell you I did get my phone log...
Koback: Okay.
***Nichol:* …** um, um, I got everything through the 13th was on my last month's billing statement, so I got a .pdf of that. I did save it. It's on my desktop, um, and it shows all my inco… incoming and outgoing in it and it… it shows where it was generated from so if I was at work it shows Platteville, and if I was at home it says Thornton, like...
Koback: Sure.
***Nichol:* …** um, I've got those.
Koback: Do you have, um, do you have my email address on my business card?
Nichol: Okay. You want me to just email that to you?
Koback: That'd be great. Then, um...
Nichol: Okay. And then I...
***Koback:* …** that'd be the easiest for both of us.
Nichol: Okay. And then my next billing cycle, uh, started on the 14th, so if you guys want home, I mean, if you want the phone records from the 14th, they're not in this nice pdf because they haven't billed 'em for me yet. They're in this weird, shitty *Excel* file and I tried to open it, and make it user friendly and readable, and I don't… I feel like it's an *Excel* sheet. I… I don't… I don't know...
Koback: It's fine. Yeah...
***Nichol:* …** what to do with it, I mean...
***Koback:* …** I know what it… it's in. You… it… it'll be fine, uh, you can send it to me however you have it.
Nichol: So you want the *Excel*? Okay, so do you want the *Excel* sheet too? 'Cause I, like I said...
Koback: Sure.

Nichol: … I have the pdf copy goes...
Koback: Yep.
Nichol: … through the 13th, and then the *Excel* is, like...
Koback: That...
Nichol: … sheet is, like, 14th on, but the date… the dates don't show up on the *Excel* sheet when I… when I downloaded it. I don't know. I gotta look at it and see...
Koback: Okay.
Nichol: … if I can get that to… to work. And if… and if it doesn't work, I mean, at the end of this billing cycle, which will be in probably, like, three weeks or so, uh, then I can give you the 14th...
Koback: Yep.
Nichol: … you know what I mean?
Koback: And then just - yeah, you can just send me everything that you have, uh, off this most recent, and then when your bill comes in if - if you'd be, uh, if you'll remember to just send that to me. And, um, we're...
Nichol: Yeah.
Koback: … we're getting those records, but again, I always like to ask… they're your records, so I always ask for you to share those with me, uh, that way, uh, it just shows cooperation, number one. Number two, if we don't have something, then I don't have to go back and write a warrant to get it. You're… you're, uh, consenting to give it… that stuff to me and… and it's helpful to our investigation and that's all that we really care about.
Nichol: I know. And I want you guys, you know, to… to… to do the best that you can and so anyway that I can help… I'm really disappointed about those texts. I just… honestly, that wasn't the first thing on my mind when I deleted them. I was just, I was so disgusted with him. I was, like, 'I don't even wanna look at this, like, you need to go away from my life, right now.' And I just boom, got rid of it.
Koback: Okay.
Nichol: I didn't even realize, like, Oh, my God. These guys are gonna need...
Koback: You ca…
Nichol: '...these.' Um...
Koback: It's okay. You… you didn't know. We… we've talked… don't beat yourself up about the texts, we'll figure it out.

Nichol: I… ((unintelligible)).
Koback: Okay?
Nichol: Okay.
Koback: All right?
Nichol: I'm - I'm hoping we can recover most of them. Um, I think I had one more thing to say to you. I don't know. The media is really ((unintelligible)). Today it's crazy. After I got off the phone with you, I literally probably got numerous phone calls from friends and numerous texts from people saying that the media is coming to their houses and asking them questions. So I don't know. I must be hiding out pretty well because...
Koback: Good.
Nichol: … they're going to great links, I've had people that I haven't talked to in a year trying to contact me, like, people, old coworkers that I hardly even know are, like, 'Hey, are you okay?'
Koback: Well, just continue to do what you're doing and your choice whether to talk to them or not. Again, you don't have to talk to them if you don't want to. Um, and just I… like we said before, your dad is probably your best ally in this and hopefully he'll take some of the brunt of, uh, these people phoning and… and tell them to go away if that's your wishes, and then, uh, go from there. But stay in touch with me. If you go somewhere, like, you know, if you're gonna leave the state or whatever, just make sure you… let me know your phone number, um, and… and, uh, an address where… if I had to send you legal correspondence, you know, I could send that to you. Okay?
Nichol… I will - I will definitely do that. I, you know, I've already discussed the situation with my dad where it's, like, you know, I really need to see, A, what's going on with my employer and, B, like, I kind of wanna wait until a lot of this media stuff happens and figure out, like, who is safe to give my new phone number to and who is and right now, I don't have an answer for that, so I'm just kind of rolling with that number that I have.
Koback: Uh, I...
Nichol: So, we...
Koback: Exactly, so...
Nichol: … we will see and I'm...
Koback: … uh, your number is, um, that information is, uh, available to, uh, the defence and the prosecution. When - when I write a re…

like, if you change your number, um, it is available to… I… I have to generate a report so that goes out in discovery, so that could be, uh, something that they would see. Now whether or not they share that with the media or not, I mean, I'm not concerned that the prosecutor's office is going to. I know my office isn't going to, um, so just keep that in mind, um, you… you know, changing your stuff, uh, you… you're almost obligated. In fact, I'll tell you you are to keep me updated because you are a witness and you're critical in this case, so we know how to - if somebody, you know, an attorney needed to get you for a… a hearing or something, uh, how to get in touch with you and that's really what it's about. Um, it's not us keeping track of you or any of that stuff, so just… just remember that.

Nichol: Oh, and I… I would definitely keep you guys in the loop. I mean...

Koback: Okay. Good.

Nichol: … and - and I guess, uh, my last question is how long does it usually take for them to find people? 'Cause I feel like I'm pretty stashed because of how I've kept my information for the last few years anyways, I think, has...

Koback: I...

Nichol: … done me some justice.

Koback: … I don't know, I mean, it just depends. I think if… sooner or later, I mean, it's… you can always find somebody, I'll tell you that. Now they have a lot of money and they have a lot of resources and… and they have a big desire to figure out who you are, um, so...

Nichol: Right.

Koback: … I mean, do I think at some point that, you know, you're gonna have to tell them, no comment or I don't wanna talk to you or give a statement, whatever you decide to do, um, yeah, I do. And… and when - I don't know, I mean, that's a personal thing for you and… and your family, how you guys wanna decide to deal with that and maybe even, um, you know, with legal counsel at some point, you might wanna have somebody just to say, 'Hey, leave my client alone.' Um, you know, I don't know. And maybe that's just your dad, uh, your dad seemed very concerned and willing to help when we met last week and maybe he's just the right person to answer that question, uh, or, you know, to tell the media, 'Look, my daughter's not interested in talking to any of you, stop.' You know, um, I… I don't know. And… and it's not really a great question for me. I'd like to tell you, uh, I mean, I know what I would do, but I can't tell you what to do. Do you know what I mean?

Nichol: Right.

Koback: O… only...

Nichol: Right.

Koback: … you can make that choice.

Nichol: Okay.

Koback: So, but, uh, you're...

Nichol: Oh, understood.

Koback: … to answer your question, I think if they wanna find you, they're not gonna stop until they do. I… I really do.

Nichol: No, I… I agree. I think… I'm… I'm impressed with the lengths that they're going to right now. It's kind of nice, but they haven't done it yet. They've been looking for two days, and they've been unsuccessful.

Koback: Well, hopefully if you wanna stay hidden you will, and if I can help in any way - not with that stuff 'cause I'm not really able to do that, but, um, you know, the rest of the stuff… I know we had you talking to Hazel and it sounds like we got that stuff going. If anything new comes up, don't hesitate to call me. Don't make it… don't think you're bothering me or this is a problem. This is what I do. This is very important getting all this down...

Nichol: Okay.

Koback: … and getting it… getting a record of it is very important, okay? So don't hesitate to call me.

Nichol: Okay. And then my question, um, can they release my name to the papers if they have, like, no information on me? I'm sure that they're trying to put two and two together at this point, but I feel like that would be a very bold statement to be, like, this is who it was when they have no idea.

Koback: I mean, so I… can they… they're… they can do anything they want really, um, is there repercussions for doing anything? Of course. Um, do I think that they're gonna be cautious? Um, I… I think that the media really, you know, they get involved in all these cases and they don't report, uh, something until they they know accurately, um, especially names because if… let's say they say that, uh, your name is, you know, Nikki somebody else and you're the wrong person. Do they open themself up to exposure to a lawsuit for slandering somebody's name? Absolutely. So I don't think that you need to worry about that, um, I do think it… like I told you this morning, there is some warrants that have gone out, um, I do believe that they're sealed, uh, that do have your name in it because of the phone information, um, some of that stuff between you and Chris. Your name is in those. Now those are sealed. When those come unsealed, I don't know. Um, that… that's a judge's decision, not mine, so a judge can continue to keep that sealed for the, you know, the length of the investigation if he wants to because it protects our investigation by not releasing information. And that's the purpose of that is so people don't know what we're doing so the media can't dig and find out what we're doing and they can't damage the case that we're building, so, um, that… that could go on forever, so I… I don't really have an answer for that. I… I don't know how long.

Nichol: Okay.

Koback: It… it varies, um, you know, depending on the judge and… and some legal decisions.

Nichol: Okay.

Koback: All right?

Nichol: All right. Well, I...

Koback: Hang in there.

Nichol: ... appreciate your time and if I think of anything else, I will let you know...

Koback: Okay.

Nichol: ... but hopefully that is the end of it and...

Koback: Great.

Nichol: ... I will send you that, um, that record just for this month and then I'll see if I can clean up the *Excel* thing, but I don't like something that you can manipulate data. I'd rather just give you… wait till the end of the month and give you the .pdf for the 14th...

Koback: Sure.

Nichol: ... moving forward.

Koback: That's fine too.

Nichol: That would make me feel better.

Koback: That's fine. And then, um, I will be in touch with you here in the next, you know probably sometime next week to try to get you set up to come in and sit down, uh, to talk about all this information.

Nichol: Okay.

Koback: Okay? Hang in there, Nicky.

Nichol: All right. Thank you.
Koback: All right. We'll talk to you soon.
Nichol: Ha… have a good night.
Koback: You too.
Nichol: Bye.

SEVEN

Fourth Police Interview - Nichol Kessinger

(TAKEN FROM DISCOVERY FILES VIDEO FOOTAGE)

23rd August 2018

Nichol - Nichol Kessinger
Koback - Agent Kevin Koback
Tammy - CBI Agent Tammy Lee
Stacy - Stacy Galbraith
Matt - Tech guy
Hazel - Victim Advocate

This is the only video interview that has been released (apparently there was another one in September which wasn't released).

Agent Kevin Koback shows Nichol Kessinger into the interview room. She is dressed in jeans and a grey long-sleeved hoodie. Her hair is tied in a high ponytail and she has sunglasses on the top of her head.

Koback: Right, here is good.
Nichol: Okay.
Koback: I'll be right back, all right? I'm just gonna get Tammy so she can come in... introduce yourself, all right?

Nichol: Okay.
Koback: I'll be right back.
Koback leaves the room and returns moments later.
Koback: You all right?
Nichol: Yeah.
Koback: These rooms are recorded. So anything you say in here is subject to recording. Just so you know.
Nichol: Okay.
Koback: And you said on your text that you might've remembered some more stuff. So let's do...
Nichol: Yeah.
Koback: ...the phones first.
Nichol: Um, I need to...they gave me a piece of paper to transfer my contacts. Wouldn't do it for me but...
Koback: You should be able to just put 'em on the iCloud.
Nichol: I don't know...
(Laughter).
Nichol: ... how to do this. They said to follow this app. I can't even find the App Store on this phone.
Koback: Is it uh Android?
Nichol: Yeah. So strange...I um...I tried to transfer all the stuff from this phone to this phone last night and so it's synching up old texts. Like stuff I don't even have saved in here.
Koback: Were any of them from Chris?
Nichol: Yeah a few but not many. It's pretty short. There's ten or twelve and there's a few from those days but most of it like...
The door opens and Agent Tammy Lee and Stacy Galbraith enter.
Tammy: Hi! Hello, Nikki. I'm Tammy.
Koback: Come in Stacy.
Stacy: Hello Nikki.
Koback: Nikki, this is Tammy.
Nichol: Hi Tammy, nice to meet you.
Stacy: I'm Stacy Galbraith.
Nichol: Nice to meet you.
Tammy: How are you doing?
Nichol: I'm all right.
Tammy: Getting through it?

Nichol: Trying.
Tammy: Yeah?
Koback: Stressing out.
Stacy: Stressing out? Yeah, you looked stressed out.
Tammy: Did you get some therapy figured out?
Nichol: I'm waiting for you guys to get back to me on that. But I'm tryin'...
Stacy: It'll help.
Tammy: Does Hazel need to...?
Koback: Yeah, we're gonna see if Hazel comes in so...Weld County's just...I had to write a letter yesterday for Weld County to approve to pay for her treatment.
Stacy: Oh.
Koback: And that's gotta go through a board. Because it's kind of unusual, since she's not an 'eye-witness'...
Tammy: Right.
Koback: But uh it sounded like there's not gonna be any opposition to it. It's just a process.
Tammy: Oh. Okay.
Koback: So when you go through the text messages Tammy and probably Stacy will be there, so you guys know each other. Or if they reach out to you, you know that they're not the media.
Nichol: Can you guys give me your cards so I just...everyone?
Stacy & Tammy: Yeah. Sure. Okay.
Stacy and Tammy leave the room
Koback: Thank you.
Nichol: And now with this new phone I've got so many numbers that I'm sure I can figure out who they are...
Koback: So...
Nichol: I need to just deal with that if you can just help me get all of my contacts from this phone to that phone.
Koback: I can get a tech guy to help me 'cause I'm bad at it too.
Nichol: They gave me instructions on it.
Koback: So this is your old phone?
Nichol: This is the one that I use for communication. This is the one that's going to you guys. This one's mine now.
Koback: This one's nicer.
Nichol: I know. I iPhones suck. I don't need to have this back.

Koback: Okay. So you're gonna...you wanna move the contacts from there to there.
Nichol: That's all I wanna do. Once you guys do that then you guys can have this phone. I mean he gave me a way to do it so I think I need to connect to Wi-Fi, and then I need to download this app and then I think, once I download it, I can sync it up. And I need to just download the app on both phones.
Koback: Let me get a guy who knows about Wi-Fi.
Nichol: Okay.
Koback: Is your password still (he recites the password).
Nichol: Yeah, that never changed.
Koback: So that's gonna be that one? And which one is getting all the new text messages, your new phone?
Nichol: Mm hmm. It only got a few and now I get what you're saying they're out of order, they're scrambled, they're missing. They don't make sense. I got super excited when I saw them because I was like, maybe it'll be all of 'em, but it's not.
Koback: So... maybe what I'll ask. We have a device that can download that too.
Nichol: This one, too? I mean I don't know if that'll work but we can try it.
Tammy and Stacy return with their cards
Tammy: Here's mine. Here's hers.
Nichol: Thank you.
Stacy: And then Kevin knows how to get ahold of us after hours if we need to do that, too.
Nichol: I appreciate that.
Koback: I'm gonna go get Matt. I'll be right back. I need him to download...
Tammy: Are you getting her a spare phone is that what…?
Koback: She has her own spare phone but when she linked her accounts, a bunch of messages between her and Chris were recovered on her new phone.
Tammy: Oh, okay.
Koback: So I'm gonna just Cellebrite on her new phone so we don't have to take all her phones.
Tammy: Yeah. No doubt.
Stacy: Are you good in here?

Nichol: Sure.
Tammy: You want some water or anything?
Nichol: Please.
Tammy: Okay.
All three agents leave the room
Nichol: Okay, so, App Store. (Nichol is talking to herself trying to figure out her phone).
Tammy enters
Tammy: Here's water.
Nichol: Thank you. I appreciate it.
Tammy: Need anything else?
Nichol: I think I'm good.
Tammy: Okay. They'll be in here in just a few minutes, okay?
Nichol: Thank you.
Tammy leaves
Nichol: (Mumbling)… wonder what that's connected to?
Nichol: (Cursing.)
Nichol: Just so much fucking bullshit.
Nichol: WTF?
Koback returns a few minutes later
Koback: All right. Tech guy… tech guy's coming to help us.
Nichol: I would do it myself but it's, like… there so many different things on here.
Koback: Okay.
Nichol: Like right now.
Koback: So it's not very new?
Nichol: This is old.
Koback: Okay.
Nichol: I haven't used this phone since 2016.
Nichol: And so all these numbers on here are numbers of people I've gotten since… What I don't want with the media and all this other stuff going on is to have a phone just full of unknown contacts.
Koback: Sure. I get it. So he's gonna come over and turn your Wi-Fi on and figure out how to move...
Nichol: All of that.
Koback: He… he knows...
Nichol: I'll let him do that. I give up.

Koback: Okay. So your phone this time-do you have any objections to us looking at everything in your phone?
Nichol: Why do you guys need that? I'm just curious. Like why do you need everything as opposed to just stuff between me and him?
Koback: So, well, because it's easier to get if we're looking at all the material. Let's say I take everything off your phone, I can put a date in. Like, let's say, August 10th through the 15th because those are critical days...
Nichol: Uh hun...
Koback: ... but other conversations between you and Chris or other text messages between you and Chris, from June or July... do make it harder for me to find all those. Do you understand what I mean?
Koback: If it's easier for them to just take everything…
Nichol: Even though it's the same phone number?
Koback: I don't know. Are they?
Nichol: Yeah. Except for when I first met him and it was his APC thing.
Koback: Okay, and then what about your phone log? It's always his 910 number?
Nichol: It's the same number all the time. Like that one or originally was his other one—
Koback: We talked about your GPS location—knowing where your phone is at certain times.
Nichol: Yeah, I mean you guys can have all that I was just like, oh my gosh, it's so many texts on here between me and all my friends. I'm like, do they really want all this stuff?
Koback: Well, is there anything in those texts that you'd be concerned with?
Nichol: Not really.
Koback: So... Well... Not really or yes or no?
Nichol: No, I mean like...
Nichol: Well the other day my dad and I decided to do some damage control because a lot of people were like, 'Hey the media's calling me. I don't know what to say.' And I just told 'em all, like, I didn't say anything, I pretty much just said, 'If the media tries to contact you, tell them no comment.' I was like, 'Please be nice to them. You do not need to talk to them'. I was like, 'I'm safe. I'm not in trouble. I didn't break

any laws.' And I was just like, 'Just send your love and support.' And that was all I said to people.

Koback: So did that prompt all the phone calls of people going, 'Are you okay?'

Nichol: No. They were prompting me.

Koback: All right.

Nichol: That is why I did that because I didn't want to say that but I was getting all sorts of texts from people that were like, 'The media shouldn't contact me. I don't know what to do.'

Nichol: I didn't tell 'em I was a witness. I didn't tell them anything about that. It was just like, 'Just say no comment.' I need you to do this.

Koback: Okay.

Nichol: And then a couple of my super… super close friends I asked 'em if they'd be courteous enough to take all the pictures that we had of each other off Facebook and social media and they said 'yes'.

Nichol: And that was a couple of really close friends.

Koback: Is there any text messages between you and friends that reference anything that would be concerning regarding this case?

Nichol: No.

Koback: Like, talking about Chris? I think you've told me that you've never really talked with...

Nichol: My friends about him? No and like my friend's dad died last night, like yesterday.

Koback: I'm not worried about that.

Nichol: No I know but she started like… OMG she was really drunk last night. She started freaking out. She's like, 'I don't know what's going on in your life.' She's like, 'I don't know if it pertains to this case.' She just sent me like a screenshot of a news article of that case. And she was just like…

Koback: What about conversations-

Nichol: I… I didn't mention that it had anything to do with that. She's like, 'I don't know if that's what it is.' 'He works at *Anadarko*.' She's like, 'I really don't give a shit.' She's like, 'I just really just need you to be here with me and my dad.' And this and this and this. She was just kind of upset because I had asked her... um ... to please say no comment to the media. And it happened to be right when her dad died. And I think she was feeling a little, like...yeah. But I mean you guys can read this. There's nothing in there of me actually saying anything about it. I just told her…

Koback: What's your phone number on that phone?

Nichol: … 720… It's the same number that's on this one. So, no. I mean you guys can… you guys can look at it.

Koback: So between… there was a conversation that I asked you about... between you and Charlotte.

Nichol: That's the same girl.

Koback: That's the same girl who was freaking out?

Nichol: Yeah.

Koback: So was there ever a conversation about kids with you and Charlotte? Like you…?

Nichol: I can't remember the exact context. I told her that I'd been hanging out with a guy who had kids.

Koback: Okay and what...?

Nichol: She has not even put any of this...

Koback: All right. So your conversations about him having kids: How did that go?

Nichol: I mean I don't know I just told her, like she...uh...

Koback: Did you delete that or is it still on there?

Nichol: Yeah. No, no, no, no, no, no, no. I have no reason to delete anything else on my phone. The reason I deleted all this stuff with Chris was because he was making me feel really uncomfortable. And I didn't want to see it in my phone anymore.

Koback: Okay.

Nichol: Um... yeah let me scroll all the way back here. Me and this girl talk a lot. No. She is like...

Koback: So let's just, while we're here, because...We talked about this before but we didn't talk about the specific context of what that message said regarding the children. So obviously, this situation that we're looking at now, with the death of two children and all the other circumstantial stuff going around in the case... It. You. I just wanna make sure there was no comments ever made by you regarding, you know, children or dislike of children... Or love of children. Either way. Do you know what I mean?

Nichol: Oh yeah, I guess. Let me find that... Uh... I think this is where this starts. I mean, you guys can just take whatever you want off of there.

Koback: So it is easier for me to just take everything than it is to single it out.

Nichol: I know.

Koback: Plus, for the purposes of this case, the less exposure, you know, we already have initially you drew concern from me when you told me you deleted everything from Chris. I've already told you that. You understand why. There's no question as to why that might cause concern.

Koback: So if there's anything else that ever comes up, I have it. And then we can just discuss it. Do you understand what I mean?

Nichol: Mm hmm.

Koback: All right.

Nichol: It's right here. This is where it starts. She starts... right there.

Nichol: She starts talking about her and her fiancé. So that was weeks ago. And she hasn't brought it up since really or connected the dots or said shit. I mean and you guys can look through all those texts. And I don't know when that was. That was definitely when things were going good so this is weeks prior I'm assuming. I think the date is at the top of whenever we started texting that day.

Koback: Okay. It looks... this is...

Nichol: We talk a lot.

Koback: Tuesday, August 7th 2018.

Nichol: Yeah.

Koback: So. I reference everything to Sunday the 12th of August, the day of the murders.

Nichol: So that's the only conversation like that on there I believe on my phone. I don't think there's anything else. And she even last night like still wasn't even...She's still so worried about her dad. Other than that, there shouldn't really be anything on there with other people. But you guys can just scroll everything off that phone if you want.

Koback: As long as you're okay with that, that's would be…

Nichol: I mean if that makes your life easier...

Koback: It's not just about making it easier, just less… so if... there's any question. Some… like I told you before... the two girls you just met did a lot of interviews in this case. They've done a lot of work. They may know things that I don't.

Nichol: Mm hmm.

Koback: There's no way that we can all know everything. So they might go, 'Oh,' because somebody else is the one who told me about Charlotte and this message.

Nichol: Well that's probably why.

Koback: I've never read this.

Koback: Potentially I'm… yeah…

Nichol: I'm assuming that's what that is because I said his name. And I don't even think she's put two and two together because last night it was just the way she was talking. She wasn't like, 'This is him. This is it.' She was like, 'I don't know what's going on. I just assumed this is it because this guy worked at *Anadarko*.' But she is not even processing....what is occurring.

Koback: What do you mean by, 'Can tell he has a lot to take care of in life'? What did you mean when you said that?

Nichol: His mortgage and he has kids... and responsibility. I mean he's a father with a house.

Koback: You're even saying in here, 'He's all about his kids.'

Nichol: Yeah, and she was asking me somewhere in there, like... I mean everything I had to say about him at that point was really positive. Like I think I made it clear that I wasn't one hundred percent sure that this was the man of my dreams and I was gonna spend the rest of my life with him or anything. But I was enjoying the time that I was spending with him at that point.

Koback: You're referencing that he has two kids. And then you don't like that? Um, because you want to have that experience with somebody else? Is that...?

Nichol: I just know that I wasn't sure if he was the one I wanted to be with, because he had already done everything.

Koback: Okay.

Nichol: Like, I was, like, it would be really nice to have kids and have my own marriage and all that stuff, but that was never anything I conveyed to him.

Koback: So she said… you said, he's handsome, huh? Did you send her a picture?

Nichol: Mm hm.

Koback: And that's not attached here. Is that because what you… from what you deleted?

Nichol: I think it's from when I deleted all my photos of his stuff.

Koback: He's kinda short.

(Laughter).

Nichol: I mean, I talked to her knowing that I wouldn't talk to him as my girl. You know what I'm saying?

Koback: I get it. I'm just teasing you a little bit.

(Laughter).

Koback: … Seems like you're just talking about shoes and…

Nichol: Other stuff.

Koback: Okay, so…

Nichol: But then she brought it up again last night.

Koback: Brought up what?

Nichol: That case, but she didn't connect the dots. She was freaking out with her dad just dying. She was really upset. She wanted me to come see her on Saturday because it's his wake…

Koback: Unexpected?

Nichol: Kinda, sorta, yeah. He had Parkinson's. So, kinda, but not… you know what I'm saying?

Koback: Mm hmm.

Nichol: It's a very drawn out thing, but she's having a really hard time with it. I knew she would and she's just… she was like, 'Can you make the wake on Saturday?' And I'm just like, I'm really hesitant to leave the house, and I didn't tell her that, but I was like, 'I don't know, I'll try'. I'm gonna go, but I'm not gonna tell her until it's right before I have to be there. And she started bringing up…

Koback: So where did she reference, 'is Chris the guy?' I'm more interested in…

Nichol: No, she didn't even ask me, and she was just like, she's like… 'I don't know what's going on. She's like… you can see it'.

(Laughter).

Nichol: Uh, hold on.

Koback: Okay. So you mentioned on your text before you'd come in that there was other information on your texts that you thought of that was important again. Wanna tell?

Nichol: Yeah, let me. Get so side-tracked.

(Laughter)

Koback: I'll look at this while you do that and then…

Nichol: I'll show you where it is.

Koback: Yeah, show me where it is.

Nichol: There's so much in here, like, I'll just say…

Koback: You guys talk a lot.
Nichol: Oh, yeah, she is, like, my… right here… so first, she sends me this. And she doesn't ask me about him. She's saying he looks like her ex. That's when she first brings him up. She doesn't even mention me at that point. I don't even think she realizes it's the same guy. Like, legitimately. I think this girl is so wrapped up in all the stuff she's got going on right now, that I don't even think it's even processing. I mean, you can just tell by the way that she talks, see…? And she's all upset 'cause I asked her to…
Koback: Mm hm.
Nichol: … not talk to the media and it happened to be the day that her dad died and I'm sitting trying to comfort her.
Koback: Is this your best friend?
Nichol: Yes. This girl is, like, my whole world.
Koback: Alright. But you're not talking about children or your relationship with Chris or anything like that?
Nichol: No. The only time I ever mentioned him was, like, that one day.
Koback: Okay.
Nichol: And I didn't even remember that I had said that to her because I know there's so much…
Koback: What's her phone number? (????). So, I'm not gonna call her but at some point we might wanna talk to her. Just so you know, I mean, sooner or later she's gonna connect the dots or you're gonna tell her, right? If she's your best friend.
Nichol: I'm not gonna tell her. If she figures it out, she figures it out.
Koback: Okay. Um, if we're gonna talk to her I'd let you know beforehand. Is that fair?
Nichol: Yes. So I can give her the heads up. And then she apologized to me because she was being kind of crazy. She was…
Koback: So, tell me about the info that you remember.
Nichol: Okay. See right her… hold on… uh, she says, 'look man, I know you work at *Anadarko*. He did too. I know he murdered his wife and kids. I know he was a doll? Dog? I know you're my best friend. I know you have a good heart. I know that that guy needs to go to jail, and he will. I know you don't want publicity. I know that, as a witness, if you say anything it can cause a mistrial. I know you don't want that

and neither do I. Fuck the media. I want my best friend here'. I never fucking said anything to her about a trial.

Koback: Okay, but…

Nichol: See, look, she goes, 'I don't even care if you flirted with him or more. I know you had nothing to do with what happened. I don't care if your job is having an open investigation. I'm not gonna ask you a single question, but my pops died and you're my best friend'.

Koback: Okay.

Nichol: And I said, 'Please stop talking about that'. And she said, 'What? Are you on house arrest?' And she kept saying 'My father died. WTF!' She was not okay last night and I was just trying to, like…

Koback: Understandable.

Nichol: … mitigate this. Um, and I was trying to calm her down. And I said, 'Charlotte, I'm trying hard to be the best friend I can be to you right now', I said, 'I don't want to talk about that case'. I didn't say the case, I said that case, like I wasn't even affiliated with it all, 'and you need to respect that. I'm here for you regarding your dad… you know that'. And then she…

Koback: But let's go…

Nichol: Freaking out, I'm freaking out.

Koback: You guys never had a conversation except for this past text message about Chris and his children?

Nichol: No, that… that was it.

Koback: That's fine.

Nichol: I mean, 'cause he wasn't really something that I super wanted everybody to know about, and I shouldn't have even mentioned it when she brought it up, like, what she had going on sexually with her fiancé and it… it happened, but at that point…

Koback: You guys are best friends, it's understandable.

Nichol: Yeah, see. And she keeps trying to talk about it. She said, 'if you're under investigation by the police, I don't care. Why can't you attend your so-called best friend's father's death? It doesn't make sense to me'. And then all I told her was, 'stop!'.

Koback: ((Unintelligible))… or her dad…?

Nichol: Yeah, and she is freaking out… And finally, I just told her, 'you, know, getting mad with me isn't gonna bring your dad back'. And that…

Koback: Set her off?

Nichol: … is when she chilled. Well, she kinda went on another rant, but it had nothing to do with Chris and then she apologized to me this morning for being drunk and sad and angry that her dad died.
Koback: What other new information?
Nichol: Uh, okay. Um, let's see, we've got so much going on, I didn't even have time to print this off for you.
(Laughter)
Koback: You… you… you make sure before you leave you see Hazel —you need some help.
Nichol: I know, I've been asking… Um, oh, he was talking for a few weeks like he…
Koback: Give me a time frame.
Nichol: Okay… Okay, so he went to North Carolina. When he came back from North Carolina I was informed sometime, either when he was on the trip or when he was getting back, but in that area, that they filed for divorce and that, um, they were gonna put the house up. And he… for sale, and he was like, 'she's the one that called the realtor. 'Cause he told me that he had spoke to her when he was in North Carolina about it and then the next day she was the one who called the realtor.
Koback: When you say she, you mean Shanann?
Nichol: Yes.
Koback: And when you say, the timeframe they came back from North Carolina, you don't remember the specific dates? Was it the first or second week of August?
Nichol: And yeah, I think I told you guys when they left. I think he left on Tuesday 31st July 2018.
Koback: I do remember you saying that.
Nichol: And I don't remember when he came home. I really don't. I don't remember if it was, like…
Koback: So, was this a phone conversation or a text conversation?
Nichol: No. Um, this happened over the phone and he told me that… I don't know… that was when I had said, 'hey, when you go to North Carolina I really think you should try to fix things with your wife', and he kept asking, 'well, what about us?' and I was trying to, kinda, take a step back and see if he would fix things before attempting to pursue things with me because I wanted to know that if all these things he's saying, like, 'yes, we're getting separated', and 'yes…' you know, all

these things he's saying are happening are happening. I wanted to know that it was, like, you were doing this, like you said you were—prior to me coming into your life. And it had nothing to do with me, you know? And so, for me, it was like, huh, I just… I really wanted them to fix it. I would've just left the situation.
Koback: So, tell me, why Shanann calling the realtor and him mentioning that they were gonna be divorced…
Nichol: Was important?
Koback: … why you think that's important?
Nichol: Um, because, so, after that he was like, ' she's the one who called the realtor'. And I remember I was like, 'damn, that was fast', 'cause I knew he told me, like, 'we're gonna put the house up', but they said, he was like, 'we didn't know how much to offer for it and we were kinda trying to find somebody', and it was like, so for the first few weeks that I hung out with him, he kind of dragged his feet on, 'hey, this is happening'. And then, after North Carolina he's like, 'yeah, she wants to put the house up, she's the one that called the realtor', and I was kinda taken aback. Not necessarily at the speed of it, given how long he said they'd been separated, but the fact that she did it like, (she clicks her fingers), the day after he supposedly sat down and had a conversation with her about, 'hey, do we fix this or do we not fix this relationship?'.
Koback: So, do you remember how many days she was back in Colorado before leaving? Do you know that?
Nichol: Uh uh. Because I don't remember when they got home.
Koback: Right.
Nichol: I don't.
Koback: I'm just trying to get your memory jogged there on that. So, this is… they get home… he had told you North Carolina that they agreed to end their—finalise their relationship.
Nichol: Yeah.
Koback: They get home and she immediately wants to sell the house.
Nichol: Yeah. And then… so, um, I mean, I started thinking, okay, well, I know… well, in Colorado houses sell very fast here so I was like, 'what's your plan?' You know? And I was like, 'because you might wanna be prepared'. And I remember back when the whole concept came up of, 'you probably need to start looking for a new place pretty quick', and that was when he was kind of overwhelmed with it and I

told him, I was like, 'look, I just moved a few months ago', um, and... uh, I was like, 'to find a place that was comfortable for me it was like... it took a lot of research'. That's when I offered to help. I was like, 'I'll help you', and he seemed pretty gung-ho about it for the first week and he seemed very grateful, and I was putting work in on it. I was calling him and kinda letting him know about places and there really wasn't that many options in Brighton. Um, I found one—I actually texted it to myself before I texted it to him because I was going... I still have that in my phone too, um... because I found it and it was great, but it was right at the beginning of my search and then I was like, I don't want to inundate him...

Koback: So, you said a week. You think you worked on that for a week?

Nichol: No. I probably spent a few hours over a few days just trying to line it up for him.

Koback: I'm just trying to think about how many days she had been back while you were working on that. Do you know what I'm saying?

Nichol: Oh.

Koback: So, you said... did you actually work on it for a week straight?

Nichol: No, no, no no, no, no. It was just like a couple of days after work. I would just spend a couple of hours if I had time at the end of my day, or if I didn't go to the gym, and just sit down and, I mean, I could give you a day of when I worked on it, 'cause I texted that one to myself. This one. I loved this one. When is this? Saturday, August 11th 2018.

Koback: That's the night you guys went out?

Nichol: Uh, yeah.

Koback: To, er, the Lazy Dog.

Nichol: Yes.

Koback: Or the two Lazy Dog's. (Laughter)

Nichol: Yes.

Koback: All right. What else?

Nichol: Um, yeah. So the reason that this is so important is because he, up to that point, seemed like he was all about it and I was respecting him. I wasn't like, 'oh, you need to get this, you need to get that' I was like, 'what city do you want to live in? What side of town is she staying in?', you know? 'How close do you want to be to work? How close do you

want to be to your kids?' I mean, I asked him everything. I just wanted him to have something that was accommodating for his whole family. And he told me that she was probably going to stay in the Frederick area, but he never said for sure. The first time I asked him he's like, 'I don't know where she's gonna go, but she'll probably stay in this area'. And I was like, 'Chris, if you're gonna get an apartment you need to figure that out because the last thing you want is to be, like, an hour drive from your kids, it's like, you know, you've gotta be close'. And so, um, I ended up asking him again a couple days later and that was when he's like, 'I think she's staying in the Frederick area', and I was like, 'okay'. And that was when I was starting to get details. And if you guys find my text you'll see it. When I asked him, like, 'where do you want to live?' like, 'how close do you want to be to work?' like, those things. Like, you know, um, 'did you care what gym you go to?' like, 'what are you looking for', you know?
Koback: We talked about this previously.
Nichol: Yeah, yeah, yeah. So, the thing was... was he was like super gung-ho about it, and then, on Saturday, that day, um, I remember being outside with him when this conversation happened, but I don't know where. I don't know if we were, like, walking into the restaurant or walking to the car but I vaguely remember being outside with him and I was like... he had told me that he had wanted to go look at some places that upcoming week. Him and I were supposed to go do that on Wednesday. And I was like, um... I asked him, I was like, um, 'what places do you wanna go see?' And I was like, 'did you really like that place that I showed you?' because it was just super-convenient for everything. It had a little playground and it had a little pool. It would've been awesome for his kids. And it was cheap. And, um... and so... and it was close to Frederick. It was close to the gym. It was close to work. It was close to me. It was close to everything. And it was in Brighton, which is what he wanted. And so, um, I was like, 'did you want to go check that place out?' and he's like, 'yeah, I guess'. And he didn't seem sure anymore. And that was the part I wanted to tell you. I just figured I'd give you all the backstory.
Koback: Sure. Um, so he's not sure about that particular apartment or about even leaving?
Nichol: So, he told me that he looked at it and he told me that he thought it was nice, but he didn't really seem like his interest was piqued. And it was like, 'did you find anything that you really wanted

to look at?' And he told me, 'yeah, I found a few', but nothing that really, really piqued his interest. And I was like, 'you might wanna get started', and he's like, 'I found one'. And I asked him, 'well, which one is it? Because I think I've looked at every apartment in Brighton and maybe I'll remember it'. And he was like, 'I don't know, I don't remember the name of it', and he kind of, just like, disregarded it. And it was kind of strange to me because the whole week prior he was so excited that I was trying to help him because he's busy, I'm busy. So I was like, 'you look, I'll look, let's see if we can try to narrow it down to four or five spots. And then we'll find something that's good for you and your girls. You know, he seemed very enthusiastic about it. Like, during the week when conversations first really started ramping up about, like, 'you probably gotta figure something out because that house is gonna sell really fast', you know? 'Or at least be prepared'. And so…

Koback: So why do you think he was removed or not interested on your Saturday night, wherever you guys were?

Nichol: I don't know, I mean, sometimes I think about these things and I feel like they're all assumptions, but, at that point, maybe he already knew something that I didn't. I don't know. So it was just a complete mood change where he just didn't even seem that interested and I was like, 'okay', and I was like, 'well, we don't have to do that on Wednesday if you don't want to'. And he was like, 'no, no, I know I need to get it done', and then I was like, 'all right'.

Koback: Okay.

Nichol: You know, because I wasn't gonna force him, to do it. If he doesn't wasn't to do it, don't do it. Just say no. And you know, I was like… and for me, I was just offering to help because I know what a tedious task it is trying to find a new place to live.

Koback: Right.

Nichol: Um…

Koback: Any other new info you remember?

Nichol: Um, that part where he was just like, really unplugged on Saturday and then there was something else that went with that. Let me just think for a minute. It was, um… I didn't realise that I just wrote that part down. I can't believe I can't remember all this stuff.

Koback: Yeah, you've remembered so much stuff already.

Nichol: Slowly comes to me all the time. Some of this stuff is just

things that you would never think about and then, now that I'm like, hindsight's twenty-twenty. I'm starting to go back. But there's something else that happened on Saturday that had to do with all of this.
Koback: Think about it for a minute and let's see of my tech guy has his equipment charged.
Nichol: Do that. Do that.
Koback: We're gonna get your phone taken care of.
Nichol: Okay.
Koback: So, again, I'm gonna have you sign this voluntary consent.
Nichol: Yep.
Koback: It's the same thing you signed in Thornton saying that, you know, I didn't threaten you, intimidate you. You have a right to say no. I want you to read the document again. We're gonna take your phone —we're gonna use a program called Cellebrite. If you go to your phone store, that's what they use sometimes. They used to do this. They used to move your stuff back and forth. It's the same thing. They're gonna take that information and then, um, an examiner who is skilled in looking at cell phone data is gonna look at it, to try to recover the deleted material that we're after.
Nichol: I hope that they can get it.
Koback: So, the deleted material is what I'm after, obviously.
Nichol: I know it is. I feel so bad I did that. I didn't even, honestly that's not even what I was thinking about, I was just so… did not want any presence from him.
Koback: So you're okay with us…
Nichol: Just take the whole phone. Just take it, 'cause I feel like we've been trying…
Koback: I'm gonna put *all data* on here just for ease, okay?
Nichol: Yes. Take what you need.
Koback: So, read that and make sure you sign it, that you understand that we're gonna take all the data. Once I have all the stuff, I'll get your phone back to you.
Nichol: That's okay. I'm not even gonna use it anymore. I'm just gonna use this one.
Koback: Okay. I'm gonna still get it back to you as soon as we're done.
Nichol: Okay.
Koback: All right, so… Next week sometime, maybe?
Nichol: Okay.

Koback: Or the week after, something like, somewhere in that timeframe. Okay?
Nichol: Okay.
Koback: All right. Relax for a minute. I'll be back in a sec.
Koback leaves the room
Nichol: Oh… I got it. I got it. I got it.
Koback returns with Matt (the tech guy).
Nichol: I remembered by the way, I got it.
Koback: Remembered what?
Nichol: In my head. What I needed to tell you.
Koback: Okay.
Nichol: Okay. So, hi!
Matt: Hi, I'm Matt.
Nichol: I'm Nikki.
Matt: Nice to meet you.
Nichol: Hello. So, this is my original phone that these guys would like to have.
Matt: Okay.
Nichol: I have a lot of contacts on here that are not on the phone that I'm currently transferring to. And a lot of them, (she giggles), I need to have. Um, it would be greatly appreciated if we could get the contacts from this phone to just go to this phone so that all the text messages and everything have names and things connected to them.
Matt: Right, okay.
Nichol: So that I can… that's all I want to do. And I went to Verizon to switch to this phone and all the did was give me this little sheet of paper to follow which seems very simple and I'm usually pretty tech-savvy except for the fact that I can't get the app store to work on this phone and I can't get the Wi-Fi to work on this phone.
(Laughter)
Nichol: So that is the dilemma that I'm in.
Matt: All right.
Nichol: So, if you would be so kind as to just sync that up so I can give them what they need to end some…
Koback: I am not good on phone things.
Nichol: I'm usually pretty tech-savvy. After working in the oil field, you gotta get creative about things. They have technology but you're like in the sticks so everything wants to malfunction.

Matt: So, are all your contacts in this phone synced to the cloud—to the iCloud?

Nichol: I don't know.

Matt: Okay.

Nichol: I mean, some messages came over so I assume that everything is? But I really don't know. So maybe I'm not as tech-savvy as I thought.

Koback: What'd you remember? You just said you remembered something besides that.

Nichol: Oh. You want to have this conversation right now?

Koback: He's an agent. He works with me. He knows about this case.

Matt: I can step out if you feel uncomfortable?

Nichol: Uh, no. I mean, I don't know. Whatever…

Koback: You tell me.

Nichol: He had a fire stick he kept talking about. Do you know what a fire stick is?

Koback: No.

Nichol: Okay. You probably do, since you're a tech guy. They're like…

Koback: Oh, you mean an Amazon Fire stick?

Nichol: Yeah, yeah, yeah.

Koback: Okay.

Nichol: Okay. So, he didn't have it in his possession.

Koback: Who's he? Chris?

Nichol: Yes. So Chris mentioned to me that on Saturday, that same day, um, that… oh, 'cause this kind of went hand in hand with the whole apartment talk. 'Cause I was like… oh, that apartment that he said he found that he was like… I was like, 'what's it called?' And he was like, 'I don't remember'. And I was like, 'well, how much is it?' He was like, close to eleven hundred. And I was really taken aback by that 'cause I pay more than that and I don't really have that nice of a place and it's not a two bedroom, it's a one. So that part kind of seemed odd to me but I'd seen a few things online that were kind of cheap and I was just like, 'all right', and he's like, 'I'm just trying to cut costs'. I was like, 'that's cool. Like, how else are you doing that?' And it was just out of curiosity and he was like, 'well, I decided to get rid of cable'. And I was like, 'okay'. And I was kinda taken aback by that too because he loves sports. Dude, the guy lives and breathes football. So I, uh, I was like, 'okay'. I was like, 'that's a good cost to you, you know, to cut back on'. And he was like, 'yeah, I think I can watch… still stream sports via a fire stick', and I've heard things before. I don't really know a lot about them. Um, but he was saying he had a buddy working on it already for him.

Koback: Who's the buddy?

Nichol: He didn't say. I didn't ask.

Koback: Why do you think that's important?

Nichol: That he had all that set up? I don't know… I mean, it made me believe that he was…

Koback: That he was ready to move out? Is that?

Nichol: Oh, I get what you're saying. Yeah.

Koback: That he was ready to go?

Nichol: Yeah, that he was prepping. It still sounded like he was getting ready for everything to happen. Then the thing that I found really peculiar about the whole situation was the fact that he just kind of seemed disconnected about the apartment thing… on Saturday, whereas in previous conversations he was the one who brought it up. And he was the one who seemed really excited about it when I offered to help him do some leg work on trying to find him a spot for him and his girls.

Matt: Right. I'll be right back.

Matt leaves the room

Koback: Okay.

Nichol: So I don't… I don't know who his friend was. It was just weird because sometimes it seemed like some of the things he said he was still really… a lot of things made sense, and still to this day make sense. And then other things that he said don't make sense at all to me anymore. Or, like, they change.

Koback: Well, you know a lot more now, well, unfortunately, you know a lot more now about terrible things that may have happened to change the way you're thinking about what he said too. So… making you think differently about those kind of… that verbiage. Right?

Nichol: Yeah, definitely.

Koback: Okay. So…

Nichol: I think…

Koback: … we talked a lot about a lot of different things.

Nichol: I hope I'm helping.

Koback: You def… you certainly are.

Nichol: I hope so, 'cause I… so… I don't like having this stuff on the top of my head that it's so hard, and so many days I can tell that my mind is trying to block it all out right now, and I think it's almost like a subliminal coping mechanism and I'm trying not to… I'm trying not to think about it so I can help you guys out and I just… that's why I…
Koback: Why don't you give yourself a break for a day or two and just live a normal life? Stop thinking about this stuff for a day or two and then revisit it. Maybe that'll help you because you look like you're tired again.
Nichol: I lost my job yesterday so that's where that comes from.
Koback: You lost your job with the geosciences place as well? Okay, I'm sorry to hear that.
Nichol: ((Unintelligible)).
Koback: You mentioned with your skillset you should be easily employable in another, uh, locale?
Nichol: I don't know. I… you know… I hope somebody hires me. I hope people don't just see my name on a resume and just not hire me.
Koback: Well, your name hasn't even made it to the papers yet.
Nichol: Not yet.
Koback: So remember you said you had some locations you could go out of state? Maybe… I don't know if that's what you're thinking or…
Nichol: Yeah.
Koback: Whatever's gonna work for you.
Nichol: Yeah. I'm… I'm thinking a lot about all of that and it's just a matter of timing and trying to figure out when to do it. Don't attempt to do it all too soon. I don't have to do it all over again.
Koback: Tell me the name of the Geosciences company.
Nichol: Tasman.
Koback: Tasman.
Nichol: I think I was just so bummed because they told me that they would keep me and then they called me back and let me go and I was just like, 'man!'
Koback: So did they essentially fire you?
Nichol: Yes. For lack of a better term.
Koback: And that was yesterday?
Nichol: Yep. They said they let me go because they hired me to do a contract job and now that contract was over, which is unfortunate, because *Anadarko* actually offered to pay me for a while and *Tasman* said

no. So… I just wish they would've been honest with me in the first place, but it is what it is.
Koback: So now you're looking for a job too?
Nichol: I haven't even tried doing that. It's not even a priority to me at this point. But I will get dol, I mean, Hazel to help me out with this lease and sell my truck and change my entire life and hopefully somebody, somewhere will give me a decent job and give me a chance and not judge for all this whole disaster. So, that's why it's…
Koback: You said Hazel was gonna… was helping you with some of your lease stuff?
Nichol: Correct. Oh, yeah.
Koback: All right, so when you're here—I think she usually comes in in the afternoon today so check with her.
A woman enters and hands Koback a phone charger.
Koback: Awesome. So he must want this for something.
Nichol: I want to charge my phone. I didn't charge it last night… I charged it…
Koback: This one?
Nichol: Here.
Koback: What's this? Oh, this is your… this is the Verizon call logs.
Matt returns
Nichol: Through the 13th.
Koback: From what date to what date? You want this one back?
Nichol: I don't… it's a month… I don't know.
Matt: Sorry.
Koback: You're good.
Nichol: I don't… it's a month so it's probably whenever thirty days was. Probably July 14th I'd assume to August 13th. You'll see it… when you open it up you'll see it. But it's a month.
Koback: Can I just take this real quick and move it off your thumb drive and I'll give you your thumb drive…
Nichol: You can do whatever you want.
Koback: Okay.
Nichol: That's yours, um…
Koback: You don't need this back?
Nichol: Um… no. I mean, you can give it back if you want.
Koback: Yeah. I'll just go download this to my computer real quick.
Nichol: There's so… I think, so it's a month. It ended on the 13th. And

that's why I was saying when they bill me next month then I can give you the 14th and past that. And I could've given you the 14th now but… because they haven't billed me for it. Like, this is a nice pdf but the… the… their unbilled one in this janky *Excel* format and you can manipulate the data.

Nichol: Like, I don't… I don't want to give you that…

Koback: So what is on here specifically? A pdf of your complete phone bill for your cell phone?

Nichol: That ends on August 13th. I think after that…

Koback: I'm gonna go put this on my phone… I'm gonna go put this on my computer.

Nichol: My lease agreement is on there and I told Hazel that you had it.

Koback: Okay.

((Crosstalk))

Nichol: So, can you go give that to her because she needs that?

Koback: Yep, I will.

Nichol: And then, um… my… there's also a computer record of me talking to the Verizon Wireless people asking them if they can restore my tests and what they had to say about it. Just so you guys know that I did the due diligence to attempt to do that.

Koback: Sure. Okay.

Nichol: So those are the two things on there.

Koback: So, there… the messages that synced up when you started are on this phone, right?

Nichol: Mm hmm.

Koback: So when she started, like, this phone is two years old?

Matt: Okay.

Koback: But when she turned it on, a bunch of deleted messages from Chris that were on that phone synced up with that phone.

Matt: Okay.

Koback: So that's the one I want to try to rip.

Matt: Okay. So we're gonna download this phone—this one get the contacts…

Koback: This one's coming and going with us. Exactly. So this one's coming with us as evidence. That one we'll just rip so she has a phone.

Matt: Okay. I need you to log in to Google.

Nichol: I'm just trying to figure this out. I don't know if I know my password.
Matt: Okay. Hmm… that might be an issue.
Koback leaves the room
Nichol: I know… (Laughter) I mean, if you guys really can't do it, I'm sure I can go through and figure out who…
Matt: Well, there's another way we can do it. So we can try.
Nichol: Man. I'm usually really good about passwords but this one I'm not. I don't know. I really don't.
Matt: Okay.
Nichol: I was messing with this before you walked in here.
Matt: Okay. And that's the only way you can download apps, right?
Nichol: Was through this.
Matt: Yeah.
Nichol: I mean… I'll have to figure it out.
Matt: I'm not… I'm not an android guy so I don't know.
Nichol: I don't know. I never… I haven't used an Android phone in two years.
Matt: Okay.
Nichol: I guess I'll have to figure this out. That sucks, but it's okay.
Matt: Nope. There's another… there's another thing that we can try.
Nichol: Sorry. It's an inconvenience.
Matt: Nope. Did you have text messages? So, when I hooked up to Wi-Fi I think you got a couple more extra.
Nichol: Oh, I got these. Yeah. Those came in on my other phone. This was right when I transferred.
Matt: Ummm… so, I think your contacts should be, um, connected to the iCloud now, so you shouldn't lose 'em. And we can use… we can try and use our down… the machine that we use to download the phones can also transfer.
Nichol: That'll be…
Matt: I've never done that, so I don't know how it's gonna go but we're gonna give it a shot.
Nichol: Okay. It's just… that would be so nice because I was looking at these messages and I was like, oh my God, like, 'don't know, don't know, don't know, don't know, don't know'. I mean, again, I'm sure I could figure it out pretty quick if I read the text, but they're all different.

Matt: Okay.
Nichol: You would save me a lot of time. And stress.
Matt: We're keeping this one?
Nichol: Yes.
Matt: Downloading and giving it back?
Nichol: Yeah. And then this one, I think, he only needs one number off it and that one you guys will take everything.
Matt: Okay. But we're keeping the phone, right?
Nichol: Yeah.
Matt: Okay.
Nichol: That's yours.
Matt: Okay. Thanks. All right. Let me go see is I can transfer the contacts.
Nichol: Do you want the wall charger to go with you?
Matt: I'll just put it here so I won't forget it, but I don't need it right now. I will be right back. Or in a little bit.

Matt leaves the room.
A phone rings several times and goes unanswered.

Nichol: I don't know what the heck it is…

Hazel (The Victim Advocate) enters with Koback.

Hazel: Hi Nikki.
Nichol: Hello.
Hazel: How are you doing?
Nichol: I'm all right. I love your little blouse, that's adorable.
Hazel: Thank you. Thank you.
Hazel: So I don't want to take too much time, but I just wanted to say hello.
Nichol: Hi.
Hazel: How're you doing?
Nichol: All right.
Hazel: I hope we can…
Koback: I'm gonna step… I'm gonna step out.
Hazel: Okay.
Koback: Do you have the…? I have that now. I have the lease. I'll give

it to Hazel, okay? Um, did he get your phone taken care of?
Nichol: I don't know. He took 'em both. He said he was gonna try.
Koback: I'll step out for a few minutes. Give you guys a few seconds.
Hazel: Okay. All right.
Koback: If you remember anything else, we'll talk before you leave. All right? Um, Hazel said she knew that you had been fired so, um, maybe get some advice on that too, about potentially leaving here and starting… starting anew somewhere else. Probably is a good… good thing. All right? I'll be back in a few minutes.
Koback leaves the room
Hazel: So, I know *Anadarko*… you got fired, but the other company as well? Thank you.
Nichol: Yeah, well, *Anadarko* just terminated my contract. I mean, I don't blame them, it's just not a good look to be…
Hazel: Yeah.
Nichol: They offered… they were concerned and they offered to pay for a few weeks.
Hazel: Well, that's… that's pretty generous.
Nichol: It was very generous and *Tasman* cut it off. They're just like, 'we don't want to bill the contractor if you're not actually working'. It's like, I respect that, you know? I just… I don't know. I think, uh… kind of disappointed because they told me… You know, I informed them of my situation and then they contacted me a day later and they said, 'oh, you're good, don't worry about it. And they contacted me the day after and, pretty much, just let me go. It's like, just be honest.
Hazel: Well, did they give you another job or another appointment?
Nichol: They would've had to of. And I kind of had a solution for that situation too, but they didn't seem like they were all about it. So, I mean, it is what it is. I've only been working for them for four months, since April 2018, and they don't really know me that well.
Hazel: Tasman?
Nichol: Mm hmm.
Hazel: And so, are they saying that your contract with them is also terminated? Or that you just aren't working at *Anadarko* anymore and they'll find you another position?
Nichol: They told me originally that if I wasn't gonna work at *Anadarko* they'd find another place to put me. And then, they came back yesterday night and said, 'since you're not con… we hired you for the

contract with *Anadarko*, and since your contract with them is terminated we're letting you go.
Hazel: Okay. Did you call the person being communicated with?
Nichol: No. I just spent all day trying to do stuff for these guys…
Hazel: Yeah.
Nichol: … so I haven't had a chance.
Hazel: I think it might be helpful to talk to him… see what he has to say about it. And see if there's any… you know… he'll probably ask you what your contract with him was. And ask you for some more details and see if there's any way that legally he can help you out or if he can create some sort of mediation or something like that. At the very least negotiate a positive, um, referral to another agency or something.
Nichol: I mean, they told me they'd give me that. He seemed really taken aback when I asked him, but I was like, 'can you at least give me a positive referral?' I mean, I did great work for those guys.
Hazel: Mm hmm.
Nichol: They're definitely gonna miss me being there on their team for sure. And he was like, 'yeah, yeah, I'll do that'. Like, okay, I mean, I didn't really know what else to do. I was… I was just like, one more thing on my plate right now. I just… I don't know what to do. I don't think anybody's gonna hire me.
Hazel: Well, I think that right now what you need to worry about… it sounds like you have a really good supportive family and people that can help you get through for a few weeks while you're looking for work. So, I think, right now, you need to just concentrate on getting your lease situation worked out so you don't have to worry about carrying two places. And getting everything worked out with the victim comp, so that you can get started into some therapy.
Nichol: Yeah, like… hire me… my name's in the media, like, why would you do that?
Hazel: Well, it hasn't been yet. And it doesn't mean… businesses won't necessarily… the hiring agents won't necessarily have watched the news or… and if they do, I think I'd just explain to them that you're doing everything you can to cooperate with law enforcement. You do what you can to have it not impact your job. And you know your work… both at *Anadarko*… is a good testament to what a good worker you are. Through all this you kept going to work, you kept

doing your job. You were responsible towards your agency. You informed them about what was going on. You did everything you needed to do.

Nichol: I just don't think people are gonna hire me. I have a feeling that trying to get by for the next five or ten years is about to be real… real…

Hazel: Okay, well, I think that thinking that way is gonna be a little self-defeating. So, let's try to take care of what we can take care of and try to build things up for you so that you have the most positive prospects for the future.

Nichol: I mean, I just don't even know where to start. Like, I have friends that can give me a referral but what I don't want to do is have my friends give me a referral and then they see the news and then they are very taken back, and then I think some people would be kind of upset if I asked then for a referral prior to the news breaking. You almost feel like waiting till it breaks to try to approach people.

Hazel: Well, have you tried thinking about a new temporary agency or something? You know, like Kelly girls? I mean, I know they don't pay well but something like that? I know that's well below your skill level.

Nichol: I don't know. I'll probably go back to the oil fields at some point. Most of those people are a bunch of societal outcasts so it might work.

Hazel: Were you happy… were you happy when you worked there?

Nichol: Sometimes.

Hazel: Yeah?

Nichol: Sometimes not.

Hazel: But wouldn't it be torture to go back to that?

Nichol: No, it's all I know.

Hazel: Well, I think, fall back at least until all this tapers off a little bit.

Nichol: I mean, if people hire me… it's hard to get a job out there 'cause I'm a woman.

Hazel: Yeah.

Nichol: They don't think you can do it.

Hazel: ((Unintelligible)). Well, you have history… and that goes a long way.

Nichol: Yeah. We'll see.

Hazel: So, I understand that Agent Koback was given… has a copy of your lease? So, I'll talk with your landlord and see where we can get as

far as getting you out of that. And then I have a list of referrals for you for therapists.
Nichol: Thank you. And did they approve it?
Hazel: They haven't yet, but they said they should by the end of the day or early tomorrow. It just has to go through a procedure. You know, it's... it's the government. They're figuring out the procedure. They're just going through the procedure. But you can get started in the meantime, calling the therapists and just... doing little interviews with them, you know, like we talked out. Just make sure it's somebody that you feel confident with. And that you feel comfortable you can say anything to.
Nichol: Understood.
Hazel: Then, I would also ask them... just because I know you have a hard time sleeping, and I know this bothers you all the time that you could wake up in the middle of the night having issues... you want to also talk to the therapist about what kind of after-hours support you can get. And do they have an emergency line or somebody that you can talk to if it is four o'clock in the morning and you haven't been able to sleep all night. And if you need some help making those phone calls, I'll get you on and I could help you.
Nichol: Thank you. Okay. I'm like, man, just doing everything I need to do every day, there's nothing else to do.
Hazel: I know you're feeling pretty overwhelmed and it just seems like it's getting, coming out.
Nichol: Getting worse and worse and worse...
Hazel: Yeah. You know we are here for you. You do have support.
Nichol: Okay.
Hazel: You do have support.
Nichol: Yeah. The media came to my house and left a letter, like, old crinkly envelope. A piece of journal paper that was all crumpled, handwritten in chicken scratch. Like, hi, I'm with the Today Show, you should call me. It's like, why would I do that in the first place? But even then, like, the lack of professionalism that my family has seen from these news reporters is absolutely ridiculous.
Hazel: And you're just ignoring them?
Nichol: Yeah. I mean, they don't have my phone number yet. They still haven't found it.
Hazel: Well, that's good and you're not at your home?
Nichol: No.

Hazel: And your dad's pretty good about saying no and walking away?
Nichol: They're contacting everybody, but so many people reach out to me, 'The media called me today'.
Hazel: And you know, all they have to say is that they don't know anything about it and they don't have to comment or…
Nichol: That's what I told them…
Hazel: … or, 'I just don't want to talk to you'.
Nichol: … no comment, or you don't know. And I was like, 'you don't have to talk to them'. I was like, 'you don't have to call 'em back, you don't owe 'em anything. Just send your love and support. I haven't said anything else because I don't really know what else to say.
Hazel: No. That's good.
Nichol: But I've had to do it with a lot of people and it wasn't something I wanted to do. I was trying to avoid that situation but I've just been inundated with phone calls and texts about it, so I was like, 'all right', talked to my dad and I was like, 'do we do damage control on the rest of these people? So they're prepared, or not?' and he was like, 'yeah, we'll do it'. So I just called my closest friends and I didn't say anything about the case and that I was a witness, I just told them… I was like, 'hey, man, I need to do this for me, like, if the media asks any questions, just tell them no comment. Please take all the pictures that you have of us off social media . I love you and I'm safe. Uh, and, I didn't break any laws.
Hazel: Ha. That's good.
Nichol: Well, 'cause they started freaking out like, 'what did you do?', and I'm like, 'no, it's okay. You just help me, please'. So, I mean, so far it's working.
Hazel: Well, and then we talked about that. How you believed that your friends and your family would at least for a while be supportive not knowing anything. Just knowing that you needed their love and support.
Nichol: I mean, it's been four days that they've been searching for me and they haven't found me yet. I'm sure they will eventually, but, I mean, four days—it's not a bad start.
Hazel: I think you're right, and…
Nichol: And they still haven't found my phone number.
Hazel: And you do have a plan… to just say, 'no', and hang up. Don't answer the door. Don't answer the phone. You'll have caller ID so

you'll know if it's your family or your friends. And it you have a voice-mail that you can… that they can leave a message if they want, if it's family. Everybody else you can just ignore. You don't have any obligation to talk to any of them.
Nichol: Right. That's pretty much where it's at. I know it's kinda just one task at a time. Every day there's something else. I'm here and they got my phone so hopefully they can get what they need.
Hazel: Good.
Nichol: Hopefully it'll help. I'm just trying to do everything they can but it's like, at this point, I don't even know what to do anymore. I really want to just start taking care of myself and not everybody else and I feel like it's just not happening.
Hazel: Oh, but Nikki, that's all you have to do right now—take care of yourself. There's really no one else that you have to take care of right now. You know, let your friends, your family take care of you. They can offer you support. You're doing everything we've asked of you. And you need now to take care of yourself and get yourself through this. And let your family support you, you don't have to take care of them. You've done what you need to do for them. You've told them, 'I'm in a situation which I just need you to support me in. Unconditionally support me'. And that's all the taking care of them you need to do right now. There'll be plenty of time for the rest of your life to take care of people. Right now, you need people to take care of you.
Nichol: That'd be nice.
Hazel: I know I asked you this before, but I'm gonna ask you again, um, are you still feeling like you're not thinking at all about suicide or hurting yourself?
Nichol: No. I'm not thinking about any of that.
Hazel: Okay, good. And you promise me you'll let us know if you start thinking that way?
Nichol: I text you guys in the middle of the night every time I'm stressing out.
Hazel: Okay, so you will? Okay. Because we want to be here to help you. We don't want this to turn into another tragedy for you.
Nichol: Understood.
Hazel: Well, I didn't know what time you were coming in today and I have another appointment that's coming in…
Nichol: That's okay. Okay.

Hazel: So, I'm gonna see what Agent Koback is up to.
Nichol: That's okay.
Hazel: So that you're not sitting here all by yourself. This is not a pleasant room to be hanging out in.
Nichol: No. Not at all… it's awkward. They have my phone and I'll just sit here.
Koback enters.
Hazel: Oh, actually, I don't have to go find out where he is.
Koback: We're trying to get your phones to work. But you don't remember your google account?
Nichol: I should. To be honest with you it's programmed into my… my… the two places I use it all the time. And so, I don't have to remember it.
Koback: So, the only way to transfer your contacts from that phone—from your iPhone to that phone is with your google account.
Nichol: I mean, if I need to, I know where to…
Koback: We're gonna print your… we downloaded them so we have the file available we can print for you.
Nichol: Can you do that?
Koback: Yep.
Nichol: That'd be nice.
Koback: But we can't… we can't move the phone.
Nichol: That's okay.
Koback: So, your phone is essentially… you won't be able to download apps or anything without your google account.
Nichol: Okay.
Koback: So, but you do know it?
Nichol: Do I know my google account?
Koback: Yeah.
Nichol: No. If I did then we wouldn't be in this situation.
Koback: But, you know, you got it somewhere else?
Nichol: Uh, yeah. I'm sure I could reset it and figure it out… at this point.
Koback: We're just making sure you have a phone that's going to be usable.
Nichol: Yeah. I mean, I can make incoming and outgoing calls at this point, that's all I really care about.

Koback: So, he's gonna download the messages that, um, uploaded when you redid your phone, so… that take… it shouldn't take too long.
Nichol: Well, there's not much on there… it's pretty short.
Koback: Should take just a few minutes and then we're done.
Nichol: They're all, like… they're not even on the right dates, some of 'em. It's really weird how they're timestamped.
Koback: Okay.
Nichol: Like, there's one on there on the 13th, and I'm like, I'm pretty sure it was a conversation that…
Koback: Between you and Chris?
Nichol: Yeah, but it was not that same day.
Koback: The 13th was a Wednesday?
Nichol: Or the 12th. I don't… I don't even know.
Koback: All right. We'll duplicate…
Nichol: It's not in the right spot. They're not in the right spot.
Koback: Maybe the date on the phone is messed up. I don't know. I'll look at the phone. We'll see.
Nichol: Well, it's out of order. Like, unless I'm confused, but I'm pretty sure the last text on there between me and him is actually probably somewhere in the middle of a text.
Koback: So, when you say out of order, like…
Nichol: Like, it's saying hey this happened on Tuesday but I'm pretty sure that happened at a different point. Only that one.
Koback: All right. So, if it's critical, we'll talk about it.
Nichol: I know.
Koback: I need to look at the texts first before I know. Okay?
Nichol: Of course. Understood.
Koback: You probably wanna go? Right?
Hazel: Yeah, I don't want to…
Koback: You have your next client coming in.
Nichol: Thank you for your time. I appreciate it.
Hazel: Oh, yeah. You're welcome and I'll send you those therapists and get started and give them a call and see who you think is gonna be a good fit for you. You can have it all ready so when Victim Com says yes, you can get started right away.
Nichol: Thanks.
Hazel: And, if you want to, try to give the guy from CDLE a call and talk with him.

Nichol: I will definitely call him. That is on my priority list at this point. I just… I just don't want to talk to them.
Hazel: No, I understand that. I understand. And then, I'm sure he'll say it depends on what your contract says. So, if you have your contract with them where your dad can get to it… It's probably at your house? If you can have it where your dad can get to it, or something to get for you to send to him, that'd probably be very helpful.
Nichol: No, I'll have it. It's all remote—it's all electronic.
Hazel: Okay. Good.
Koback: Thank you so much, Hazel.
Hazel: And call, or text me anytime, okay?
Nichol: Mm hmm.
Koback: All right. I'm gonna see where he's at. Well, anything else while we're here? That you can think of or want to address or you remember?
Hazel leaves.
Nichol: Sometimes I feel like I remember stuff but it's vague. Like I'm, like, I can't… I don't know…
Koback: And not everything's important, obviously.
Nichol: Yeah.
Koback: I know I've tried to get you to remember as much as I could, because a lot of the stuff that you have told me over the last coupla conversations is relative and it's important and I appreciate you going back and looking at calendars and doing all that stuff, but stop thinking about this for a while. I think we've got everything. I don't think you can remember anything more. We've had a lot of conversations about this case, so just give yourself a break. Go have dinner with one of your friends and have a… nobody know who you are.
Nichol: Not yet.
Koback: So, even better to make that happen. Whoever you trust in, like Charlotte, or whoever your other friends are, go have a normal night and not sit at your house and dwell on this. It might do you wonders, okay?
Nichol: Ah. Are they gonna post anything if they don't find out anything? 'cause I'm just surprised they haven't posted anything yet.
Koback: About what?
Nichol: About me. I mean, it's been four days.
Koback: You know that they are dying to find out who you are.

Nichol: I know. They haven't even reached my inner circle yet and it's been four days.
Koback: You've got good friends.
Nichol: Yes, I do,
Koback: So, be thankful for that and I… we've had this conversation. Is it… you know, you said you were thinking about going somewhere else? Go.
Nichol: I don't know when I'm gonna do that. Can you guys help with a name change? Like, dude, I'm serious. Please?
Koback: So, I can't do anything for you. That's a legal process. It's, um, it's really not that difficult. Uh, there's just paperwork that needs to be filled out. I think your best bet would be to call, maybe ask an attorney to help you with that, or seek advice from… I don't even know who you call. Honestly, but people change their name all the time, when they get married. Uh, so, it's probably the county clerk. But it's gonna… I think it would have to be at a state level to make a name change. But I don't know specifically how to do that. I don't.
Nichol: Does that become public? Because that would defeat the purpose.
Koback: I don't know. I know it can be done. I just don't know how to do it. And I wouldn't even know who to reach out… I mean, I could find out and let you know. But I don't know how to do it. Um, you know? Like witness protection thing is very, very rare.
Nichol: I'm not expecting that.
Koback: Yes. I… he's not going anywhere. He's not gonna hurt you. All those things. So…
Nichol: No. I'm not expecting that. I don't even know. A part of me… I keep getting really scared that it's going to be really hard to find good employment for a really long time. Like, years and years and years of my life. I feel like people aren't gonna want to hire me.
Koback: If you go to another state this is not headlines in that state. You realise that.
Nichol: I mean. I… I… yeah, I do.
Koback: And if I do a background on you, you're a good employee. It doesn't come up that you dated Chris Watts. And you're involved in this case. It doesn't work that way.
Nichol: But, I mean, I don't know. I just feel like this is one of those things that if it goes to court it's gonna be huge.

Koback: Well, I mean, it's national right now, but it's not like… you know, it's not the theatre event that happened in Aurora seven years ago, right? So, I get it, but I don't… I don't think you need to just step back for a minute. Take a breath. Figure out what you're gonna do. Obviously, you have some serious—very serious decisions to make over the next, you know, couple months.
Nichol: I know. I'm trying to find out how to do all this without spending all my savings. Saving up for a house and I'm just like, dammit.
Koback: Well, at least you have savings to fall back on too. A lot of people can't say that.
Nichol: Yeah, that is true. Well, since they fired me, hopefully I'll get unemployment for a little while so I can get my mind right, go to therapy and then go back to work at that point. 'Cause I'm not ready, so…
Koback: Going back to work might be a good thing for you though, than, you know, sitting and thinking about this every day.
Nichol: No, I know. I agree with that, but finding a job is the big task. That's what I told her, she's like, 'why don't you reach out to some of your friends… about a job'. It's like, well…
Koback: But they don't know who… what's going on.
Nichol: No, they don't now, but what I don't want is for somebody to give me a reference and then they find out what's going on. I think that's really disrespectful.
Koback: I think you reach out specifically to an employer not a person. Other… I don't know anything about the oil industry, but other companies like, who you work for. I have this skill, I'd like to come and work for you.
Nichol: I've been thinking about it. I was thinking about reaching out to some old employers. I've always been a really good employee to those people. Everybody when I leave is pretty disappointed. This is the first time I've ever been terminated from a job. So…
Koback: Sometimes that can be tough to get over too.
Nichol: It's hard. This was the dream job. I feel awful about all of this. I wanted that for so long to get out of the oil fields. I was so tired of living on oil rigs. It's such a rough life. I just want to be in the office somewhere doing environmental for an oil company and I finally got it and all this happened.

Koback: Well, you have that skill set now, so maybe you can move back into that.

Nichol: I hope so. We will see. Um, I forgot what I was gonna say. Are you guys… am I in trouble because I deleted his texts.

Koback: No, you're not in trouble.

Nichol: I didn't know what was going on at that point.

Koback: So, is there a ques… does that cause questions?

((Crosstalk))

Nichol: Of course it does.

Koback: Now, there is… but is it criminal? No. Is there concern that you're hiding something? Potentially. That's why I want 'em or I wouldn't be asking for 'em.

Nichol: I know. I'm trying to give you guys that.

Koback: You've been up front with me about everything. I don't have a concern that you ever told Chris, 'I don't want you…', you know, 'go kill your wife.'

Nichol: No. Hell no.

Koback: Or, 'get rid of your kids'. Or 'I don't want to date you if you have kids'. None of these things ever came out of your mouth—we talked about that.

Nichol: Yeah.

Koback: So… but until those text messages that are deleted, um, are there, you know, and all that… it's just speculation. But it's kinda like, hmm, why did you do that? And I get your excuse. I understand what you're saying. That on Tuesday, you realised who this man was and what he had done. You didn't want him to be part of your life anymore, so you got rid of it.

Nichol: I didn't even want to see it in my phone. It was freaking me out. 'Cause I remember I had, like, deleted them and then he sent me another text and then I deleted that one too.

Koback: Right.

Nichol: 'Cause I was like, 'I don't want to deal with this. By the way, when you're looking through those texts, look for his APC phone for that one conversation we had where he screen-shotted me what he did on Monday. Remember that?

Koback: Mm hmm.

Nichol: Yeah.

Koback: And you said… that's his *Anadarko* phone?

Nichol: Mm hmm.
Koback: Okay.
Nichol: And that should be the only recent. Like, there's probably stuff that if you guys are able to pull up, like way, way back that we talked, but nothing…
Koback: The thing we talked about was him proving that he went to the oil field.
Nichol: That he went to work.
Koback: That he went to work that morning. At whatever site he was supposed to go to… to check on the leaks.
Nichol: So that will be in there. Okay, okay, all right. And then, um, I don't know… am I allowed to address my friends and tell them, please, no comment to the media?
Koback: You can say anything you want.
Nichol: I mean, I haven't been telling them anything else.
Koback: I would not talk with anybody about this case.
Nichol: Oh, no.
Koback: Except, I know you talked to… you need to talk to… a therapist. And I'm sure you're talking to your dad. Probably your closest person.
Nichol: To some extent. I mean, what's not… when he's not here for this I don't tell him about this. I tell him I'm coming down here, but he doesn't need to know any more—he's so stressed out.
Koback: You're an adult. You made some decisions that caught you in a bad situation. But there's nothing wrong with you talking to somebody. I just wouldn't go into details.
Nichol: No. I didn't even tell people I'm a witness or anything…
Koback: Certainly your best… I mean, if I was you I'd be confiding in my best friend, like, 'hey, this is what's happening in my life and I need help'. Is there anything wrong with that? No.
Nichol: I mean, that's about as far as confiding has gone with me telling her about some guy I was hanging out with but that was way before any of this.
Koback: Yeah. And you need support right now, too. So, you do… there is no… we're not… you're not in trouble. There's no charges against you. You're simply a witness.
Nichol: I just don't want to get in trouble for talking to my dad or asking a friend for help.

Koback: About what?
Nichol: Well, I mean what my dad already knows. You know what I'm saying?
Koback: Right. There's nothing to get in trouble for. (Laughter).
Nichol: Okay. I don't know how that works. That's why I'm asking… this is one more thing I don't need on my plate. 'Cause I just… oh my God…
Koback: You're not… you're not in trouble. And talking to your friends and family about what's going on isn't gonna get you in trouble. Okay?
Nichol: I don't even want to talk to my friends about it. I don't even want anybody to know. I mean, they're gonna find out, but I figured, the reasons that I think I'm staking out from the media as long as I have been is because nobody knows anything. And 'cause my inner circle's really awesome.
Koback: Maybe.
Nichol: I don't know. They haven't reached my…
Koback: Or they just… because you're not on social media?
Nichol: At all. But I mean, I eliminated all of that, like, even have the ability to go through… I went and found everybody. I knew that had any public posts and was just like, 'this needs to be cleared'. It's all gone.
Koback: Right. So, you've made it very difficult for them to find you. But do I think, eventually, that at some point they are gonna find you? Sure. Of course.
Nichol: Do you think they're gonna find where I'm staying at? I think that would be really tricky.
Koback: I don't know—you haven't even told me where you're staying.
Nichol: Nobody knows.
Koback: I don't know how it's connected to you or your family. So, I mean, if it's in your family's name, certainly it wouldn't be that hard to figure it out. So, if that… you know? There's ways to find out where people are staying, but they're limited. Unless somebody knows about this place that talks to 'em.
Nichol: Nobody. All right. My dad doesn't even know where it's at.
Koback: Let me check on this. Let me check on this phone.
Nichol: Oh, yeah. That's right. I'm like, 'am I ready to go?'

My phone…
Koback: I know you're ready to go. (Laughter). So, he's printed the… your contacts. Be back in a minute.
Koback leaves the room and returns a short while later.
Koback: Okay, there's those. And he's still messing with your phone. Give me a few minutes, okay? Be back in a minute. Did you sign that?
Nichol: Yes. Should be…
Koback: There it is. All right. Do you want a copy of that?
Nichol: Ah, sure, that would be…
Koback: I'll be back in a minute.
Koback leaves again and returns
Nichol: Oh, you guys got this all printed up.
Koback: You all right?
Nichol: One more question for you.
Koback: Yeah?
Nichol: I have jury duty on September 17th. Is that something that I can do?
Koback: Of course.
Nichol: Given the fact that I'm, like, mid in this mess.
Koback: Yep.
Nichol: Okay.
Koback: So just answer the questions. They're gonna ask you a bunch of questions. Answer 'em truthfully. Um, yeah, I wouldn't… I wouldn't avoid it.
Nichol: I just didn't know.
Koback: Have you ever gone to jury duty?
Nichol: I was supposed to go once and they didn't need me, but I just wanted to double check.
Koback: No. It has no bearing on what's going on in this. So, you're all right. I think he's still trying to get your phone back together.
Nichol: Oh… can I use the restroom?
Koback: Yeah. You need to…
Nichol: Can I leave my stuff in here? And come back in here?
Koback: Yep.
Nichol: Thanks.
Koback: I'll be right back.
Nichol and Koback leave the room. Nichol returns first then Koback joins her.

Koback: Thanks, man. Ah, that's all right. Just having a bad day. Okay. Will you show me the messages that downloaded? I'm gonna take photographs of 'em because the device that we're using doesn't want to work.
Nichol: ((Unintelligible)).
Koback: I don't know.
Nichol: Oh, for those?
Koback: The messages that came from Chris that you said showed up on the phone.
Nichol: Yeah. I don't think any of the ones from the *Anadarko* phone came in, but I don't know that number.
Koback: Okay.
Nichol: I didn't see 'em but maybe there's… maybe you guys can give me the number, we can check that out too.
Koback: Um, I can probably get it real quick. Show me the ones that you think came from him, though. Is it 9…?
Nichol: I'll show you… 901… just give me a sec. Boom. Right there.
Koback: Okay. So I am going to take photographs of these in lieu of downloading it.
Nichol: Do you want me to just screenshot and send them to you?
Koback: Well, but there's no way to do that.
Nichol: No. I mean, just screenshot right here.
Koback: This isn't hooked up to Wi-Fi or anything, is it?
Nichol: No, but I'm saying if…
Koback: Oh, I see what you're saying.
Nichol: It'll come in clearer, that's what I'm saying. You can watch me do it.
Koback: Yeah.
Nichol: I'm gonna screenshot em and text them to you right now.
Koback: Or you can email 'em to me.
Nichol: I'll just send 'em to you right now while we're here.
Koback: Okay. That's fine.
Nichol: Okay. You know what's scary? I read this one, back on June 27th… that's when I first started talking, and look at him… thoughtful, loyal, truthful, dedicated, doesn't play games. It just makes me so sad to read this and think like…
Koback: So, are these some of the ones that you deleted?
Nichol: I deleted everything that he sent me. These are so old. Like,

look how old.
Koback: And is there any from those dates?
Nichol: Yes. So, look like these… 6-27, 6-29, these are old and then they seem to be... see, and then we're missing the 2nd and 3rd and then there's the 4th.
Koback: Okay. So there's a lot of messages.
Nichol: Kind of, yeah. But then there's no 5th, 6th, 7th or 8th. And then there's the 9th but it's only one text. And then the 17th—one text.
Koback: And you guys text how many times a day?
Nichol: All the time. I bet you guys have hundreds of messages you need to recover. But, yes, so here's the 11th, but look, there's only one from the 11th.
Koback: Can I see what it says?
Nichol: Yeah, yeah, yeah, yeah. And the only text I think might be out of order. Might… is the one at the very end. I just wish they were more complete, and I don't understand why they're coming in bits and pieces. Like, what's causing that?
Koback: So, the 10th… oh, and you went to the Rockies game?
Nichol: Yeah. I didn't see him that day. I was with my friends, but I stayed with him that night.
Koback: Okay, So, this one's Sunday night?
Nichol: Yeah.
Koback: At 4:07pm. What's he talking about, 'pounding fruit'? Is that you or him?
Nichol: That's him. Oh, so he was talking about that birthday party he was gonna go to. Whoever was hosting it… I don't remember, like, he told me the name.
Koback: Jeremy?
Nichol: I don't even remember to be honest with you. Like, the only names that I remember very well was, like, Nick and Mark. Those are the only two that I'm… could be, like, oh yeah, like, I can tell you maybe a little bit about these people.
Koback: Those are his friends?
Nichol: Yeah. Kinda. Um, they went to the birthday party and he said oh, this guy always barbecues. And then he was saying, oh, he didn't barbecue, so, he was saying he had fruit and asparagus. Yeah, 'didn't do any BBQ that time. He did hot dogs. So, he was saying he avoided that. He was trying to eat healthy.

Koback: So, this is the point when…
Nichol: This is the one I don't know if it's in order. I'm not sure exactly why this is referring to, but I think this one at the bottom, 'OMG that's absolutely ridiculous. They would freak out!' That… do you remember when I told you I was always trying to incorporate his kids into stuff. I mean, even if it wasn't directly, like, me and him. But just, like, I was always thinking of cute stuff when I'd see stuff. I was like, 'oh my God, little girls would like that!' I would show him and I found this box of lucky charms that was unicorn lucky charms…
Koback: Okay.
Nichol: … and I thought they were really cute. And I texted it to him and I was like, 'do your little girls know about these because they're awesome?' and I was like, little stuff like that.
Koback: So, that's…?
Nichol: I don't think that's the 13th because I don't think I talked to him that day. What night was the 13th?
Koback: It was Monday.
Nichol: Was it Monday?
Koback: I think. I gotta look. 'Cause I can't…
Nichol: I think, well, no, well… maybe these are in order. Monday was the day that I sent that I sent that text.
Koback: Yes. That's Monday morning at 2:44pm. So that's in the afternoon. Monday—does that sound right?
Nichol: I was at work when I texted it to him. Okay, so that's in order. It is in order. And this makes sense.
Koback: And this is the 12th?
Nichol: So, that's Sunday, right? Okay, so they're in order, they're just missing a whole bunch.
Koback: That's Sunday? He's basically saying he's still at that barbecue.
Nichol: Barbecue.
Koback: And that fits? Okay. Perfect.
Nichol: So, no. So then, this is in the right place. I was thinking 8-13 was Tuesday and I'm like, I don't think him and I had a pleasant conversation on Tuesday.
Koback: Wanna screenshot all of those to me?
Nichol: Yeah, yeah, yeah. How do you screenshot?
Koback: And then, I turned this off.

Nichol: Oh, this phone is weird. You, like, Ninja chop it. Whoa. I think that worked. Okay, so that takes us down to 6-29 and then I'm gonna scroll up to 6-30.
Koback: Ninja chop. That's old… old school.
Nichol: I had to do… ((Unintelligible))… permissions at my house last night. I did not like it. I'm, like, this is scary. That's cool. I got to… (Unintelligible)) …
Koback: So, while you're doing that, let me ask you about the texts with you and Charlotte.
Nichol: Yes.
Koback: You talk about children and he's got his own kids and that makes you, kind of, uncomfortable, because you'd like to have your own family. Put that in context for me. Is that a fair statement, the way I'm saying it?
Nichol: I guess. It was never anything I said to him, though.
Koback: Okay, that's what I want to know. Did you ever say anything to him, like…?
Nichol: Never. Never.
Koback: Anything about his kids being a problem?
Nichol: No.
Koback: Anything about his wife being a problem?
Nichol: Never. Never. I always tried to be so inclusive with them. And even with her when I was talking to her it wasn't that his kids were an issue. It was just this man already has a life. Should I go build my own? You know, with somebody who hasn't done that, yet. And then, she was the one that was saying, you know, I was engaged once and it didn't work and now I'm engaged again. She was trying to tell me it doesn't matter, I'm on my second time of going through this, and she's like, I love this man very, very much and she was saying he's not gonna love you less because he's already been through marriage once and been separated and already had kids. Like, he's not gonna…
Koback: Those references were never made to him though, about children?
Nichol: Never. Never.
Koback: So, Charlotte. That's who you were talking with, right?
Nichol: Yes.
Koback: Did you one time tell me Charlotte's a lesbian?
Nichol: No. She's engaged.

Koback: You… were you talking about one of your friends that might have been a lesbian?
Nichol: That's not the case. I don't think so. I don't…
Koback: You never said that about any of your friends that I inquired about?
Nichol: I don't think so. I don't think that was the case.
Koback: I think, like, on the first day we talked with your dad there I inquired about Charlotte. Um…
Nichol: Yeah, you asked me about Charlotte and eHarmony and I looked on my text messages, like, what are they talking about? And I couldn't find it so I was wondering maybe if somebody referenced both those to you but not together.
Koback: Okay.
Nichol: I'm wondering if that's where that came from.
Koback: Okay. So Charlotte is your friend? She's your closest friend?
Nichol: Yep.
Koback: You guys had this conversation, but it never went anywhere besides her and you?
Nichol: Yeah.
Koback: You never mentioned it to Chris? You never said anything about your kids… or his kids, pardon me… damaging your guys relationship?
Nichol: Nooo. Nooo. No, no, no.
Koback: Or nothing like that?
Nichol: Never. And I mean, even in that, I wasn't like I never said his kids were a problem. Like, he already has a life. I don't know about that.
Koback: So, in light of what's occurred, though. What I'm trying to make sure was that there was never a conversation that you guys had that and he might have thought that you, um…
Nichol: Ah, no…
Koback: You were saying, 'I can't be with you if you had kids'.
Nichol: I wouldn't… I wouldn't be with him if I couldn't accept that.
Koback: Okay. I'm just making hundred percent sure that those…
Nichol: I promise you I really want you guys to pull up these texts because all the stuff I've been telling you will, like… She bangs her hand on the table. … sync up.
Koback: And I hope we can. I haven't been very lucky with your

phones yet. And they've been nothing but a pain, so this one's coming with me. Geez.
Nichol: I think I know this is a task. I'm gonna… some of these might be duplicates but, whatever, I'm gonna send these to you. Um, no. That was just kinda something between me and her and it wasn't even really the kids, it was that he had already been married before and I was just, like, I don't know if I like… a long-term relationship with this guy, is that something that he would eventually want? Because that's something that I would eventually want. You know? I just don't…
Koback: So, your concern was more about his prior marriage than his children?
Nichol: I guess… honestly, I wasn't really that worried about him at that time. Like, if you read the majority of those texts it's very, very flattering to him in all the many things I have to say about him. It was just that I wasn't one hundred percent committed to him, yet… I mean, I was monogamous with him… I wasn't seeing any other men, but I wasn't, like, hey, this is the guy I want to spend the rest of my life with. And part of the reason that I was uncertain, I mean, yeah, he'd already built a life but honestly, he wasn't out of the marriage that he was already in.
Koback: Okay.
Nichol: So, I mean, I felt horrible, I mean, I'd got this guy, and, you know, I'd take in his kids, and we're gonna do this, and we're gonna do that. Because I didn't have any problems with them, it's just…
Koback: Okay.
Nichol:… Um, I know the context of that text now, looking at it, it looks so bad.
Koback: You have to look at it from the perspective that I'm looking at it.
Nichol: Yeah.
Koback: And how it could be misconstrued or made out to sound something another way that's why I wanted to give you the opportunity to say what it really means. Okay?
Nichol: No. I don't mean any harm towards those kids. I always thought they were so cute when he showed me those pictures. He was all about 'em, you know? And not only that, but it's like, once you guys get those texts you will see there's not very much mention of his children, and if there is such mention, it's always cute stuff where it's like,

'hey, you should show them this', or, 'hey, this apartment's great for them', or, you know, 'what do you think of bunk beds? And, you know, like, they, those little girls reminded me of me and my little sister. They're the same age.

Koback: You said that before.

Nichol: Yeah. I mean it was so cute, he would call his little daughter, the younger one, CeCe, he called her rampage. He's like, 'she's wild', and it just made me… because my little sister was totally rampage. And it was just, kind of like, spot on, you know? And so like… it just made me think okay, these guys are going through a divorce at the same age that I was at when my parents went through a divorce. I was like, how did I handle that? You know? Like, tell him, you know, this is what happened when my parents were separated when we were this old. And just try to give him a reference because I gave a damn.

Koback: Right. Okay. Um…

Nichol: I mean… but just because I care about the f… him, and I care about his kids and all of that doesn't mean that I'm ready to turn around and commit everything.

Koback: Did he ever say anything like that? Like, 'do I have to get rid of my kids?'

Nichol: No he…

Koback: Or do I, you know…?

Nichol: This shocked me just as much as I think it shocked the rest of the world. All of it. Like, he lied so much, now I go back and think about all the shit that I'm, like... it's lies. His friends that he spent the night at their house… he even fooled them as much as me. He lied to everybody. He had all of you fooled. And everybody stood up for him. His friends stood up for him. I really thought she left. I was like, 'let her fucking go', you know? 'She'll come back in a day… she'll be alright… let her cool down… she'll be here… it'll be okay'. You know? Like, had me convinced. I think she's just upset. And then… and then… never would I have guessed. I mean, even now, when I go back through this stuff that, I'm like, it doesn't make sense, you know? Or seem a little off. That stuff still doesn't send a red flag to me, like, hey, this guy is gonna murder his family.

Koback: Sure.

Nichol: You know?

Koback: You didn't think there was any… you didn't have any indication, and, by all accounts, it didn't seem like anybody did.
Nichol: No. I just, like, ah… you know? Sometimes, I like… sometimes, I think what that man is thinking, you don't know, you know? But it's like, how long has his brain been shifting to this paradigm shift where he feels the need to do this? It's like, I just don't believe that's something that just happens, in a day… or two days. I don't think it happens in two months. I think it's something that takes a very, very long time to develop and I don't…
Koback: Right. So that scares you when you look back at it?
Nichol: Yeah. Because I like, I think about it and I'm like, he could've had that capacity to do that whether I was in his life or not. He could've had that capacity to do that, maybe not even just to them… it could've been me. It could've been our co-workers. I mean, the more I think about it… I mean, I think… I think a lot of people are gonna probably assume that I was the catalyst for his movement, but I don't think… you know? Not me instructing him, but him deciding to do that because he had me in his life and because he was so infatuated with what we had going on. But, you know, I try to put the reason to it at the end, like, why would you wipe out your family to be with me? Like, it doesn't… it doesn't compute. It's like, how would that go? Like, hey, my family just disappeared. And you think I'm just not gonna be concerned about that? And not only that. He was so about those little girls, and I was trying to push him to do that. Like, I told you there'll be days where he would want to come over my house after work and I'd be, no, go hang out with your kids… your kids are home. Like, that was me. That wasn't even him. That was me pushing that. And he would go do it. You know? And he spent time with them, but he was never like, 'oh, I don't want to hang out with them'. He just said, 'can I see you for a few hours?' And I'm like, 'if your kids are awake, go hang out with your kids'. You know? If they're sleeping and you want to talk you can call me, but don't do that while they're up', like, 'spend time with them'. And… and… and I just, uh… oh my God. That is the part that I have the hardest part swallowing. Where it's like, why would you take them out to spend time with me? Like, it doesn't fit. It doesn't fit at all.
Koback: Mm hmm.
Nichol: You know, I…?
Koback: But you said he was infatuated with you.
Nichol: But even then, if he's, so, all about me and I support him

being with his kids, you would think that he would want to do what would make me happy.
Koback: That's a good point.
Nichol: And what would make me happy…
Koback: Was him hanging out with his kids.
Nichol: … was his kids. It's in texts. It's in phone conversations.
Koback: We'll look into it.
Nichol: It doesn't…
Koback: That one particular context in that… it's so open kind of it interpretation whether or not you said… that's why I wanted to address it in particular.
Nichol: Okay. Yeah, there's nothing like that in our texts. I can tell you that right now. Never.
Koback: Did you send those?
Nichol: Yeah. I'm working on it, sorry.
Koback: How'd you ever get any work done? You get sidetracked.
Nichol: I actually get a lot of work done.
Koback: (Laughter). I'm just teasing you.
Nichol: It was a lot easier in the oil field than it was in the office though. Are you…(she recites Koback's phone number).
Koback: I am.
Nichol: Okay. Just want to make sure.
Koback: Yeah. Don't send those to anybody else, please.
Nichol: Let's see if I can do it in… screenshot.
Koback: You can probably send them all.
Nichol: Activity not done.
Koback: How about email? If you emailed it, could you select each one and attach it to the email?
Nichol: I mean, I just want to do it here so you know I did it in its entirety.
Koback: Okay. That's right. You don't have Wi-Fi on that phone right?
Nichol: No. I don't have anything on here. Okay. I think this is all I… just… this is gonna be a slow process you must bear with me. Yeah, I don't know. Sometimes I just feel like… it's not even sometimes, I legitimately think that that man's cheese was sliding off his cracker long before I came into his life.
Koback: Have you stayed away from the media for the last couple

of days?
Nichol: Yeah. I guess they know where I live. I'm like...
Koback: I mean, no. What they're reporting about him or the case?
Nichol: No.
Koback: So you've been watching that?
Nichol: Kind of. I, uh, thought...
Koback: So you saw the video of him talking about relationships?
Nichol: Oh, I don't really... I can't even bring myself to watch most of that stuff.
Koback: Okay.
Nichol: I will scroll the headlines if they look different than what I... uh, previously, like, knew about the investigation. Kind of looking for my name so that I know when it happens. So, I can deal with that, but, other than that, no. I don't, uh, I never actually watched that video.
Koback: Okay.
Nichol: I don't really, like... I have a hard time looking at him now. It's kind of the same thing, like, when I deleted the texts, I saw his mugshot and I looked at it the first time and I saw it and it scared me. And now, when I see it, I just move past it.
Koback: Okay.
Nichol: Because I find it to be... I don't get it. I just don't know. I don't know how to work this new phone now. Attached. Oh my goodness. I think some of these are repeats, I'm sorry.
Koback: That's okay. As long as I have them all that'd be great.
Nichol: I think you do.
Koback: You look like you've been drinking way too much coffee.
Nichol: Because I'm shaky?
Koback: Yeah.
Nichol: I think it's from sleep loss.
Koback: They're coming.
Nichol: You know the one at the very bottom... oh, you do...? No, you don't. No, you don't. You're missing the last one.
Koback: Send me the last one and I'll send you out of here. And then, don't think about this stuff for a while.
Nichol: I'm trying, but it's hard. So much easier said than done.
Koback: And then, when I'm done with your phone, um, I'll get this back to you.
Nichol: I mean, if you're gonna need it, keep it.

Koback: No. We don't need to keep it because… what it's gonna do, if I take everything, then it's just easy. I'll get it back to ya. Okay? So, the examiner that's gonna look into it, she comes back early next week, um, and I'll try to corral her to do that as early as possible. So, we can download your phone and get it returned to you.
Nichol: All right. I think I sent them all. The phone is so different from my phone.
Koback: Totally different than an iPhone. I know that.
Nichol: This has been a long time... it's been years and years… I actually had this phone…
Koback: Oh, let me go see if I can find this *Anadarko* number real quick. I'll be right back.
Nichol: Yeah, yeah, yeah. And then I can do this on here.
Koback: Totally forgot about that. Right back.
Koback leaves the room and returns a short while later.
Koback: Okay 720… You just reading those?
Nichol: I haven't seen these in so long.
Koback: Look for his *Anadarko* stuff so then you can get out of here. Can you read my handwriting?
Nichol: 310… Let's start at the top. I just resent you all of those.
Koback: That's fine.
Nichol: 720… So, that would've been on the 12th or the 13th. What day was Monday?
Koback: Um, 11th was Saturday, so the 13th would be Monday.
Nichol: Okay. So what happened on the 13th… ((Unintelligible)).
Koback: It's okay.
Nichol: Didn't mean to take it, I'm so sorry. I really didn't, like, I didn't know.
Koback: It's fine. Don't beat up yourself about it. We've already been through this ten times. It is what it is.
Nichol: I know.
Koback: Is there any older ones, potentially, from this *Anadarko* phone?
Nichol: That's a possibility.
Koback: Is there a way to search those?
Nichol: I don't know. I don't know.
Koback: Can you go here and search?
Nichol: Maybe. What about this? Because I haven't used this phone in years.

Koback: Search.
Nichol: Search.
Koback: Cool.
Nichol: Yay! 720… it's gonna be like, 'that's everybody'.
Koback: Nope. Okay, not on your phone.
Nichol: Okay. I tried.
Koback: How about in your call log? That was text messages. In your call log did you ever converse with him on that phone? I mean, this phone's pretty old.
Nichol: I don't think…
Koback: Oh, but… how about we just look at your call log and just see?
Nichol: Let's see… let's see if it downloaded. Nope. Eleven, oh, two, two thousand sixteen.
Koback: Okay.
Nichol: And then all these. These are all 2016. So it didn't update the call log. All it did was today, once I got… okay…
Koback: Is that Samsung?
Nichol: Galaxy 5. Yeah, I just thought it was so weird all those messages started showing up and I was like, 'we have all of them'.
Koback: That would be so nice.
Nichol: Wouldn't it?
Koback: It would make my life too easy. All right. You ready to get out of here?
Nichol: Yes, I am.
Koback: All right. Take your stuff. I will call you. Probably won't be next week. I'm gonna be busy all next week, so I'll just call you the week after when your phone's done. Uh, and then I'll get back to you. And then, at that time, if there's anything new, we can talk about it then.
Nichol: Do you think he's gonna take this all the way to trial?
Koback: I do. Right now.
Nichol: Have they gotten the discoveries yet?
Koback: No. They have some stuff.
Nichol: Do you think it's gonna change when they get them? Do they know I'm one of your witnesses?
Koback: Um, yeah. They have to know. Do they know what you said yet? No.

EIGHT

Plea Deal (With the DEVIL)

On the 6th November 2018 Chris Watts filed a ***WRITTEN WAIVER AND GUILTY PLEA*** to the District Court in Weld County, Colorado.

Between: ***The People of the State of Colorado vs Christopher Lee Watts***.

It is said Chris agreed to this in order to avoid the death penalty, and Shanann's family approved it. Shanann's mother reportedly said, 'He made the choice to take those lives, but I don't want to be in the position to take his'. However, as soon as this happened, the investigation was immediately halted leaving a ton of unanswered questions. Here are some of the details…

WRITTEN WAIVER AND GUILTY PLEA

I am the defendant in this case.

1. **I have had enough time to talk to my lawyer about this case, and he/she has discussed the evidence against me. I have fully explained my side to him/her.**

2. **I believe that the District Attorney has enough evidence to convict me at trial.**
3. **I am satisfied that my plea of guilty in this case is in my best interest.**
4. **I understand that I have the right to exercise any or all of the following rights, even against my lawyer's advice:**
5. **The right to remain silent about this case;**
6. **The right to have my lawyer represent me and be present with me during any conferences or questioning by anyone about this case, at all court hearings, and at trial;**
7. **The right to plead NOT GUILTY and have a jury trial; and,**
8. **The right to appeal my case to a higher court if I am convicted at trial.**
9. **I understand that the right to the jury trial includes:**
10. **The right to help select the jury;**
11. **The right to confront witnesses who testify against me, and to have my lawyer cross-examine them about their testimony;**
12. **The right to be presumed innocent, unless and until the District Attorney proves my guilt beyond a reasonable doubt;**
13. **The right to have my lawyer call witnesses to testify for me if I want and, if necessary, to have the judge order witnesses to come to court.**
14. **I have read and understand the elements of the charge or charges that I am pleading guilty to, as shown on the attached sheet(s).**
15. **I have read and understand the possible penalties that I could be sentenced to, which are shown on the attached sheet(s).**
16. **My plea is freely, intelligently, and voluntarily given. I know that I am giving up all the rights described above. I understand these rights. I am**

giving up these rights and pleading guilty of my own free will. No one has pressured me or tried to make me plead guilty against my will. I have not decided to plead guilty because of anything I have been told except for the agreements shown on the attached sheet(s).

17. **I understand that the record may be further supplemented by police reports, affidavits, or other documentation attached or provided at the time of sentencing.**
18. **I understand that if I am not a citizen of the United States, this guilty plea may cause collateral consequences, including, but not limited to deportation, exclusion from admission to the United States, or denial of naturalization**
19. **I understand that following the sentencing in this matter, I have, in certain circumstances, the right to appellate review of my conviction and sentence. A Notice of Appeal must be filed within 7 weeks (or 49 days) of the sentence. I also understand that if I am determined indigent by the court that I have the right to the assistance of appointed counsel upon the review of my conviction and sentence and the right to obtain a record on appeal without payment of costs. Additionally, I understand that I may have the right to seek post-conviction reduction of my sentence in the trial court within 18 weeks (or 126 days) of the imposition of sentence pursuant to Crim.P. 35(b).**

The document was signed by Chris, his attorney and the District Attorney.

<u>ELEMENTS</u>

<u>COUNT 1: MURDER IN THE FIRST DEGREE (F1):</u>

On about the 13th day of August, 2018, in the County of Weld, State

of Colorado; CHRISTOPHER LEE WATTS, unlawfully, feloniously, after deliberation, and
with the intent to cause the death of a person other than himself, caused the death of Shanann Watts; AFTER DELIBERATION means not only intentionally but also the decision to commit the act has been made after the exercise of reflection and judgement concerning the act. An act committed after deliberation is never one which has been committed in a hasty and impulsive manner.
WITH INTENT - A person acts intentionally or with intent when his conscious objective is to cause the specific result proscribed by the statute of defining the offence. It is immaterial whether or not the result actually occurred.
PERSON – A human being who had been born and was alive at the time of the homicidal act.

COUNT 2: MURDER IN THE FIRST DEGREE (F1):
Between and including the 12th day of August, 2018 and the 13th day of August, 2018, in the County of Weld, State of Colorado; CHRISTOPHER LEE WATTS, unlawfully, feloniously, after deliberation, and with the intent
to cause the death of a person other than himself,
caused the death of Bella Watts; AFTER DELIBERATION means not only intentionally but also the decision to commit the act has been made after the exercise of reflection and judgement concerning the act. An act committed after deliberation is never one which has been committed in a hasty and impulsive manner.
WITH INTENT- A person acts intentionally or with intent when his conscious objective is to cause the specific result proscribed by the statute of defining the offence. It is immaterial whether or not the result actually occurred.
PERSON – A human being who had been born and was alive at the time of the homicidal act.

COUNT 3: MURDER IN THE FIRST DEGREE (F1):
Between and including the 12th day of August, 2018 and the 13th day of August, 2018, in the County of Weld, State of Colorado; CHRISTOPHER LEE WATTS, unlawfully, feloniously, after deliberation, and
with the intent to cause the death of a person other than himself,

caused the death of Celeste Watts; AFTER DELIBERATION means not only intentionally but also the decision to commit the act has been made after the exercise of reflection and judgement concerning the act. An act committed after deliberation is never one which has been committed in a hasty and impulsive manner.
WITH INTENT - A person acts intentionally or with intent when his conscious objective is to cause the specific result proscribed by the statute of defining the offence. It is immaterial whether or not the result actually occurred.
PERSON – A human being who had been born and was alive at the time of the homicidal act.

COUNT 4: MURDER IN THE FIRST DEGREE (F1):
Between and including the 12th day of August, 2018 and the 13th day of August, 2018, in the County of Weld, State of Colorado; CHRISTOPHER LEE WATTS, unlawfully, feloniously and knowingly caused the death of Bella Watts, a child who had not yet attained twelve years of age, and the defendant was in a position of trust with respect to the victim; KNOWINGLY – A person acts knowingly with respect to conduct or to a circumstance described by a statute defining an offense when he is aware that his conduct is of such a nature or that such circumstance exists. A person acts knowingly with respect to a result of his conduct when he is aware that his conduct is practically certain to cause the results.
POSITION OF TRUST – one in a position of trust includes, any person who is a parent or acting in the place of a parent and charged with any of the parent's rights, duties, or responsibilities concerning a child, or a person who is charged with any duty or responsibility for the health, education, welfare, or supervision of a child, including foster care, child care, or family care OR institutional care, wither independently or through another, no matter how brief, at the time of the unlawful act.

COUNT 5: MURDER IN THE FIRST DEGREE (F1):
Between and including the 12th day of August, 2018 and the 13th day of August, 2018, in the County of Weld, State of Colorado; CHRISTOPHER LEE WATTS, unlawfully, feloniously and knowingly caused the death of Celeste Watts, a child who had not yet attained twelve years of age, and the defendant was in a position of trust with

respect to the victim; KNOWINGLY – A person acts knowingly with respect to conduct or to a circumstance described by a statute defining an offense when he is aware that his conduct is of such a nature or that such circumstance exists. A person acts knowingly with respect to a result of his conduct when he is aware that his conduct is practically certain to cause the results.

POSITION OF TRUST – one in a position of trust includes, any person who is a parent or acting in the place of a parent and charged with any of the parent's rights, duties, or responsibilities concerning a child, or a person who is charged with any duty or responsibility for the health, education, welfare, or supervision of a child, including foster care, child care, or family care OR institutional care, wither independently or through another, no matter how brief, at the time of the unlawful act.

COUNT 6: UNLAWFUL TERMINATION OF PREGNANCY IN THE FIRST DEGREE (F2)

On or about the 13th day of August, 2018, in the County of Weld, State of Colorado; CHRISTOPHER LEE WATTS, with the intent to terminate unlawfully the pregnancy of a woman, namely Shanann Watts, feloniously and unlawfully terminated the pregnancy of the woman.

Further, the woman died as a result of the unlawful termination of the pregnancy. WITH INTENT – A person acts intentionally or with intent when his conscious objective is to cause the specific result proscribed by the statute defining the offense. It is immaterial whether or not the result actually occurred. PREGNANCY means the presence of an implanted human embryo or fetus within the uterus of a woman. UNLAWFUL TERMINATION OF PREGNANCY means the termination of a pregnancy by any means other than birth or medical procedure, instrument, agent, or drug, for which the consent of the pregnant woman, or a person authorized by law to act on her behalf, has been obtained, or for which the pregnant woman's consent is implied by law.

COUNT 7: TAMPERING WITH A DECEASED HUMAN BODY (F3)

On or about the 13th day of August, 2018, in the County of Weld, State of Colorado; CHRISTOPHER LEE WATTS, believing that an official proceeding was pending, in progress, or about to be instituted, and acting without legal right or authority, unlawfully and feloniously wilfully destroyed, mutilated, concealed, removed, or altered a human body, part of a human body, or human remains with intent to impair its or their appearance or availability in the official proceedings OFFICIAL PROCEEDING means a proceeding heard before any legislative, judicial, administrative, or other government agency, or official authorized to hear evidence under oath, including any magistrate, hearing examiner, commissioner, notary, or other person taking testimony or depositions in any such proceedings. WITH INTENT – A person acts intentionally or with intent when his conscious objective is to cause the specific result proscribed by the statute defining the offence. It is immaterial whether or not the result actually occurred.

COUNT 8: TAMPERING WITH A DECEASED HUMAN BODY (F3)

On or about the 13th day of August, 2018, in the County of Weld, State of Colorado; CHRISTOPHER LEE WATTS, believing that an official proceeding was pending, in progress, or about to be instituted, and acting without legal right or authority, unlawfully and feloniously wilfully destroyed, mutilated, concealed, removed, or altered a human body, part of a human body, or human remains with intent to impair its or their appearance or availability in the official proceedings OFFICIAL PROCEEDING means a proceeding heard before any legislative, judicial, administrative, or other government agency, or official authorized to hear evidence under oath, including any magistrate, hearing examiner, commissioner, notary, or other person taking testimony or depositions in any such proceedings. WITH INTENT – A person acts intentionally or with intent when his conscious objective is to cause the specific result proscribed by the statute defining the offence. It is immaterial whether or not the result actually occurred.

COUNT 9: TAMPERING WITH A DECEASED HUMAN BODY (F3)

On or about the 13th day of August, 2018, in the County of Weld, State of Colorado; CHRISTOPHER LEE WATTS, believing that an official proceeding was pending, in progress, or about to be instituted, and acting without legal right or authority, unlawfully and feloniously wilfully destroyed, mutilated, concealed, removed, or altered a human body, part of a human body, or human remains with intent to impair its or their appearance or availability in the official proceedings OFFICIAL PROCEEDING means a proceeding heard before any legislative, judicial, administrative, or other government agency, or official authorized to hear evidence under oath, including any magistrate, hearing examiner, commissioner, notary, or other person taking testimony or depositions in any such proceedings. WITH INTENT – A person acts intentionally or with intent when his conscious objective is to cause the specific result proscribed by the statute defining the offence. It is immaterial whether or not the result actually occurred.

PENALTIES

COUNT 1: MURDER IN THE FIRST DEGREE (F1): The minimum sentence is life in prison without parole; the maximum sentence is death.

COUNT 2: MURDER IN THE FIRST DEGREE (F1): The minimum sentence is life in prison without parole; the maximum sentence is death.

COUNT 3: MURDER IN THE FIRST DEGREE (F1): The minimum sentence is life in prison without parole; the maximum sentence is death.

COUNT 4: MURDER IN THE FIRST DEGREE (F1): The minimum sentence is life in prison without parole; the maximum sentence is death.

COUNT 5: MURDER IN THE FIRST DEGREE (F1): The minimum sentence is life in prison without parole; the maximum sentence is death.

COUNT 6: UNLAWFUL TERMINATION OF PREGNANCY IN THE FIRST DEGREE (F2): 16 TO 48 years confinement with the Colorado Department of Corrections; a sentence to the Department of Corrections requires an additional mandatory parole period of 5 years for crimes committed prior to July 1, 2018 and 3 years for crimes committed after July 1, 2018. A fine from $5,000.00 to $1,000,000.00

may be assessed in addition to or in lieu of any sentence of imprisonment.

COUNT 7: TAMPERING WITH A DECEASED HUMAN BODY (F3): 4 TO 12 years of confinement with the Colorado Department of Corrections; sufficient mitigating circumstances may reduce the minimum to 2 years; sufficient aggravating circumstances may increase the maximum to 24 years; a sentence to the Department of Corrections requires an additional mandatory parole period of 5 years for crimes committed prior to July 1, 2018 and 3 years for crimes committed after July 1, 2018. A fine of from $3,000.00 to $750,000.00 may be assessed in addition to or in lieu of any sentence of imprisonment.

COUNT 8: TAMPERING WITH A DECEASED HUMAN BODY (F3): 4 TO 12 years of confinement with the Colorado Department of Corrections; sufficient mitigating circumstances may reduce the minimum to 2 years; sufficient aggravating circumstances may increase the maximum to 24 years; a sentence to the Department of Corrections requires an additional mandatory parole period of 5 years for crimes committed prior to July 1, 2018 and 3 years for crimes committed after July 1, 2018. A fine of from $3,000.00 to $750,000.00 may be assessed in addition to or in lieu of any sentence of imprisonment.

COUNT 9: TAMPERING WITH A DECEASED HUMAN BODY (F3): 4 TO 12 years of confinement with the Colorado Department of Corrections; sufficient mitigating circumstances may reduce the minimum to 2 years; sufficient aggravating circumstances may increase the maximum to 24 years; a sentence to the Department of Corrections requires an additional mandatory parole period of 5 years for crimes committed prior to July 1, 2018 and 3 years for crimes committed after July 1, 2018. A fine of from $3,000.00 to $750,000.00 may be assessed in addition to or in lieu of any sentence of imprisonment.

AGREEMENT

Defendant will plead guilty to all counts set forth in the Complaint and Information:

Count 1, Murder in the First Degree – After Deliberation (Shanann Watts), a class one felony;

Count 2, Murder in the First Degree – After Deliberation (Bella Watts), a class one felony;

Count 3, Murder in the First Degree – After Deliberation (Celeste Watts), a class one felony;

Count 4, Murder in the First Degree – Child Under 12 (Bella Watts), a class one felony;

Count 5, Murder in the First Degree – Child Under 12 (Celeste Watts), a class one felony;

Count 6, Unlawful Termination of Pregnancy in the First Degree (Nico), a class one felony;

Count 7, Tampering with a Deceased Human Body, a class three felony;

Count 8, Tampering with a Deceased Human Body, a class three felony;

Count 9, Tampering with a Deceased Human Body, a class three felony;

All sentencing options on all counts are open to the court. However, in exchange for Defendant's guilty pleas the Office of the District Attorney agrees that it will not seek the death penalty. Whether sentencing on separate counts run consecutive or concurrent to each other is open to the court, with the exception that, at a minimum, the parties stipulate the sentencing on Counts 1 through 3 and count 6 shall run consecutively as each charge references a separate victim. Defendant will not be permitted to waive a factual basis for any charge. The parties further stipulate that the Defendant will pay restitution as determined by the Court, including but not limited to the expenses for funeral and burial expenses for Shanann Watts, Bella Watts, Celeste Watts, and Nico Watts. Furthermore, the Defendant agrees to pay restitution covering the actual costs of specific future treatment pursuant to C.R.R. 18-1.3-603(1)(c).

Finally, the parties stipulate that the People may withdraw from this agreement if the Defendant commits a new felony offence while awaiting sentencing.

There are a lot of opinions on this plea deal, one of them being that the plea deal was taken unlawfully. It certainly seemed to have been dealt with faster than is usual in such a high-profile case like this. Chris was never made to confess the entire truth—to explain the hows and whys in their entirety. We, the public, didn't get to hear what caused this once seemingly perfect husband and father to perform one of the most heinous of acts. We can't be the only ones who felt cheated by this.

And, now, according to Chris, he feels he is entitled to an appeal, the main reason being he claims he might not have been in the best state of mind at the time of confessing the crimes in the manner in he did.

But can he actually appeal, considering he confessed to everything and waived his rights to a full trial? Well, according to the state of Colorado a defendant can file a 35c motion. He may raise any issue of constitutional magnitude in his Rule 35c motion. One of the most common issues in post-conviction litigation is the question of ineffective assistance of counsel. The defendant in a criminal case has a constitutional right to the effective assistance of counsel. A violation of that right may result in the defendant's conviction or sentence being overturned.

What would Chris hope to gain from an appeal? Unless he had some further evidence proving he didn't actually kill his family then he would most certainly still receive life sentences. He could even receive the death penalty. So why would he risk this, unless, of course, he has something quite substantial to gain from it?

NINE

Sentencing Hearing

(TAKEN FROM LIVE STREAM FOOTAGE)

On the 19th November 2018 in the Weld County Courthouse, Colorado, Chris Watts, handcuffed and dressed in orange prison attire, is led into the courtroom to face his victim's family for the first time since the murders. His fear is palpable.

The Judge is Marcelo A. Kopcow.

DA Michael Rourke is the first to address the court.

'Your Honour, present in the courtroom are Frank Rzucek, Sandy Rzucek, and Frank Rzucek Junior. They are Shanann's mom, dad, and brother. They have been fully advised on the nature of the proceedings today. Also, based upon the order that the court entered last week, I can tell the court that Ronnie and Cindi Watts are present in the courtroom as well. They've also had opportunity to meet with representatives from my office over the weekend to discuss the nature of the hearing today. I believe that we are fully in compliance with the Victim's Rights Act.' DA Rourke returns to his seat.

'Thank you,' Judge Kopcow said. 'So, what I would like to do is explain the procedures that we're going to use regarding the sentencing hearing. Let me first say that I realise that this sentencing hearing is emotional for many of us. And I expect that your behaviour in the courtroom, both in this courtroom and the overflow courtroom is appropriate. If the court determines that your demeanour/behaviour while in the courtroom during the hearing is not appropriate, I have advised the deputies that I will be asking you to be escorted out of the courtroom, so please be mindful of your demeanour during the sentencing hearing. Also, as a reminder, all electronic devices must be turned off. The only electronic devices that I have authorised to be used are those through the expanded media coverage order. If deputies see that you are using electronic devices not authorised by the court the deputies will take action on that. So please be mindful of that. If you need to turn off your electronic devices, please do so now. So, these are the procedures that we are going to use for the sentencing hearing. First, the prosecution will have an opportunity to present evidence. Once the prosecution finishes, the defence will have an opportunity to present evidence. Then, if there are any victims under the victim's rights act, including Cindy and Ronnie Watts, that have been called by the prosecution or the defence or any other defined victims under the victim's rights act they will have an opportunity to make a statement to the court as it relates to the victim's rights act. Thereafter, the prosecution will have an opportunity to argue. The defence will have an opportunity to make an argument. If Mr Watts chooses to, he will have an opportunity to make a statement and then the court will impose a sentence in this case. Does everybody understand? Okay. And so, Mr Rourke, are you going to be speaking on behalf of the prosecution?'

'Yes, your Honour, I am.'

'Then you are welcome to present the evidence.'

'Thank you.' DA Rourke gets to his feet. 'Your Honour, if may I approach… ((unintelligible)) … would have been marked as sentencing exhibits one through twenty-one inclusive. I have provided copies of these to defence counsels.' He approached the judge and handed him some paperwork.

'Thank you.'

'Your Honour, photographs one through twenty-one… sentencing exhibits one through twenty-one represent a number of different photographs that are in Discovery that Shanann's mother and father wanted the court to have for your consideration as you impose sentence today. They may allude to those and I've asked them to do so by way of sentencing exhibit number, but that's the substance of exhibits one through twenty-one.'

'Thank you. And you have individuals who would like to make a statement?'

'I do, your Honour. If I could first call upon Frank Rzucek to join me at the podium.'

'Thank you.'

Shanann's father gets up and approaches the stand.

'Good morning, Mr Rzucek,' Judge Kopcow said.

'Good morning.' Frank unfolds a piece of paper. He appears distraught and has large circles under his eyes. 'I'd like to say to the court that…' Frank steps backwards and appears unsteady on his feet. '… Shanann, Bella and Nico (this was clearly a mistake as I'm sure he meant to say Celeste here) were loving and caring people that loved life, that loved being around people who loved them. They always had good times. This is the first time they went to the beach this year and they loved it. But God only knows what happened that night. Life will never be the same without Shanann, Bella and Celeste and Nico… had all their lives to live and they were taken by a heartless one. This is the heartless one. The evil monster how dare you take the lives of my daughter, Shanann, Bella, Celeste, and Nico. I trusted you to take care of them, not kill them. And they also trusted you, the heartless monster, and then you take them out like trash. You disgust me. They were loving and caring people. You may have taken their bodies from me, but you will never take the love they had from me. They loved us more than you will ever know. Because you don't know what love is, because, if you did, you would not have killed them. You monster. Thought you would get away with this. I don't know how. The cameras do not lie. You carried them out like trash, out of the house, yes, I seen the video tape. You buried my daughter, Shanann and Nico in a shallow grave, and then you put Bella and Celeste in huge containers of crude oil. You heartless monster. You have… you have to live with this vision every day of your life and I hope you see that every time you close your eyes at night. Oh, I forgot, you have no heart or feelings, or love. Let me tell you something. I will think of them every day of my life and I love them every day of my life. Prison is too good for you. This… this is hard to say, but may God have mercy on your soul. I hope you enjoy your new life—it's nothing like the one you had out here. May the courts have no mercy on you. It's hard every day—it hurts in so many ways. I have heard people say that you're not a monster. No you are not—you're an evil monster. Thank you. Love you Shanann, Bella and Nico. Love your Pop-pop and Dad. And one other thing… and Shanann says she is super-excited for justice today.

Thank you, your Honour.' Frank folds up the paper and walks back to his seat.

Chris sits stock still, his eyes firmly fixed downwards. A male member of the defence team pats him supportively on the back.

DA Rourke returns to the stand. 'Your Honour, Frankie Rzucek Junior. He has asked me to read his statement for him. But he would like to stand with me if that's ok?'

'Of course. Sir, if I could just have you state your name for the record.'

'Frankie Rzucek junior.'

'Thank you for being here.'

'Your Honour, the past three months I've barely slept because I've been going through a lot of different emotions because I did not see this coming. You went from being my brother, my sister's protector, one of the most loved people in my family, to someone I will spend the rest of my life trying to understand. What gave you the right to put your hands on a woman? Let alone my best friend, my beloved sister your daughters and your son? Why weren't they enough for you? In the blink of an eye you took away my whole world—the people who mattered to me the most. Everything in my life I loved, your children. They trusted you. They loved you. They looked up to you because you promised to keep them safe, instead you turned on your family. My blood is boiling as I write these last words because they are the last you will ever hear from me. I can't even think of the right words to describe the betrayal and the hate I feel, and, to be honest, you aren't even worth the time and effort it takes to put my pen to this paper. There isn't a day goes by that I don't cry for my family. They were my whole world. All I do is ask myself why. Why would you do this? You don't deserve to be called a man. What kind of person slaughters the people that loved them the most? Did you really think you would get away with this? Did you really think that this was your best option? To throw away your family like they were garbage? They deserved better and you know it. I hope you spend the rest of your life staring at the ceiling every night, being haunted by what you've done. None of us deserved this. Hearing my mother and father cry themselves to sleep in this hotel room, causes me anguish that is beyond words. I can't describe how this feels. How badly my heart is breaking for my poor parents. We trusted you. You have taken away my family from this Earth but you can never take them from my heart. You took away my privilege of being an uncle to the most precious little girls I've ever known. I will never hear the words Uncle Frankie again, but you will never be called Dad again either. You'll never be able to put your hands on another woman, let alone my best friend, my beloved sister, and your son. I just can't comprehend how they weren't enough for you. Shanann, Bella and CeCe loved you more than anyone. You were their hero. How could you destroy the people who loved them the most? I pray that you never have a moment's peace or a good night's rest in the cage that you will spend every day of your life in. A cage you are privileged to live in because my family isn't evil like you. We begged the District Attorney to spare your life, because, despite everything, we believe that no-one has the right to take the life of another. Even someone like you. I feel sorry for your family. I know the pain that they must feel knowing that they can't hug you, because that's how my mother and father and I feel every time we cry for our family. Nothing hurts more than watching or hearing my family weep for their loved ones I just wish that you would tell the truth, but I know that is asking for more than you are capable of. I stayed up all night writing this statement. I don't sleep because of you. My life will never be the same because of you, but at least my conscience is clear. I get to live free, but I can't say the same for you. I haven't slept in two days because I've been anxiously waiting for this moment. The moment I get to tell you how I feel, how this has affected my family and I. My family and I can finally grieve after today. If anything, we will come out of this stronger today than we were before and we will continue to pray for your family. Sincerely, Frankie Rzucek.'

Frankie thanks DA Rourke and pats him on the shoulder before heading back to his seat.

'Your Honour, Sandi Rzucek would like to address the court,' DA Rourke said.

Sandi makes her way to the front of the courtroom.

'Good morning,' Judge Kopcow said.

'Good morning, your Honour and thank you for this moment.'

'If I could just have you to identify yourself for the record.'

'My name is Sandra Rzucek, Shanann's mother. I wanted to say thank you for this moment. I want to take a moment to thank everyone who has prayed for our beloved family—who has sent gifts, cards to us, from all over the world. I know God will put the Evil people where they need to be. I also wanna take the time to thank the town of Frederick, Greeley FBI, the DA's office, the CBI for exceptional work. We thank Nickole Atkinson, Shanann's neighbour, Nathan, and his family. To me they're our heroes. They really are, God bless. God makes no mistakes on who he puts in your life, marriage is about love, trust and friendship, and unity. We marry in sickness and health till death do us part. Our daughter Shanann loved you with all of her heart. Your children loved you to the moon and back. Shanann's family was her world. Shanann put a crown on your head. But unfortunately, the day you took their life God removed that crown. We loved you like a son. We trusted you. Your faithful wife trusted you. Your children adored you and they also trusted you. Your daughter, Bella Marie, sang a song proudly. I don't know if you got to see it, but it was Daddy, you're my hero. I have no idea who gave you the right to take their lives, but I know God and his mighty Angels were there at that moment to bring them home to paradise. God gives us free will, so not only did you take the family of four—your family of four, you took your own life. I want the world to know that our daughter and her children were so loved by us. They will always be protected by God and his mighty Angels. I didn't want death for you because that's not my right. Your life is between you and God now, and I pray that he has mercy for you. From Shanann's mother, Bella Marie, Celeste Katherine, and Nico Lee's nonna. Thank you your Honour.'

Chris sits rocking back and forth, clearly affected by Sandi's words.

'Your Honour, that's all the witnesses I had intended on calling,' DA Rourke said. 'And I know the court addressed this and the procedural posture. And I'm aware that Mr and Mrs Watts would also like to address the court. I would certainly invite the court if you want to call upon them or we can certainly do it after any evidence that the defence has as well.'

'Sure. Does Cindy or Ronnie Watts wish to make a statement, under the victim's rights amendment?'

Jean Powers—attorney, Ronnie and Cindy approach the stand.

'Good morning, Miss Powers' The Judge says.

'Good morning, your Honour.'

'Could I have you introduce yourselves for the record?'

'I'm Cindy Watts.'

'Ronnie Watts.'

'I have authorised you to make a statement to the court as paternal grandparents to the children. And if you choose not to make a statement but your designee, Miss Powers, chooses to she can do so as well. How would you like to proceed?'

Cindy and Miss Powers have a short conversation.

'Who's going to be speaking today?' The judge presses.

'Your Honour, initially, they've asked me and they're hoping that they have the strength to speak, but if they do not, they've written out their statements and asked me to finish for them so…'

'That would be fine. Who would like to go first?'

'If I could start, your Honour,' Miss Powers said. 'On behalf of the Watts', your Honour, and to the community, we thank you for the opportunity and the recognition under the victim bill of rights. We come today as the grandparents and the parents of the daughter and children whose life was taken in this case. We are not here to ask for leniency. We are not in any way condoning or tolerating the crime that has occurred and the pain that has been caused. We join in our daughter-in-law and grandchildren's family in saying this should never have happened. This is not condonable. This is something that we will never get over. We appreciate the consideration that everyone has paid, most especially the families that have lost everyone. We appreciate that they begged for Christopher's life. We agree and echo what they have said, that it is not his place to take anyone's life, nor would it be our place as a community to take his life. So we thank you for the opportunity and for every consideration and effort that's been put out. The prosecution in this case has in fact respected the victim bill of rights. They took the time to explain that the information that my clients had at the time that they were interviewed was not correct. They were misinformed. They were searching for answers. They were not intending to cause any pain to anyone. And they appreciate that the prosecution answered their questions and gave them the time and the respect and the consideration so that they could tell this court and everyone in this community that the interview content was not their message. That they accept that their son has done this. That they accept that he chose to plead guilty. That he sought and requested their consent and agreement for a life sentence. They appreciate that he is given the opportunity to serve that life sentence. It is his responsibility. It is his sentence, and it is not enough to make up for what he has done. We understand and we join the family in that we have questions. We don't know how such a thing could possibly happen. Or that a man that was responsible for raising his children and protecting his wife would take the steps that he did. And that he would disregard their bodies and the love that he had for them and they had for him and everyone else and take the gestures and put this community through the investigation and the discovery and the responsibility of bringing justice. We do not understand that. We do not think it was appropriate. We cannot begin to think that an explanation will ever justify it. My clients indicate that they understand that a full opportunity for a confession with all of the responsibility and accountability has not occurred. And they support the family in the request that that happen if not today, at an appropriate time, in an appropriate manner, so that everyone can have peace. To understand to the best of their ability the details that they need and to have their questions answered. And by giving this opportunity of a life sentence we hope that he embraces that moment. That had the death penalty been pursued there would not have been an opportunity to be accountable and to give a full confession. And had the death penalty been sought, council would've fought for his life, the prosecutors would've been engaged in a multiple year battle, the families would've been torn apart, this community would've had to subsidise it and endure it and we have so much respect and gratefulness that that did not happen. We would strongly encourage Christopher Watts to give that full confession in the tone and in the timing that he thinks is appropriate with the guidance of his council. We feel it will be appropriate and helpful to ease the pain and the suffering. But we also say that we don't think that there's anything he can say that will ever account for his behaviour. There is nothing that can be done to cure the harm he has caused, and he has the responsibility to serve his sentence with dignity and with regard for everyone. And to spend every breath that he has left in atonement for what he has done.'

Cindy Watts takes the microphone.

The judge asks her to state her name for the record.

'Cindy Watts.'

'Thank you.'

'My name is Cindy Watts. I am the grandmother of two beautiful granddaughters, Bella Marie, and Celeste Catherine Watts. I am also the mother of Christopher Watts who I will be directing most of my statement to. First, I'd like to begin by recognising the absolute horror of this crime and acknowledging the devastating loss that both the

Rzucek family as well as our family have faced. Our families have been irreparably broken by the needless deaths of Shanann, Bella, CeCe and Nico. This is something that we will never get over. We will always mourn the loss of our family, and in that, we are united in our grief. I am still struggling to understand how and why this tragedy occurred. I may never be able to understand and accept it, but I pray for peace and healing for all of us. Now, to my son, Christopher. I have known you since the day you were born into this world. I have watched you grow from a quiet, and sweet, curious child who Bella reminded me so much of, to a young man who worked hard in sports and later mechanics to achieve your goals. You were a good friend, brother, father, and son. You have… we have loved you from the beginning, and we still love you now. This might be hard for some to understand how I can sit here under these circumstances and tell you although we are heartbroken, although we can't imagine what could have happened that led us to this day, that we love you. Maybe you can't believe it either. As the Lord said, in Jerimiah 3:31—I have loved you with an everlasting love, therefore I will continue my faithfulness to you and you, as your mother, Chris, I have always loved you, and I still do. I hate what has happened. Your father and sister and I are struggling to understand why, but we will remain faithful as your family, just as God remains faithful because of his unconditional love for all… for us all. We love you, (she turns to face Chris), and we forgive you, son.'

The attorney steps up once more. 'Judge, if I could read Mr Watts statement?'

'Yes.'

'My name is Ronnie Watts, and I am the grandfather of Bella, Celeste, Nico Watts. And I am the father of Shanann. I am the father of Christopher Watts as well. And one of the most important things I've done in my life is to raise my children and to watch as they started their own families. I spent many years coaching little league, and talking to my son, taking him to the races, and sharing my love and knowledge of cars with him. He was just as involved with his girls. I believe he loves his girls. I know he does. This tragedy has impacted my family in so many ways. Beyond losing my precious grandchildren, our beloved daughter-in-law, we are forced to question everything. We still don't have all the answers. And I hope one day, Christopher, you can help us. Chris, I want to talk to you as a father and son. You are here today, accepting responsibility, but I want to tell you this now, I love you. Nothing will ever change that. And I want you to find peace. And today is your first step. The bible says if we confess our sins, God is faithful, and just, and will forgive us. Chris, I forgive you. And your sister forgives you. And we will never abandon you, and we love you, Dad. Judge, thank you for the opportunity to address the court.'

The three make their way back to their seats.

'Are there any other statutory victims under the Victim's Rights Act that would like to make a statement today?' The judge asks.

Somebody say's 'Your Honour I'm not aware of any.'

'For the record, nobody is raising their hands,' the judge says. 'Mr Walsh would you like to present any evidence?'

'We have no evidence, your Honour.'

'Thank you. Mr Rourke is there any statements you would like to make on behalf of the prosecution?'

'Yes, please.' DA Rourke returns to the stand. 'Your Honour, there are no words to adequately describe the unimaginable tragedy that brings us before this court today. By my comments, I'm not gonna even try to express the horror, the pain, or the suffering that the defendant has caused to these families, to this community, and to all who were a part of this investigation. However, I do want to spend a few minutes sharing with the court the details of the crime, and so far, you've only had opportunity to review the affidavit and a few facts here and there that have been offered to the court in the motions and pleading that have been filed. The questions that have screamed out to anyone who will listen, since August 13th of 2018 are why? And how? Why did this have to happen? How could a seemingly normal husband and father annihilate his entire family? For what? These are the questions that only one individual in this courtroom or on this planet knows the answers to. I fully expect we will not receive the answers to these questions today. Nor will we at any point in the future. I don't expect that he will ever tell the truth about what truly happened. Or why. Even if he did, there's no rational way that any human being could find those answers acceptable responses to such horrific questions. The best we can do is try to piece together some kind of understanding from the evidence that is available to us. And the evidence tells us this… the defendant coldly, and deliberately ended four lives. Not in a fit of rage. Not by way of accident, but in a calculated and sickening manner. Shanann was thirty-four years old. She had married the defendant in the November of 2012. Over the weekend leading up to August 13th she had been at a work conference in Phoenix, Arizona and returned home in the early morning hours of August 13th. We know that she got home about one-forty-five in the morning. The doorbell camera on their home shows her arriving back home from the airport. Shortly thereafter, at least, according to the defendant, they had a… what he referred to as an emotional conversation about the state of their marriage and about what their lives would look like going forward. What was said during that emotional conversation only he knows. What we do know, is that shortly after that the defendant strangled her to death with his own hands. We know that he slowly took her life the morning of August 13th. We know that this was not done in an uncontrolled vengeful manner that he tried to describe to the agents of CBI and the FBI. If that were the case you would expect to see horrible, vicious bruising about her neck, shoulders and face. You would expect to see the hyoid bone in her neck broken. You would expect to see some kind of defensive wounds on his body as she struggled and fought for her own life. None of those are present. The only injuries that were on Shanann's body were one set of finger… or bruising which appear to be fingernail or finger-mark bruising to the right side of her neck. We know that our experts tell us it takes two to four minutes to strangle someone to death manually with their own hands. The horror that she felt as the man that she loved wrapped his hands around her throat and choked the life out of her must have been unimaginable. Even worse—what must Bella, age four, and Celeste, age three, must have experienced or thought as their father, the one man on this planet who was supposed to nurture and protect them was snuffing out their lives. They both died from smothering. Let me say that again. The man seated to my right smothered his daughters. Why? Imagine the horror in Bella's mind as her father took her last breaths away. Your Honour, I understand very clearly, Bella fought back for her life. The frenulum, the connective tissue between her upper lip and her gum, had an inch and a half… 'scuse me, had a centimetre and a half laceration. She bit her tongue multiple times before she died. She fought back for her life as he father smothered her. Celeste had no such injuries. In fact, she had no external injuries at all. But, according to the medical examiner, she was smothered none the less. The defendant then methodically and calmly loaded their bodies into his work truck. Not in a hasty or disorganised way. He was seen from the neighbour's doorbell camera backing his truck into the driveway, going back and forth into the house, and back out to the truck three different times. One time for each or their bodies. He then drove them away from their family home one final time, intent on hiding any evidence of the crimes that he had just committed. In one final sign of callousness for his wife, his daughters, and their unborn son and their remains, he drove them to a location that he thought no-one would ever find them—to one of the oil tank batteries of which he was so familiar. He knew this was safe. He had texted a co-worker the night before saying, *I'll head out to that site. I'll take care of it.* He had carefully ensured that he would be alone in the middle of the plains, to secrete away the remains of his family in a place that he hoped they would never be found. In one final measure of disrespect for the family he once had, he ensured they would not be together even in death. Or so he thought. He disposed of them in different locations. He buried Shanann and Nico in a shallow grave away from the oil tanks. Bella and Celeste were thrown away in the oil tanks at this facility. Different tanks, so that these little girls wouldn't be together in death. Imagine this, your Honour. This defendant took those little girls and put them through a hatch at the top of an oil tank eight inches in diameter. Bella had scratches on her left buttocks from being shoved through this hole. A tuft of blonde hair was found on the edge of one of these hatches. The Defendant told investigators that Bella's tank seemed emptier than CeCe's because of the sound that the splashes made. *These were his daughters.* Significantly, that when his co-workers arrived at the tank battery later that morning, to a person they all described him as acting completely normally. It was a normal workday, even while his daughters sank in the oil and water not far away from him. And then his efforts at deception truly began. We've all seen the emotionless interviews that the defendant gives to the local media, asking for help in locating his family. We watched as he claimed that the house was empty without them. And that he hoped they were somewhere safe and that he just wanted them to come home. He told investigators that they were at home sleeping when he left for work that morning. And that Shanann had told him that she was taking the girls to a friend's house for the day. What is striking about this case, your Honour, beyond the horrors that I've already described to you, is the number of collateral victims that he created by his actions. While he stood in front of TV cameras asking for the safe return of his family, scores of Law Enforcement Officers, neighbours, friends and family scoured the area, fretted for their safe return. They texted him begging for any information and sending him their best wishes, all-the-while, he hid what he had done. The list of indirect victims does not end there. Think of the fire-fighters and the Colorado State Patrol Hazmat experts who had to don protective suits and who were called upon to pull Bella and Celeste out of those oil tanks. Or the coroner employees who had to conduct these autopsies, or the victim assistance who had to frantically ease the suffering of those affected. All of this, your Honour, for what? Why? Why did this have to happen? His motive was simple, your Honour. He had a desire for a fresh start. To begin a relationship with a new love that overpowered all decency and feelings for his wife, his daughters and unborn son. While Shanann texted the defendant over and over again in the days and weeks leading up to her death, attempting to save her marriage, the defendant secreted pictures of his girlfriend into his phone and texted her at all hours of the night. While Shanann sent the defendant self-help and relationship counselling books, one of which ironically enough was thrown in the garbage, he was searching the internet for secluded vacation spots to take his new love and researching jewellery. And while Shanann took the girls to visit family in North Carolina, the defendant went to car museums and the sand dunes with his new girlfriend. The stark contrast between the subjects of their internet and text content is absolutely stunning. Even the morning after he killed them and disposed of their bodies, he made several phone calls. One was to the school where the girls were supposed to start, telling the school that he would… that the girls would not be coming to school anymore that they were being unenrolled. Presumably to get him some more time before Law Enforcement notification about them going missing. He contacted a realtor to start discussing the selling of his house, and he texted with his girlfriend about their future. None of this answers the question of why, however. If he was this happy, and wanted a new start, get a divorce. You don't annihilate your family and throw them away like garbage. Why did Nico, Celeste, Bella and Shanann have to lose their lives in order for him to get what he wanted? Your Honour, justice demands the maximum sentence under the agreement reached by the parties. As you will recall the agreement calls for life sentences as to Shanann, Bella and Celeste and all of those to run consecutively together. It also calls for the count of unlawful termination of a pregnancy as to Nico, to run consecutively to counts of one, two and three. I would suggest that the extreme aggravation present in the defendant's conduct, and in the efforts that I have described mandate that the sentences for counts seven, eight and nine, for tampering with a deceased human body, each be the maximum of twelve years and that those sentences run consecutively to one another. It is very clear that each of these acts… excuse me, that these were not the subject of one act, but each oil tank that he walked up with his daughter's bodies, and the hole that he dug for his wife and unborn son, mandate a mandatory consecutive sentence. It's been alluded to this morning, but the defendant was certainly eligible for the death penalty in this case, under the existing law in the State of Colorado. As you heard, Shanann's family strongly opposed my office seeking the death penalty and being bound to the Criminal Justice System for the next several decades. That's in large part, as you've heard, why we've reached the agreement that we have. Four lives were lost at the hands of the defendant on August 13th for reasons that we will never fully understand, nor will we know. In the end, the Rzucek family was much more merciful towards him than he was towards his wife, his daughters and his unborn son. Prison for the remainder of his life is exactly where he belongs for murdering his entire family. Thank you.'

'Are you seeking ninety-one days to file a clause for restitution?'

'I am, your Honour, please.'

'I'll grant that request. Mr Walsh, will you be speaking on behalf of your client?'

Mr Walsh half rose to his feet. 'Your Honour, Miss Herold will address the court.'

'Good morning, Miss Herold.'

'Good morning, your Honour. Mr Watts has asked us to share this morning that he is devastated by all of this. And although he understands that words are hollow at this point he is sincerely sorry for all of this. Thank you.'

'Thank you. Mr Watts, as I indicated when we began, you have the right to make a statement if you choose to. Would you like to make a statement?'

'No, Sir.'

'Thank you. So, the court has considered the arguments made by the attorneys. The court has considered the statements made by the victims in this case. The court's gonna find that the plea agreement is fair and reasonable under the circumstances. I want to acknowledge the Rzucek family as well as the Watts family that um, showing mercy on Mr Watts is understood. And I respect that decision to request that the District Attorney not seek the death penalty in this case. And so the court is going to accept this plea bargain under the circumstances. Words that come to mind when I hear the evidence in this case are, a senseless crime, and the viciousness of the crime and equally aggravating in this court's determination is the despicable act of disposing of the bodies in the manner in which they were done in this case. I've been a judicial officer now for… starting my seventeenth year, and I could objectively say that this is perhaps the most inhumane and vicious crime that I have handled out of the thousands of cases that I have seen. And nothing less than a maximum sentence would be appropriate and anything less than the maximum sentence would depreciate the seriousness of this offence. So the court is going to sentence Mr Watts as follows. With regard to count number one–murder in the first degree as relates to Shanann Watts, the court is going to sentence you, sir, to a life sentence in the Colorado Department of Corrections with no possibility of parole. And that is gonna run consecutively to all but counts three and four. With regard to count two as it relates to murder in the first degree, with Bella, the court is going to sentence you to life in the Colorado Department of Corrections with no possibility of parole. With regard to count number three, the court is going to sentence you as it relates to Celeste, to life in the Colorado Department of Corrections with no possibility of parole. With regards to counts four and five, relating to Bella and Celeste, as a different theory of first degree murder, the court is gonna sentence you to life in the Colorado Department of Corrections and legally those sentences must run concurrently as a different theory of first degree murder. Recognising um, the unlawful termination of pregnancy for the unborn child that has been named Nico, the court absolutely believes that the maximum sentence of forty-eight years would be appropriate and will run consecutive to the other charges, with an additional mandatory parole period of three years set forth by statute. With regard to count number seven, as it relates to tampering with a deceased body, as well as counts eight and nine, each a class three felony, the court is going to impose a maximum sentence of twelve years each for those counts to run consecutively to the other counts. The court is going to order that the statutory fees be paid and court costs. The court is going to grant the prosecution ninety-one days to file a notice of restitution and that will be the sentence of the court. We will shortly be in recess. I would respectfully ask the parties that you remain in your seat. There is a plan by the deputies on allowing people to exit the courtroom so please remain seated until you are authorized to leave the courtroom based on the direction of the deputies. Deputies, I would respectfully ask that you take this defendant into custody and have him serve the rest of his life in the department of corrections.'

TEN

Final Chris Watts Prison Interview

TAKEN FROM DISCOVERY AUDIO FILES

February 2019

Apart from Chris being moved to Wisconsin Department of Corrections, little had been heard about him after the sentencing hearing in November. However, that doesn't mean everything had settled down. In fact, the opposite was true in the online crime circles. The Discovery files had been released and amateur sleuths around the world trawled through every page and studied the footage frame by frame. It was during this time a member of the public spotted the shadows underneath Chris's truck on the morning of the murders. Had Nate's CCTV footage caught much more than originally thought—evidence the girls had been still alive when Chris put them in the truck? Is this what prompted the unplanned prison interview?

Transcript taken from the Discovery's audio file.
Please note: Although every effort has been taken to present a true account of the following interview, sometimes it is difficult to distinguish which detective was actually speaking.

Tammy **-** CBI Agent Tammy Lee
Grahm **-** FBI Special Agent Grahm Coder
Dave **-** Detective Dave Baumhover
Chris **-** Christopher Watts.

Chris is surprised by the detectives visit.
After reintroducing themselves, Grahm goes on to explain the reason the three of them are there.

Grahm: … the last time that we talked to you was a different situation. Our investigation was open and your case was open. That's completely different now, so, your case is completely closed. Nothing about what we're gonna talk about today has anything to do with an open investigation. So, we're not here to get more charges on you, or get any statements from you that are gonna jam you up any more. Right, that's all done. So, all of our cases are closed, and the court case is closed. So, there's nothing that we're gonna talk about today that's gonna get you in any type of trouble, at all. Um, and so, that's… I wanted to make sure you knew that's not why we're here.
Chris: Okay.
Grahm: Okay. But why we are here… so, um, the three of us we're from three different agencies, right? Quite a bit different, um, CBI, FBI, and Frederick PD. Different goals, and the things that happened with you are what brought us together. And as the months have passed on, since everything happened, we just keep in touch with each other, and keep talking to each other, and we've all separately kind of said, um, did Chris seem unique to you? Me and Tammy have talked about this, Dave and I have talked about this. Did Chris's situation seem different to you? And, we keep having that conversation and we can't quite put our finger on it. Right? Um, we think that your life, leading up to all the things that happened, were very interesting to us, and, for me personally, I don't know if you remember but one of the last things you told me was, hey, Grahm, I'm sorry that I started lying to you. Um, and that stuck with me for the last couple of months. It's been ringing in my head, right? I've never, ever worked a case like this where someone told me that. Ever. And so, as I walked away, I thought Chris is different, Chris is a little bit unique in that regard, um, so, talking with Tammy and talking with Dave, um, I said, you know, what did you feel like when it all went down? When we were there and we were talking to you guys, we all kind of, in our own different way and our own wording said, it all happened a bit too quick for us. Right? Um, so, when we saw you last, and we were talking and talking and talking, um, about your family, about your parents, about everyone, then, the next thing you know, me and Tammy and Dave, the next thing we know the

patrol officers came in and arrested you. Um, and that was far quicker than we hoped it would happen. Um, and you understand why that happened, and we understand why that happened, but it left us with a thousand questions that we didn't get to ask. Um, and then, even more importantly, I think it probably left you with a thousand things you didn't get to talk about with us. I don't know if you feel that way or not. And so, that's why we're here today, we wanted to kinda talk to you a little bit more about everything, you know. Um, I think there's a lot of things that you didn't get to talk about. Um, and so, you know, that's why we're here, um, and it sticks with me, that to this day, there's not one person that's told me, 'I saw it comin'. I knew Chris was like that, I knew it. Not one person. So, it's just… it's interesting to me, right? Not one. Um. So we wanna talk a little bit about that. Some of the people that we work with, er, your family, Shanann's family, um, have said, you know, if you get to talk to Chris would you tell him some things for me? So we have that to talk about today, and it's good. I think you'll like it. I think it will give you some closure. Um, and so, really, that's why we're here. Are you available to talk to us?

Chris: Yeah, definitely.

Grahm: So, off the bat, if you have any questions, just tell me, and if there's something that you don't wanna talk about, that's okay. We might press you a little bit. We might say well do you mind if just maybe we ask one question? Um, if something makes you uncomfortable, just tell us. If you need to take bathroom breaks, take bathroom breaks, um, you know, anything like that, we'll need bathroom breaks and water breaks ourselves too. Um, so then, is there anything about your schedule today that makes it that you can't talk to us?

Chris: No, there was like, a pass for this in the am and pm.

Tammy: Yeah, they reserved the room for the whole day. Just in case.

Chris: Okay, I didn't know if it was for two separate things…

((Crosstalk))

Tammy: I think you have to go back for lunch to get it um, counted for or something. Accounted for.

Chris: Oh, yeah. I think lunch is, like, eleven but the count is, like, twelve-fifteen, so…

(Crosstalk))

Grahm: So, in general, how's it been?

Chris: It's a lot different than Colorado.

Tammy: Is it?
Grahm: Good or bad.
Chris: It's better I think. Here I'm actually around other people. In Colorado it was just like, I was segregated, and there was pounding on the walls all night. ((Unintelligible)). I was climbing the walls…
((Crosstalk))
Grahm… From other people?
Chris: They were telling me, like, how I should kill myself and what they were gonna do to me…
Tammy: Oh!
Chris: This… this is a lot different. People here seem to… it's not that they don't care, but it's just kinda like, they don't… they don't judge you as soon as you walked in. Colorado was like, they knew why… why I was there and that was it. It was like, they just, had one second alone with me, it would've been…
Grahm: Really?
Chris: Yeah…
((Unintelligible))
Chris: … I don't know what it was like in the OC there, but they had to lock down the jail for me to walk down the hallway.
Grahm: Wow. So they had to make sure you were completely separated from anyone else?
Tammy: Wow.
Chris: Like, I couldn't… I didn't see anybody else there, if I was next to somebody, I never saw them.
Tammy: You'd just hear them?
Grahm: How did they know who you were?
Chris: I don't know. They… they make phone calls in there too…
Grahm: Oh, right.
Chris: … and they got the newspaper in there before I got... got in there, so.
Grahm: How is, er… have you been able to talk with family?
Chris: Oh, yeah. Definitely. We get, er… I get from six pm to seven-thirty… ((Unintelligible)).
Grahm: Really? And do they charge you for it?
Chris: Yeah, it's just like Colorado… it's like… ((Unintelligible)).
Grahm: And how do you make money to pay for that?
Chris: Um, they put money on the phone.

Grahm: Oh.
Chris: So, if I was to call… if I was to dial somebody's number they would have to have, like, a phone account set up.
Grahm: And so, who you call pays for it?
Chris: Yes.
Grahm: Oh, okay. You're able to talk to like, family members and parents and that?
Chris: Yeah, Mom and Dad and my sister.
Dave: Is that a good thing?
Chris: That's a good thing.
(Laughter).
Chris: If they don't hear from me they're like, what's wrong?
Dave: And how is it with them?
Chris: So far so good.
Dave: Yeah. It was hard to hear your parents at sentencing.
Tammy: Yeah.
Chris: I didn't know what they were gonna say.
Tammy: Mm hm.
Dave: And so… I really appreciated what they said, I don't know about you.
Chris: I didn't expect them to be there. They were there on the sixth, but I didn't think they would fly back.
Dave: And then I liked what your mom said.
Grahm: Um. Well, so we have a thousand questions, I'm sure that you do too. Is it okay if we start or do you have any questions for us?
Chris: Go ahead.
Grahm: So, one of the things that we're battling with is, um… and I shouldn't… I won't make assumptions today so are you aware that this is a national story?
Chris: After… after a little while I was. I didn't talk to my parents while I was in Colorado, so I didn't find out… ((Unintelligible)) … So, I made one phone call and that was in the segregation area there, but my dad didn't… he thought it was some kind of marketing dudes.
Tammy: Aw.
((Unintelligible, crosstalk)).
Tammy: So they didn't answer?
Chris: So, they didn't answer but… I didn't talk to anybody but what the… what some of the deputies were saying… my attorney kept

coming in saying, 'you've got people from Australia, England and all kinds of people trying to figure out what's going on.
Dave: Did you get any of the letters, like fan mail or anything?
Chris: I got letters and I could keep 'em. So I could read 'em but I got a bunch of letters that had no return address. Stuff that was, you know… not very good letters.
Dave: They came from a weird perspective, didn't they? From what we've heard.
Chris: Definitely there is… there was one person I guess that was writing me four times a week tryin' to come visit me. And there was just a lot of people like… ((Unintelligible)) … saying you're awesome, or you're… all kinds of crazy stuff.
Grahm: Well, I don't… we're gonna talk about hard issues today but, I don't intend to take you to a dark place today.
Chris: Okay.
Grahm: I hope that when we're done you'll feel better. I hope it'll be therapeutic. Um, we're gonna talk about, obviously, what happened with your family. So that's gonna be hard to talk about. I appreciate anything you can tell me about it. If you need to take time out, if you need to get a tissue, that's fine. Right? Um, I think it'll be very good for you, good for us. And so, one of the reasons… ((Unintelligible)) … is, we're aware you were getting a lot of letters, um, a lot of interest, then, us personally as law-enforcement, we got so many people who claimed to have known you, claimed to have been with you, dated you, slept with you and ninety-nine times out of a hundred they were just crazy people, right? And so, maybe that's a good place to start. Um, had you heard about any of them?
Chris: Uh, John Walsh told me about one dude from Wyoming…?
Grahm: Yeah.
Tammy: Trent.
Chris: Yeah, that guy, that blew my mind, I was like, who is this guy?
Grahm: Who told you that, now?
Chris: Attorney John Walsh.
Grahm: Um, do you mind if we talk about him?
Chris: Yes.
(Laughter).
Tammy: Grahm and I interviewed him.
Chris: Did you have to?

Grahm: Waste of our lives.
Tammy: Yes.
Grahm: So, Trent, in summary, Trent came in and said, um, he met you online on a dating app, um, had a few, you know, er, casual but quick sexual encounters with you, and let me be very clear, not only are we not here to jam you up today, we're not here to judge you. If there is anything like that, you can imagine we've heard way worse… ((Unintelligible)) … so, um, if it's true you can just, you know, casually say, yeah, this happened, it wasn't as bad as you said, but maybe this happened. So, his story was he went online, met you, and it was a time when you were experimenting with maybe men. And so, he said you met a couple of times, met his friends, you went to an apartment, you had a couple of meetings in a parking lot, and that was basically it. Any of that sound familiar?
Chris: No, I've never met the guy.
(Laughter).
Tammy: He talked about being in your truck with your girls, like, the whole nine yards. So…
Chris: No. I've never even been to Wyoming, let alone driven up there to see somebody.
((Crosstalk)).
Grahm: Do you have any gay experience?
Chris: No.
Grahm: Okay. Any interest?
Chris: No.
Grahm: Okay. Ever had a time you experimented… wondered…?
Chris: No.
Grahm: Okay. Is it possible that he found you instead of you finding him?
Chris: I… from what John told me, he found me on like, that WhatsApp. I don't even have the app. You have my phone so you could've saw what Apps I have. I've never even heard of the app, but…
Grahm: Okay.
Chris: … apparently, he told me, we met at the rehab centre or something?
Grahm: Is that what they say?
Tammy: No, that was another guy.
Chris: Oh okay.

Tammy: Yeah.
Grahm: Yeah.
Chris: It was totally… I
Tammy: So, did you see a picture of him on the news or anything?
Chris: John showed me a picture.
((Unintelligible- crosstalk))
Tammy: So you saw, and you were like, no way. Big lips—did you see them?
Chris: Mm hm.
Tammy: His giant lips.
Chris: Yeah and I was just, like, I have no clue.
Grahm: He's somewhat memorable.
Tammy: Yeah.
Grahm: If you met him, or talked to him, or got to know him, you might remember. Um, he's… he's… he was kinda meek.
Tammy: Yeah.
Grahm: And also, a little bit, um, flamboyant.
Tammy: Mm.
Grahm: His big lips, well, not big lips, but injections…
Tammy: Aha.
Grahm: You know, the skincare and makeup, um, and he mentioned that, one of the times, just as a gift, you got him some skincare products…
Tammy: Mm hm.
Grahm: … does any of that sound familiar?
Chris: No.
Grahm: Okay. You can imagine all this stuff we're dealing with… okay. So, that's one…
Tammy: Mm hm.
Grahm: Trent Bolte. There was another gal that you were dealing with…
Dave: Amanda McMahon—have you ever heard that name?
Chris: No.
Dave: No?
Chris: John showed me a picture of her, nothing.
Dave: Okay.
Tammy: So, you did see a picture of her too?
Chris: Yeah, like…

((Unintelligible – crosstalk))
Grahm: Does that look familiar?
Chris: That's the same picture he showed me I was like, nah! and he was like, oh, you don't know her neither?
Grahm: Yep.
Chris: I was like, no.
Grahm: Yeah.
Chris: He said it was a *Chick Fillet* parking lot rendezvous or something.
Dave: Right…
Grahm: And that's just not…
Dave: … that's what she's claiming.
Grahm: Okay.
Chris: All I know is one *Chick Fillet* in Colorado, that one down in Broomfield? Highway seven? That was it.
Grahm: Okay. Do you feel comfortable enough today to tell us if there were other people?
Chris: Yeah, it was just Nichol.
Grahm: Okay. And that was it? Okay. Um, as these people come out… for the most part, we've not given their stories much credit… they're just crazy people that want attention, um, and so… but, when that does happen it does make us think, um, you know, there may have been others, so Nichol was the only one?
Chris: That was the only one.
Grahm: Was there ever a one-night-stand with someone else, out of the blue…? ((Unintelligible))
Chris: No.
Grahm: Okay. Do you mind if we talk a little more about Nichol?
Chris: Okay.
Grahm: So, walk me through it because that was one of the things we never really got to ask you about.
Tammy: Right, we didn't talk much about that.
Grahm: We just kinda skipped on… you know, talked about where the girls were. So what happened there?
Chris: So, it was probably around, June first or somethin' when I first met her, and, uh, it was just a work conversation, like, she messed with the gas metre set, you know, we were out in the field, and I was messin' up and… ((Unintelligible)) … after that, you know, we just ran into

each other a few times in the office and, I think it was probably the fourth time meeting, um, she asked me, it's like… we were talking back and forth, I would say, um, you know, like, we moved here from North Carolina, stuff like that… And she said, what's all this we stuff? And I took out my phone, showed her a picture of my girls on the phone, and she was like, oh, okay. I didn't wear a ring to work, 'cause… ((Unintelligible)) … 'cause I lost all that weight, so… but um…

Grahm: You lost so much weight that your fingers lost weight?

Chris: Yeah. I was out in the snow one time, and I was like that… ring went off in the rocks, so… I was like, I was panicking trying to find it and I was like, I can't wear this thing to work…

Tammy: Hm.

Chris: But, um, so, after that, she left me alone for a couple of days, and she text me… ((Unintelligible)) … after that, we just kept texting back and forth, and there was… you know, she used to work in a… ((Unintelligible)) … North Dakota, thing, and uh, we just sent story's back and forth about what we did and everything, then, one day it just, kinda, went to a dif… different level, and then, I never thought it would go to that level, but, she was talking about meeting up after we got back from San Diego.

Grahm: When you went with Shanann?

Chris: Yeah. We were in San Diego from twenty-second to the twenty-sixth of June and, er, we met up after we got back and, um…

Tammy: How did you guys meet up?

Chris: Er, at a park in, er, Thornton? Yeah, in Thornton somewhere, um, and… after that we just kept seeing each other for most of the month of July.

Grahm: So, let me ask you this, um… you tell me if I'm wrong. You strike me as somewhat a shy person, so, when you guys were meeting was it just very initiatory, like, flirting at first?

Chris: Yeah.

Grahm: Okay. From both sides?

Chris: Yeah. We were just, kinda like, feeling each other out, you know?

Grahm: And so, texts… any calls?

Chris: More nearer the end of June.

Grahm: Okay. And what makes you remember it was June that it happened?

Chris: We didn't call each other before I left to go to San Diego.
Grahm: Oh, okay. All right. Um, at first, did you think something might happen?
Chris: I just thought it was just flirting, I didn't think it would actually, like… something that would actually happen.
Grahm: Yeah. Well, it's only natural, right? Everybody flirts at work, right? Um, because the relationship between men and women is different, so, if you're working with a girl at work, it's just kinda natural to flirt.
Chris: I wish I was on the field more, so I didn't go to the office… that was…
Grahm: Yeah, I can kinda see it in your eyes. That's er, that's kinda where the past started isn't it?
Chris: Yeah, I mean, if I was, like… I was a field… when I went from a rover to a field coordinator, like, I would spend the morning time in the office trying to get everything situated where we were gonna go, everything like that, you know, if I was a rover I'd be more out in the field instead of going to the office for more than an hour…
Grahm: Right.
Chris: … which gave me more time to run into her, pretty much.
Grahm: Yeah. Okay. What did she know about you? Did she know you were married at first?
Chris: She did, once I showed her the pictures on my phone, you know, the home screen picture?
Tammy: So, was your wife in that picture or was it just your girls?
Chris: It was just my girls right there, but my wife was, like, the lock screen. She knew I was married and had kids.
Grahm: Okay.
Tammy: Are you aware that she said she didn't know you were married?
Chris: No.
Tammy: What do you think about that?
Chris: She's just tryin' to save face, tryin' to… I just… tryin' to… something my sister said, it was like, uh, she was trying to keep things together...
Tammy: Yeah.
Chris: She phrased it in a different way but just kinda like… it's like ground control, she's trying to control everything that's going on

around her. I'm sure she got bombarded by all different sides of the media and, everything, so…
Tammy: Have you talked to her at all?
Chris: No.
Tammy: No?
Chris: No. I'm hoping she hasn't written to me with a different alias or something, I'm not… ((Unintelligible)) … that way.
Tammy: Aw…
Grahm: Are you… you know you're not allowed to talk to her?
Chris: I would hope not.
Grahm: Okay. No one's told you that, though?
Chris: No, I mean, I would expect, like, er, I thought, like, at Colorado we had a DOC list, like, if you're on the victim list you can call them.
Grahm: Oh, right.
Chris: But here, I'm not sure. I've just talked to my sister, parents, some friends of my parents, so…
Tammy: Do you wish you could talk to her?
Chris: Maybe once, just, uh…
Tammy: Just to get some closure?
Chris: … just to say, like, I, you know… just once.
Tammy: Yeah.
Chris: Just to say, I'm sorry this all happened. I'm sorry… I'm not sure what happened afterwards, like, what you went through, you know, like counselling, if you're like, you know… if you're, like, in a different state, if you had to leave everything behind, but I just wanted to let you know, I'm sorry. And that's something I never saw happening with somebody else either.
Dave: Would it be alright if we told her that?
Chris: That's fine.
Grahm: Do you want us to? Do you want us not to?
Chris: If she would wanna hear it, talk to her, yes. I'm not sure… I'm sure she'd answer your phone call more than an attorney phone call that she didn't wanna call… answer.
Tammy: That was your attorney tried to call her and she wouldn't answer?
Chris: Yep. Yeah, cos I remember… I remember her phone number, but after that, they figured out that's where she lived, they left a call…

business card there. And she just pretty much, after the fifth attempt, they said, she said, stop.
Tammy: Yeah.
Chris: Yeah.
Tammy: I'm sure she's getting bombarded, like everyone else, so…
Chris: Well, hopefully it's calmed down since, but… but, er, I'm sure, like, I just hope she can, like, I'm not… ((Unintelligible)) … for her. She's on the outside, but hopefully it can get that way at some point. I'm not sure if she had to leave Colorado or not, but… surely, that would've been hard if she did.
Tammy: Mm hm.
Chris: *Anadarko* was her dream job, so that's one thing I always asked my attorneys, was like, er, did she have to leave? Like, er, did she have to do anything at work? Because that was one thing she always thought that was a good job, so…
Dave: Oh, really?
Chris: Yeah.
Dave: What did she mean?
Chris: Oh, like, an oil company like *Anadarko*, I mean like, unless you work at, like, *BP* or *ConocoPhillips* or something.
Dave: Oh, I see what you're saying.
Chris: *Anadarko's* a big company.
Grahm: Big leagues?
Chris: Yeah.
Dave: Can I ask kind of a tough question?
Chris: Yeah.
Dave: Um, did you love her?
Chris: It felt like it was true.
Dave: I think so too. I think it was the same for her.
Chris: Yeah.
Dave: Okay. Tell us about the time you spent with her.
Chris: Well, I mean, it felt like it was, you know… I think that all I can tell you guys… I've never been pursued by anybody before… it's like, I was the one, you know, trying to pursue. Because, you know, when me and Shanann got together it was like… she was always pushing me away, kind of like, you know…
Grahm: She was sick for a while, right?
Chris: Yeah, she had just got diagnosed with lupus and she was on a

bunch of different medications and stuff and she was, um… it was… I guess I was… I guess I just wasn't her type.
Grahm: You weren't her type?
Chris: I wasn't her type. She's… she told me when I first… when we first met…
Dave: She told you that?
Tammy: (Laughter).
((Unintelligible crosstalk)).
Chris: When we first met, like, it was at a movie theatre. My cousin's ex-wife set us up.
Tammy: You were dressed like shit, weren't you?
They all laughed.
Chris: I think…
Tammy: That's what you told me…
Chris: … I didn't know, like, that…
Tammy: So, she was fancy, and you was in, like, shorts and…
((Unintelligible crosstalk)).
Tammy: It was a fancy theatre, right?
Chris: … in Charlotte, they call it the epicentre. Apparently, if you like Champagne…
Grahm: Oh, this is a fancy date night for you.
Chris: Yeah.
Tammy: I think he handled it… I think he came like he was going to a Cinemax…
((Unintelligible crosstalk)). Much laughter.
Chris: No, I don't know if you… you could watch a normal… normal movie but you, like, drink Champagne, you know? Cos I had a beer and just sat there and whatever… but yeah, that was when she first saw me, she was like, I just probably just turn and talk to the bartender a little more… Yeah, it was… I was persistent trying to… I mean, even on our first date, I couldn't eat anything really, I was just...
Dave: Really?
Chris: Yeah, I was just… she was just chowing down and she was like, you eat like a bird and… ((Unintelligible, crosstalk)).
Dave: That's funny.
Chris: She talked to her parents, you know, months later, she was like, 'this guy never ate, but he's like a trash disposal…' Trash disposal! I was like, that wasn't me—I was embarrassed. ((Unintelligible)). But, um,

yeah, I was always pursuing her and finally I just… ((Unintelligible)) … medications and stuff—she had, like, eight bottles of medications so I was giving her day and night and I would put them all in that little flip over…
Dave: Pill box?
Chris: Yeah. All that kind of stuff, and, you know, I would always, you know… I even went to her colonoscopy, and then after that she knew I was, kind of, a keeper. It was like, who goes to a colonoscopy after two months with somebody?
Grahm: Right.
Tammy: That's a little soon.
(Laughter).
Chris: Well, she asked… she needed a ride, I'm like, yeah, she's like, 'do you wanna go to my colonoscopy?' I'm like, 'sure, why not'.
Grahm: Right.
Chris: I even sat with her while she drank that nasty stuff all day.
They all laughed.
((Unintelligible crosstalk)).
Chris: Yeah, it was, I mean, it felt like a great relationship. Everything was… everything was great.
Grahm: Right. You're talking about with Kessinger?
((Crosstalk)).
Chris: No. With Shanann. And, erm, the first… first year, you know, like… and my parents they were… Mom, my mom was always, kind of, hesitant.
Grahm: Why?
Chris: I… I was the baby I guess. I never… plus I never had a girlfriend in high school so, she never left me or saw me with, like…
Dave: Oh, interesting. So she's kind of watching her baby walk out, a little bit?
Chris: Exactly. I mean, I'd turned eighteen, I graduated, I never went back.
Grahm: Okay.
Chris: At all. And my sister moved back and forward all the time, so.
Grahm: How old were you when you met Shanann?
Chris: I was twenty-five.
Grahm: Okay.
Tammy: So, no serious girlfriends before that?

Chris: Nothing more than six months or so. Yeah, there was some girls here and there but nothing… they weren't, like, you know. The last girlfriend I had before Shanann… she was, just actually got divorced. I should never have done that, but I was more, like… I was kinda, like, helping her get through her divorce, it seemed like.
(Chuckles).
Tammy: Mm hm.
((Unintelligible)).
Grahm: You're the rebound guy?
Dave: Rebound guy.
Chris: Pretty much…
Grahm: Would you say then in your relationships with women, um, it seems to me… you tell me if I'm wrong… it seems to me you're attracted to maybe a more dominant personality?
Chris: It seems like it because I'm more of a… just reserved, like, I kinda like, just go with the flow…
Grahm: Yeah.
Chris: … it's like, Shanann usually made all of the decisions, it seemed like, so…
Grahm: I get that. I'm the same. Yeah. I don't know what it is…
Tammy: Yeah. I don't think that's very… ((Unintelligible)) … but… (Laughter).
Grahm: So, then, I know it's hard keep bouncing back and forth, but it, erm, one of the reasons we're here is… we just keep telling ourselves, Chris just does not fit the mould.
Tammy: No.
Grahm: It just blows us away what happened. Right? And so, we will do a little bit of bouncing back and forth and that's just to get to know you a little better. Because we never really got that chance, did we?
((Unintelligible crosstalk)).
Chris: … probably about three of four times, probably.
Grahm: So, then with… do you call her Nikki or Nichol Kessinger?
Chris: I would call her Nikki.
Grahm: Okay.
Chris: There's so many Nikkis and Nichols in this… I got 'em confused.
Grahm: So, we'll call her Nikki. So then, with Nikki was it different?
Chris: It just seemed like I was more in control seemingly, and that

never happened. Like, she'd actually ask me my opinion on a lot of things, like, what I wanted to do, and I was just, like, okay…

Grahm: It was new, wasn't it?

Chris: Very new.

Dave: That's fascinating to me. And so, did it feel more like an equal partnership? Or…

Chris: It seemed like it, yeah.

Grahm: Okay. So then, when it was date night, what did you guys do? Would you guys talk about it? Would you ask to go somewhere? Or would she say I wanna go somewhere?

Chris: I… no… the first time we went out it was to a movie, we were in the orchard, we'd walked over there… and then I asked her, I was like, hey, do you wanna go see this movie? And like, yeah, I'm like, okay, cool. When we got there it was sold out, and, you know… ((Unintelligible)) … to wait two hours or just go home but no, she just wanted to walk around and talk. I was, okay!

Grahm: Oh, wow.

Chris: So that was… that was different. And, you know, she wanted to go to the car museum—Shelby museum, in Boulder. I'd never been there and…

Grahm: That was right up your alley.

Dave: Yeah.

Chris: … and I was just like, that was awesome. I was just walking around cars… it was just cars… and then, you know, drag race, and yeah.

Grahm: Okay.

Chris: I haven't been to a drag race since 2008 and that was in Charlotte.

Grahm: Okay.

Chris: I went to the… ((Unintelligible)) … drag ship over there. This is like the NHRA… the top car stuff, like, me and my dad used to go there all the time. And then, like, uh, we went, uh, camping, in sand dunes national park. And I'd never… I'd never been camping. I'd always wanted to do it, and she'd done it, like, countless times.

Grahm: Oh really? Okay. She's outdoorsy?

Chris: Yes.

Grahm: Okay.

Chris: She was… I guess… every time she needed to clear her head she'd just go by herself.
Grahm: Oh. So she's a completely new type of, er, person then… relationship?
Chris: Yep.
Grahm: Okay. All right. Um, well, what were you thinking this whole time, like…
Chris: At the back of my head I was telling myself what you doing. You know, every time, you know, I opened up my phone I would see pictures of my wife, and my kids and I'd just say what am I doing? And then every time I was with her it seemed like, I didn't think. It seemed like it was like a blinder was up in my face.
Grahm: Oh.
Chris: And it was… every time I look back on it, like, you know… I have pictures of my wife and kids in the cell and, like, every night… you know… every morning and every night I still talk to 'em, you know. I say, like… I got this book, er, I used to read for CeCe, and I… I remember that book, so, I read it out to them, like, every night. And there's some scripture and stuff I read to 'em, so, I just try to, you know, I just try the think back, I wish… this second, I wish, that blinder hadn't come on my head, right in my eyes, and I would've seen what was going on, like, you know? I was havin'… everybody said oh, you're just out there havin' fun, while your kids, you know, are… your kids and wife are on vacation. I'm just like, no, it wasn't like that, but it seemed like… that's what it looked like, you know? You're going, you know, you're going to camping, you're going to drag race… going, all of the other stuff that you have fun doing but you're doing it with somebody else, it's not your family, it just didn't seem right.
Grahm: Okay.
Chris: You know, I'm with her and it's just like I didn't see that anymore…
Grahm: Okay.
Chris: I was there at her house almost every night, and I didn't have that time at home just to, like, think about anything. 'Cause, literally, I… I was only at home from when I got home from work, worked out, I ate dinner, and then, I went over to her house. Like, I was never home… I never slept at my house for the whole month of July.
Grahm: Now, talk me through that though. When you said you were

at home and then you were at her house, was that while Shanann was gone?

Chris: Yes.

Grahm: Oh, okay. So you weren't at your house?

Chris: No.

Grahm: This all happened so quickly didn't it?

Chris: It did. It was insane. I mean, I was like… she even told me she was never in a normal relationship. She would never have somebody over her house more than one or twice a week, but she felt like she wanted me over there… she said she felt comfortable with me over there. So, it was just, like, that's what was different, like she wanted me over there, but, um, I just wish that all that would just go away. I just wish I… almost… I… I know it's wrong to wish I'd never met somebody, but I wish, you know, maybe met her at work and then just kept it that way.

Grahm: I think, if we had a time machine, I don't think this would happen again.

Chris: No.

Grahm: And some people, when this happens, you're like, well, if it wasn't this time it would've been next time, or the next time. It just wouldn't have happened with you would it?

Chris: Uh huh.

Grahm: It happened so quickly that… you tell me if I'm wrong… you're not the type of guy to take control, but sometimes when you need to… it seems this is what happened.

Chris: I didn't take control of the situation. It was like the situation controlled me.

Grahm: Right, it just happened. I get that, man. I'm somewhat passive myself and it's like, you know, this situation, why did I let that keep going?

Chris: Why? It was like a rollercoaster ride that I kept punching the ticket on and was never gonna get off.

Grahm: Yeah. Can we talk about a harder subject? Um, cos when we were talking, the last time we talked, um, the last thing we talked about was where the girls were. But we never really got to talk about that night. What happened?

Chris: So, nothing really happened that night, it was in the morning.

Grahm: Okay.

Chris: It was, you know, me and Shanann… she got home at two o'clock. And, uh, you know, I felt her get into bed and I just… ((Unintelligible)) … thought I heard like… ((Unintelligible)) …make sure I left my phone out at two o'clock... make sure she's in there and I could kinda feel her kinda stirring around a little bit. Ah, she… I just had a feeling that she knew, like, what was going on. 'cause, I mean, like, obviously I didn't use an Anadarko gift card, you know, that I had gotten, I used my actual credit card and I kinda just felt like she knew what was going on and, she uh, started rubbing her hand on me and we ended up having sex, but, uh, I guess that was more like a test…
Grahm: Oh?
Chris: I woulda thought.
Grahm: Interesting, okay. That makes sense.
Chris: 'Cause when we talked… when I woke up later on in the morning, you know, I pretty much told her, you know, I didn't think it was gonna work anymore. And she was like, what happened…what was last night? You know, I figured that was a test after I've gone through everything in my head.
Grahm: That makes sense.
Chris: And, she just told me, you know, like, to get off of her and she's like, I knew there was somebody else… I knew there was somebody else… I knew there was somebody else. I couldn't bring myself… I couldn't just say just yes, there is somebody else but then she said, 'you're never gonna see your kids again, you're never gonna see them again, get off me… don't hurt the baby'.
Grahm: Is that what she said?
Chris: *'Cause* when, like, when I climbed in bed, I was pretty much on top, pretty much straddling her like you do.
Grahm: Yeah. Okay.
Chris: She thought I was gonna, you know, hurt her or hurt the baby or something so… 'cause she knew that, you know, something happened. She thought I was just trying to check out or something, and that's when that happened.
Grahm: I know it's hard, but do you mind if we talk just a tiny bit deeper about that? So, she comes home, uh, you know, she touches you, you guys have sex, it seems like she's doing her test… which I understand. It sounds like you do too

Chris: I'm sure that, you know, like, Nikki or Nickole Atkinson or Cassie probably told her, you know?
Grahm: That's what I was thinking, right? They talked about it during that whole weekend.
Chris: One of them... my parents have told me there was like a... going through, like, text messages, it's, like, all pretty much they all kinda just told her he's with someone else type of deal.
Grahm: Yeah, and she spent a lot of time with the gals. That's what they did probably all weekend, is talk about it—give her advice, I think that's what we found, right?
Tammy: Mm-hm.
Grahm: Okay, so she comes home, you guys have sex, and then did you fall asleep between then and going to work?
Chris: Yes.
Grahm: Okay, so then, at some point, does she wake you up or is it you waking up for work?
Chris: My alarm wakes me up.
Grahm: Oh okay, and you're going to work out?
Chris: Mm hm.
Grahm: But that's when she started wanting to talk more? She was pretty mad?
Grahm: Okay.
Chris: Yeah, she... I mean, it was... I already kinda knew that, you know, using that credit card was kinda, it was...
Grahm: *W*as that intentional?
Tammy: Yeah?
Chris: I had no other way to do it...
Grahm: Oh.
Chris: ... like, I had got *Anadarko* gift cards from, you know, doing good stuff at work and stuff like that and I'd used them all.
Grahm: Oh. Was part of you just like, aw, screw it whatever... I don't care. I'm using this card?
Chris: I... I... part of me just wants to say, Nikki could you pay for this? (Laughter). I don't know...
Grahm: Yeah.
Chris: ... even... I think, from what my attorneys said, she even noticed I used a different card, like, a blue card and maybe she thought, you know, I felt comfortable enough just to use a normal bank

account or something. I told her I was going to a Rockies game and I told you guys I was going to a Rockies game. Even… it felt like, you know, like, looking back at everything and reading the scripture more and more now, I can see like, you know, God told me, like, gave me opportunities to get out… Even my friend, Jeremy Lindstrom, he even invited me, 'cause it was his daughter that came and watched the kids on Saturday… that Saturday night… and he was like, 'Hey instead of going to a Rockies game you wanna go with me to a Broncos game and watch the Arizona Cardinals?'. Like, in my mind it was like, you know, don't. Just say, hey I can't find a babysitter…

Grahm: To Nikki?

Chris: Yeah. And maybe that would have been, like, you know, a light switch in my head goes off… a light switch in her head goes off… maybe just like, goes different directions.

Grahm: Mm hm.

Chris: That was kinda like, my last opportunity to get out it seems. I wish I woulda just said, yeah, let's go. I think that woulda just put me on a different trajectory.

Grahm: So then, Shanann, did she actually say, you're never gonna see the kids again?

Chris: She said it to me before.

Grahm: Yeah, that must be hard to hear.

Chris: Yeah, 'cause she said to me before she went to Arizona, 'cause I wasn't really sleeping in the bedroom I was sleeping on the couch or in the basement bed or something and she had slammed the door, said, you're never gonna see the kids again…

Grahm: Did she get fiery like that?

Chris: Only once in our entire relationship have I ever seen her act that way.

Grahm: Yeah? And that was a time before or was that the night that happened?

Chris: No, it was back in North Carolina.

Grahm: Oh.

Chris: Yeah, it was one it was just like one of those… it was just a fiery argument. I never raised my voice to her or anything, I just got mad and I slammed the door and she's like, oh, like, you shouldn't have slammed the door.

(Laughter).

Dave: Is that when you were in North Carolina that last week?
Chris: No. It was… this was 2010–2011…
Dave: Oh.
Chris: … it was like early, early, early.
Dave: Okay.
Chris: At the old house.
Grahm: Before kids?
Chris: Yes.
Grahm: Were you dating or were you married at that point?
Chris: Dating.
Grahm: Oh.
Chris: Yeah it was just like… I… I don't remember what it was about, I think some… I think some girl maybe texted me from my past or something and I was just like… and she said, you know, 'Don't have that happen again', and I'm just like, what, I can't have friends that are females? I don't even talk to this woman anymore. It was just like… he whistles. Nope!
Grahm: Was she fiery? Did she have that Italian blood that her mom has?
Chris: Lord, yes!
(Laughter).
Grahm: Was she always like that, or was she, er… did she snap at things?
Chris: She wouldn't snap at me, but you could tell, like, you know, if something… something really irked her a little bit, it would come out.
Grahm: Zero to one hundred type thing, or what?
Chris: Uh, yeah. Zero to two hundred.
Grahm: Oh, interesting.
Chris: She's… she's… she gets activated about something, it's like, alright, it's gonna happen…
Grahm: Well, that's why she was probably so successful at *Thrive*, right?
Chris: Oh yeah, she had done a couple other direct sales businesses, but this one was different.
Grahm: Why?
Chris: This one, like, 'cause I think she had done, *Origami Owl* and something called, *It Works,* and then a couple other different things, some bags and stuff like that, but this supplement stuff, 'cause it worked

with her and it worked with me, and she was like, okay, I can kinda use this as, like, alright this is what it's doing for us, and then, after a little while, she could see how people were above her, how it was helping them, and then it was just, like, trickle-down effect. It was a good system, about commission wise and everything. She could use all the business IQ she has from running those cell phone shops and from the *Dirty South Customs* shops and all that, she's business minded she knows how to do accounting books like the back of her hands. So, it all just fell into place with all the…

Grahm: So then, on that night, was it just a new type of fight you never had or what?

Chris: Yeah, it was just a totally different type of fight, you know, it was… it just felt like, I noticed more anger than anything else, there was emotion to it at first and then it felt like it was just anger there was just, like, no love there it was kinda like… what we were saying… what she was saying was just, like, it's almost like you knew, like, something was combating at each other we didn't know… it wasn't ourselves.

Grahm: Really? Anger from you? Or anger from her?

Chris: I think it was more anger from me and more desperation from her, 'cause she wanted to fix it. And she knew… she knew something wasn't right. When that whole thing with my parents happened with the whole… somebody… my parents called it *Nutgate.*

Grahm: What happened?

Chris: Nutgate?

Grahm: What's that?

Chris: The peanut… the peanut thing…

Grahm: Oh, yeah…oh… with her family?

Tammy: Pistachio ice cream or whatever?

Chris: Yeah, they call it *Nutgate.*

Tammy: I haven't heard that.

(Laughter).

Chris: I guess that's what people are calling it, but that was, like, another *out*, like, maybe I coulda just stopped everything with Nikki and just concentrated on helping whatever happened there. Shanann had a story, my mom had a story. Whatever happened… I coulda asked my ten-year-old nephew, he probably could tell me what actually happened.

Grahm: Well they both had their feelings for good reasons and they both didn't see it the other person's way and…
Chris: Yeah, and, like, I didn't talk to my parents from then on, 'til like August 6th, and, like, you know, my dad took the whole week off…
Grahm: *Y*ou didn't talk to your parents from then on?
Chris: Yeah.
Grahm: Oh, okay.
Chris: 'Cause Shanann was like, 'do not talk to them, do not call them, do not do anything'.
Grahm: Is that what she said?
Chris: Yeah, and CeCe's birthday was the seventeenth but I think the actual birthday party was a couple days after.
Grahm: In August?
Chris: In July. And, er, my… my mom and my dad was gonna go, but then there was a post on Facebook about allergies and stuff like that Shanann had made and my dad was like, 'nah, I just can't do it anymore…'
Grahm: He perceived that as her taking a shot at him?
Chris: Yeah.
Grahm: Okay.
Chris: She always said she never, you know, put those posts directed at anybody but I know... she…
Tammy: If you read them you know who she's talking about.
Chris: Yeah, she had a method to the madness and you could see it…
Grahm: Mm hm.
Chris: … but, um, I wish I coulda just took more time just to fix that. I was… I wanted my parents to be involved since, you know, the whole wedding thing and then after that, it's like, my mom and my sister are always combatting with Shanann and Shanann combatting with them. My dad was always cool. He's just like me, he's just like, you know, go with the flow. I just want everybody to get along type deal…
Grahm: Chicks, man!
Tammy: I loved your dad.
Grahm: He's the best.
Tammy: Isn't he? I loved your dad.
Grahm: So… I'm sorry… keep going.
Chris: That's cool. I just wish I coulda, like, when we were at the beach in August, like, my dad was supposed to take the whole week off

just so he could see the kids and see me and grab a cookout at my sister's house or something, and then... but we just pretty much spent five days at the beach and Shanann... ((Unintelligible)) ... I don't want to say, like, punishment for them not to see the kids, but, like, I wanted them to see 'em. I wished I could've fixed it all, fixed all that, even, like, when I was at the beach I told Shanann that it was more like... what was going on was more of like I... I feel like... 'cause, you know, my dad's my hero... I feel like I lost something in my life. I hadn't talked to him for three weeks. He couldn't see the kids for three weeks, FaceTime, or anything. I wanted them to be able to have that relationship. She was pretty much gung-ho, like, she tried to kill my daughter by giving her peanuts. I was like, I don't think she gave it to her!
Grahm: Was that her stance? That your mom...
Chris: Put something in front of CeCe.
Tammy: Like, to kill her? Or just...
Grahm: Didn't care... didn't pay attention...
Chris: No, to just, like... she thinks that allergies, in this day and age, people think, oh, you're fine.
Tammy: ... like it's a made-up kind of thing?
Chris: It'll be fine, you'll have a rash, it'll be fine. I've seen CeCe, you know, like, I've seen a picture of when she had a cashew the first time... it wasn't good. Then she had kiwi the second time and same thing happened. And, um, I know it's real.
Tammy: So you know it's serious, yeah?
Chris: Yeah, it's not, like... it wasn't like her throat closed up, but she broke out in a full body rash that looked really crazy looking. Luckily, like, you know, nothing with her throat happened. But, um...
Tammy: So, did that make you angry at your mom for doing that?
Chris: Yeah, I mean, I was just like, Mom, I told her, you need to think, you need to, like, you know, pay attention, just because another kid could have something doesn't mean another kid could have something, 'cause we were at that birthday party at Jeremy's that Sunday, you know, and they had this cake there, Bella wanted it so bad. I'm like 'you can't have it sweetie, 'cause CeCe can't have it'. She was like, yeah okay, and all the other kids were like, they can't have the cake? You know. I just kinda took them off and gave em one of those frozen pops or something. You know, it's just that, she had to learn that just because one kid can have something there's another kid that can't have it for a

legitimate reason, like, she couldn't have done it, but you know, that's the kinda talk I had with her. Shanann had called me I think it was maybe the middle of July or something when she told me all this had happened, that's when I called my mom and talked to them for a while and there're just like, you know… they just couldn't deal with her anymore. Shanann just kinda like, you know, flipped out and my nephew told Bella to go hide behind a curtain because, I don't think your mommy's gonna let you come over here again, or something like that.

Tammy: Aww.

Grahm: So, it got heated?

Chris: Oh, they were… it was bad.

Grahm: Really?

Chris: It was like a last straw between them, I think.

Grahm: In the same room or over the phone?

Chris: No, they were at the house

Grahm: So they were really heated?

Chris: At my mom's house, yeah. 'Cause CeCe and Bella and my niece and nephew were there.

Grahm: Okay.

Tammy: How did Shanann find out about the ice-cream thing?

Chris: 'Cause, er, Shanann was there and, er, I guess they were all sitting one… one of those couches, kind of like a U, and my niece went into the kitchen and… she knew where the ice-cream was 'cause she's been there before.

Tammy: Oh, so it's not like your mom gave it to her?

Chris: Oh no, she went into the freezer and got it, went out and sat beside CeCe and started eating. But it's just a matter of CeCe could go like… like that. I don't know what would have happened if she just got it on her hand…

Grahm: Right.

Chris: … but, like, I know on the prick test, on the back, it's like a welt.

Dave: So, were they staying there at your parent's house during that time?

Chris: Yeah it was, er… so, they would go from my… from Sandy and Frank's house for a few days or five days and go to my mom and dad's house for a couple days—back and forth

Dave: So it happened during that time when they were there?
Chris: Mm hm.
Dave: Okay.
Grahm: So, there were so many things that happened, weren't there, that were just little tiny ingredients to this recipe?
Chris: ((Unintelligible)).
Grahm: It's nuts, Chris. I mean, it's just so many things just didn't go your way.
Chris: Everything was like, someone was stirring a pot. You it just…
Grahm: That's exactly what it was like. So then, I know I keep bringing it up… can you walk me through just the last few minutes before Shanann died?
Chris: It was pretty much just… I had gotten dressed for work and then, like we started talking…
Grahm: Did she come to you?
Chris: No, I was just right there in bed.
Grahm: Oh, okay
Chris: Yeah, so I was just like I got my blue shirt on and my jeans and everything…
Grahm: You were ready to go?
Chris: I was ready to go and…
Tammy: Was she asleep? Or did you have to wake her up to finish your conversation, or…
Chris: I wake her up, 'cause she… she got home at two o'clock, so she was pretty much out of it. But I never knew, like, if her plane got delayed or if it was something she just told me and she just sat around with Nickole and just, like, talked for a while and then came home or something. I'm not sure if that was…?
Dave: Yeah, it was delayed, yeah.
Chris: But uh, yeah, when she came home and everything, but yeah, I woke her up to talk to her.
Grahm: Oh, okay.
Chris: Yeah.
Grahm: And is that because it was just eating at your brain?
Chris: Yeah, I knew, like, you know, something like, something doesn't feel right with me. I know, like, she knew, I just… I just knew she knew. I just felt like maybe, like maybe the kids weren't gonna be there when I got home that day.

Grahm: Oh. Interesting. Now, um, I don't mean to offend, but I have to ask… is that really the truth?
Chris: I really felt there was… they weren't gonna be there when I got home that day.
Grahm: Oh.
Tammy: Like, she would take them somewhere? Or…
Chris: No, I just, I just felt like either… maybe I wouldn't go home, or maybe they weren't gonna be there or I wouldn't be allowed in, type thing.
Tammy: I think I saw some text messages where Shanann talked about, um, that she would take the kids to another state or something 'cause she wouldn't be able to afford to live in Colorado or something… did she say that kinda stuff to you? Or…
Chris: Yep
Tammy: What did she say about that?
Chris: She said she couldn't afford to live in Colorado by her… on her own and that, uh, I told her well, I mean, she could try it. She pretty much makes the same amount I do.
Tammy: *Yeah.*
Chris: But she said she wouldn't, she wouldn't wanna try just because, you know, Colorado just… price of living there was a lot higher than North Carolina
Tammy: And this is just so I'm clear, you thought maybe she was… she… in your mind, she thought maybe she would take the kids somewhere else or, like, lock you out of the house, or…?
Chris: Or just, you know, I wouldn't wanna make it seem, like, you know, I'm trying to pound on the door trying to get in or anything like that…
Tammy: Mm hm.
Chris: … I just feel like, you know, that is what I did on Sunday, was kinda like… or Saturday night it was kinda like the last straw, kinda like going out with somebody and using the actual bank account card and, like, not trying to hide it at all.
Grahm: So, walk me through it though, because she comes home, she touches you, you guys have sex, you fall asleep, you wake up for work all natural, all, you know, a normal days work type thing.
Chris: Yeah.
Grahm: What was it that made you think, I just can't do this anymore.

I have to talk to her?
Chris: It was eating away at me. I knew, like, something… everything that I did… I know that when I was with Nikki it was, you know, different, like, I wasn't even in the realm of, I'm a dad, I'm a husband, type thing.
Grahm: Oh.
Chris: And then, like, I was saying, when I'm never at home, like, sleeping in my own bed… and I have no concept of that anymore.
Grahm: Interesting! So in your mind and heart you had moved on?
Chris: It kinda felt like if I wasn't at home, I didn't think about it almost 'cause, like, if I wasn't sleeping in my own bed, like… I think there was one point, like, Nikki had gone to the mountains with friends for a few days, like, end of June, first part of July, and then, like, you know, that part, you know, I'm obviously at home, but from that whole month of July on, was like I was never home. I never had all those reminders, I never had, you know, like… every time my wife called me I would be at Nikki's house.
Grahm: Oh, while she was in North Carolina?
Chris: Yeah…
Grahm: Okay.
Chris: … and I would like, you know, walk outside talk to her while next to the car or something like that. I would never be at home, like, looking, like… to have all these pictures around me, just being in the same bed, seeing my kids in bed, seeing everything that we'd built for that last six years.
Grahm: And so, did you just want to once and for all, get it out in the open?
Chris: I just wanted to tell her how I was feeling at that point in time, like I didn't feel like me and her were compatible anymore. I honestly didn't feel like that 'cause what was going on with Nikki, it was new… it was new.
Grahm: Right. Absolutely.
Chris: Anything that's new always feels better than the old.
Grahm: Yes.
Tammy: You were probably just bitten by the love bug…
Chris: Yes.
Tammy: … is how a lot of therapists talk about it?
Chris: Yeah, unfortunately it was just like I never felt that. I mean,

even with new relationships in the past it always feels different for the first couple weeks and then, you know… but it just… something with Nikki felt different. I don't know what it was. Maybe it was just like you said, like, you know, I was more in control and it was more of me coming out, 'cause Shanann always said it always seemed I was more myself around other people, like, you know, her cousin Cody. Like, she… Cody lived and came out and visited us a little bit while we were in Colorado for a little while and Cody always talked about oh 'Chris is so funny, Chris is like…' Shanann was always like, oh you're never like that with me. I'm just like, well, maybe I always feel nervous around you.

(Laughter).

Grahm: There's only so much oxygen in the room, right? I say this to some people, when dominant personalities, you know…

Chris: I just always felt nervous. I always felt like I was, you know, never could actually just be myself. With Nikki I was myself, like, all the time. It was just different.

Grahm: Well, and it seems as though… and again, it's hard to talk about and you tell me if I'm wrong, but it also seems… er, is it accurate to say that sexually you were able to say, Nikki this is what I would like, this is what I'm into and blah, blah, blah, and maybe not with Shanann?

Chris: Nikki just wanted, I mean, she wanted what she wanted. She wanted to do it pretty much all the time. I was just like, '*o*kay, that's fine with me'. With Shanann it was just like, hey, sometimes it happens, sometimes it didn't, but that wasn't the case it wasn't just, like, sexual. I was more myself, I could… just not think about what I was going to say or plan what I was going to say or say something stupid…

Dave: A little bit of freedom.

Tammy: Can I ask you something about that morning that you had sex with Shanann? Did you feel at all like, maybe you were kinda of cheating on Nikki by doing that?

Chris: I felt strange. I felt like, you know, the first time I was with Nikki I felt weird and then the last time I was with Shanann I felt totally strange. I just like, I... I didn't know who I was. I didn't know who I had become, I didn't… I felt like I had become… ((Unintelligible)) … on TV, and that did not feel right with me. Like, I didn't know what had happened to me.

Tammy: *Mm hm.*

Chris: Nikki even asked me, are you… have you ever done this before, have you ever strayed away? I'd never even thought about it. She's like what's different? And I was like, I guess it's just you that's different, 'cause I've just never actually… I've seen girls smile at me before—never done anything about it. With her it was like… it was like she had a leash on me, and she tugged me away. As soon as she walked in I'm like, what the hell is going on? So…
Grahm: And Tammy brings up a very good point. I wonder if that last time with Shanann having sex had a… somewhat of a role in you thinking, I've gotta do something. I've gotta say something. We've gotta have a talk. Something's gotta change. Is that accurate?
Chris: It is. I felt like maybe it was a trigger point or something like… like, you hit the push button on a bomb and it just blows up. Something in my head, something was irking... I had to say something.
Grahm: Ok. So exactly what did you say and what happened?
Chris: So, I woke her up, and was like, hey we just gotta talk. I just told her I don't feel compatible. I don't feel like this is gonna work. Can we cancel the trip to Aspen? 'Cause she'd booked a trip that week to go to some mystery four-star luxury hotel or something.
Grahm: Just the two of you or the whole family?
Chris: Just me and her.
Grahm: *Okay.*
Chris: She had Amanda Thayer coming to watch the kids that week that weekend or something.
Grahm: Okay.
Chris: I was just like, can we cancel that, can we, like, do something, like, from what I remember I even said, can we move to Brighton? (Laughter). To get away from this house. And, like, I'm not sure if that was in the beginning or end part of the conversation or what not. That conversation went so many different ways, it had gone from staying together, to not staying together, to just like, all of the above.
Grahm: Ok. So this is half an hour, an hour or what?
Chris: Definitely not more than a half hour I don't think…
Grahm: Okay.
Chris: … I don't think.
Tammy: Are you crying? Is she crying?
Chris: It's back and forth. She's got mascara… she didn't wash her face when she got home, so she had makeup on, so mascaras running

all over her and stuff like that. And it was… nothing about that convers… I just wish I could take it all back… just the whole Nikki thing back—everything.

Grahm: So when did it turn?

Chris: As far as the conversation?

Grahm: Mm hm.

Chris: Just at the end when I was telling her like, I… I told her I didn't love her anymore. That's when it happened.

Grahm: What happened?

Chris: She told me to get off her and I put my hands around her.

Tammy: Did you say she said something like… that you're hurting the baby, or something?

Chris: Yeah, that was before that, 'cause when I was straddling her it was kinda like around her waist type deal.

Tammy: Why did you get on her like that?

Chris: I just… when we got on… got on the bed…that's… that's just where I got on.

Grahm: Is that so she would listen to you?

Chris: I felt like she could probably listen to me just laying beside her, but I got on top of her. And every time I think about… I'm just like, did I know I was gonna do that before I got on top of her? I don't know.

Grahm: Really? That's an interesting thought, Chris.

Dave: *Mm hm.*

Grahm: You don't know if you knew.

Chris: It's like, you know, everything that happened that morn… I just I don't know, I try to go back in my head- I didn't want to do this but I did it. Everything just kinda like…

Tammy: Felt like you had to?

Chris: It just felt like it was… I don't even want to say I felt like I *had* to, I just feel like there was already something in my mind that was implanted, that was gonna do it and I woke up that morning and it was gonna happen, and I had no control of it.

Grahm: You never thought about it before?

Chris: It was just like I don't want… like… like in the sentencing hearing, the prosecutor said it takes two to four minutes for something like that to happen. Why couldn't I just let go?

Grahm: Well, that's interesting.

Dave: Was it feeling like it's in motion and you just couldn't stop it?

Chris: Yeah it was just like… I don't even wanna know what she saw when she looked back at me, honestly.
Tammy: Did you look at her? What was she doing?
Chris: She wasn't fighting.
Tammy: Why do you think she wasn't fighting?
Chris: I don't know, maybe she was praying, maybe she was… I read the Bible it said, you know, like, uh, I read a Scripture that said don't er… er… forgive these people for they do not know what they do. Maybe she was saying that I don't know what she was saying in her head. Like, when you guys told me, take off your shirt, and checked for defensive wounds, there wasn't gonna be any. She didn't fight. I don't know why.
Tammy: She didn't gra… could she grab your arms, or were her arms pinned down or…?
Chris: No, not that I remember. I don't think so. I mean, I don't think, like, I moved to where my knees are around her arms or anything, but… it was just kinda, like, when I got on top of her we… we started talking and that was it. It's kinda like in my head, or the back of my head that was gonna happen and just like… at the end of the conversation, it was just like, that's what happened. I just wish I could have let go.
Tammy: Did it seem like it was that long? Two to four minutes? How long did it seem for you?
Chris: Almost kinda felt like it was… like it was longer almost, 'cause it felt like time was standing still. It's kinda like I just saw my life disappearing before my eyes but just, like, I couldn't let go. It was like somebody else, like, like if you picture somebody else around you holding your hands, holding you to keep you from not letting go.
Dave: At some point there was a statement about rage. Do you feel like you were in a rage at that point? How do you…?
Chris: That's the only way I can describe it, honestly. Like a snap. Something, else… I don't know, I guess my attorney had said something, you know, strangulation is more of a like a… I don't know… passionate type thing. I don't know how that can be passionate.
Tammy: It's just intimate 'cause you're right in there, using your own hands. It's a lot different than someone standing across a room and you shooting them or something like that, so…

Chris: I guess it just felt like somebody was behind me, just like… just… I just couldn't let go.
Grahm: It's interesting to me because there was a lot of things in your life that were like that, right? Where you was, like, maybe you just felt out of control, or maybe felt like, I don't know why I couldn't take a step back or, you know, like, even when you said your buddy was like, let's go to the football game, you wanted to say yes, you just couldn't.
Chris: I wanted to, like, I… I hadn't been to a football game since North Carolina, so I was just, like, yeah sure, like… I wanted to say that. I wanted to just text yeah… yeah, babysitter fell through… nope, can't go.
Grahm: So, then what?
Chris: After, you know… Shanann was like, once that was… once she was gone… it was just like, I didn't know what was going on. It feels like a traumatic event type. Everything… I was like, I was shaking. I didn't know what had happened. I didn't know what to do. I didn't know what I had done. I still wasn't in that right state of mind. I don't think, like… like, I wasn't in control of what I could think or what I could do in that point of time. Most people say, like, why didn't you just call 911? Unless you're in that situation you don't know what you would have done. It's easy to play Monday morning quarterback.
Tammy: Mm hm.
Grahm: I agree with that.
Chris: Like you said, if someone shoots someone you don't know what was going through their mind at that point in time. You don't know what you would have done.
Grahm: So what happened next?
Chris: Bella came in the room.
Grahm: Is that what happened? Bella came in? What did she say?
Chris: ((Unintelligible)).
Grahm: Did she hear something? Is that why she came in?
Chris: Obviously, I think.
Grahm: Okay. What did you tell her?
Chris: Mommy don't feel good.
Grahm: And then, did that happen with Bella right in that room?
Chris: Not in our room.
Grahm: Okay, what happened?
Chris: She walked in, she thought, you know… Shanann was sleeping.

Grahm: Did you take her back to her room?
Chris: I put Shanann in that sheet, that's like…
Grahm: Okay, and then what?
Chris: Carried her downstairs, backed my truck up.
Grahm: At that point were the girls still there?
Chris: Mm hm.
Grahm: Okay. So, Shanann's in the truck, then you went back to the house?
Chris: Got everybody back in the truck.
Grahm: Was Bella first, or was CeCe first?
Chris: In the truck?
Grahm: I'm sorry. So, Shanann was first, and then Bella was next? Was Bella alive when you guys got in the truck? Oh, okay, what happened?
Chris: They woke back up
Grahm: Okay.
Chris: I don't really want to talk about this part, honestly.
Grahm: Okay.
Chris: Those are my kids, my babies. I have to talk to them every night. I don't see how it coulda happened…
Chris is sobbing.
Grahm: Okay.
Chris: Every time I see pictures of them, I don't know how this could have happened. Being a dad was the best part of my life. I took it all away.
Tammy: I think that's the hardest part for us, Chris, is we see those videos, we see that love you had for your girls, like, it's obvious to us, and even to us, we… it's hard for us to understand how a dad who's giving piggyback rides and, you know, making snacks and watching princess movies and those kind of things, um, how you get to that point, you know?
Chris: I know, just… like I said, it was like something else was controlling me that day and I had no control over what I was… no fight back.
Tammy: Yeah.
Chris: When that prosecutor said Bella bit her tongue, like, repeatedly, I just want to just bang my head up against a wall.
Chris sniffs loudly.
Tammy: So, you put Shanann in the truck and then you put the two

girls in the truck? Were they just sitting in their car seats or…? I guess they probably didn't have car seats in your truck did they?
Chris: No, they were sitting in the back in, like, that bench seat.
Tammy: So, Shanann was back there, too?
Chris: She was on the floor.
Tammy: What did they say about Shanann being on the floor?
Chris: Is Mommy okay?
Tammy: What did you tell them?
Chris: I said she'll be fine.
Tammy: Did you have their stuff with them? Like their toys and their blankets and stuff?
Chris: They had something with them that they carried. One of them had, like CeCe and Bella had a blanket or something with them. Like a pink blanket or…
Tammy: What about the dog? I think one of them had a stuffed dog, right? That talked?
Chris: Yeah, one of them had a little barking dog.
Tammy: Was that with you too, do you know?
Chris: I think it was. It's hard to remember if they had, like, the big blanket, small blanket…
Tammy: So, I think I saw, um, on the video that you put a gas can or something in the back of your truck, is that right?
Chris: Mm hm.
Tammy: Did you have different plans for when you put that in there?
Chris: I don't know what was going through my head. I feel maybe I could just get rid of myself at the same time if I was doing all of this, honestly.
Tammy: Yeah.
Grahm: Did you think about that?
Tammy: What did you think about that?
Chris: I didn't feel like I deserved to live after that happened.
Grahm: Was there any thought to the whole family going away that day, to include you?
Chris: After everything happened that was a definite thought.
Grahm: See, it's interesting to me… um, we had all kind of wondered if there was a point when you were all together and if you were all going to pass together. That to me makes sense, even though it sounds crazy, that's what a family man does, right?

Chris: A family man doesn't do what he did.
Grahm: No, I know. I guess what I mean is, it seems like you guys were going to be together forever in that way. Is that maybe what was going through your head?
Chris: Honestly, I just felt like after I didn't deserve to live. Whatever judgement I was gonna come upon myself, you know, I just didn't deserve to be on this earth anymore after what happened.
Tammy: So, what made you not do that, do you think?
Chris: I don't know it was more of just… I like a… 'cause with the site… maybe it was just more of like, I would have hurt more people than just me and everybody else. I know there was other people out there, not like at the site, but other people maybe out in the area. I didn't want something on the site to catch fire and blow up, and then other people around would get hurt in the same…
Tammy: So you were thinking initially about starting a fire out there or an explosion or something? Or…?
Chris: No, not for that, maybe I could take care of myself out there.
Grahm: How?
Chris: With gasoline, that's the only thing… I mean… I don't… I don't have a gun, anything like that. It's not like I could just commit suicide that way.
Grahm: So, just to blow yourself up?
Chris: Yeah, it was just… I wasn't thinking. I don't have weapons. I've never hunted before in my life. I don't what… nothing was right that morning.
Tammy: I remember you kept telling me that. You kept saying, I didn't know what I was doing, Tammy, I didn't know!
Chris: When you asked about the sheet, like, what were you doing? It's like, I don't know what I was doing.
Tammy: I think you were just in automatic mode or… seemed like. So, did you drive straight out there? So, what were you thinking on the way out there?
Chris: I was- kinda like what I'm doing right now, I'm just nervous, shaking, not knowing, like, you know, what's going to happen.
Tammy: Yeah.
Chris: I know my life is completely changed. I don't know what's happening. Like, honestly, I try to picture that whole ride. It's a forty-five minute to an hour ride out there. And it's just, like, couldn't I have

saved my girls' life? Couldn't I have done something? Why did I do that? I don't know. This is my flesh and blood. This is what I wanted all my life was to be a dad, just to have, you know, kids, and they love me and they… all that, and nothing makes sense. Like, the oil tank… nothing makes sense. I'm just like, what are you doing?

Tammy: So, what happened when you got out there?

Chris: I took Shanann out. Just to place off to the site.

Tammy: Mm hm.

Chris: Then…

Tammy: What were the girls doing when you were doing that?

Chris: Just sitting in the back of the truck.

Tammy: And then what happened after that?

Chris: CeCe was first. She did have a blanket. She had a blue blanket. A Yankee blanket.

Tammy: So was she alive when she went into the oil tank? No?

Chris: No. I put the blanket over her head.

Grahm: And that's how she passed? Couldn't breathe?

Chris: I put the blanket over her head. I didn't want to know. I strangled her right there in the back-seat.

Grahm: Okay.

Tammy: What was Bella doing?

Chris: She was sitting right behind her.

Grahm: Did she understand? Did she know what was going on?

Chris: She didn't say anything.

Grahm: And then same for Bella? Just without the blanket?

Chris: With the blanket.

Grahm: Oh, okay.

Chris: I didn't look. I think every time I close my eyes I start to hear her saying, Daddy, no! And that was it.

Grahm: That's what Bella said?

Chris: I hear that every day.

Grahm: Do you really? Sorry, man.

Chris: Sorry doesn't take anything back I did.

Grahm: I know. Is it possible that, in your mind, you didn't want them to suffer through their life? Was this like a mercy thing?

Chris: I mean you can say that after the fact, but it was just like I don't…

Tammy: You didn't feel like that during that?

Chris: I just didn't… I feel like there was just anger with Shanann, with everything and that I was just taking it out on everybody that was in front of me that morning.

Grahm: Yeah.

Chris: I mean, kids growing up without their parents, depending on what grandparents… whoever they grow up with seems to be fine, but it was just like it was an anger thing, it was just like…

Tammy: And what were you so angry at Shanann about? Like, if you could pinpoint it?

Chris: Nothing that… nothing that makes anybody want to do this. You could be angry at your spouse your whole life but you should never have done anything like this. You should never let it get to that point. I let it get to a point where I've never… I mean, I've never been angry before. And this was like the epitome of being angry. The epitome of showing a rage. The epitome of… of like, losing your mind. Some people in here have said, dude what the heck happened? You must have frickin' snapped and I just walk away. It's just like, you know, I don't see it my mind. When I look outside every day I'm like, what could we be doing right now? You know. Right now, I'd have a five-year-old, a three-year-old, and, likely, a one-month old son, and a beautiful wife, and just, like, right now it's just me.

Tammy: I watched that video of you finding out that Shanann was pregnant. You don't seem excited. You seem like kind of in shock and…

Chris: Scared?

Tammy: Yeah. Like, oh fuck. Like it's already complicated, and now this.

Chris: Well, it's like, er… when we had talked about it a couple… it happened fast. With Bella it was like, we almost gave up trying then she bought me a like a supercharger for my car. And then with CeCe we tried, tried, tried, and then *finally*. But with Nico it was once or twice and like two weeks later, she's pregnant.

Grahm: Is that what happened?

Chris: Yes. It's just like… it was more of a surprise, scare… wait, what? We just talked about this. Like, you know. And people have brought up the fact like, oh she was probably pregnant before you guys even talked about it. I'm just like no, that's not… no. But it was insanely fast. I'll give it that. Like, that's the only reason I gave that

notion, like, even a moment of thought 'cause it was like faster than any other time that she had gotten pregnant.
Tammy: You just didn't seem…happy. Like, you know what I mean, like…?
Chris: Yeah, I don't remember the video much. I know she was wearing a 'oops we did it again' shirt, I think, and I was walking in with my cooler or something.
Tammy: *Mm hm.*
Chris: I don't remember my actual reaction, like, watching the video but like, I could see where you guys see it like that. It didn't seem like he was jumping for joy, type thing.
Tammy: Yeah, it didn't seem like that.
Chris: Did you watch the one of, er, where I found out about CeCe?
Tammy: Uh-uh.
Grahm: No.
Chris: Oh, okay.
Tammy: Is it totally different?
Chris: Yeah, it was.
Tammy: Yeah?
Chris: It was 'cause, er, Bella was in the crib and it had an eviction notice on it.
Tammy: Oh yeah, you told me about it. Yeah, I never saw it, though.
Chris: Yeah, I picked up Bella and spun her around and whatnot. This time it was just me and Shanann and she was in the kitchen. I don't know, like, I forget what date it was, maybe like June 3rd or 5th or 7th…I'm not sure what date it was in the video but, maybe I already felt guilty about talking to Nikki at work.
Tammy: Yeah.
Chris: Maybe that was going through my head.
Grahm: Is that the potential timing? Does that make sense?
Chris: I don't remember the date or what day the video was, but I knew, like, I had kinda met Nikki around June 1st. I knew she, like, told me afterwards.
Grahm: When you say, met her, you mean, like, went on a date with her?
Chris: No. No, I didn't go on a date with her until Shanann was in North Carolina.
Grahm: Oh, okay.

Tammy: Just like flirting and stuff?
Chris: Yeah, I mean, it was natural flirting back and forth. I was just like… I just, I knew, like, with that video timing I probably just looked like I felt guilty for even talking to a girl at work.
Grahm: Well you probably did, right?
Chris: Yeah.
Tammy: Did you guys fight before—you and Shanann? I know you talked about, like, not really raising your voice and stuff. Was there… because I want to say… didn't a neighbour talk about them fighting and stuff?
Dave: Yeah, but that was embellished and exaggerated. He retracted that.
Tammy: Oh, he ended up doing that?
Dave: Yeah, he retracted it.
Tammy: Did you guys ever fight? Did you ever? Was there any domestic violence in your house?
Chris: No we never…
Tammy: This is strange to us
Grahm: Even from her to you? She gets mad when she's pregnant and grabs a knife or scratches you or smacks you around or… nothing?
Chris: No, she never, like… nothing.
Grahm: Okay.
Chris: That's what makes all this even more hard to understand from my standpoint, and I know from yours too.
Dave: Yeah. Did she ever belittle you at all? Did you ever feel that way, maybe?
Chris: What was that?
Dave: Did she ever make you feel like she belittled you? Or you felt belittled by her?
Chris: I mean, there was always points in a marriage where, you know, the dominant person takes control of everything, but I was… my whole life I just went with the flow, like, I never put myself in the centre of attention. I didn't wanna be. I just kinda… I just wanted to be in the back row. If she did belittle me I couldn't think of one at that point in time.
Dave: So you never really felt that way.
Chris: No, I mean I always knew I was the introvert and she was

the… you know, she took control of most situations, like, when people came over, like, I knew what I… what my role was.
Tammy: I watched videos of, like, cooking, or she'd make power balls, or, you know, like, protein balls or whatever. You just don't seem like you want to be in those videos.
Chris: No.
Tammy: I feel like you were being forced to be in those videos. Correct me if I'm wrong, but that's what it seemed like to me.
Chris: Yeah, I hated being in those… I hated… I mean, I did it for her…
Tammy: Right.
Chris: … because it was for her business, and stuff…
Tammy: Sure.
Chris: … but, it was… you know, I hated just being out for everyone to see. That's why the whole gender reveal thing I was just, like, hmm. I didn't want it to be, like, some live Facebook video. I'm just like, no. I just… but I never wanted to be out there.
Grahm: Yeah.
Chris: I felt like…
Grahm: Well, you know when she was… because we talk about this a lot, Tammy and I and Dave… you know, I think it was Florida, on some LeVel or Thrive thing and she's like, here we are! And it's all expenses paid!
Chris: Oh, and I was like…
Grahm: And I'm thinking, like, he is not into this video right now.
Tammy: No, you don't look into any of the videos to be honest with you.
Dave: I wouldn't be either.
Tammy: Yeah. I mean, I remember you talking to me about she would even post stuff for you, like, because you were technically a salesman too for *LeVel* or *Thrive*
Chris: Yeah, she put me underneath her and… not like anything, any of my friends or stuff… anything I do would help her. So, it was just, you know, I would send her pictures, like, I took a picture with your patch, send it to her and then she'd make post about it. Eventually, she was like, I need you to take more control over your business and stuff, I was like, I don't know what to talk about. Like, if I went up to talk to somebody at the mall or the pool or something, like, about this, I'd just

stumble over my words and be like, okay, bye. But no. I'm not a salesman. She could sell everything you're wearing back to you…
Tammy: Right.
(Laughter).
Chris: … and you wouldn't even know it, you know… like, wait, I just paid for my shirt…? Those videos were not me. I did it just to support her, you know, like…
Tammy: Could you tell her no? Could you tell her I don't want to be in that video? Or was that not an option?
Chris: Probably not an option. She'd probably be like, this is to help our family. This is to help this and that', you know? I couldn't have told her no. It would have made her mad. I wouldn't even start that because it's for the business it's for the family, you know. I was gonna try to help out wherever I can.
Tammy: Right.
Grahm: Did that actually make money?
Chris: Hm.
Grahm: So, not only just more sales, but it actually put money in you guy's pocket?
Chris: Hm. She made probably… in that last year, probably as much as I did.
Grahm: On commissions basically? I know that's a simplified version of it but…
Chris: Yep, I mean, it's a…
Dave: MLM?
Chris: They don't take taxes out on it so, that was, like, the good thing, and they paid for your car.
Tammy: Mm hm.
Chris: So…
Tammy: Did they give her an allowance or something to buy a car…
Chris: Yeah, they…
Tammy: … or lease it?
Chris: Mm hm. If you're a certain level, like, er, 12K or above, they give you a car allowance once a month. I'm not sure how they even made money, the owners doing that, they did. Unless there's just an insane mark-up on the product, which I guess there is.
Grahm: Probably is.
Chris: I'm not sure how much it costs for them to make it.

Tammy: Did you feel like a different person wearing those patches?
Chris: Yea especially like the duo, the burn patches. Like the Apple watches, like if you look on it, like when it tells you your exercise and stuff, it says exercise, like, all day. My heart rate was up. Just from those patches.
Grahm: Were they just full of caffeine, or what?
Chris: Ah, they had something in them. I mean, the Black Label ones, the longer black ones, those have caffeine in them, but they never had that effect. I mean, the Duo Burn ones, the ones that were more of the fat loss type, it felt like I was working out all day even though I wasn't.
Grahm: Were you tired?
Chris: I mean I know at some points even Nikki said I'd fall asleep on the couch – her couch- when I was talking to her, and then pick back up like I never knew I fell asleep, which I don't know if it was an insomnia thing or what. I wasn't sleeping much.
Tammy: They had a lot going on then.
Chris: Yeah. That was the only patches I felt a real big difference on, just because it felt like I was working out all day.
Tammy: Mm-hm. You don't feel like they changed your personality or anything like that though?
Chris: I don't know. I don't really know. I just know I felt different on those than any other patch. I felt like I could just go long and longer each day. I'm not sure if that – that was probably a bad thing. I don't think I was sleeping more than probably three hours a night.
Tammy: When Shanann was gone would you stay with Nikki and then go home to get ready for work?
Chris: Yeah, I'd just wake up at like four, four-thirty go home and get ready for work and leave. Then I'd just work out when I got back home.
Grahm: What were the conversations with Nikki as far as um, at some point you guys were talking about her helping find you an apartment? So what did you guys talk about as far as your future together?
Chris: That didn't really happen until I got back from the beach, so I told her, like, I lied to her, like, hey, you know, I had talked to Shanann about getting a separation-
Grahm: And that talk hadn't happened yet?
Chris: No, I mean it kinda, like… no… she knew something was going on, we weren't sleeping in the same room and she even

mentioned the fact like hey you know, Colorado is a fifty-fifty state, or something like that. Ok, I guess she looked it up. But that actual talk that hadn't happened. I thought it was gonna happen.
Grahm: So when you had conversation with Nikki, I get it- you're telling her the progress towards the divorce is a little bit more than it was. So what were you guys planning?
Chris: So it was more of like she's gonna help me find an apartment that's affordable that's around Brighton or maybe close to work, like, Fort Lupton or something around there. That's kinda like where my area was.
Tammy: Did you talk about moving in with her?
Chris: She didn't want that.
Tammy: She didn't want that? Would you have done that if she would have been cool about that?
Chris: Uh, it would have been a little too soon I would have thought. We had only been really seeing each other for a month and just talking for two months so that would have been really... 'cause she called her house... her apartment... like, her... kind of like her shield or she had another word for it, but...
Tammy: Her safe place?
Chris: Yeah, safe place or something like that. And she said people like to invade it but that's why she would always let me come over because she said she felt like I was fine her dog liked me and everything. Should you belong here type thing, okay. So...
Dave: So you and Shanann, did you talk about selling the house? At what point did you? There was some discussion there with Anne Meadows.
Chris: Yeah she had sent an email to Anne about we'd go about selling the house and I think Anne told her about get— Anne was always about getting pre-approved just like if you're selling your house get pre-approved for another house so it's like, you know, much faster.
Dave: Yeah, so you can just quickly transfer from one to the other. When did that happen, do you remember?
Chris: I think it was either right before we left... no, it would have had to have been first week of August somewhere around there I think she may have contacted her.
Dave: Okay, so the plan was maybe to buy a house I think you told me in Brighton, you were thinking of buying a house in Brighton?

Chris: Yeah, she liked that Adams 12 school system or something, so. I think that's what Brighton is.
Tammy: What were you thinking about when you called the school that day? On Monday?
Chris: I was freaking out I was thinking in my head what I just did, what I had done and I didn't know it was stupid to do anything, to call the school, to call Anne, to call anybody. They were right to be suspicious about anything because I probably sounded eccentric on the phone and out of sorts, and just, you know, I don't even know what they were thinking when they heard me.
Tammy: I think they thought it was weird…but I don't know how you would not sound weird, you know, like you said, so.
Grahm: So are you a hundred percent sure the girls were still around and alive when you drove out? Okay. So that's completely accurate nothing else about that?
Chris: No, they got in the truck.
Grahm: Okay.
Tammy: Where did the blanket go?
Chris: It either- it was probably in the trash can or something, I think. It wasn't, like, it was still in my truck.
Tammy: We thought we had saw some GPS where you stopped by near construction, a roll-off dumpster. Is that true?
Chris: Yeah. I think that I dumped my clothes in there.
Dave: So that would have been on the way back to the house?
Chris: My neighbourhood.
Dave: Yep. When Officer Coonrod was there? Okay. Was it one of those red construction dumpsters?
Chris: More than likely.
Dave: Okay, got it.
Tammy: Did you pack new clothes? How did that work?
Chris: I already had some in there, 'cause like in case we have a spill or something. If you ever get crude oil on you. I had two pairs of boots, I had all different kinds of things in there just because one time I had to clean up a spill and I had defrost on and I had a headache for two weeks 'cause it's the crude oil, so I always have something in there.
Tammy: So where did you keep them after you took them off? Did you just change up there into your new, other clothes?
Chris: Uhh, see I dumped my clothes in that dumpster.

Tammy: But wasn't that on the way back? When you were coming? Like you had already worked the whole day, right?
Chris: I worked 'til eleven or so…
Dave: That was back when Nickole Atkinson—
Chris: Yeah when she was at my house. The doorbell.
Tammy: Did you think right then like, oh fuck, here we go… or what were you thinking then?
Chris: I didn't know why she was there. I didn't know like, maybe she had an appointment or something with Shanann. I didn't know.
Tammy: What did you think that day, like, what you were going to say? Like what was your plan? Were you just gonna go home and be like, report to the police that you family's gone or—?
Chris: I… I had no idea what was gonna happen after everything. I mean, I don't even know how I was even acting even to all the people that I was around. *'cause* when Troy and Cody and Chad and Alyssa and all them, like, when they showed up, I don't even know how I was even being somewhat even coherent what I was saying. But apparently ,they understood me. I didn't know what was gonna happen. This wasn't some Criminal Minds—
Tammy: —well thought out thing?
Chris: Yeah, it wasn't nothing like that. I had no idea what was going on.
Grahm: So once the girls were gone, was it also just a minute by minute thing as far as the oil tanks?
Chris: Yeah. I didn't know what to do. I mean just thinking about an oil tank makes me want to throw up.
Grahm: And was that just because it was in front of you, and there it was- it just presented itself? Or was it a plan beforehand? Okay, was there any reason why the separate ones?
Chris: No, it was like you said going up the stairs and I didn't know. What Frank said, I was trying to separate everyone, that's not true. I don't want to separate anybody.
Grahm: What was the reason?
Chris: I… I… I can't even tell you. Like I said it was like something else was in control of what I was doing and I was doing something I never thought I would do in my life.
Tammy: Did you think there would be less chance of someone finding them if they were in separate tanks?

Chris: I don't- no, I couldn't- whatever my reasoning was in my head that day it wasn't sound because nothing was right.
Grahm: And you don't even remember thinking about it?
Chris: No, it was just a reaction, of something that I wasn't even thinking about.
Dave: Can you talk about the trash bags? Do you remember that?
Chris: Oh, with the—
Dave: There were two.
Chris: Oh, okay, yes. Trying to… 'cause the sheet kept… the one coherent thing I guess I had, I didn't want the girls looking at Shanann while they were in the backseat.
Tammy: So what did you do?
Chris: Put a trash bag on one end of her feet and one on her head, so they didn't have to see.
Grahm: And they were just too little to kind of figure out, right?
Chris: Yeah, they didn't know what was going on.
Grahm: Okay.
Chris: I just know that when I was driving up there, they were just, you know sitting there just kind of asleep or kind of just holding onto each other, laying in each other's laps…
Grahm: Do you remember having any thoughts of thinking about why not just putting them all together with Shanann?
Chris: Honestly, honestly, it was just happening so fast I had no time to really have a thought that was my own.
Grahm: Okay.
Chris: I wasn't dutifully trying to separate anybody pass them away, or trying to keep anyone separate. Everything Frank, Sandy and Frankie said I don't hold it against them. They can hate me… I think they have a right to hate me for the rest of their lives.
Tammy: They don't, they don't hate you.
Dave: In fact while we're on the subject, I speak with them weekly and I told them we were gonna come here and hopefully you'd speak with us and they told me to tell you, understandably, they're you know, devastated, but they actually said that they love you. They still love you. Sandy explained it, you know, he's our son… son-in-law… for eight years. I can't just turn that off. So they don't hate you… they don't.
Chris: That's amazing to hear that.
Dave: Yeah and I can tell you Sandy was the one that was most resis-

tant to penalties in this case, she told me that from the very beginning. She didn't want that- it's God's decision, it's not her decision and then she told me that even then. So it's not just a one-time thing that she has said it to me, it's been over the whole course of the event, so that's probably one of the most honest things someone's ever told me. It's pretty amazing. Faith is… well… she's obviously a believer. So am I. So, I get it. I understand it.

Chris: That's amazing to even hear that.

Dave: Good people.

Chris: I would have figured they would have hated me.

Dave: They don't. I mean anybody would think that. I certainly would, but... I have to admit, I was surprised. Really taken aback by that, but they certainly don't, so.

Chris: So what'd they say when they knew you were coming out here?

Dave: Um, they said they want to know, you know, details because they need closure and that's really all they want and they want to keep it private and I said absolutely, you know, we'll talk to him about what you told us just so they can put it past them because they're having a hard time dealing with it. They're trying to get past it all and I think that may help, just to…

Chris: Closure, you know, I mean my parents still think… I told them I pled guilty for a reason. And I told it to them and when they had that video phone thing Colorado the day before I pled guilty. Like, I pled guilty for a reason. I didn't just… I knew other people were watching I didn't just go in and be like, just say anything, like, they seemed to take it okay.

Tammy: What made you do that, Chris? What made you plead guilty?

Chris: I didn't want them to go through this for two or four years. I didn't want my attorneys to lie for me for four years. I mean, they would have done anything I told them to do. I don't see how they can do that, that's what attorneys do, like, they take their defendant and say, hey, what happened, okay we'll go with that story. Like I told them everything I just told you guys and it's just like they got together well, if they ever offered plea deal would you ever want it? Just plead guilty to it? I'm like, yeah, if we can end this, end this. Back in September I told them that.

Tammy: Really?

Chris: Yeah but, it was way too early and prosecution was still doing their investigation, grabbing evidence and all kinds of stuff. That wasn't on the table. I think it was around Halloween, I think that's when the prosecution went to Frank and Sandy and Frankie's house and was talking, if we could end this would you be open to that? And that's when the whole death penalty all of that conversation happened. I guess they were surprised that it would just be over.
Tammy: Yeah, we were all in shock, I'm not gonna lie.
Chris: Yeah that was like…
Tammy: It was like we were going a hundred miles per hour, and we hit a brick wall. That's what it felt like to all of us, so I mean obviously you had more time to contemplate it then us.
Chris: I mean I told John and Kate and Sophia and Amy if we can just stop this, I know everybody's telling me to fight this, there's not enough evidence for this and that and I'm like, no. Honestly, this needs to end. For Frank and everybody to have to fly back to Colorado every single time and get reminded of this, I'm sure it's never going to go away, but to have to come and talk about it, have other people talk about it, have, you know, all three of you get on the witness stand and say what they saw, what they've seen, what they heard on tapes and everything that…I don't want people to have to relive that over and over and over again for years. Like, if I could just end this for everybody and there was any closure at all they could start then instead of 2022, that way it would only get worse…for everybody.
Tammy: So did it have anything to do with you not having the death penalty?
Chris: No, honestly, when I was sitting in that cell, I felt I should die. I was listening to everybody telling me like, hey if you do this and this you can hang yourself from that cell. You can do this and that.
Tammy: They were telling you stuff you could do?
Chris: Yeah, that you could drown yourself in the toilet if you wanted to fill your toilet bowl up or something like that – they've been there a bunch of times and at one point I was listening to them. I was just like, you know, I just felt like maybe there's a different purpose for me somewhere. Maybe it's here. I don't know. I prayed to God every day that *He* would move me away from Colorado, move me away from the DOC there. They were saying there was a hit on me. They said if I was going to a DOC in Colorado I'd last a week and I'd be dead. There's the gangs and all the kind of stuff. So I just feel like God moved me here for

a reason and hopefully I can help people that way. I didn't want my family, I didn't want Shanann's family and all of our friends having to go through that because after a while I knew that this stuff was everywhere and I knew all her *Thrive* friends and everybody… it would just… break that hole in their hearts a little bit bigger every time. I didn't want that. I knew it would have gotten worse. I didn't want it to get any worse than it already was.

Grahm: Did you ever think about, boy, you know, it could be very believable what I told them. It could be very believable that Shanann did end the girls, and so maybe if I try to convince people that- maybe if I fought with my attorneys on that, maybe I could lessen it somehow. Did you ever think about that?

Chris: Honestly, I never thought about the story until you guys mentioned it.

Grahm: Yeah?

Chris: Yeah.

Tammy: I wondered.

Chris: I never even thought about it till you guys mentioned it.

Tammy: What did you think about it once it got mentioned?

Chris: Just like I just went with it. I knew my dad was out there and I knew they would probably believe it because my mom and my sister just never really liked Shanann. I mean, through all this I got letters from some of my friends even said, you know when we were over your house we could see Shanann was more of a dominant personality and you're always helping with the kids and everything and you're a great dad and everything. We could see a couple things I never saw and whatnot. Even my best friend Mark even said, you know there's always something that I didn't really get with Shanann, and I'm just like nobody ever told me any of this stuff. But yeah, I never thought about that story. That's what my attorneys were going with and then like, I think it was probably the second week I told them what really happened.

Tammy: What did they say after that?

Chris: They were quiet, they were writing it down. They said they wouldn't judge me, so I told them. I told them about everything that happened and they, you know, appreciated it. I guess most of the time other defendants or their defence don't tell them actually what happened they just tell them, get me out of here, this is what happened, but I told them what happened. I didn't want them going… if this was going to go anywhere in court, I didn't want them to be under a false pretence and get surprised. 'cause I know there were probably things that you guys probably knew that, I mean, if I lied to them and just told them , no this is what happened, it would have made them look, you know, foolish and stupid and just unprepared and I'm just like, *this* is what happened, and they appreciated me telling them that so now they would be prepared and that's when they were saying if we ever went to them, the prosecution, and said, we could end this, would I be open to it? I'm like, if this could end, end it.

Tammy: I know there was like, wasn't her phone found on… on the couch or between the couch cushions? Like, did you plant all that stuff?

Chris: I just threw it in there.

Tammy: You just threw it in there?

Chris: Yeah…

Tammy: Why did you do that?

Chris: I don't know what was going on that morning… (Laughter). Even, like, her watch, her phone… if I planned this, I would have probably just taken it out to the field with me, you know?

Tammy: What about her ring and stuff? What were you thinking about that?

Chris: It's like, you know, maybe she wanted… maybe she actually really wanted a divorce. Maybe she didn't want to fix it. I just put it there on the counter.

Tammy: She took it off? Or did you take it off?

Chris: I took it off.

Tammy: Okay. Oh, so that would look like she was saying I want a divorce— I'm leaving it here when I'm taking off. I see.

Dave: So, the phone and her watch in the couch, was that that morning before you left to go to Cervi?

Chris: Yeah, I think Nickole's son found it or something?

Dave: Yeah.

Tammy: What other things did you do that maybe we even missed?

Chris: The phone and the watch. I think I threw the therapy book she wanted me to read in the trash.

Tammy: That was that morning?

Chris: Probably. I think so.

Tammy: Were you trying to make it look like she threw it in the trash?

Chris: I don't know I just didn't think nothing was ever gonna work again. I didn't know what was going on.
Tammy: Did you go down to the basement? I thought the basement door opened?
Dave: Yeah, the door was open. So, there was a lot of movement I think it was around 4:26am or something. The garage door opening, the basement door opening, and then the living room censors at all. Do you remember at all what you were doing around that time? Other than opening up the garage.
Tammy: You had a lot of steps—I'll just say that.
Chris: So, like, the basement I'm not really sure, the only thing I really have down there is my workout- the bench press and what not.
Tammy: Do you remember going down there for anything or opening that door for anything? Did you think about, well maybe I'll take her out that way? Is it a walkout basement? I wasn't at your house.
Chris: No, it's like a garden level basement, but I don't remember really, I don't think I worked out that morning.
Tammy: Were you packing your lunch in the kitchen, did you have to do all that normal stuff?
Chris: Yeah, oh yeah, I packed a lunch and everything did all that. I don't remember about the basement or anything unless I just worked out that morning and I just don't remember… I don't think I did. Unless there was a trash bag down there.
Tammy: Oh, you get trash bags from there?
Chris: Maybe I did. Maybe there wasn't any in the garage and I went down there and got one.
Dave: Do you normally carry a roll of trash bags in your truck?
Chris: No.
Dave: There was a roll in your truck.
Chris: There was?
Dave: Yeah.
Chris: Maybe I just grabbed and brought it with me then.
Tammy: That would have been kept in the basement, maybe?
Chris: The basement or the garage.
Tammy: I'm sorry, what were you saying, Grahm?
Grahm: Um, one of the more kind of poignant or tender moments in all this was seeing you with your dad when he came in. What was it like when you picked him up from the airport?

Chris: It was… it was very strange. It was kinda like I almost knew this was probably the last time I'd ever see him on the outside. In my head I knew that.

Grahm: Yeah? What did you guys talk about?

Chris: Honestly, he just wanted to talk about sports, he's always kinda like you know, distance himself from a problem type thing. You know when, like if there was ever an issue or anything, he'd always want to talk about- just bring up…. Like, when I'd try to get him to quit smoking, like all the time, this was after I graduated high school and what not he would…

Tammy: Are you talking about cigarettes?

Chris: Yeah. And uh, he would always just like, change subjects. He'd say ok yeah, yeah, I'll get to it, and then boom, something else. I kinda felt it was kinda like that. He maybe asked a few questions like, do you know where they're at? Do you think you know where they're at or anything like that? And I just, you know, told him no, and then, like, just wanted to talk about sports and just normal things and just, kinda… I'm not sure if he maybe knew anything? You know, maybe he kinda figured out maybe something happened and just wants to talk to me as his son.

Grahm: Is it possible he saw that you were in a stressful situation and wanted to do what he always did, what he thinks is comfortable?

Chris: Yeah, I think that was a good way to put it.

Grahm: I bet you picked up a lot of that from him.

Chris: Yea, in stressful situations, the grey hair doesn't show it, but I try to be not stressed. When I worked on cars there's a lot of stress 'cause it's on commission you get paid what you do, not by showing up. *Anadarko* was a little less stressful 'cause I get paid just to be there, but…

Tammy: Was your dad's marriage like yours and Shanann's marriage as far as, like your dad was more the passive one and your mom was more dominant?

Chris: Oh yeah. My mom was always the more aggressive one.

Tammy: Was she like Shanann in a way? Like, were you attracted to Shanann because she was kind of like how your mom and dad's relationship was?

Chris: It was like… it almost mirrored her mom and dad's relationship, honestly, 'cause her dad is like my dad, they're both, like, kind, calm, cool, collected, and her mom is more like…

Grahm: Sandy rules that roost
Chris: Oh yeah, yeah, very. And it's just, like, you know, I kinda related it to that. *'Cause* her mom always told Shanann that she would marry someone else kinda like her dad, and I felt I was kinda like her dad. I couldn't build a lot of things he could, but our personalities were kinda alike. I think he really liked me the first time he met me because I was helping Shanann with this… she had got this car from a dealership she worked at and she was driving around and it felt like the wheel was about to fall off and I pulled over where her dad was and I got underneath and jacked it up and I was, you know, trying to fix everything. He said any other guy she ever dated would have just stood by and watched me do it. So I think that's when he really, kind of liked me. I was always wanting to help people. Not to hurt anybody.
Grahm: Well you helped her through her Lupus, and you were at the colonoscopy, and you were jacking up the car and…
Chris: Yeah, I mean anytime she had an issue with a car at the *Dirty South Customs*, I would just drive it work, see what I could do with it. Do everything I could to help.
Grahm: Yeah. I think one of the reasons Frank and Sandy work so well is because Frank lets Sandy be Sandy. And they probably both saw in you that you let Shanann be Shanann.
Chris: I just… I didn't try to change her. I just let her be who she is. She's gung ho. She knows what she wants and she's gonna go get it. I didn't say, No, you can't do that, that's what her first husband did. He controlled everything. He tried to be Sandy and it didn't work. And she turned into almost like me. She just kinda, like, laid back and let him do what he needed to do and I think she learned after that she could just be herself, and with me she could definitely be herself. So that's how it worked.
Grahm: So, do you think your dad had any inkling? Because I'm trying to remember the timing. He showed up when you were still walking around, you weren't in any trouble yet when Ronnie came.
Chris: Yeah, I had met with you the night before, like for three or four hours, then I was at Nick and Amanda's house and that's when I went to go pick him up.
Grahm: Okay. And you picked him up— it was early that morning, wasn't it?
Chris: Yeah, it was ten-thirty I think when his flight came in.

Grahm: And from there you guys probably drove home and then to the police station.
Chris: Yup.
Grahm: And the talks there were… no type of confession from you?
Chris: No, it was just like, you're just gonna wait. If you're hungry there's that barbecue joint down the street, and, like, it's good, and you told me he never left.
Grahm: He did not. I wasn't lying. He's faithful.
Chris: I don't know how he lasted that long without food!
Tammy: We ended up giving him food.
Grahm: He was great. And the reason I ask is because when I look back and watch the video, now knowing what I know after talking to you today I can see how genuine he was, but I just didn't know if you guys had come up with some sort of plan.
Chris: No. We never talked about anything like that. If I had told him anything, he would have probably just told me tell them right away
Grahm: I think you're right.
Chris: He would have still loved me either way, but he would have told me you need to tell them, like, right now. I didn't think I was gonna be there for fourteen… or however long it was, ten hours. I don't know how I did it that day.
Tammy: You were there a long time.
Chris: Yeah but it was… he woulda told me just to say… just to tell you.
Tammy: Did you know walking in there that you were gonna tell us? Or did you think-
Chris: I didn't, I mean, I knew there was a reason you brought me back in, I know for the, uh…
Tammy: What did you think about the polygraph?
Chris: That was horrible.
Tammy: Why do you say that?
Chris: I don't know how you do that.
Tammy: Why do you say that?
Grahm: *'Cause* Tammy's a torturer?
(Laughter).
Tammy: I am not!
Chris: You asked me questions for what, like three or four hours

beforehand, then you do the polygraph and it's like you just break down someone's brain to like…

Tammy: To mush?

Chris: To mush! Jello. It's just like, I know you guys have a job and a plan and you execute it.

Grahm: She's thorough right? There's no way to get out of there without the truth.

Chris: No, I mean, I kinda knew where… 'cause right when you asked me about Saturday night when I told you about the Rockies game I was like, man, she is going through her head, *that's a fucking lie.*

Tammy: Well we did know. We found out about Nikki right before the polygraph.

Chris: I figured that out after meeting with John and everybody that she had met with somebody from CBI, like, the 14th or 15th. I was like, they were talking? Oh, okay. You already knew. So, but…

Tammy: I mean, I didn't know how extensive it was, but yes, we knew.

Chris: Walking in there that day… just walking into that room I knew I wasn't walking out. Just the feeling I had walking in that room. Just the – I mean, I don't remember if the polygraph stuff was already in there…I think it was... but it was, I knew…

Tammy: I just feel, sometimes, when people, you know, do… do that bad thing, and they stay, some part of me thinks, well, I think they're here because they really want to tell us what happened. It's not normal that you want to keep all that in. That just kills people on the inside and I could tell it was killing you that day.

Chris: Yeah, I mean, it was like, the 13th when I slept in that house, nothing. I don't think I even slept two hours I finally got so tired I just fell asleep. I turned every light on, nothing felt right.

Tammy: What were you thinking about during your media interviews?

Chris: I didn't want to do it.

Tammy: Why did you do it? Did you feel like you had to do it?

Chris: I felt they would have just kept knocking on my door until I answered it and I didn't even set it up. Nickole Atkinson set it up. She told me, hey, Fox is gonna be at your house at seven-thirty. I'm like, what? Okay. And, you know, I even called you about it. What do you recommend I do? And he's like, it's kind of up to you.

Tammy: It didn't look good. Obviously, we can't say, oh we knew right then he was lying, but I think we all watched it together, and went, this might be bad. I had that feeling after I watched it. I could kind of see it in your face.

Chris: I was just lying to more and more people and it's just like…

Dave: Do you have internet access here?

Chris: No.

Dave: I would say just don't get into that trap of putting in, watching all that. The social media trap and all that, it's just ridiculous.

Chris: No, they don't let you have social media here. I think some of the GP guys are getting these little tablets that are the size of an older iPhone. I think they can use email but I'm not sure about social media. Definitely no social media, I'm not sure about internet or not. This place is probably a dead zone probably for phones anyway I would think.

Tammy: I don't know, we're getting service which is weird! I didn't think we would!

Tammy: Did you talk to Nikki afterwards… after all this happened?

Chris: On the 13th and the 14th.

Tammy: And what was that conversation like?

Chris: The 13th was kind of like, you know, it was more text and then maybe a phone call like, one phone call and then she thought maybe Shanann like, took off with the kids. *'Cause* I was telling her I didn't know where they were and all that. And then the 14th, I think, she thought maybe something might have happened because they hadn't come back.

Tammy: And why do you say she might have thought that?

Chris: Her… you know, she kept asking me some weird questions, like, she kept asking questions that only I would know. But she was testing to see if it was actually me on the phone.

Tammy: What do you mean?

Chris: Like, she would ask, what's my dog's name? Or what yoga studio do I go to? Or something like that. I would just answer, like, and then she's like, I'm not sure if this is you. I'm like, Okaaay…

Tammy: Is this through text or is this through calls?

Chris: Text.

Tammy: Oh, okay. So she wasn't hearing your voice… okay.

Grahm: Is it possible she thought you had been arrested, and *we* were on the phone?
Chris: Either Shanann had my phone or somebody else had my phone or, like, maybe… maybe she thought it was you.
Tammy: Well hopefully Shanann would know all the answers to those questions, right?
Chris: No, this was Nikki asking me.
Tammy: Yeah but if she's asking you the name of your dog and what yoga studio, wouldn't Shanann know that?
Chris: Maybe she thought I was with Shanann and she was just trying to figure out where she was.
Tammy: Hmmm.
Chris: Some of the conversation on the 14th got a little bit weird. I think that's when she met with CBI or something, or FBI, I'm not sure who she met with first.
Tammy: So she talked to you after she met with…?
Chris: Nope, she didn't. She told me, this is the last time you'll probably hear from me I'm going to stay at my friend Jim's place while this is all going on. She said not to contact her until this is done. She told me I needed to delete everything. I didn't delete everything. I'm not sure why I didn't delete everything, but it probably helped you guys out a little bit.
Dave: She told you to delete everything?
Chris: Delete all conversations.
Dave: Did she tell you why?
Chris: She just said delete it. Which I don't think you can ever delete a text message.
Tammy: We're pretty good at getting deleted text messages.
Grahm: When your dad came in one of the first things you guys talked about, you said kind of quietly, I cheated on her, I cheated on Shanann. Your dad didn't know until that time?
Chris: When I was in North Carolina I spent most of the time with my parents and my sister. You know I told them something like, I don't think this is going to work. With what happened with the nuts and everything and them not being able to see the kids, they're like you know, this is the first time they had talked to me, pretty much.
Grahm: Oh, because you went three weeks or something, right?
Chris: Yeah, 'cause Shanann had told me to call them when I was at

the beach just to smooth everything out. She was like, alright, whatever is going on in your head you need to fix this. But she didn't want the kids to see them, she didn't want to see them and then, when I did see them after I went and saw my grandmother—she's in a nursing home—she still wouldn't go see my parents or anything with the kids, so I just told her to leave me there and then come pick me up. I spent the whole day there. They said they wanted to see the kids, they just didn't know if they could ever forgive Shanann for everything that happened that day. I mean, I'm not sure everything that was said that day when they had that argument, but apparently it was a knock-down, drag-out, bomb that went off in there.

Grahm: Pretty hurtful things?

Chris: Yeah. I'm guessing so, and they just don't know if they could ever forgive her or not. I never told them about cheating on her. They even asked me, is there somebody else?

Grahm: Oh, did they really? So they could kind of sense that maybe something was going on?

Chris: Yeah, 'cause Nikki was texting me the entire time I was over there so they could kind of see I was texting somebody, but it was like… maybe they kind of knew? Like, when I was in San Diego talking to my friend, Mark, I told him about Nikki. But I didn't tell him I was going to meet up with her.

Grahm: Okay.

Chris: I should have told him right then. Maybe that would have helped me. I know maybe he had an instance where maybe some girl was coming after him. She was engaged and he ended up getting with her and they were together and then she cheated on him.

Grahm: Is this before he was married or during?

Chris: It was after

Grahm: Okay.

Chris: Like, he could have helped me, honestly. I never told him the whole thing. It was a lot further along than I wanted it to be.

Grahm: That's interesting to think about, right? Your dad could have given you some good advice.

Chris: Yeah, everybody, but this is my friend, Mark.

Grahm: Oh, oh. I'm sorry, okay.

Chris: While I was in San Diego.

Grahm: Oh, I got you.

Dave: So you think you told Mark about that hoping maybe he'd question you about it?
Chris: Mark is my best friend, you know. I grew up with him. I've known him since I was eight or nine years old. So, like, he had been married before and it didn't work out. They were stationed together or something over in Korea. And it actually just kind of came out in the whole story you know, like, I just told him there was this girl at work that I've been talking to, but I'm distancing myself from her, but that wasn't the case. I was just letting it exponentially get worse. If I had told him, hey you know he would have been like, *w*hoa man, alright, take a step back and look. And don't fall into that trap. You're going to be alone for five weeks. There's times, you know, like, I wish maybe Shanann didn't have to go away for five weeks. Maybe we all just went for one week. Nothing would have ever happened. Five weeks alone, I mean, that's the only reason really that was even almost allowed to happen.
Grahm: There are quite a few people who would tell us, and do tell us, you need to look into Nikki more. Nikki Kessinger. All the way from the extreme end of things being, Nikki is the one who ordered the hit.
Tammy: She was there hiding in the basement!
Grahm: So the extreme is, she is the one who told Chris to do it. She is the real problem. All the way, that's the extreme side, and then all the way to, well there are these texts where she was infatuated, she was in love, she was saying how good Chris was in the sack, and, maybe we should look at her more. What would you say to those people?
Chris: She had her moments where I had to talk her off a ledge, kinda deal.
Grahm: What does that mean?
Chris: Like, I guess after the fact there was videos of her where she was recording herself because she was bipolar or something? I never knew that. But it's like she would get worked up about nothing. She came to my house once**,** 'cause I think it was July 4th. I didn't have to work that day, so I didn't get up at like four and go home and Shanann had called me, like, ten times in a row. I didn't hear it because I was sleeping. And, she was pissed, Shanann was pissed. And I called her outside like, *w*here are you at, like, what are you…? I was like, I didn't have to work today, you called me at 5:30am. And she's like, well the kids want to talk to you, it's seven-thirty. I'm like, I was sleeping. She's like, she's just like, screw you. I don't know where you're at, and I went

back inside and I told Nikki, I've gotta go, and she was just like, okay, are you coming back? I'm like, probably not.
Grahm: So, wait a minute, you kinda lost me there. Were you at Nikki's place when Shanann called you?
Chris: Yes, yea.
Grahm: Ok so you were sleeping in her bed?
Chris: Yeah 'cause I wasn't going to work that day.
Grahm: I gotcha.
Chris: 'Cause I didn't have to that day. It's the first holiday I've ever had off and, you know, Shanann was pissed and, you know, it kinda pissed Nikki off too that I left, but I think that's when she, uh… I called Nikki later and she kinda realized that she'd always be like the second, she said, second bill. And I said I probably wouldn't come back that day. I don't want to be anywhere else when Shanann calls, she was already pissed. So, it was stuff like that where she would go, she said she would go online websites and look at, like, will our relationship work? Will a mistress turn into a relationship?
Grahm: That's what Nikki was looking up?
Chris: Yeah.
Grahm: She would tell you that or your…
Chris: She told me that. She said that she would go on websites and look at stuff like that. I was like, why do you even look at stuff like that? She's like, I just want to see what other people have experienced.
Grahm: But that confuses me though, because I thought earlier you were saying *she* thought you were headed towards a divorce. So why was she looking at herself as a mistress?
Chris: This was later on
Grahm: Oh.
Chris: Like, you know, in August, like the first week of August when I told her, like, I had had that talk with her about separation, that's when she started looking at apartments and stuff. Like, during our July relationship type thing, that's when she was looking up like, will it actually work. She told her friend Brittany about it, I guess, and Brittany told her not to do it but she said she already made her decision.
Grahm: Okay. And so, are those people absolutely wrong about Nikki? She wasn't asking you to get rid of your family?
Chris: No.
Grahm: Are you sure?

Chris: Yeah, I'm sure.
Grahm: Okay. And no part of any of this was because she put it in your head or asked you to or…?
Chris: No, she never… I mean, this whole relationship contributed to it.
Grahm: Sure.
Chris: But she never, it never, no…. she didn't want me to do this.
Tammy: Was it ever like, I wish you didn't have kids, I want to have kids of my own with you?
Chris: She never knew if she wanted to *have* kids, but she said that, you know, at one point she said, I'd like to give you a son.
Tammy: Well, did she know that Shanann was pregnant with a boy?
Chris: No.
Tammy: Did she know Shanann was pregnant?
Chris: No.
Tammy: And why is that? You just didn't tell her?
Chris: I didn't tell her. *'Cause*, like, we had met—
Tammy: But Shanann put that on Facebook! Like, how did she not see that?
Chris: I don't know. Maybe she did and waited for me to tell her or she put it on her end?
Grahm: Can I ask you a question? A lot of people think you named Nico after Nikki. So what was that about?
Chris: Nico was actually a name that Shanann liked.
Grahm: Okay. Shanann thought of that one?
Chris: Yeah, I actually wanted to spell it like N-E-K-O, I thought it was like *Neko* that way, but she said N-I-C-O. I thought it said like *Nick-O* or something.
Grahm: Okay.
Chris: I guess Nico is more of an Italian name, and to leave her my middle name and my dad's and all that, but Nico, that's a name that she always liked.
Grahm: Okay.
Tammy: Did she name all the kids? Did she name Bella and Celeste?
Chris: Yeah, because Bella in Italian means *beautiful,* Marie, her mom's middle name, Celeste because her grandmother's name, Cathryn is Shanann's middle name.
Tammy: Did you have any input in their names?

Chris: I said I liked 'em. I was like, if we had a third child, you know, and we could have Lee in the middle name, I know the girl's names. I love those names. So I was like, that's cool. Especially since we have little nicknames for them like Bell and Bellabean and CeCe, obviously.
Dave: Can we go back to the house on the 13th? So at one point right when you got back there, Coonrod… Officer Coonrod -, and Nickole was there. You went in the house and were there for about a minute or so before you let everybody in. Do you remember what you were doing in there at that time?
Chris: So I went in through the garage and then I ran around and I opened the front door- did everyone come in through the garage or the front door?
Dave: Everyone came through the front door.
Chris: Yeah so I came in, I went in through there, I came in and opened the front door, uh, ran upstairs. I acted like I was looking around.
Dave: Did you go around the house at all before you opened the front door?
Chris: No, I didn't run around the house, I stayed down the bottom floor and went and opened the door.
Dave: Yeah, yeah, ok, I was just curious.
Chris: I ran upstairs with everyone else, that's when Nickole's son found the phone and I was going through…acting like I was walking through the house.
Tammy: Shanann had her bra on? Is that normal that she was sleeping in a bra?
Chris: Mm… every once in a while. She just got home from the plane, so she didn't even take off her makeup or anything. Maybe she was just that tired, but normally, I don't know?
Tammy: Did it not come off when you guys had sex?
Chris: I don't think so. Sometimes she just keeps her shirt on and she doesn't want me to… she wants what she wants, she knew what she wanted.
Tammy: Was it just missionary sex?
Chris: Yup.
Grahm: And her final resting place, was that just naturally what she was wearing? You didn't change her or anything like that?
Chris: No.

Tammy: Did you have to see any of that stuff? Pictures or anything?
Chris: No. I asked not to.
Tammy: Okay.
Chris: They said I could I was like, no, I don't want… I've prayed for those Hazmat workers that, I'm sure it's like Hazmat, right?
Tammy: We were all there.
Dave: We were all there.
Chris: I'm sorry. I never wanted to see it. I prayed for those that had to be there. I don't ever want to know what the aftermath was. They said if there was ever a preliminary hearing that I would have to see them, just to be prepared and not have a reaction… an initial reaction… but I don't want to see them.
Tammy: Do you feel like your lawyers were fair to you?
Chris: Yeah, they were my only human contact really. So they were almost like a guidance counsellor almost.
Tammy: Did you feel like you were driving the bus though? With your decisions you made or no?
Chris: Yeah, there was a lot of things I didn't know were going on behind the scenes. Maybe there were a lot of things they never told me. Like, you know, stuff that came out afterwards like that whole Nikki Kessinger article in the Denver Post, they told me afterwards and everything. I always felt like anything I was telling them they were fair, they were gonna do. Like the whole taking the plea deal and everything. I told them that's what I wanted to do. They asked me, it seems like a hundred times, are you sure you want to do this? Up until sentencing I had time to back out, before we walked into the courtroom they were like, are you sure? I said, yeah, this is it. They never told me this is what you have to do. They always just said this is your decision if you want to take this farther. Even John said… he had all kinds of motions, written all kinds of stuff that was really creative 'cause he had never been in something like this before. He was ready to fight and I was like, I didn't want you to have to do that. Not for me. Not for something that the story isn't right…isn't true. It would have only gotten worse for everybody. For all three of you, for everybody that was involved in it.
Grahm: Are you still glad you did?
Chris: Yeah, I mean, I never thought I'd be in prison the rest of my life but I don't want people to have to keep going through this every day of their lives knowing that, you know, there's a trial hanging over

their heads. I didn't want people to have to relive it every day. Did they ever have to see the pictures?
Grahm: *Say that again.*
Chris: Did they ever have to see the pictures? Frank and Sandy and all them?
Dave: No, they never saw them. They saw some things. They didn't see anything bad. We shielded that from them.
Chris: Okay. I didn't want them to have to see anything or hear anybody talk about… or, like, you know, anyone bash their daughter, you know, to hear… if some of my friends had a negative impact from her or had a description of her that didn't match, you know, something like that. I didn't want them to hear that either. I didn't want anyone to have to trash her memory. I wanted them to know she was a loving wife, she was beautiful, she always helped everybody else, all her friends, her Lupus friends, everybody. I just wan… I don't want anybody to take away what she did.
Tammy: We tried to get you to say that that night…
Chris: I know.
Tammy: I know, but, um, do you remember that?
Chris: I remember. I was just like…
Tammy: I know, you obviously weren't ready to say that then.
Chris: I know, I remember after my dad left you both came in, like, *alright, we got most of the story, let's get to the true story.* I just… I just wanted to bang my head against the table.
Grahm: Well, in the end I think you did the right thing, and even though it's hard to hear, um, there's a lot of people who thank you for what you did. I think your whole life has been thinking of others except for one, brief moment. You know? I think you really did think of others when you made that choice. So, I personally thank you, right. It would have been hard for the three of us to go through. Not this hard or for everyone else—not that hard, right?
Chris: Anybody that was family or friends would have just been exponentially harder for everybody.
Grahm: Yeah. You did the right thing.
Tammy: So you haven't told your parents what happened, you just told them, I'm pleading guilty for a reason?
Chris: I've told them on the phone. Even, 'cause they're-they're still…
Tammy: *You should fight it… You should…*

Chris: I… I… they've-they've got letters from Australia, from England, I mean, I was like the 35C Colorado and stuff, you know, proper council or something.
Tammy: An effective council.
Chris: I mean, Effective Council. And some of the stuff they've, you know, said about the *Thrive* patch, how it's not FJA approved, how it can alter somebody's mind, like, um, er, like, it… it was some kind of condition. But there's something else they call CPSD complex, er, post-traumatic stress disorder, something like that. And then some people from England have had it and it's like… they've been emotionally abusive relationship. Like, some of the little subjects in there, it's like, yeah, I can relate to it. But it doesn't make up for the fact what happened. But they've… they've got a lot of support. They've had a lot of hate mail, a lot of phone calls, a lot of, you know, stuff like that. You know, I wish it never happened. But they... they give us some support, which is good, but on the phone they still think that, you know, there's a chance that I could get out.
Tammy: Yeah. I mean, you don't wanna ever think your kid's going away forever, like…
Chris: Yeah, they…
Tammy: You don't wanna fathom that.
Chris: … they tell me to fight it, you know. Not every day, but on their bad days.
Tammy: Yeah.
Chris: You know, I'll get a bad message, or a bad letter and I just call her back.
Tammy: Is it more your mom or your dad?
Chris: My mom, she loses it a lot on the phone. My dad's usually tryin' to, you know, don't talk about this stuff on the phone, because it's just gonna rile you up and it's gonna make him go back to his cell and he's just gonna, kinda, think about that all night.
Tammy: Right.
Chris: And that's… that happens a lot.
Tammy: Yeah.
Grahm: Would you ever want them to know what you're telling us today?
Chris: I'd rather just tell them myself.
Grahm: Yeah.

Chris: They're coming… I think they're coming for a visit, like, May or so.
Grahm: Do they still think Shanann killed the girls?
Chris: They still believe that, even though I've told them I pled guilty for a reason, they think that I was, their words, like, railroaded.
Grahm: By?
Chris: ((Unintelligible)). Because they, they think that they pressured me to do it.
Tammy: Do you feel like that?
Chris: No.
Tammy: No.
Chris: No. They asked me plenty of times, and this is like, they wanted to fight. Like, if I'd said fight they would've just, you know, gone…
Tammy: Put on their gloves?
Chris: Yeah. Just got in there and did it. But I said, no, I can't have you do that.
Grahm: So, Chris. You care about others deeply, I can tell. You worry about others. Um, and I may have asked you a bunch of times today but, you're not just telling us that you did it because you feel bad for Shanann's memory?
Chris: No.
Grahm: You did it? Okay.
Tammy: I have to say, you know, after this was all over, you know, people would bring up, oh, my God, I bet you're gonna find out that Chris used to torture animals, and, you know, all this stuff. You can imagine, you know, hearing that someone's capable of that, what have they done in their past, those kind of things. Can you think back to your past at all, like, your childhood and think about any other moments that maybe you felt the same rage. I mean you obviously didn't do anything like that, but maybe you felt that rage and what would've triggered that, or anything like that?
Chris: Not really. I mean, I was always someone who would try to coax people down. Like if somebody wanted to fight somebody else. I mean, I got in a fight when I was in third grade, but it was like, you know, we'd rip each other's shirt and I went away crying. You know, and I was stupid. I was like, why did I do that? And, maybe, that was the final bad thing I did in school. So, I can't think of any…

Tammy: Did you feel it on the inside whether you didn't act it out, like, did you feel, like, like if someone bullied you at school or someone whatever… would it still be inside of you, like, did you feel like that even though you didn't actually act on it?
Chris: I don't believe so because I was always… I mean, I never really talked to many people. So, I never… I mean, people knew who I was, but I didn't really… I mean, I never really spoke to many people. That's why I never had a girlfriend in high school, I mean, I was always kinda, just flying under the radar.
Tammy: Did you feel like you had low self-esteem?
Chris: I wouldn't say low self-esteem. It was just, like, I didn't wanna be… I didn't wanna be part of, like, a group or a clique. I just, you know, I had a couple friends. I sat at the lunch table with them or sat out in what they call the fish-pond area, you know. ((Unintelligible)). I didn't really even want a whole lot of friends. It was kind of close knit-ted. It just wasn't out there, for me. People know who I was but, it just wasn't… it wasn't awkward or anything.
Tammy: Mm-hmm. Can you attribute that to anything in your child-hood, why you were like that?
Chris: My sister was always the popular one.
Tammy: Ah-ha.
Chris: She was more like my mom, more outgoing and, like, me and my grandma would always sit outside middle school waiting for her to come out and pick her up, you know, she'd always be the last one out because she would talk to everybody in the hallway. And my grandma would always be like, where is she at? Does she know we're waiting? But, you know, it's… I was just the opposite of her.
Tammy: Mm-hmm.
Chris: And it was like, sometimes you have kids that are the same and sometimes you have opposite and me and my sister were the opposite. Maybe I just drew on that, that I didn't want to be the popular one. I just wanted to be just the regular, you know, regular guy.
Tammy: Mm-hm.
Chris: So there was never any bullying, not like I remember. Nobody ever came up to me or wanted to fight me or…
Tammy: You never got made fun of? Never…
Chris: Nah. I mean, I was… I had braces and I had a bowl cut for a while, but I didn't get made fun of.

Tammy: Most kids did, right?
(Laughter).
Grahm: The eighties and nineties were cruel.
(Laughter).
Chris: Yeah Jim Carey cut—with a bowl on your head. But yeah, I don't think there was anything that would… that would be pent up inside me…
Tammy: From childhood.
Chris: … from childhood.
Tammy: I know you talked about your dad having an addiction when I was talking to you.
Chris: That was after I left. I'd left home.
Tammy: Is that… was it cocaine or something?
Chris: It was some type of powder. I'm not sure. I guess it was cocaine.
Tammy: How do you think that affected you?
Chris: I don't think it affected me… Well, it did affect me, but it didn't deep down, it didn't hurt as much as I thought it would. It was kinda weird. 'Cause, I'm like, I think my mom and my sister told me. Like, when they talked to him about it, it didn't seem to register, I mean, he would just change the subject. And, when I talked about it he eventually… er, immediately, changed the subject. I'm, like… 'Cause they found, like, cuts on his CDs and stuff where he would, you know, like, separate it…
Tammy: Oh.
Chris: … and stuff like that. 'Cause at the car dealership you find guys that would do that all the time, I guess. But he was just coping with… I'd never came back home and, it was just before I met Shanann, and it was just…
Tammy: Did you feel guilty that he was now using drugs because you never came back home? Like he lost his kid?
Chris: No, because I never really knew why he was doing it. After the fact it was that he was coping with that. But I never really knew why he turned to drugs when Mom thought he was having an affair because all his money was going somewhere else, but it was drugs. But, um, like, myself, I never used drugs, so I always tried to tell him what's going on? Like, why do you need to use this, and it's like, he could use it for a whole lot of better things, you know, just don't throw your life away, I

mean, because, you could see in his face, you know, it was like, eyes were getting like, you know, what drugs do to your face, and the skin was getting all loose, and he was losing a lot of weight, his nose was bleeding all the time, and kinda like stuff like that, and I was like, 'hey, you know, you've smoked, like, every day of your life since you were, like, fifteen or sixteen, and I can't get you to stop that, but I'll get you to stop this.

Tammy: Right.

Chris: And then, he put it away, I guess, pretty quick after I talked to him about it.

Dave: Do you think you're closer to your dad than your mom?

Chris: Mm-hmm. Yeah, we always went to the races together, you know, and like, that together. You know, he always came to my sports… I played a couple school sports, rack ball, all that sort of stuff, you know. Mum would come too sometimes, but my dad was always there. Even if I wasn't playing, he would just come there just in case.

Tammy: Aww,

Chris: So, it was cool.

Tammy: Yeah. I wondered if they hadn't visited because they didn't… weren't ready to visit, or if it's a money thing, or, you know, like…

Chris: Here?

Tammy: … could get time off.

Chris: Here?

Tammy: Yeah, you.

Chris: Visit here?

Tammy: Yeah, visit here.

Chris: Well, I was told, like, they can't drive in the snow.

Tammy: Oh, these roads are bad.

Chris: Yeah, it's um… I think it's like an hour… ((unintelligible)) … where it is. I told 'em, like, to wait till springtime.

Grahm: Good advice.

Tammy: Yeah.

Grahm: It's pretty brutal.

Tammy: It was yesterday.

(Laughter).

Grahm: Did they have money to get here?

Chris: They sold my… ((unintelligible)) … to get some money to come out here, so… yeah, so they'll come out here in… they said April but I was like, you know, maybe push it till June, because they can still have a blizzard out here in April sometimes.

Grahm: Yeah, late spring blizzard, yeah.

Chris: The lake affects stuff, crazy.

Tammy: Yeah.

Grahm: And how are you… ((unintelligible)).

Chris: Yeah. The first time I… when I first came… I mean, I didn't know I was coming here. Honestly, I just… when I was at the RDC…

Tammy: Swooped you up, didn't they?

Chris: I was there a week. The first day I got there they put me through a ringer, like, I had, like, eleven tests to do, like, mental tests, like reading, math, that kind of stuff to see what my IQ was and then I just sat there the rest of the week and then Sunday came along and after dinner they said, right, strip down and put this on. I said, okay, then I walked outside and they put me in a van. It's like… Good. I had no idea what was going on. Then we stopped in Sterling which really freaked me out, I was like, I don't wanna do this… because I'd heard so many horror stories about that place, and uh, they just stopped to use the bathroom then they kept on going.

Tammy: In the prison? Did they use the bathroom at the prison?

Chris: Yeah it was like, uh, at the wash tower outside.

Tammy: Oh.

Chris: And, uh, we went to Nebraska, to the Sheriff's office there, and another Sheriff's office in Iowa. We stopped to eat breakfast then got here. And I asked them… I talked to them once, I'm like, can you tell me where we're going? A destination state? And he's like, *I don't know*. It was like, one of those transport vans where you have just the middle, where I was sitting there and I could see out the window and I could see… they would put in an address each time. Like, they had four sets of addresses. But they would never tell me where we were gonna end up.

Tammy: What did they say your IQ was?

Chris: I was like one, forty. One, thirty-five, something like that.

Tammy: Is that high? I don't even know what…

Grahm: I think it's above average.

Chris: Yeah, it took me back to high school for real, like…

(Laughter).

Grahm: Parts of the city and all that stuff?
Chris: Yeah there were a lot of work problems a lot of, uh, geometry, a lot of, you know, patterns, like, if this was this way, and it was like, like a series of 'em… ((unintelligible)) … just a lot of-a lot of stuff like that, but, like, the further you got along the harder it got, I was just like… they gave me this little thing… take that pen, and took the little tube out of the middle… ((unintelligible)) … sheets and everything.
Grahm: It's like high school, yeah. Do you know how long you're gonna be here?
Chris: No.
Grahm: Neither do I, by the way. Do you know, are you going to get a job?
Chris: I wouldn't be, uh, if uh, since I'm staying here, uh, since I've got staffed here, maybe after work.
Grahm: Oh. So what's your job now?
Chris: I don't have one yet.
Grahm: Okay.
Chris: They had to move me out of the accept-acceptance of the valuation. Assessment of the valuation.
Grahm: Are you still in that phase? Okay and how long will that take?
Chris: Well, right now, seven months after, I'm just waiting to be moved over to a different unit.
Grahm: And are you in gym park right now?
Chris: No. No, I'm in a unit—there's eleven or twelve of us in there. There was twenty-two when I first got there but they've been transferred to the other prisons around.
Grahm: And what are the other guys like?
Chris: They're… they're fine. Like the first time I'm like, I sat out and ate a breakfast or lunch with them I was… I was scared.
(Laughter).
Chris: It's just like, it doesn't happen, like, since. It's never happened. Except they lock the hallways down, like up in Colorado.
Grahm: In Weld, I'd heard that.
Chris: Yeah. So, it was like, you know, being next to… like, right, like this, eating next to somebody, I was just like, he could take his fork and kind of stab me or something. But it's totally different here. I mean, people know who I am but they don't, you know, run at me or jump at me, because apparently they, um… the guys that work here, they know

that other maxes are locked down for twenty-three twenty-two hours a day.

Grahm: Oh, so this is an alright place to be?

Chris: For, like, the max… for the max guys. They say it's the best max but the worst medium.

Grahm: Oh.

Chris: Because, er, if you're max, you're working, so, you know, you're out of your cell working. You know, if you're a clerk or working in the kitchen or the rec area or doing something.

Grahm: Okay.

Chris: But, er, yeah, they said that if you get sent here, it'll be best for you. Plus, they said it's not like, it's not as rowdy as some of the other places.

Dave: Yeah. That's pretty intense.

Chris: Yeah. So, I mean, I'm going to the GP area, I just don't know when.

Grahm: And you think that will be while you're here?

Chris: Mm-hm.

Grahm: Okay.

Chris: They say, I guess it could take… it takes a lot to get moved from max to medium 'cause Colorado I was classified as minimum restrictive. But with the charges it would've been medium, but here it's automatically max.

Grahm: And what are the other guys in for, do you know?

Chris: Er, they said most guys are in here for like, gangs, snitches and, uh, sex offenders, and… mainly people who have twenty years or more.

Grahm: So, people who are in for a long time and who would otherwise have a pretty hard time in a jail?

Chris: Yeah.

Grahm: For whatever they did, whether it be snitching or…

Chris: Yeah, like, you know...

Grahm: … children or…

Chris: Yeah, there… there's some people who are from other states here, as well. And I guess there's a coupla cops here too.

Grahm: Okay.

Chris: Just, you know, things have happened, and they just don't think it would be better… it would be a lot better if they're here and not at another prison.

Dave: Yeah. So what kind of jobs are available?
Chris: Well, it's like… They'll probably have me out in the kitchen more than likely. That's where everybody starts out either washing dishes or, like, you know, putting food on the trays or helping clean pots and pans, something like that.
Dave: Right.
Chris: But they have libraries, they have, you know…
Dave: If this is the PSU area, or psyche area…
Chris: So they'll have like, different guys doing clerk stuff around here. I mean, they've… they have over three-hundred GP guys here, that live here. So, they have a job for every one of them.
Dave: Oh.
Chris: There's even a guy that shovels sidewalks.
Tammy: I think we saw him…
Dave: Yeah, we saw him.
Chris: Yeah. I don't know if I wanna be that guy.
(Laughter).
Dave: Not here.
Tammy: Do you, um, do you go to therapy? Do you have… see a psychologist. Do you…
Chris: There is actually… the one I s… ((unintelligible)) … or something like that. She's, uh, she sees me, like, once a month. But she's actually from Aurora.
Tammy: Really?
Chris: Yeah it was weird, I walked in and saw a Bronco flag and I'm like…
(Laughter).
Chris: I'm like, who are you? But, um, yeah it's…
Tammy: Does she give you therapy or...?
Chris: No, she just talks to me, just to see if I need anything or, like, if I need psych meds or anything like that. I've declined all that stuff, but most people on my unit have meds.
Tammy: Just to have 'em or do you think they need 'em?
Chris: Well, it's a special management unit. Like, they just put me on there to keep me away from GP and most people are either… they have some type of medication they're on.
Tammy: But you don't take anything?

Chris: No. They just keep me on there until the security advisor says, you know, I can get moved to GP down the hall.
Tammy: What kind of stuff, like food and stuff, do you miss the most from the outside?
Chris: Food?
Tammy: Yeah.
Chris: I know, from last time in North Carolina, Bojangles, that was really good. You guys ever go out to North Carolina?
Grahm: Is that a barbecue?
Chris: It's like, it's chicken and biscuits
Tammy: Mm-hm.
Chris: And that barbecue place down the street from PD.
Dave: Mm-hm. Smoke house? George boys?
Chris: Yeah. ((Unintelligible)) … I miss that. I miss Shanann's cooking that's for sure, like, her spaghetti sauce and fried pizza.
Grahm: Fried pizza?
Tammy: I've never heard of that. What is that?
Grahm: I've never heard of that.
(Laughter).
Chris: Her mom has… I think it was her mom, has her grandmother on her mom's side has this dough, home-made dough you can make. She'd just make up the dough and she would make it up with Bella and stuff and sometimes she'd make up a smaller one, but she'd make a really big one. And then, um, she would, um, put it in the oven, the bottom oven and it would sit there for a couple of hours, not with it on or anything, just to let it rise. And then, once it's done, take it out for a minute throw the spaghetti sauce she has spread it around and fill it with mozzarella and pepperoni and put it in the oven at three-fifty.
Grahm: But what part is fried though?
Chris: Well they have some parts you can put on the grill or put it on the stove too.
Grahm: Okay.
Chris: It's really good. I mean, it's really thick.
Tammy: I think we need this off Sandy.
(Laughter).
Chris: I will work on that.
Tammy: Yes. Write a note.
Grahm: Are you able to stay out of trouble here?

Chris: Yeah.
Grahm: Nobody's getting in any fights? You're not getting… ((unintelligible)) … or anything?
Chris: I try to keep a low profile here, 'cause I don't wanna… 'cause they say if you get two ((unintelligible)) reports, they'll ship you out.
Grahm: To another location?
Chris: Yeah.
Grahm: Oh, so then, does that incentivise people to keep their nose down?
Chris: Yeah, 'cause a coupla guys got busted for having a cell phone.
Tammy: No kidding! Like, that stuff just baffles my mind how that stuff gets to…
Chris: They won't even let me… like, if someone sends me a letter and it has even… someone sent me a Christmas card with glitter on it and they won't let me have it because it has glitter on it. They were just like, it's contraband, so, yeah, I don't know how people get, cell phones and stuff.
Tammy: So what do you do with all these letters that are coming into you?
Chris: Most of 'em. I just have, like, this… if somebody writes me once, I'll never write them, just because I don't know who they are or where they're from. I'll keep it if it's a letter. If it's a weird letter I'll just shred it up and throw it away. If it's a supportive letter, I'll keep it around, just, you know, like a supportive letter. And then, like, I've had some people write me a second and a third time, but they've changed the way they talk or they've said different things. There's this dude in California that wrote me. He's like a… he's a senior high school, he's like, okay dude, I looked up the name, I'm like okay, shred it up, threw it away. He wrote me again, like, two weeks ago, totally different. Like, he never mentioned his age, never said, hey, I support you, and all this and that, like, if I didn't recognise his name, I wouldn't know he was just some eighteen year old kid trying to, trying to just probably just get some information. Trying to, you know, because there's been some journalists, and people. I can just kinda tell, I mean, they ask a lot of questions. But I try to take into effect who's writing me, and not to respond. I mean, I've not responded to a few people, just because, either my parents have talked to them on the outside, and I don't know if it's a real person. But, there are some people who're like, they seem

like they're just trying to get help for themselves too, you know, some people ask for some, like, just for some spiritual advice.
Tammy: They're asking for spiritual advice from you?
Chris: Yeah. Yeah, like, you know, if they're not asking about the case I'll write 'em back… if they ask about the case I don't write 'em back.
Tammy: Do you think you'll be in love again? Because there are a lot of women out there that are in love with you.
Chris: No. I don't think that's gonna happen. I'm not the guy that's down the street going through whatever it is.
(Laughter).
Chris: I've heard enough about that guy since I've been in here.
Tammy: What have you heard about him?
Chris: He got engaged over a letter.
Tammy: He did, yeah.
Chris: That's-that's pretty insane. But yeah, I don't see myself being in love ever again.
Tammy: Do you have some ladies that are giving you a lotta… just telling you, you know, that they're in love with you, and that kind of stuff?
Chris: Well, I've had a couple letters that have been, like, you know, I've used to get love letters from lady friends who tell you all you need to know, and I'm like, I don't get those letters. Trust me, I guess there was one letter in Colorado that someone sent me a picture of them in their bikini, and it was like, went on from there. That was the only letter I ever got, but the press took it and just went with it.
Dave: Yeah.
Grahm: Did you ever get a request from the press?
Chris: Mm-hm.
Grahm: And how does that work?
Chris: Tear it up, I don't really…
Grahm: So, are you personally… ((unintelligible)).
Chris: I don't, you know, write back.
Grahm: Would they allow you to talk with them? Would they allow them in here to talk with you?
Chris: I don't know, uh… I guess some stations have asked to come in here to talk to me, but they have told them no. But then, but, uh, I got letters from Denver pla… uh, Denver stations and what-not wanting to talk with me and their quotations, off the record—I'm like, yeah right.

(Laughter).
Chris: Anything I write…
Grahm: Yeah. You're right.
Chris: So, I just tear it up and throw it away.
Tammy: Have you thought about writing a book, or… anything with that?
Chris: No. You know, I… nothing like that. My mom and dad have said that maybe you should write down how you feel or, you know, how you've been dealing with this type thing, you know, just write it down. And that would feed my story but I'm just like, I'm just not… I'm not write… that's not… that's not me. I've always been… had a really crazy imagination, from when I was a kid, I even convinced my teacher I was going to Japan over the summer, or China or something. But she said I should just write down my story, you know, how you've coped with this.
Tammy: Why did you convince your teacher you gone to another country?
Chris: It was just like, what did you do over the summer? And I was just, like, oh, China… and just started writing.
(Laughter).
Chris: And she actually believed it, I was really convincing.
Grahm: So you're a smart dude?
Chris: Yeah. It was… ((unintelligible)) … said, how was China?
(Laughter).
Dave: So, earlier you were saying about this experience you wanna help people. What do you mean by that?
Chris: So, this couple of letters I've gotten, like, this one-this one girl, she's in an abusive relationship and she just can't find a relationship with God. And I've read… I've never read the bible before all this, and… well, in County I read it, because in the segregation, hold area it was like, that was the only book I got and I was like, okay. I read it cover to cover. And I never thought I could, I mean, I mean, how many pages are in the bible? But it stuck with me. And I've been reading it more and more here, and I got a different version in here and I've just been reading it and trying to, um, a coupla scriptures a day. Like, I've got my mom and dad and make them a little journal and stuff like that. My uncle Jonny, and, uh, his wife, um, Martha, they're actually missionaries, and, um, and one of my cousins is actually as well, and

they've been helping my mom and dad. They took 'em a couple of my letters and they were amazed at how mature I've gotten with the bible and everything... the scriptures, and one thing... one gift I did get was a good memory, as far as I can memorise stuff, and I guess that happened with cars and with the oil field I can memorise acronyms like that, and I've been memorising a lot of different scriptures and I can just, I kinda like, help people that way. It's, there's been inmates that have left my unit and went to a different place and they may just ask, can you get me a coupla scriptures to help me through this, like, do you know of any? I just help somebody that way.

Dave: Yeah. That's good.

Tammy: Do you need to go to school or anything?

Chris: No. ((Unintelligible)).

Tammy: Oh, they don't?

Chris: They're an accept or evaluation prison, so they don't... ((Unintelligible)).

Tammy: Do you need to go in them?

Chris: No.

(Laughter).

Chris: No, I was always asking, why do people go in there, and they were like, you don't wanna go in that class.

(Laughter).

Tammy: Yeah, you stay away from that class.

Chris: So that's the only thing they have here, but they have other, like, that's like a map of the prisons, they have here.

Dave: Yeah, I was looking at that earlier.

Tammy: Oh, wow.

Chris: They have a lot here.

Dave: Like three right in this area.

Chris: Yeah. I was just amazed that, when I... one thing I did see out of that window when I first arrived is, like, there's a neighbourhood that's right next to the prison.

Grahm: Yes, I thought the same thing.

Chris: Yeah. I was like, that's weird. Because in Colorado, they're all, like, out in the middle of nowhere.

Grahm: That's right. ((Unintelligible)).

Tammy: Hey. Easy!

Grahm: Well, um, we might take a little break right now.

Tammy: I think it's almost time for you to get lunch.
Grahm: Yeah.
Tammy: Like twenty minutes.
Chris: It's like the polygraph, everything just like, voof!
(Laughter).
Chris: I looked at the time and I'm like, oh wow!
Tammy: It's been four hours, holy cow.
Grahm: They might let us come back and talk to you. And there might be a couple more things we wanna go over, ((unintelligible)) … and then the other thing is, we might be back, in a month, in a year, two years, if you're up for it? Now, that's way down the road, but, I guess, maybe, in the back of your mind, just think about that and, um, I hope so far today's been alright for you.
Chris: Yeah, it's been… honestly, when I walked in, I was just like, wait, I know these…
Grahm: Where do I know these guys from…?
(Laughter).
Chris: I looked at you and I'm like, that's… that's not the psych councillor, that's… oh my gosh. Okay.
Tammy: The Colorado people.
Chris: I passed that eighties sergeant and I'm like, that's not the eighties…
Grahm: So, there's a possibility we might not make it back today, I just wanna let you know but, we might. Um, so, we really appreciate you talking to us.
Chris: Total, took me off guard, I didn't know any of this, so.
Grahm: And again, the case is over. It's closed, and that's not what today's about. We really appreciate it. You dealt with a lot of things really well, really good. You made a lot of good decisions, and obviously we're here because of one bad decision but you've taken steps to get past that, um, so, yeah, we might come back after, lunch, if that's alright?
Chris: That's fine.
Grahm: Okay.
Chris: Cool.
Grahm: I'll just go and see if I can grab somebody.
Chit-chat about the weather.

Dave: If we don't come back I just wanted to let you know I talked to your dad the other day, just to get your property.
Chris: Oh, the phone, and stuff?
Dave: Yeah, the phone and um, what else?
Tammy: Wallet.
Dave: Yeah wallet and we had some other things too, but I had to wait for the DA to release all that stuff…
Chris: Okay.
Dave: … red tape crap. But we'll send it off to him.
Chris: Thank you. Yeah, I know he wanted my phone just to get pictures off it, and stuff.
Dave: That's what he said, yeah.
Chris: I think I had that phone since 2016 so there's a good amount on there.
Dave: Yeah.
Grahm: If we don't make it back today, it's because of some other scheduling it's not that we don't wanna talk to you no more.
Chris: That's fine.
Grahm: There's more things we can talk about but if we don't make it back, that's why.
Chris: Okay. Yeah, it's the holidays up here so I figured it would be pretty much open.
Grahm: Okay.
Chris: Because I didn't see many people walking through the hallways when I came down here. Usually there's a ton.
Grahm: Of visitors, or what?
Chris: No, just people, like workers walking up and down.
Tammy: It did seem pretty sparse.
Grahm: Yeah it did seem sparse today.
Chris: That was one thing I was shocked about when I walked around here. I was always used to seeing everybody in handcuffs walking down the hallways. Here they just walk up and down.
Dave: That is interesting. I thought the same thing. I couldn't tell who was who.
Chris: Yeah, it's just… you see the red tag, it's like, an inmate, but it's somebody else that works here.
Dave: Oh.
Chris: Or somebody like an actual civilian who works here.

Dave: So then you're not in shackles and hand-cuffs that often?
Chris: I haven't been since I got here.
Dave: You're kidding me?
Chris: I was… that's when I was amazed. When the guy took me in the hallway I was like, anything? No? Just keep walking.
Dave: Yeah.
Chris: That's just my… ((unintelligible)) … when I first got here, but now it's just like max or something.
Tammy: Hm.
Chris: It was just like, you know, if you… if you wanna act up they'll…
Grahm: You'll lose it… they'll put those shackles back.
Chris: Oh, yeah, they'll put you in hand-cuffs and take you to the hole.
Grahm: Yeah.
Chris: I didn't know shit till I got here.
Grahm: Do they have solitary here?
Chris: Oh yeah. They'll shackle you up real good. Can't move.
Grahm: A reminder—behave, right?
Chris: Yeah, it's like, don't pass through, don't pass anything that's not yours otherwise you're gonna…
Tammy: Do you get to buy commissary and stuff?
Chris: It's different here. It's like a bubble sheet. In Colorado it's like a little touch screen you do.
Tammy: Ah-ha.
Chris: Here it's like a little scan tron. You send it off to Missouri, I mean, it's the same company but it's, uh, it just takes longer to get here.
Tammy: Like what kind of stuff can you buy?
Chris: Like ramen soup and peanut butter, oatmeal, stuff like that. I usually just get the oatmeal.
Tammy: Do your parents put money on your ((unintelligible)).
Chris: Yeah, I'm not sure how that restitution stuff's gonna work, I'm sure Dad, or whatever, whoever sends me money or Mackenzie will take a little it… of it too.
Tammy: Okay. Thank you.
Grahm: Thank you.
They break for lunch.
Tammy: We came back. How was lunch?

Chris: It was macaroni and cheese and a bun and some milk.
Dave: Sounds good.
Tammy: Chocolate milk or regular…
Chris: Oh, just regular. Chocolate milk's just… I don't know.
Tammy: That's special? It is a holiday today, you know that?
Chris: I know. But I think I had chocolate milk on Christmas.
Tammy: Oh, really?
Chris: Yeah, they got milk there because it's the dairy state.
Grahm: The dairy state?
Chris: Yeah, we have cheese with a lot of stuff too, so.
Tammy: Macaroni and cheese.
Grahm: We brought you some non-lactose Power-aid if you'd like it?
Chris: Seriously?
Grahm: Yeah. All yours.
Chris: Thank you.
(Laughter).
Chris: That's cool. Thank you.
Grahm: So, we don't wanna take you all day, so… and we really do appreciate being able to sit down and talk with us, um, there's a few things we wanna kinda clear up, wrap up, and then see if you have any questions for us that'll be okay. Did you wanna talk about Ronnie real quick?
Dave: I talked to your dad while we were at lunch and, uh, a couple of things we talked about—your property and waiting for the DA's office. But then he also… the reason he called was… Dave Colman? Was going to pick up some of your personal items out of the house, that's all.
Chris: Okay. All good.
Dave: Yeah, that's all.
Tammy: We didn't tell him anything about what we talked about.
((Crosstalk))
Tammy: And he doesn't even know we're here.
Chris: Okay. He just lives round the corner from me so…
Dave: Yeah, a lot of time when anybody goes over there they usually call, so it'll give everybody a heads up and that way no-one will have an issue. Neighbours call and say somebody's getting into the house.
Chris: Okay.
Dave: So that's why we do that.

Chris: Okay. Has anybody been checking on the house making sure, like, pipes haven't been broken, that kind of thing?
Dave: Water's off. I do know that.
Chris: Okay. I was worried about, you know, sprinklers and that sort of stuff, just… I usually blow them out, and all that kind of stuff but I wondered if anyone was actually going through it and watching it, that kinda thing.
Dave: The water's been off a while but the power's still on.
Chris: Oh, it is?
Dave: Yeah.
Grahm: So, um, fortunately or unfortunately—I don't know how you wanna look at it, but we need to get a tiny bit more into the weaves and into the mechanics of the time that you showed up at the house when officer Coonrod was there, till the time when we were all done talking.
Chris: Okay.
Grahm: So that includes at the house, that includes at the oil site, um, and everything.
Chris: Okay.
Grahm: And part of the reason we need to get into that is, um, I mentioned before how we just really wanna get into the mind-set of what happened. And you can imagine this is really important for us in the future, for when we're talking to a guy that's in your position to say, you know, this isn't really a monster this is more like a Chris Watts, and boy, I remember with Chris, had we asked this or had we done this a bit better and so that's why we wanna get into the mechanics of it a little bit more with you. Um, and that's gonna mean exactly how, exactly when, where were you, what was Shanann wearing or all of that. Right? So we really just need for you to take a deep breath and get into it with us. Would it be alright if we ask you some specific questions? Okay. So, one of the first things we wanna talk about was when you came home, so this is after they've passed, you came home and met with Officer Coonrod, um one of the first things we see on the video is you walking into the garage and into Shanann's car, do you remember what that was about?
Chris: Into her car?
Grahm: Yeah, did he open a door or something?
Dave: Yeah you opened the passenger door and, you know, it looks like

you're looking for something or maybe you picked something up there. Do you recall what that was?
Chris: Not that I'm aware of. Not like… not looking for anything, maybe just opening the car door to see if, like… see if… ((unintelligible)). Nikki was saying, I think I see the car seats still there.
Dave: Yeah.
Chris: Something like that, and when I opened up the door I looked in just to… I don't know, it's a first reaction. Like, everybody's just waiting. Pretty much waiting to get in the house.
Dave: Right, right. Okay.
Chris: So I didn't, I don't remember looking for anything as far as spes-spes-specific or anything but I was, ah, just reaction going in there and saying I know everybody's there and I don't know what's gonna happen when they get in the house.
Dave: Sure. Nervousness maybe?
Chris: A lot of it was nervousness.
Dave: Sure. Okay.
Grahm: And then backing up a tiny bit—we've come forward too far. Um, so, she comes home at two in the morning, um, she gets into bed. Was, when you guys had sex together was that pretty quickly after she came home?
Chris: I think it was around two-thirty because she had… I felt she'd been in bed for a little while.
Grahm: A little bit. And forgive me, it's not a pervy thing, but. She woke you up?
Chris: Yes, she was… I could feel a hand on me, like rubbing my leg or my chest or something.
Grahm: And that was a signal like, let's go time, kinda thing?
Chris: Pretty much.
Grahm: Okay.
Chris: Yeah.
Grahm: Okay. I get it. And that was maybe a half an hour after?
Chris: Mm-hm.
Grahm: And, after that, is there any talking? Or was it kind of a… ((Unintelligible)).
Grahm: … quiet in the middle of the night?
Chris: Yeah. I just felt her hands around me and I'm just like…

Grahm: Time to go? Yeah. That's funny. Alright, um, then, a couple hours of sleep. Alarm goes off.
Chris: Mm-hm.
Grahm: Okay. I guess what I don't understand is… so then there was some talking? And then, how did you get on top of her? How did that happen?
Chris: It was like, when I got into bed… she was laying… while she was sleeping she was laying face down which she generally never does.
Grahm: Okay.
Chris: And I was… I got into bed and I kinda nudged her, and then she kinda rolled over and then I was just right there on top of her.
Grahm: Okay. And so that was after you'd gotten ready?
Chris: Mm-hm.
Grahm: Alright, and so, you go down, you make your food…
Chris: Yeah, I get cottage cheese and another couple things out and made my food for that day.
Grahm: Okay. And then… so this is… we talked a little earlier today about, you know, all of these things playing in your mind, where you don't wanna go another second without having this conversation… without some sort of completion, right?
Chris: Mm-hm.
Grahm: And then, so, you come back, she's asleep, and then, you just kind of nudge her?
Chris: Yeah, I just kinda like, okay, wake up for a second.
Grahm: And was there, nudge, talk for twenty minutes or was it nudge, and all of a sudden you're on top of her.
Chris: Nudge and pretty much on top of her.
Grahm: Okay, so that happened very quickly?
Chris: Yeah, that was how we pretty much talked. I was just right there.
Grahm: And was there talking?
Chris: Yeah.
Grahm: Okay. So, a nudge, a talk. She's laying down and you're standing up?
Chris: I was on… I was, like… I crawled back… I got on my side of the bed.
Grahm: Uh-huh.
Chris: I just nudged her like that.

Grahm: Oh, okay. And then you're talking while you're on top of her?
Chris: Mm.
Grahm: Okay. That seems confusing to me. Is that actually what happened? Okay. Um, and so…
Tammy: She was fine, like, just laying there and you're trying to talk to her while you were on top of her?
((Crosstalk)).
Chris: … she thought we were just gonna have sex again or something.
Tammy: Oh, okay.
Grahm: Okay. And how long did you talk?
Chris: About fifteen-twenty minutes.
Grahm: Really? In that position? Okay. And was there any sex?
Chris: No. Maybe… I'm… basically, from… ((unintelligible)) … maybe she maybe thought I'd try to go again, I don't know.
Grahm: Okay. And I don't wanna harp on it too much, but, I'm just trying to think if my wife's four months pregnant, and it's five o'clock in the morning, and I wanna talk, and I wanna get on top of her, that's just not gonna fly. And that's why I'm confused. Is that really what happened?
Chris: Yeah.
Grahm: Okay. And then, talked for about fifteen minutes and then it's heated and then your hands are on her neck?
Chris: Yeah.
Grahm: Okay. Alright. Um…
Tammy: What did this… what did this talk consist of?
Chris: Basically, just, about how… at first it was just like the selling the house type of thing. And about not going to Aspen and trying to maybe go at a different time, and then just switched all to the, I don't feel like I'm in love with you anymore and we're not compatible, like that. And that's when it got to the heated part of it.
Grahm: Okay.
Dave: Did she ever say at some point, get off of me, or anything like that?
Chris: At the end. That's when she said, I don't want you… 'cause where I was she didn't want me to sit down, or hurt the baby or anything.
Tammy: Did she accuse you of cheating at that point?

Chris: Mm-hm.
Tammy: So what did she say?
Chris: She said, I knew there was somebody else. I knew there was somebody else. I just couldn't come out and say that there is somebody else, but she obviously already knew.
Tammy: And your response to that was what? Did you say, no there's not, or deny it?
Chris: I just denied it but, I mean, at that point, because I was… she'd accused me at the beach and I was like, there's nobody else, there's nobody else, you know. And then when we got back home she always said there's got to be somebody else because she'd always talked to her friends like Christina and somebody on text messaging and they all would say there's got to be somebody else. If he's not wanting to sleep with you… he's getting it from somebody else. So, there's no… there's no, I mean… she couldn't really say that I was getting it anywhere else because I was using *Anadarko* gift cards so it was just me getting distant. But she knew and I just… that's mainly the reason why I talked to her because I knew that after that night, it was like, it felt… I felt guilty. More guilty than ever before.
Grahm: Yep. And then, it seems to me… I'm sorry, a lot of thoughts here. So we know what happened. And we can talk about it today kind of openly but what I need from you is that to say, I know it sounds bad, I know I feel this way, but basically this is exactly what happened. Um, so if you could tell us that, it seems then that it would've had to be a pretty quick transition from two people talking to this.
Chris: Yeah.
Grahm: Right is that what happened?
Chris: Yeah. It was like, I don't wanna… I'm trying to think about the last things we were talking about but it was, you know, I love you, I don't love you anymore. And then she was like, you're never gonna see the kids.
Grahm: That's perfect, Chris. That's exactly what we need. Okay. And I know it's hard to walk through that again. But that's exactly what we need. So then, as soon as you started talking like that, then it was on? Okay.
Tammy: And it was you saying that you didn't love her/ Yeah. Okay.
Grahm: And her saying you're never gonna see the kids?
Chris: Yeah.

Grahm: Okay. And I can imagine how that made you feel. I'm sorry.
Chris: It didn't... didn't warrant what I did.
Grahm: Yeah. Um. And then, the fact that she didn't scratch at ya or anything is that just because it was so powerful?
Chris: I don't think it was... I mean, it didn't feel like it. I've never done that before, put my hands on anybody before, so I don't even know what kind of force I was putting on her neck.
Grahm: Okay.
Chris: Like I said to you before, I don't know if... ((unintelligible)).
Tammy: Did you cover her face at all during that time?
Grahm: Both hands on her neck? Okay. And so, if it's done right, I mean, that can be a matter of seconds before on their carotid loses oxygen to their brain and is out, right. Did it seem like it was that quick or...? Okay. Maybe a minute? Maybe two? Okay. Screaming? Okay. Did you see eyes go bloodshot or anything like that?
Chris: Mm-hm.
Grahm: Okay.
Tammy: You kept talking about the mascara—did you see mascara on her face?
Chris: It looked like... it was like... that's what I attributed it to.
Tammy: Was she crying? Is that why? At what point did she start crying?
Chris: When I was talking about the relationship—talking about not being compatible. And when she was talking about being with somebody else and she started crying. That's why I thought, you know, mascara. I don't know if it wasn't...
Tammy: I don't know.
Chris: I don't know... I don't know.
Tammy: Was there a pillow or something you wanted to ask about?
Dave: Yeah, so there was... was there ever at any time a pillow or a sheet or anything involved in that? On the face specifically? No?
Chris: Not unless... the sheet I wrapped around her downstairs.
Dave: The one that was at the site? Okay. And then the other sheets that were in the trash... at what point did you put shoes in there?
Chris: That was...
Dave: Obviously after I was in the house?
Chris: Yeah. I think it was probably the next day or so.
Dave: Okay.

Chris: I think it might of… I'm not sure what happened… this is hard to talk about, like, when…
Dave: Yeah.
Chris: … you strangle someone sometimes, I guess, they use the bathroom.
Dave: Yeah.
Chris: So that was… I think that was one of the reasons why because I think that's what happened.
Dave: Oh, okay.
Grahm: And you said she was sleeping face down at one point? Was her face in the pillow or was it turned to one side or…?
Chris: Kinda like on the side. She was a side sleeper, but she was more down than usual.
Grahm: Okay.
Tammy: But then she turn… rolled completely on her back when you started talking to her?
Chris: Yes.
Grahm: Um, now as hard as that was, we need to talk about the girls too, okay? Um, so with the girls, you talked about how they got into the truck with you and were alive. Okay? Are you one-hundred percent sure that's true? Okay. Um…
Tammy: Do you wanna… can I ask you to go back just a second… um, you talked about before that Bella walked in though, into the bedroom. Can you tell us about that? Before you left.
Chris: Yeah it was… I was just getting the sheet off the bed and she walked in and she had her… ((unintelligible)) … blanket with her. And she was like, what's wrong? What's wrong with Mommy?
Tammy: And where was Shanann at that point?
Chris: She was pretty much on the bed, but she was face down.
Tammy: Wrapped in the sheet?
Chris: Yeah.
Tammy: What did you say?
Chris: I just said, you know, she doesn't feel good right now, that's when I started carrying her downstairs.
Grahm: Shanann?
Tammy: Did you carry her like this? Did you drag her? What did you do?

Chris: I attempted to pick her up and take her down, but I lost grip after a little while and… ((unintelligible)).
Tammy: Did Bella see you do that? What was Bella saying?
Chris: She started, er… she was crying a little bit and she was like, what's wrong with Mommy?
Tammy: And what did you say that time?
Chris: I said… just that she doesn't feel good. She's a smart girl and she knows what… ((unintelligible)).
Tammy: Mm-hm. Did she ever touch Shanann? Try to wake her up or anything? No.
Grahm: She didn't want to see her, or ask to see her or anything? And so that initial time did she see you put, uh, Shanann in the truck. So, she was kinda following you? Okay. So she followed you and you put Shanann in the truck?
Chris: Yeah.
Grahm: And then what?
Chris: I got… CeCe wasn't up yet, she was just in her room. She was just getting ready to get out of her bed. And then they were just walking around the house. I put the… I put my lunchbox in the truck and stuff, grabbed the kids and them on a sheet in the back.
Grahm: Okay. And so Shanann, is she kind of on the floor in the back? And they were just on the bench? Okay. Um, and they were both alive at that point? Okay. Is there any reason you would feel uncomfortable to tell me they're not alive at that point?
Chris: No.
Grahm: Okay.
Chris: It wasn't on the video or anything?
Grahm: Um, it's hard to see. And I believe you. Obviously um, I'm trying to make sure I give you all the opportunities to be comfortable enough to tell me anything. Okay.
Chris: They were alive.
Grahm: Okay.
Chris: I hear that every day when Bella was talking to me at the site.
Grahm: Oh, really? What do you mean?
Chris: When she said, Daddy, no. When we were driving to the site she said, Daddy it smells.
Grahm: Oh. Okay. So, that goes back to maybe Shanann evacuating herself.

Chris: I don't know if it was that, you know, that smell like a skunk maybe sometimes?
Grahm: Oh.
Chris: I got some kind of… I smelt it that way, but I don't know what that was from.
Grahm: And was that maybe outside of the truck or was that in?
Chris: I don't know.
Grahm: Okay. What did you guys talk about on the way out?
Chris: They were quiet, they just, you know, lay next to each other.
Grahm: Okay.
Chris: Maybe Bella in her lap and CeCe in her lap, just back and forth.
Grahm: Oh, just trading off like little ones do?
Chris: Mm-hm.
Grahm: Okay. Were they awake?
Chris: I think one would kinda fall asleep the other would… CeCe would kinda trade off back and forth.
Grahm: Were they talking to you?
Chris: Just about, you now, just saying Daddy it smells.
Grahm: Oh, right.
Chris: It was early in the morning… ((unintelligible)).
Grahm: Okay.
Tammy: Did you have to… you didn't have to wake CeCe up?
Chris: No there was noise from kinda getting Shanann down the stairs.
Tammy: Did she kinda fall down the stairs?
Chris: No, it was more like trying to get her down and, you know, from the steps, maybe her foot caught the next step kind of thing. ((Unintelligible)).
Tammy: Oh.
Grahm: So then, once you get to the site, tell me what happens.
Chris: I get to that one site and I get Shanann out and just pull her over to the… ((unintelligible)) … of the site there.
Grahm: Okay.
Chris: The girls are still in the truck.
Tammy: Did they ask you what you were doing? Taking Mommy out, or…
Chris: Yeah, I can't remember what I told them. But they did ask that.

Grahm: What did they as… what did they say specifically?
Chris: It was something like, what you doing to Mommy?
Grahm: Okay. And then is that when you buried her?
Chris: I didn't… I don't remember if I dug a hole first or… but they didn't watch me do that.
Grahm: So then, you pulled Shanann out and she's maybe just sitting there on top of the ground?
Chris: Yeah, like, off to the side.
Grahm: Off to the side. Close to where she ended up?
Chris: Oh, yeah.
Grahm: All right. And then the girls, right?
Chris: Mm-hm.
Grahm: You mentioned Bella was first?
Chris: Cece.
Grahm: CeCe was first? Okay. Um, where exactly was she when it happened?
Chris: In the back-seat.
Grahm: Was she just right next to Bella?
Chris: Mm-hm.
Grahm: Okay. And so… so once again was it hand over her face? Was it…?
Chris: Just the blanket over and then my hand.
Grahm: And then your hand. Okay. And then that just stopped her from breathing, that type of thing? Okay. Did she struggle at all?
Chris: I don't think so. My… I was blocking her face and my hand was just here.
Grahm: Oh, okay.
Tammy: You had one hand here and one hand over her mouth?
Grahm: Just pushing her into the back-seat type thing? Okay. What was Bella doing?
Chris: Sitting there next to her, she didn't know what was going on.
Grahm: Okay. Could she see you? Okay. Um, and then, did that take a minute or two?
Chris: I think so. I didn't… I don't have no concept of time.
Grahm: That's fine. Okay. Tell me about what you were thinking?
Chris: I wasn't. I was thinking… ((unintelligible)). If there was any partial hint of what I feel for those girls and what I feel for my wife then none of this would've happened. I wasn't thinking.

Grahm: Okay. So she's in the back-seat? Okay. Um, and then, once she's gone, is it Bella next or did you pull CeCe out?
Chris: I pulled CeCe out.
Grahm: Okay, so once CeCe's gone, Bella's still there, in the car alive, and you pull CeCe out. What did you do with her?
Chris: Put her in the tank.
Grahm: So, she went into the tank and Bella's still in the back of the truck alive? Okay. With regard to that tank, did you bring up CeCe, put her down, and open the hatch?
Chris: Brought her up, opened the hatch…
Grahm: And then put her in? Okay. When we talked the very first time we met, we were talking about this. It was a matter of just lowering her down? Okay. And so she went in feet first? Okay. Was she able to fit pretty well? Was it snug?
Chris: I don't know. I think so.
Grahm: Okay. Did you have to move her around a little bit and get her in there?
Chris: I think so.
Grahm: Okay.
Chris: I mean, I didn't have to, you know, hit her, you know, or anything like that.
Grahm: It's not like you stomped her in…
Chris: No.
Grahm: Okay. Um, and then, closed the hatch?
Chris: Yes.
Grahm: Okay. And then what happened with Bella? Tell me what happened there.
Chris: She said, what happened to CeCe… What she asked was, is the same thing… is that same thing gonna happen to me as CeCe?
Grahm: Did she ask you that? Okay. Bella's pretty smart. How did she sound when she asked you that, Chris?
Chris: Just that soft voice she always had.
Grahm: What exactly did she say?
Chris: Is the same thing gonna happen to me as CeCe? And I said… I don't even remember what I said.
Grahm: Okay.
Chris: I don't know if I just said yes like a horrible person or if I just put the sh… put the blanket over her and didn't say a thing.

Grahm: Same blanket, same way?
Chris: Mm-hm.
Grahm: Okay.
Chris: She said, no, Daddy, and that's the last thing she said.
Grahm: Did she say, no, Daddy, like, Please, no, Daddy, type thing? Did she say it like, don't do it?
Chris: She just said, no, Daddy.
Grahm: Okay. Same way, hand on neck, hand over mouth or hand over blanket which is over mouth?
Chris: Yes.
Grahm: Did that take a couple minutes?
Chris: Felt like it.
Grahm: Okay. Then… then what?
Chris: I just know that she had a couple of spots like over her eye or something. I picked her up and same thing.
Grahm: Um, and we talked a little bit earlier today about it, you don't remember why a different tank?
Chris: No.
Grahm: Okay, and there was no reason?
Chris: There… I mean, they're both same tanks, I mean, I don't know why I did two separate tanks.
Grahm: Does one… I never got up there, does one catwalk lead to both?
Chris: Or you can go to either tank.
Grahm: Okay. But if you go up one set of ladders does that…
Chris: Yeah, just one catwalk.
Grahm: Okay. Now Bella was a bit bigger, was she harder to get in?
Chris: It felt like it a little bit.
Grahm: Okay. And so, was it a matter of just kinda manoeuvring her? Alright. Um, so then, they're both in there, um, is there any reason to think they were alive…?
Chris: No.
Grahm: … when they fell in? Okay. You're pretty sure? Okay. So, once that's done, then what?
Chris: I go over to Shanann, and I clear away some leaves and dig a hole.
Grahm: Okay. Did you have a shovel?

Chris: Yeah, ***WE*** had a shovel, a rake, and a weed-whacker as far as the tools… ((unintelligible)).
Grahm: With that rake, if I remember right, it was…
Chris: Part of it was sitting there because it was broken.
Grahm: Oh. Did it break as you were digging or something?
Chris: No. I was rak… I was smoothing the ground over.
Grahm: On this day? It broke when you were doing that? Okay. Was that after you were all done? And it seems as though maybe the first people that got there saw… was it stuck in the ground?
Chris: I guess it was, like… not standing up, but it was, like, laying down.
Grahm: Oh, okay. Were you planning on coming back?
Chris: I mean, I don't know. I don't think so.
Grahm: Yeah. At this point then, this is just before then, is a couple of hours you would make it back home?
Chris: Mm-hm.
Grahm: To see Officer Coonrod?
Chris: Mm-hm.
Grahm: Okay. So, once she's buried, then what?
Chris: That's when people start showing up.
Grahm: Did you notice was she cut, or broken, or bleeding in any way?
Chris: No. I mean, I noticed the bloodshot eyes you were talking about I noticed that at that point, other than that, no.
Grahm: Um, had she partially given birth?
Chris: No.
Grahm: Do you remember?
Chris: Yeah, I remember. I remember she had a shirt and I think blue underwear on.
Grahm: Okay. That's what that point…
Chris: ((Unintelligible)).
Grahm: Thank you. I know that wasn't easy.
Tammy: Can you… can you tell us about… obviously you know, um, the District Attorney got up and talked about Bella's injuries and stuff?
Chris: I… I didn't wanna hear about that.
Tammy: Right. Can you tell us about that?
Chris: As far as, like, her biting her tongue?
Tammy: And ripping her frenulum, which is that connective skin

from your lip to your gum, was gone. Her gums had like a… what looked like a hole in them from… the pathologist said it was from her obviously struggling to get away.

Chris: I didn't know that. I didn't know what that meant.

Tammy: Yeah.

Grahm: Could it be that that's what happened?

Chris: So like… I didn't put my hand, like, over her… like that. Is that what you're talking about?

Tammy: Well, it would've been just downward pressure on her… this area.

Chris: I didn't… I didn't see any of that when I got back up. I mean, it wasn't like… her lip was, like, missing or something?

Tammy: No, see the skin that connects that? That was ripped—it was gone.

Chris: I don't…

Tammy: That would make a hole in her gum.

Chris: I'm just thinking, maybe, it's like, maybe it's like her mouth… not her… her head was twisting back and forth—would that have done that?

Tammy: Yeah.

Chris: She had a blanket over her. I don't know like…

Tammy: Did you feel her doing that thrashing? Or trying to get away, or…?

Chris: I felt her head moving back and forth.

Tammy: You did?

Chris: But I didn't know that that would happen.

Tammy: Could you tell she was trying to yell or say anything, or…?

Chris: The only thing was, Daddy, no. And then, like, the… some grunts here and there. Kinda like, trying to breathe.

Tammy: Mm-hm.

Grahm: During that time do you remember getting phone calls from Nickole Atkinson?

Chris: After uh… before she got to my house or after?

Grahm: Just any time during that morning.

Chris: I think I didn't get one till I saw her on my doorbell camera.

Grahm: And that was, like, what—ten o'clock?

Chris: Yeah it was right around there.

Grahm: Okay. And so at that time had everything been done out at CERVI-319?
Chris: Yeah. I was at a different site… ((unintelligible)).
Grahm: Okay. So you went from there when it was all done—so, the girls are in the oil, uh, Shanann's in the ground, and did you do a bit of a clean-up? Um, was there any questions about the sheets or any garbage cans? Or, or garbage sacks?
Chris: No… ((unintelligible)).
Grahm: Okay. So then you went from that site to work?
Chris: At that CERVI-319 there was a little spill. That's what happens… everyone shot up there because they knew that was up there and we were trying to figure out what happened.
Dave: While we're on that subject, just back up. The night before you had some text messaging about going out there?
Chris: Mm-hm.
Dave: Can you talk about that a little bit?
Chris: Yeah, that was, I think, Friday, that we'd figured out we had a spill out there from like… it's an old site set up a little different. So, what had happened was there's a down-comer and a side-comer going into those oil tanks and one of the down-comer's is tied in to the back-pressure line that'd split. Every time it was dumping oil it had spilt on the ground and it was… the oil was coming up…
Dave: Okay.
Chris: … out of the ground, and we decided just to go out there on Monday, because it was Friday and he had, like, switched it on… either he had shut it in or switched lines or he'd covered it up and seeing if it was just gonna come back up.
Dave: Okay. And, more specifically, you talked about… or, you texted about how you would go up there and take care of it.
Chris: Yeah, I was going to take care of it for him because I'd gone out there plenty of times.
Dave: Okay.
Chris: But like… I used… when another guy was out there as far as another foreman, you'd shown me around out there, and like, you'd still go and I just got… ((unintelligible)) … with the place, and I'd just help him out.
Grahm: And so that was a genuine…
Chris: Yeah, that was genuine.

Grahm: … it wasn't pre-um…

Chris: No. No.

Tammy: Because there's a lot of people who had said that you wouldn't normally do that.

Chris: That I wouldn't normally help somebody?

Tammy: No, like a field… your position, not you specifically, but your position doesn't do that kind of stuff.

Chris: Well that's the thing, like, when I was a roader and… ((unintelligible)) … tried to do everything. I wasn't good at delegating stuff. I just used to do stuff on my own. Or just, like, taking care of it for somebody else.

Tammy: Right.

Chris: I wasn't good at the whole, like, hey, you go and do this, you do that, while I just sit over here.

Tammy: Well, you can see how it looks to us. You know. When it came up, we were like…

Chris: I know. I know.

Tammy: … making plans to be out there, you know, that day.

Chris: I know.

Grahm: But that's not what it was. It was just natural.

Chris: I was just askin' to help 'em.

Grahm: So how long were you there… what time do you think you were done with the girls?

Chris: It's hard to tell. I think everybody started showing up there by around seven forty-five—eight o'clock.

Grahm: Okay. And then you were there… did you move to a different site?

Chris: Yeah, it's like the ten-twenty-nine or the six-twenty-nine—something like that.

Grahm: So how long were you at that site?

Chris: The rest of the day until I got called away.

Grahm: So then that was… you were there for at least a couple of hours until you heard Nickole Atkinson on the doorbell?

Chris: Yeah.

Grahm: And then… I think it was even more time after that until you started coming home?

Chris: Yep.

Grahm: And you got home at two? Two-something?

Chris: No, it was closer to one-thirty. Around there.
Grahm: So, somewhere around, you know, nine o'clockish, all the way till twelve-thirty or twelve or one or something? And then you came home?
Chris: Yeah.
Grahm: Okay. Um, there was a lot to do about coming home, a Metallica song—have you heard about that?
Tammy: Battery.
Chris: I've heard of the Metallica song that people have been… someone sent me the lyrics to called Battery.
Grahm: Do you remember doing that?
Chris: That was, er, Nikki Kessinger, she liked the song, or she just wanted to know what it meant.
Grahm: Oh.
Chris: That's why I…
Grahm: So that's why you looked it up?
Chris: Mm-hm. I just kinda looked up the… I didn't have the CD with me, so I just kind of looked up the words.
Grahm: And was that on the way home?
Chris: Hm.
Grahm: Oh, that was just a different time?
Chris: That was a different time.
Grahm: And… and so…
Chris: It's just a coincidence because it says Battery.
Grahm: Right. Okay.
Chris: But it's, you know, it's like a more about a family coinciding as a battery.
Grahm: Okay.
Chris: Not like, you know, hitting somebody.
Grahm: Sure.
Tammy: Why did Nikki wanna know what it meant?
Chris: I dunno it was kinda strange, she… she's very into different types of music and, I mean, I never really thought I'd listen to. And she got me into a few things there as far as music-wise, but Battery was a song that she asked me… because I knew… I knew Metallica pretty well and I was like, hey, what's this… this lyric mean? I just… just looked it up just to look at all the words together and put it in my head again. That's why it was strange I put those lyrics in that letter.

Grahm: Oh… so, does that make sense?
Chris: Yeah. Someone sent me the lyrics to it. That guy from California.
Tammy: Oh. The kid? Senior?
Grahm: Um, with regards to, then, when you get home, you and the officers saw… you mentioned you took the ring off her finger, um, and then the book… did you throw that out in the trash? Okay. Um, there was another book, Body of Evidence…
Tammy: That you had in your cell.
Chris: Body of Evi… um, Patricia Cornwell?
Grahm: Maybe. Does that sound right?
Tammy: Probably.
Dave: Did you have that over in County?
Chris: Mm-hm.
Tammy: What was that about?
Chris: That was just one they gave me.
Tammy: Who gave it to you?
Chris: The, er, deputies.
Tammy: Not your attorney's or…?
Chris: Oh, no they don't give me books. Any book that I had was given to me by their book cart that they had.
Tammy: So you didn't ask for that book, or…
Chris: No, they just, kind of, give it to me. Like, I got outdoor books, um, military guy, and Patricia Cornwell. My grandmother always read her books and thought it was… I mean, she was always… she loved those books and… I'm not sure, but that was probably one of the first books I read… probably the second book I read there. It was like, they had… they gave me four books to choose.
Tammy: What other book did you read, do you remember?
Chris: The first book they gave me when I was on suicide watch was… I don't know why, Murder at something… And I was like, I looked at them and they were like, that's the one we got and I was like, okay.
Grahm: They handed you that book by itself, no other choices?
Chris: No, the next book I got, another guy that was… I guess they're overcrowded in there… he was sleeping on a cot outside my door, he was like, try this one and that was based in, like, the eighteen hundreds.

It was more like a situational book—like a time-period book. That was a little more calm. That was the first book they gave me.
Tammy: You don't remember what it was called… Murder at something…
Chris: Murder at the Truman Centre?
Tammy: Truman Centre?
Chris: Yeah, I think it was, um… maybe the Kennedy Centre. Um, I think it was written by Margaret Truman.
Tammy: Did you read it?
Chris: Mm-hm. Yes. It was decent. I'd never read a book in a long time, so it was… it was different, but some of the books they gave you, like, when you're in the hold, well, they don't have books in there aside from the Bible, but the, er, the counsellors there let me have a couple of books and they were the ones to choose from… just the ones they had… I told 'em I like mystery books or something like that…
Tammy: It's kinda crazy that they would give him, like, murder or murder mystery books.
Grahm: You'd hope that it wasn't some sort of insult or, you know, you can only hope… okay. What do you think of yourself now?
Chris: I don't… I, humph… Back, back when all this happened, when I was in Weld County, I definitely didn't feel like myself anymore, and when… my attorney would talk to me and like, you know, talk to some of my friends and, like, some of the stuff they would say, like… they can say good things but I'm just thinking to myself, how can you… anybody say those things about me now, being… what happened. It's like, people that I knew and that I never talked to again, and back in the day, or went to school with or, something like that, maybe… now they're gonna say, that's Chris Watts, the guy that's, you know, did all this horrible stuff to his family. Now, like, I know I shouldn't, really, you know, take to heart what other people think about me so much, it's just a matter of, like, what God thinks about me, what his opinion is—not anybody else's. Everybody can have an opinion about everybody. Before I got in trouble, I mean, I was always the guy that judged somebody on TV, you know—that guy that's in the orange jumpsuit. That guy that killed that guy, you know—that guy's horrible. Now I'm the… and it's like, when we come out at, like, six o'clock at night and there's something on the news, like, I try not to even pay any attention to it. It's like I don't wanna be in that position where I'm judging somebody else, 'cause that's, you know, what people were doing to me.

Grahm: Yeah.
Chris: And I don't wanna be that person anymore. But, I just hope that I can, you know, step back and kinda look at everything that I've done in my life and then, up to that point, it's just like, I did some good things, but the matter of the most important thing, I screwed up the worst. Let's hope that I can at least help somebody and, uh, I don't know how much time I have left.
Tammy: Was… was it your intent the whole time when you were taking the girls out there, that you were gonna do that to them? Honestly?
Chris: It's like when I got… when I got there I didn't think… are you talking about the tanks or…?
Tammy: Yeah. Like, well, just…
Chris: The thought process and all this… none of this makes sense. I know why you guys keep asking these questions, but it doesn't make sense to me. At all.
Tammy: I… I mean, did you… you could've done it before you guys left.
Chris: I know.
Tammy: And not had 'em, you know, alive in the back-seat. They could've been with Shanann on the back-seat.
Chris: I didn't think about anything really. Like, as far as, like, how everything that was gonna happen, I don't know why I … why I left everything out there in the field and why, like all this stuff. None of this makes sense. At all.
Grahm: But to Tammy's point, did you think that they might be coming back or did you know they wouldn't be coming back?
Chris: I dunno it's… I mean, the whole trip out there it's as though I was on… I mean, I wasn't thinking, it's like… In my mind right now I'm I'm hoping that I wasn't like that I wasn't coherent enough to make that decision where I knew I was gonna kill my girls… I'm like, I was just hoping that no father would want to do anything to hurt his… his blood and flesh, but I did that, and I just don't understand how it happened. I even read books that say, you know, no dad would ever do anything to hurt their… hurt his children. But this happened. So, I always think to myself, like, did I… was I even their dad at one point? I don't know. But it just… it's just gonna take a long, long time to… guilt and everything… to get this through.

Tammy: Have you asked for forgiveness, from God?
Chris: Mm-hm. It just takes a long time for me to forgive myself. That's one thing that's not going well. I just hope that they can one day forgive me too.
((Crosstalk))
Tammy: I think you said earlier that you were so angry at Shanann, or whatever, that you were gonna, you know, that anyone in your path of destruction, or whatever, was gonna get it. Basically, kinda, is what kinda made it sound like. I'm not saying it exactly right but… why were you so angry at Shanann?
Chris: I don't know if it was just because of the… separating me and my family, pretty much, because, I mean, it happened at the wedding, like, that's the reason they didn't come to the wedding. I blew up at my family to a point where I said some horrible things to them back, you know, back in twenty-twelve, that I'll, you know… I pretty much told my family that I don't need them anymore. That I had… I said, you know, I cussed my mom out, and I did all this kind of stuff. I never thought, you know, and… I dunno if it was just, like, Shanann coached me on to do it, or it was just rage that was like I'd never seen before. And I don't know if it was just everything that happened in July with, I can't see my kids, I'm not sure if they're ever gonna go see 'em again, I don't know. And it was just like, I dunno if that had something to do with it or if something inside me just triggered it and I just like, all that pent up from the wedding any everything, just like, it was like a long fuse that finally just burnt to its end.
Grahm: What happened in two-thousand-twelve?
Chris: There was, uh, my mom and Shanann just, like, like from when I proposed to her it was at the beach and from then on it was like… she always said to Shanann, I didn't need a ring like that when I was your age, I didn't need all those fancy things when I was your age, and this just kept blowing over and blowing over and I just kept… they'd never agree on anything. It was just like, you know, we didn't really need their help to do anything it was just like, we'll pay for it ourselves and all that kind of stuff, you know. It was just back and forth and, I think, maybe, mom just never thought she was good enough. She always thought she was hiding something from me.
Grahm: She always thought Shanann was hiding something? Like what?
Chris: Stuff from her past or like, you know…

Grahm: Oh, I see.
Dave: Was there conflict at a barbeque when all the families got together? One of the first… maybe a barbeque that Shanann put together for everybody to get… to meet each other? Two families we call that.
Grahm: Like, when you first started dating?
Chris: Oh, I know we did have something like that, but I didn't recall any kind of arguments that took place like that. I know, when I proposed to her Shanann had her family come down to the beach too and they stayed at a separate house, but as far as a barbeque I don't remember one that was like that.
Dave: Way before then?
Chris: Yeah. I remember… I remember the time when I asked Frank to… if was it okay if I asked Shanann to marry her. I remember that little get together. I don't think…
Grahm: So then, what was the boycott of the wedding about?
Chris: It was just my mom and pretty much my sister just didn't like her.
Grahm: Oh.
Chris: They just thought, you know, that they… that Shanann had taken me away from them. Yeah. To Colorado.
Grahm: Oh.
Chris: 'Cause we, we were in Colorado and we flew back to get married.
Grahm: Oh, okay.
Chris: 'Cause I… we had… we went to Colorado for thanksgiving to visit some friends, and we decided to move out there, like, a couple of months later.
Grahm: Okay.
Chris: So it was, like, that was, like, April. I moved out there April twenty-twelve and we got married November twenty-twelve in North Carolina, so they always thought that she's taken… that she took me away out there. And then…
Tammy: Was there something with invitations, or something? Your sister was supposed to send invitations or something.
Chris: Yeah, there was… okay, now you're bringing some memories back. Um, it was something to do with that and then my sister wanted to know her kids hold… my sister wanted her kids to be the ring bearer

and something else… ring bearer and flower girl. And then Shanann was like, no. She told her no. Or wait, either she told her no or Jamie backed out because of something else. And then it just all blew up.
Grahm: And is that pretty close to the wedding?
Chris: Yes. Yeah. Within a coupla weeks.
Tammy: Did they go to the wedding? Your family?
Chris: Uh, my grandma did.
Tammy: But your parents and your sister did not go?
Chris: No.
Grahm: Ronnie wasn't there either?
Chris: No. Nobody was there. My grandma was there and the, like, the dance where the groom dances with his mom, like that, I danced with Mark's mom and my grandmother.
Grahm: It's sad isn't it I mean it all comes from a place of love, you know. Them loving you and not wanting to get ((unintelligible)).
Chris: It was a… it was a great day, I mean, everybody was really happy, I mean, it always just rang in the back of my head that they weren't there and every time they took a picture it was just, oh where's… oh, they're not there. I never knew if they actually were gonna come anyways, as far as I can… Sometimes, I thought they would just… Ah, I'm gonna go just to be there, but I never knew if that was the case.
Grahm: And so, then, when Tammy was asking why were you so mad at Shanann, um, it was part of this whole family strife?
Chris: That's the only thing I can think of right now, because, I mean, there's no other reason. I mean, to be mad at her, but we took care of each other for the last four years. It was a good relationship. I mean, it's just like, if I never met Nikki would I ever have, you know, thought our relationship was bad? Probably not.
Grahm: Interesting.
Chris: That was one thing I always thought about, even Nikki asked me, she said I don't want you to leave your wife just because of me, I'm just like, what do you mean? She said, well, if you just met me would you have known? I'm like, no. Because I never thought I would've strayed away from her at all. I've never followed, or like tried to follow anyone, you know.
Tammy: Was Shanann checking your phone, or …
Chris: She always had my phone.

Tammy: She was always checking your phone? So how did you get past that?
Chris: I used my work phone.
Tammy: To text? And you had some secret apps thing?
Chris: That was on my personal phone.
Tammy: Were you using anything else to contact… have contact with her?
Chris: No. Nah, I just text her with my work phone, and, like, er, when Shanann and the girls went to North Carolina I used my personal phone. She just told me, put the pictures in a… in a app. I found that calculator app. I just searched on the app store, like, hidden pictures and the calculator app popped up.
Tammy: Like, if your iCloud and whatever is together she would know if you were getting apps. You know, downloading apps and stuff like that.
Chris: They used to be a long time ago, but, when we got different phones, or when our phone… phone contact list had to be synced up from the cloud, I just, I couldn't have… she had tons and tons and tons of phone contacts. I couldn't have all that, but it was still kinda linked up at one point. But as far as asking to get on my iCloud account… that freed it up a little bit.
Dave: How about your Facebook account? You deleted that at some point, when did you do that?
Chris: It was when we got back, August seventh? I'll have to work it… I think it was August eighth. That's when, um, Nikki told me she'd told her friend about me and I just knew they'd try to look me up on Facebook and they'd see that Shanann was pregnant. Nikki already probably already found them, but that's the reason I did that.
Tammy: Did you and Nikki ever fight?
Chris: We never fought but, I guess, that I had to calm her down a bunch of times.
Tammy: Yeah, you started to mention that when I was talking to you before about how her getting upset about some video or something about being bipolar, or… what were you talking about?
Chris: I think either my dad told me about that, or John Walsh told me about it. She made a couple of videos when she was talking to herself, saying she was bipolar or something like that. A lot of things, like, when she realised she was the other person in the relationship and

that I'd always put my wife first over her, and that's what made her kinda take a step back a few times. And then I'd have to calm her down.

Tammy: Tell me about those times. What did it look like?

Chris: So, the first one is probably around July fourth when I had to leave her house because she wanted to spend most of the day together before she went to a baseball game or something. And when I had to leave, it kinda like said, it just made her like, take a step back and wonder what she was doing. I just, you know, told her just because of... just because I had to leave it doesn't mean, like... I was just... I was comforting her at some point. I don't even know why I was doing it. Maybe I knew I was too far gone at that point, but it was...

Tammy: 'Cause this is when Shanann's pissed because she's called you ten times—you were sleeping, it was your day off and then you go outside to talk to her on the phone and tell Nikki that you need to go home just in case she calls back...?

Chris: Yeah.

Tammy: ... and all that, right?

Chris: Mm-hm.

Tammy: So what did she say to you, Nikki?

Chris: She was in the shower—she said okay, and then that's... like, when I talked about when I had to calm her down, it was on the phone.

Tammy: And was she like, we're breaking up, like, we're not gonna... I can't do this. Or...

Chris: No she said she didn't wanna, like, she didn't think it was safe for her. She didn't think it was good for us to see each other anymore that day.... the rest of that day, because of all that. And I said, okay, that's fine. And she asked me to come over, like, later on after she got back from the baseball game.

Tammy: And so you did that?

Chris: Mm-hm.

Tammy: So what was the second one like?

Chris: It was basically about the same thing. She was, you know, I didn't really note it at one point, but I guess she had, um, set up a couple of dates on a harmony app or something and he never showed up. And, uh, she'd already made plans with me...

Tammy: What do you mean, she'd set up dates when she had plans with you?
Chris: Yeah.
Tammy: Why would she do that?
Chris: I think she'd figured out they were not gonna show up. She went… I guess when she went to the baseball game, they never showed up. And then there was another one that never showed up either.
Tammy: So she's actively dating other people while you were together?
Chris: I didn't know it until a couple of weeks later.
Tammy: And how'd you find out?
Chris: She told me.
Tammy: What did she say?
Chris: It was one conversation where I actually, kinda, fell asleep on the couch, and then she tells me, like, not much pressure why she told me about it, but it was very random and she could tell it took me back a little bit because I figured she would've told me that if she was actively still, like, looking around. I mean, she didn't have to tell me, but I figured she…
Tammy: Do you think she told you though so that it would hurry you up and…
Chris: Make a decision?
Tammy: … you're making a decision?
Chris: It might've been. But, you know, it's… she never had anybody who tried to fix things as far as you know, hey, I like where we're at as far as the relationship goes and actually, I did stuff for her around the house, around her little apartment. Like, and nobody's ever done that, and… so that was different.
Dave: What about her male friend, where does he stand? What's his name?
Chris: Jim?
Dave: Jim.
Chris: Um, he worked in the oil field, North Dakota I believe. And I guess he's been a friend of hers for a long time. And he's kinda-like a shoulder to cry on, he's… somebody who's always been around for her. I guess he's had a couple of girlfriends and, I guess he hasn't had much luck in that department, as far as girlfriends, and him and Nikki have always been good friends.

Dave: Platonic friends?
Chris: Yes.
Dave: As far as you know?
Chris: As much as I knew. I think they've just been friends for a long time, from the oil fields, North Dakota or wherever he's working now, either Wyoming, ((unintelligible)) … he goes all over the place.
Grahm: When, um, Sandy and Frank lived in the house for fifteen months, what was that like?
Chris: It was, you know, it was tough. Yeah it was tough, because, I mean, to go from just me and Shanann and Bella and CeCe to, you know, two other people and then now four dogs.
Grahm: Right.
Chris: ((Unintelligible)) ... heat seeking missile everywhere. But it was cool having more people around, but it was stressful.
Grahm: Yeah.
Chris: Like, I mean, 'cause, with Shanann, having two dominant personalities in the house, you know, with her mom there, it was kinda… like, her mom would tell her how to raise the kids sometimes, or, like, do this, do that, you know. Whenever they were sick she was like, alright, you know, rub peroxide on their feet and they'll be fine. I was like, what? Okay… And er, I wouldn't do it, you know. And Sandy was like, just do it, Chris, it'll be okay. Just little things like that…
Grahm: Yeah.
Chris: … and it was like a clash every day. It was kinda like, every time I got home I didn't know if Shanann was pissed or if she was okay. 'Cause, when we first… when they first got there they hadn't got a job yet and so they were around all the time, but once they got jobs and stuff, like, I think it was a little better for Shanann, because, you know, they weren't around the house all day. But it was definitely stressful, vacuuming every other day. And, just like… cooking was great. That was awesome…
(Laughter).
Tammy: Was she a good cook?
Chris: Yeah, that was always… because they were down the basement, so I was always trying to keep the girls upstairs while they were sleeping, not running around downstairs. I didn't want them to wake up and… I know Frank always told me that, trying to wake up Sandy

early is not good. So that was just, you know… just, kinda like, walking on eggshells a lot.
Dave: Yeah. It was stressful?
Chris: Yeah.
Dave: Do you think that stressed your marriage at the time, or…?
Chris: It was sixteen months—it was fifteen, sixteen months and it was a long time. It was great around the holiday times, because they're already there, and you know, all that was great, and…
Dave: Sure.
Chris: But yeah, definitely… we never really had much alone time. Because we always had to kinda plan it out. So…
Dave: Yeah. What was their purpose for moving out there?
Chris: They just wanted to be closer to the kids, because, you know, we saw them a lot but it's not the same as, like… with two kids it's hard to fly back and forth. I mean, when they went back to North Carolina this past time, that was the first time CeCe's been there and she was three. First time her brother had ever met her.
Dave: So were they trying… were they trying to move to Colorado permanently or were they just…?
Chris: They were thinking about it at that point, though.
Dave: Okay.
Chris: But it, you know, Frank was saying that he didn't wanna leave but Sandy…
Dave: She wanted to go back?
Chris: Yeah.
Dave: Yeah.
Chris: Yeah, it was just a matter of… they knew their house wasn't being taken care of… they just, they wanted to go back and… they'd put their house up for sale for a little while but never bought.
Dave: Hmm. Okay.
Tammy: What about your financial stresses?
Chris: Bankruptcy was something I never thought was gonna happen. You know back in, like, twenty-fifteen, twenty-sixteen something around there. I never thought that was gonna happen. And I never… a lot of it was from the wedding because we put it all on credit cards.
Dave: Hmm.
Chris: And… and then the doctor bills from, you know, endoscopy to just, like, the girls, it just seemed they were sick every month, it seemed

like. Some type of ear infection which just figured out they had to put some kind of tubes in their ears and, you know, different operations here, a couple of overnight stays in the hospital for breathing, stuff like that. There was just… it all mounted up. I never thought it was that far gone, but… you know.

Grahm: Was any of that from Shanann's neck surgery or were those bills pretty well paid up?

Chris: Well I think the bankruptcy never touched the medical part of it because you have to be like, like, to survive the medical part of it, like medical bankruptcy and then there's regular bankruptcy.

Grahm: Oh.

Chris: I don't think that bankruptcy ever touches student loans or medical stuff. You have to, like, be specific with that. But the one thing it just took away, like, a lot of the furniture that we had bought and then, a couple of other things inside the house—it kinda alleviate all the… I mean, it took… we had to make the house payment by phone every month and that was because of the bankruptcy still, like, every time. And it's just like, I didn't know how long it was gonna take, but apparently once you're in bankruptcy you pretty much never get out of it.

Tammy: You guys… weren't you guys behind on your mortgage? You know, when I talked to you…

Chris: Yeah, I think earlier in December twenty-seventeen and then January, February, and March twenty-eighteen. That's when I took the 401k out... the loan out to pay for that.

Grahm: How was it that you were spending so much money? What was it…?

Chris: Just, you know, kids and just other bills that we had and… just every… I mean, I knew that I was getting paid four or five by the bell. I never really asked. You see, I mean, I didn't even have access to the bank accounts on my phone.

Grahm: Oh.

Chris: So, I never really asked to see what it looked like, like how far… I just know she called me and tell me you need to pay the mortgage today, and I'm like, cool. And that was, you know, from the… from my little four-wheeler incident where I sold it without paying it off yet, and she thought, well you're never touching the accounts ever, ever. So I'm like, okay, that's cool with me. But, it's… I never saw the account, it was just like, here… like when I worked at I got my cheque I just brought it to her. So…

Grahm: There was a haircare company, I think it was called Monat, does that ring a bell? Do you know anything about that?

Chris: Hm-mm.

Grahm: Maybe hair dye?

Chris: I don't know.

Grahm: Do you know she did an auto order. The company has stuff delivered… like a haircare product or haircare dye.

Chris: That's some… I mean, she had little… some little gift packs she had delivered once every month or once every two months, and like they were different… an array of different products in it.

Grahm: You don't remember where it was from?

Chris: No. Did you say Monet?

Grahm: Monat. M.O.N.A.T. No?

Chris: Doesn't ring a bell.

Grahm: There was an order that was made at two-fifty-one, that's why I asked if it was, like, an auto order, type thing.

Chris: It might've been an auto order.

((Crosstalk)).

Chris: It might've been something that… I know that Nickole Atkinson, she used to be into all that stuff… I mean, maybe Shanann got her something or maybe it was something she recommended?

Dave: How about the HOA thing. What happened there?

Chris: She mailed it to the wrong address. They changed their address and she mailed the wrong address for a year. We got a letter in the mail… we were getting, like, sued over it. We hadn't… ((unintelligible)) … for a year. So we had to pay double for either a whole year or a couple months. That sucked.

Grahm: What happened to all the money she'd sent to the wrong address?

Chris: I don't know. They said they wouldn't… ((unintelligible)) … or anything. I wasn't even sure what that address was. She said it was something that she didn't see. I'm like, I'm not gonna… because she did so much so I'm like, I'm not gonna, like… ((unintelligible)).

Tammy: So, Chris. What do you think we could've done better? What could've made you tell us the truth that night? What did you need to hear from us that you didn't?

Chris: I'm not really… I'm not sure what really goes through people's minds when they're in the interrogation room. For mine… for when I was in there with you, I was… I was, you know, nervous. I was… I mean, I knew I'd done something wrong, and I knew you probably already knew or were going to find out. It's just, like, you know, watching the, you know, I hate this, the TV shows to see what's gonna happen next type-thing. I never know if that's right, but, I think it's just the… the horror of knowing what you did and trying to tell somebody else what you did. That's what kept me from doing it because I… I didn't even wanna admit to myself that I had done anything. I knew… I knew what I had done. I knew how bad—horrific it was. I knew how bad it'd hurt other people. I didn't… I just couldn't even admit to myself that I'd done it. I couldn't even tell my attorney's I'd done it until two weeks later.
Tammy: So, were you trying to save us from the horror of it?
Chris: No it was just a matter of… I couldn't admit it to myself, how could I admit it to you?
Tammy: So do you think any amount of us asking you things different ways would've helped or… do you think anything would've helped?
Chris: I think if maybe you didn't ask about if Shanann hurt the kids… if you would've asked the other… if, you know something in that… a different order of questions maybe it would've came out a different way. Because that's the only reason I went with that story because…
Tammy: Well you weren't giving us anything else.
Chris: I know.
(Laughter).
Tammy: That's the problem. So, if… you think if we would've said, what, do you think?
Chris: If you would've said, you know, I think you would probably have to… if the video had showed them in the truck you'd have probably had to have lied and said, we saw the kids in the truck. I mean, I hate to say that you would have to have lied to get me to say what you wanted me to say, but I think it might've been that.
Tammy: That we saw the kids in the truck?
Grahm: When we were talking, there was a point where you just said, can I talk to my dad? Did you just wanna tell him first?
Chris: I just, you know, wanted to tell him that I loved him and that

it's probably the last time you're gonna see me, as far as, you know, outside of a… outside of a cell, pretty much.
Grahm: Are you looking forward to them coming?
Chris: Yeah, 'cause I was just talking to them on the phone, you know, it's just totally different when you see 'em. See their face, you know. It's like, when we got on that little video conference at Weld County it was just, like, it was all I could do to stop, like, stop breaking down on that phone. So…
Grahm: So it'll be…
Chris: It'll be good to see them.
Tammy: What do you get to do when they're here?
Chris: Like this.
Tammy: Like, in a room like this?
Chris: There's a visiting room, visiting centre down from my unit and I don't know what it looks like but I know it has tables and… it's pretty much, they… they set up a time and you get a couple of hours.
Grahm: That would be good.
Chris: Yeah just in that little centre—I'm not sure what else is in there, but, I just know there's tables, nothing like vending machines, stuff like that. But it'll be good to see them. Unfortunately they can't make the ((unintelligible)). I was hoping they could maybe show me a video or two, but that ain't gonna happen. Or a picture. But they pretty much only let you come down with your ID—that's it.
Grahm: Can they mail you a still photo or anything like that?
Chris: Yep, they can do the still photo—sometimes they try to play a video over the phone for me but it's really like fuzzy and crackled lots.
Grahm: Do you have any other questions for us? Did you ever wonder… I wonder why they did this, or I wonder why the investigation went this way, or…?
Chris: I mean… I mean, I think the first time I was brought in, it was the fourteenth I believe, when I met you that night.
Grahm: Mm-hm.
Chris: You told me that there was a bunch of other people coming in for statements—was that true?
Tammy: Yeah.
Grahm: There was a couple people.
Tammy: Yeah.
Dave: There were a lot.

Tammy: There were a lot, actually. Yeah. A whole board worth of people listed and agents out.
Grahm: They didn't get the attention you got that night, but … (Laughter).
Chris: I just… I just wish none of this had ever happened, honestly. Like, you guys could've… never had to come… never had to meet me… anything like that. None of it ever felt real. Especially when they put me in that… that suicide watch cell, the last thing that one of those guys said was, good luck. He slammed the door and I kind of knew from then on that was it.
Grahm: A deputy said that?
Chris: Er, one of the guys, um, one, like, they're called the SAR guys, special operations group at the Weld County Jail.
Grahm: Yeah
Chris: That was it. The next morning when I got up to take a shower I saw a newspaper with a big piece cut out of it, I don't know what that was about. I just kinda saw my last name, I'm like, oh. ((Unintelligible)).
Grahm: If we came back to talk to you some day, would you be inclined to talk to us again?
Chris: Yeah.
Grahm: Okay.
Chris: Today just caught me off guard—I had no idea.
Grahm: Yeah,
Tammy: Well, we didn't really wanna tell you we were coming just because we didn't want you to have anxiety about us coming, or…
Chris: I would've had anxiety.
Tammy: Yeah, so we figured the blitz attack was probably the best course today.
(Laughter).
Chris: Just like the first time we met?
Tammy: Right. Oh, you knew when you were meeting me.
Chris: I did, yeah. You just didn't have all your props here today.
Tammy: That's right. What's all the props man? It's …
Grahm: Sophisticated equipment…
Tammy: It is.
Grahm: … right?
Tammy: That's right. Sophisticated instrument.

Grahm: I don't know if that's ever gonna happen. We might not ever see each other again, but…
Chris: I didn't think we would, honestly.
Grahm: Your experience is definitely interesting. Um, you, yourself are definitely interesting. Um, we see things in you that we didn't expect to and we don't see things that we expected to see. So, it's very interesting to us. I hope you can take to heart that today was a lot about us learning how to do better. How to talk better, how to do an investigation better.
Chris: I mean, I'd never talked to a police officer before. Or FBI, CBI, anything like that, so that was all new to me, like. Everything that I've ever seen as far as the authorities has been on TV. So I… I didn't know what to expect but once got into that interrogation room it just felt exactly what it looked like, just like you guys cook and prod and then leave. Come back in, it's like, give me time to stew give me time to, you know, think—it's like, it works. It just really drills more questions into your own mind instead of, you know, just staying in there, asking questions all the time.
Tammy: Mm-hm. You liked it when we took breaks—you think that worked on you?
Chris: I did.
Tammy: So, you were watching videos of the girls at one point. Do you remember that? Them giggling and laughing and…
Chris: Like when I was in the interrogation room?
Tammy: Yeah.
Chris: I don't remember that.
Tammy: You don't?
Chris: I-I didn't… I thought you always had… you already had my phone at that point.
Tammy: No. We didn't take your phone towards the end… till towards the end.
Chris: Okay.
Tammy: That was weird for me.
Chris: It's… it's like when you put that picture in front of me.
Tammy: Yeah.
Chris: Asked what made me do it. It's… it's… I didn't have a signal in there, it's like, the videos that I had on my phone, which is sick. I wish I'd taken those videos out more often, for all that had happened, but it's

definitely… definitely got in my head, a lot. I don't know where that picture was from because I'd never seen that picture.
Tammy: The one we showed you?
Chris: Mm-hm.
Tammy: Really?
Chris: I'd never seen CeCe in that dress before.
Grahm: Really? We talked a lot about that dress.
Tammy: Yeah. And you were saying…
Grahm: Were you making it up?
Chris: I never saw her in that dress.
Tammy: You were even telling us about when she last wore the dress.
Grahm: And the boots…
Tammy: And the boots…
Chris: Not that dress.
Tammy: … those were her favourite winter boots, and she wore them all summer.
Chris: Oh, the winter boots, yeah but that white dress was different. I've never seen that picture.
Tammy: No. Because you talked about buttoning it up. You said, I remember because I was… she just wore it the other day and I had to button up at the back.
Chris: It must've been a different dress. Not that one.
Tammy: Hah.
Chris: 'Cause that… that picture… was that North Carolina? Or was that…?
Grahm: I don't know.
Tammy: I don't know where that picture came from.
Dave: I pulled it off Facebook. Shanann's Facebook.
Tammy: So maybe it was when you weren't there, or something?
Dave: Might've been, yeah.
Tammy: 'Cause you don't recall that, huh?
Chris: There's a lot of pictures I guess I hadn't seen from when they were in North Carolina. At my parent's house. Especially, like, fourth of July, and stuff. And they had fourth of July dresses on and stuff that I never saw.
Tammy: Aw.
Chris: Some I had on my phone, but that white dress, I'd never… like they were… she was going to church or something. I just never saw that

white dress. And Bella's little dress that she had, and that little awkward smile there at the back. Yeah, that… that definitely got in my head. It did that.

Tammy: When we had that picture out for you? So, like, to us it didn't …

Chris: I know I didn't show any emotion.

Tammy: … feel like that because you didn't elicit any emotion.

Chris: I don't show emotion that much. It's like my dad, we don't show emotion, like...

Grahm: Were you fighting it down or were you not a guy to show it

Chris: Most of the time, I'm not the guy to show it. I hold it in as much as I can, like, you know, in my cell, I've cried a lot, obviously, but I'm not really a guy to show it.

Grahm: Okay.

Chris: I don't like, I don't know, I try to hold it as much as I can.

Dave: Well, you were a difficult guy to read—especially at the house that day. That makes total sense now.

Chris: I knew I was… I don't know if I was in shock, or just disbelief or just like… 'cause some people say I looked like I was a heartless, no-soul person—a soul-less person when I did the TV interviews or something. And I'm just glad I never saw it. I don't even wanna know what I looked like or sounded like.

Dave: But you were obviously feeling it then you just weren't …

Chris: Yeah. Like…

Dave: … showing it.

Chris: … nothing registered at all. Everything was just harboured deep down and then I think it was one night, when I was in my cell, it all hit me at that point. Not the fact that I was in jail, but the fact that everybody was gone. And none of it… I think if it was like… like, if something happens to your family in an accident–like a car accident, something horrible, that registers at one point—you did it! I don't know, it doesn't register at one point. It's like in my head it never registered.

Tammy: Does it seem real now?

Chris: Oh, it felt… feels real.

Tammy: It does?

Chris: Like every day. Like I see pictures, I just know where they were at when they were doing that. You know, where… when I first had some type of hearing over the phone and I heard Frank and Sandy and Frankie and they're on the phone and, I forgot what kind of hearing it was, something about a probate hearing or something, but I knew exactly where they were, I could hear the birds on the back deck , and back in my cell I just bawled my eyes out because I knew where they were. And I don't know how many times the girls were out the back there, it's… it's just weird how emotions process differently for me than for everybody else.

Tammy: Mm-hm.

Chris: I sometimes… like, you said, um, if you lost your kids in the grocery store for five seconds you'd be a mess…

Tammy: Mm-hm.

Chris: … and then, you know, for me it'd be… and I'd be panicked but I probably wouldn't cry. I'd be trying to find them but it processes different for me. I've never knew why… never known why. I don't think I'm a cold-hearted person. It's just a matter of… I just don't show it. I don't show emotion as much as other people do. Even when, you know, the girls left North Carolina, you know, her… Shanann's brother, mom and dad were all crying when they left. It was just kinda like, you know, I never really saw my parents get like that when they left. Kinda like, I don't know if you're born that way.

Tammy: Like your family didn't show emotion like that, is that what you're saying?

Chris: Yeah, like, you know, my dad couldn't really speak at the sentencing hearing 'cause he said he was kinda like… he said he was gonna lose it. Like, lose his emotions. That really hit me because I've never really seen him like, you know, like that.

Tammy: Like vulnerable?

Chris: Mm-hm. And nobody's ever seen me that way either, like, maybe I…

Tammy: Was it ever like you're a sissy if you're like that, or was it just something you just never did?

Chris: No. I never saw my dad cry. So, maybe it's just something that, you know, was just imprinted in my brain that I should never cry. Maybe, I don't know.

Tammy: Was your mom a loving mom? Like a doting mom? And, you know, would give you affection and hugs and kisses?

Chris: Yep. Oh yeah, she would always ask me, you know, what was

going on. She said that I was always hard to read—she never knew what was going on.
Tammy: But did she still try to give you affection, even growing up?
Chris: Mm-hm. Yeah, she always… with my sister it was always apparent what was going on. Always, she was always open with me, I was always just, you know, closed off. And she always wanted to know what was going on—how I felt, it was like, yeah, okay… that's all I gave her. Even if… even if something was wrong, like, I would've probably never said anything. 'Cause I would just, like, deal with it myself. But I don't know if it was just growing up that way that just kept me that way.
Dave: Deal with things on your own kinda thing?
Chris: Build up so much that you can't deal with them. They… once they take a hold of you, you never thought in a way they'd take hold of you.
Dave: Do you think this was a result of bottling up for so long?
Chris: Definitely.
Grahm: What do you remember your dad saying at sentencing?
Chris: I remember there was a scripture, one John one dash nine, and then, like, a lot of it, the other, the representative said, for him. My mom said a lot… my mom spoke but everything my dad had written down the other person said. Like, you know, he always… he was talking about going to little league games and races and stuff like that. Going to… being my coach and everything like that. So, you know, I could experience the same kind of joy doing that for my girls.
Grahm: I remember your mom saying she loves you and she always will.
Chris: Yeah.
Grahm: That was pretty important to hear.
Chris: Yeah, I think after that she said, I forgive you son.
Tammy: Mm-hm.
Grahm: That's big, right?
Chris: Mm-hm. Yeah.
Grahm: And your dad… when we came here today we were just hoping and praying that you'd take your dad's advice. Do you remember what he said? I hope if you ever get a chance to talk, you can talk about it.
Chris: Okay.

Grahm: And I think that's what today was. Don't you?
Chris: Mm-hm. Yeah, I think it was. I just didn't expect it to be today.
Grahm: Yeah.
Dave: So the DA made some comments during the sentencing hearing about your emotions and having no emotions or… do you remember all that?
Chris: Yeah, he just said, you know, he lied to us from the start, and a couple other things. I believe that's what he was saying.
Dave: What do you think? Do you think he was anywhere close? What do you think… or what is your opinion on what he said in that?
Chris: I mean, it's gonna be, you know, taking all his evidence and putting it into the story that you wanted to convey and, like, if you don't know me, that's the way you're… that's what you're gonna portray. Like, if you take everything from August 13th to now, that's how people are gonna… that's how people… there's no other way that people are gonna opinionate themselves about me just by what they see right there.
Dave: Right.
Chris: They're gonna say, okay, they look at the guy that did that did the… the interview on the fourteenth and see a guy should be on his hands and knees crying his eyes out and what's he doing? He's just talking. And they're just like… I know, they maybe got some information maybe from her friends saying he was cheating on her, something like that, he's a cold person, he was, you know, trying to do this and that… it's like, they don't know me, that's always gonna be their thing about me, 'cause, like….
Dave: Mm-hm.
Chris: … there was one church service, the only one I've gone to in here and they said do not be defined by one moment in your life and, I think that's, like… people are defining me by one moment in my life. They don't know what happened before or what can happen later.
Dave: Yeah.
Chris: So I just hope that, you know, may… hopefully they stop judging me. There's tons of people in here, you know, I don't even wanna know what they did 'cause I don't wanna judge 'em.
Dave: Hmm.
Chris: I'm not that person, you know. They know what I did, I not gonna ask them what they did, you know.

Dave: Makes sense. You did show some emotion during that hearing. What part do you think it felt most emotional?
Chris: I think I felt… when Frank was talking about, you know, he… I didn't know what to expect when he started talking, but you know, he… all… he said I was an evil monster and that… that… that rang in me. He said I tossed them away like garbage and that hurt. And, you know, Sandy was talking about a video about uh… Bella was calling me a hero and that… that triggered me a lot there. And then when Frankie was saying I'll never be called uncle again but you'll never be called Dad again… that really stung. You know. Then my parents got up there, and just hearing my mom and dad talk, you know, it was just like, they couldn't look at me but I was still, like, everything they said. Saying that they forgive me and that, you know, I'm still their son—no matter what. You know it's… I know, like… you know my attorneys told me you need to show a little more emotion because I guess they… the first time I went to the court room I didn't, you know, I didn't know what to expect I was still new to everything. Just in shock about what was going on and… they said I was just a cold person just looking at them, so that was when I did the plea and at the sentencing hearing I just… all of it felt more real than anything.
Grahm: I remember growing up my pastor used to tell me, it's better to be one foot out of hell facing heaven than one foot out of heaven facing hell.
Chris: Mm-hm.
Grahm: So I think that's you. You've been to hell and now you're facing the right direction.
Chris: Definitely. I definitely feel like it's… I never knew I could have a relationship with God like I do now but I just … just like the amazing grace with all this but I just want you to know what I had to pay and the kind of price for this. I know there's a purpose for everybody, I just hope that I can find mine.
Grahm: Well, I think you're seeking peace, right? That's good.
Chris: Probably the only thing I can do right now is to seek peace. And hope and pray that everybody can find it too.
Grahm: Good.
Chris: For everybody that was involved. For all of you and all your team and everybody. Friends, anybody that was involved.
Dave: What do you want to happen with this information?

Chris: I mean, I know you're probably gonna tell the… Frank and Sandy and Frankie. You'll just try to give them a little closure, right?
Dave: Yeah, I don't know how much I'm gonna tell them. Obviously, you know Sandy a little better than I. She wants to know everything. Um, but, um, I'm gonna digest it a little bit before I talk to them about it. Um, so I don't think there's any rush on that. And then, um… but other than that, I have no intention of talking to anybody outside of law enforcement. But, uh… what would you like to see happened with it?
Chris: I mean, I'd like to tell my parents, you know, when they get here, instead of finding out anywhere else.
Dave: Yep.
Chris: 'Cause I know they've been bombarded with information from, you know, from the Amanda girl to the track guy, from people going on inside editions saying they knew me and went out with me or had whatever else with me. And, just like, I don't want them to think there's other false information going on out there, because people are getting hold of information and it's like, where are they getting this information from, type deal?
Tammy: Would you like to see people charged?
Chris: No. People taking advantage of situations and… you know, they gotta… honestly, they need to look into themselves and figure out why they did it themselves. So, I mean, I don't think charging them will help. I think they'll work out their… work out whatever they got going on within themselves. I mean if…
Tammy: Did you ever have a profile on Tinder or anything like that? Any of those dating websites, or anything?
Chris: No. I just had Facebook and I had Instagram. I didn't even know what the WhatsApp thing was called until… ((unintelligible)).
Tammy: You've never heard of that?
Chris: No. I'm like, I don't even know what that is, man. This guy's fishing for something. So I'm sorry you had to waste your time and go out there and talk to him.
Tammy: It was a big timewaster.
Grahm: It was a big waste of time.
Tammy: Yeah. But you would not want to be listed as a victim in that case? As far as him being charged with false reporting?
Chris: Nah, I mean, it's… he's… whoever's gonna try to get their five

minutes of fame… whatever they wanna do with this, I mean, that's on them. I mean, if he's willing to do that, he needs to figure out what's going on with himself before, like… I-I don't think charging him with something's gonna fix it. So it would just be a waste of time.
Grahm: Anything else reported sent anywhere?
Chris: Um…
Dave: Don't be afraid to ask.
(Laughter).
Chris: How's things in Colorado now? I mean, since all this… after… everything's quiet now? Everything's cool?
Grahm: Yeah.
Tammy: Well, we had another guy murder his fiancé—girlfriend—whatever you wanna call it, so… that's… ((unintelligible)) … you've probably seen it on the news. No?
Chris: ((Unintelligible)). I think the only thing here was that Jayme Closs thing. Have you heard about that?
Tammy: Oh yes. We were just talking about that out front.
Dave: Is that the girl who was kidnapped?
Tammy: Yeah.
Chris: She escaped after, like, ninety days.
Dave: That's insane.
Tammy: Yeah. That's crazy.
Chris: He'll probably come here. Everybody comes here.
Tammy: Yeah. They said he's in some County Jail, is that right?
Dave: Yeah, brow… brow…
Tammy: Barren or something?
Dave: Brown or Barren County. Yeah.
Chris: Yes, so, all I see here is the stuff that kinda… it's like everything happened here. So, I guess I'd better watch out.
(Laughter).
Chris: I'm sorry.
Tammy: Definitely. Do you mind if I take a picture of you, just to show what you look like now? You just looked so different then.
Chris: I just, you know, like…
Tammy: It's not gonna go on social media or…
Chris: Okay.
Tammy: … it's just for our own records.
Chris: Okay.

Tammy: Is that okay?
Chris: That's fine.
Tammy: Were you asking him something while I was doing that? I'm sorry.
Dave: No, I was just gonna say it's like to go… the roads and that are scary enough…
Tammy: I know. But when it's snowing it's horrendous.
Dave: You need an ice bracer.
Tammy: Some ice… ((unintelligible)).
Dave: Yeah, we had spikes on the tyres.
Tammy: Oh.
Grahm: Right, Chris we're gonna let you get back to your day. Do you want another minute to finish your drink?
Chris: Yes. They won't let me take that back.
(Laughter).
Chris: Yeah, I had to shave. They recommended I change my appearance. That they'd already ((unintelligible)) … though.
Tammy: Why is that? Just so people didn't recognise you? No?
Chris: Yeah, I just shaved it all off. That razor… except the razor that they have here… it's like a… it's a single blade. So, like, I'm…
Tammy: A safety razor, right?
Chris: Well, it's more safety than actually a razor.
(Laughter).
Tammy: That's why it doesn't shave.
(Laughter).
Chris: It's like a sharp rock or something.
Tammy: Yeah right.
Chris: Just imagine shaving the same spot for five minutes. And then finally
Dave: Something starts coming…
Chris: Something starts coming off. You have to warm it up or something, I don't know.
Tammy: You'd probably be better just plucking them out with your fingers or something.
((Unintelligible)).
Chris: Everything here's for safety, so, like…
Dave: Yeah, I think so.

Chris: They said if I got to GP or something I could get something different.
Tammy: Oh, that makes sense.
Chris: ((Unintelligible)) … unit to have razors.
Tammy: Well that makes you feel better probably? Like…
Chris: Well, they don't have to watch me. Other guys, they stand next to 'em while they shave, but that would be kinda weird.
Tammy: Oh.
Dave: So do they have any other jobs, like, if, uh… like fleet. Would you be able to go and work fleet maintenance or anything like that?
Chris: If I was a minimum. or a low… a low medium. They have guys who like, run across the street to a wreckers building and work over there. I don't know, like, you know, I guess it takes a while to get classed down from maximum to medium.
Dave: Yeah.
Chris: So it's… I'm not sure, like, if they… ((unintelligible)). I don't know if they'd take me back to Colorado. I don't know what the… ((unintelligible)) … might be.
Dave: Right.
Chris: I'm not sure if that happens or not.
Dave: Yeah. That's all pretty secretive right up to the minute they do it.
Tammy: Mm-hm. Definitely.
Chris: You guys gonna do some exploring around here?
(Laughter).
Tammy: Everything's covered in snow. And it's freezing.
((Crosstalk)).
Grahm: … winds when we walked out.
Dave: Maybe we can make a snowman.
((Interference)).
Tammy: So if you just said I want this more education stuff would you get moved to another place? Or is it fully up to them whether you could do that?
Chris: It's already out there because I'm not sure how it gets paid for.
Tammy: Right.
Chris: So it's… whatever they want me to do, that's what I'm gonna do. If they want me to go back to Colorado I'd be like, why? Why would you want me to go back to Colorado?

Tammy: I would say I told you that, you would question that.
Chris: Oh, always. After a while… if I was here for a long time, and then, it's okay since you levelled down, we'll be back. I'm like… like what? I don't know how that would go.
Tammy: Are you scared to level down now?
Chris: No. I mean, it'd take a… it'd take years for that to happen but, like, I don't know. I don't know how it would be in Colorado in the DOC there. My PSE counsellor, she worked in the DOC in Colorado and California she said. Colorado looks like California.
Tammy: Really?
Chris: She said… ((unintelligible)) … any violence, kinda thing.
Tammy: I can see that.
Dave: Yeah. I can see it. It's definitely changing. I think people in that part of the country are just different overall. It's really… I talked about that earlier. Colorado's not like it used to be. People here just seem to be nice.
Chris: Been a lot of transplants probably move into Colorado from other states.
Dave: Yeah.
Chris: Probably that, because I know Dave Malone, he said people are going to Florida just to get away from Colorado because it's changed.
Tammy: It's just so expensive and…
Dave: Everything. It's crazy.
Tammy: Mm-hm.
Chris: Houses just keep going up and up before any kind of… like a half-an-acre of land, whose gonna pay seven hundred grand? Here I think it's a lot cheaper, but the pay is a lot… much lower I think.
Dave: Yeah, yeah.
Tammy: Mm-hm.
Dave: Yeah, I was doing a little reading on the area and the median house price is a hundred-and-sixteen thousand. I mean, you can't even buy a mailbox in Colorado for that.
(Laughter).
Tammy: No that's true.
Dave: That's nuts. It's nuts.
Chris: I was reading Pittsburgh is kinda like the same way. It's like… wha… it's a crazy thing about how much it varies. From like state to state, city to city.

Dave: Is Pittsburgh expensive?
Chris: No, it's like…
Dave: Oh, inexpensive?
Chris: Yeah. Hundred, hundred and fifty-thousand for a house.
Dave: Jeez.
Chris: You can deal with the weather and deal with all that kinda stuff.
Dave: Yeah. There's a reason for that, right?
Chris: Yeah, I guess you get from April to September. That's your only good months here. The rest of the time you're in your house.
Grahm: Yeah. I don't think I could handle that.
Dave: Unless you have snow mobiles.
Tammy: I wouldn't even like that.
((Crosstalk)).
Grahm: … when you start using a snow mobile for a necessity, that's a problem.
(Laughter).
Grahm: … taking it to the store.
((Crosstalk)).
Tammy: That's a problem.
Dave: Kinda walk around, tied down all the time.
Tammy: Are they coming, or…?
Grahm: Yeah, they just said they just literally walked away with another person.
Tammy: Oh, they did?
Grahm: They've got to get to the other end of the wherever and come back.
Tammy: This place is huge.
Chris: It's a long hallway.
Tammy: So how far is your pod or wherever you're staying? From here?
Chris: It's all the way down that side.
Tammy: All the other way?
Chris: I think this is like the west side of the building here. I haven't gone much farther than this. Like, all my stuff's on the east side, but they've got, like, they got huge pods that've got… ((unintelligible)) … in 'em. But they do, like, forty or fifty people out each day.
Tammy: You have a cell-mate, right? Someone said…

Chris: No.
Tammy: Oh, you don't have a cellmate?
Chris: Nope. But when I go to GP I probably will.
Tammy: Mm-hm.
Chris: Most of the cells on my unit are single cells—there's like three that are doubled up, but there's… they don't have the overcrowding they have… that issue they had when I first got here.
Tammy: They were just saying, there was four-hundred extra inmates that they ended up shipping out to different places, so…
Chris: Yeah, I never knew what the assessment part of it was, apart from, like, how many people they had coming in and out, but it was like a… that had people coming in, out, everywhere.
Dave: So is it a general supervision type thing like Weld County is? Like a big room with pods on the top?
Chris: No, it's like, they have a sergeant desk at the front and then a hallway of twenty cells that you just, kinda, walk back and forth. You already see with, like, you have, like, like a cul-de-sac of cells three tiers. And then the… the perch for the sergeant right here. And he can see in everybody's cell just looking around.
Dave: Wow!
Chris: But this one they've gotta walk up and down. This used to be a mental hospital or something back in the day. It's definitely old. You can hear those pipes vibrating around the wall. And it's just like hope they don't bust.
(Laughter).
Tammy: Is it exceptionally freezing in here?
Grahm: It just went cold over the last twenty minutes.
Tammy: Yes.
Chris: It gets, hooh! Depending on which way the wind's blowing, depends on which side of the building gets cold. It gets cold.
Tammy: It's pretty chilly.
Chris: There was a six-foot snow drift outside my window for a little while. It's finally starting to go down. Some days it was negative fifty.
Tammy: That's crazy.
Dave: Yeah, it's a little too cold for me.
Tammy: I mean, we're the ones that chose to come in February, but…
(Laughter).
Tammy: She's ready for you now.

Chris: Oh. It was good to see you, guys.
Tammy: Good to see you too. Take care of yourself, okay?
Chris: Thank you. Have a safe flight.

So, we have reached the end of book two and presented the facts as we know them.

Like us, you may think there are many questions never asked that remain unanswered.

Do you believe Chris Watts acted alone, or was there something more sinister at play?

Join us in book three, The Truth Within the LIES, where we discuss the many controversial theories.

For anyone new to this case, the first thing they ask is why? And unfortunately no amount of reading, or watching, or studying will answer that for you. The only person who knows the absolute truth is Chris Watts himself, and for some reason he has refused to confess all up to now. Oh yes, he's confessed to much of it, but there are so many discrepancies, changed statements, obvious lies and omissions. The online True Crime Community is rife with scenarios and theories and some of them are eye-poppingly, jaw-droppingly valid. So we've given you the facts, and now we intend to put forward some of the theories to see if we can work out which truths have been weaved through the lies and vice-versa.

Please note: These theories are not the opinions of the authors and in no way are they saying these events are actually true. But they are most definitely food for thought...

The Truth within the LIES

DISCOVERING CHRIS WATTS - PART THREE - THE THEORIES

NETTA NEWBOUND
&
MARCUS BROWN

THE TRUTH WITHIN THE LIES

DISCOVERING CHRIS WATTS - PART THREE · THE THEORIES

Amazon Link

Acknowledgments

We'd like thank the following…

Our respective families for their never-ending support.

Gloria Nuckols for all that you do.

Mel Comley and the wonderful ARC Team.

All of the beta readers - Gloria Nuckols, Michelle Cooper, Pat Fox, Sue John and Donna Tolero.

With Love… Netta & Marcus xx

About the Authors

Netta Newbound lives between glorious New Zealand and The UK Lake District with her husband, Paul, and their adorable grandson, David.

Marcus Brown lives in North Wales with his partner, Jon, their cat Tobias & two adorable dogs, Sally and Sammy.

For more information or just to touch base with Netta & Marcus you will find them on:

Facebook
Twitter
Instagram

Also by Netta Newbound & Marcus Brown

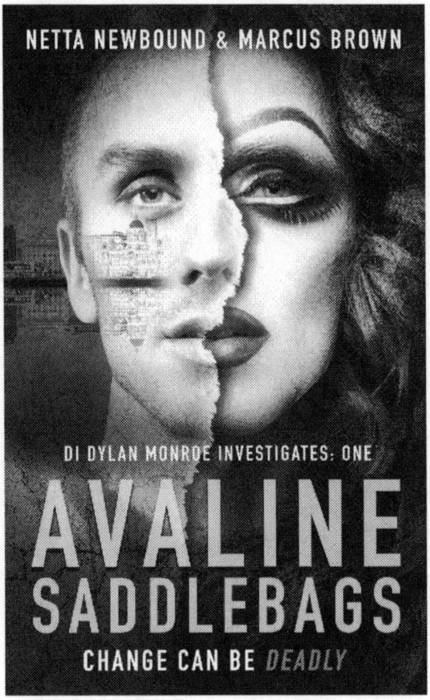

Avaline Saddlebags

Avaline Saddlebags is a gripping, often amusing, psychological thriller with an astonishing twist that will take your breath away... change can be DEADLY!

Made in the USA
Middletown, DE
01 September 2024

60182964R00239